ANNUAL EDITIONS

World Politics 11/12

Thirty-Second Edition

EDITOR

Helen E. Purkitt
United States Naval Academy

Dr. Helen E. Purkitt obtained her PhD in International Relations from the University of Southern California. She is Professor of Political Science at the U.S. Naval Academy. Her research and teaching interests include political psychology, African politics, and emerging national security issues. Currently, she is an African Research Fulbright Fellow at the International Tourism Research Center of the University of Botswana. She is also coordinating a research project at the U.S. Naval Academy designed to develop a wiki database related to the nexus between jihadist terrorist groups and other transnational illicit networks operating in and through Africa, Latin America, and world-wide. She is the editor of a recent volume entitled, *African Environmental and Human Security in the 21st Century* (Cambria Press, 2009). Past research findings about emerging security threats tied to dual-use technology are summarized in a monograph she co-authored entitled, "Good Bugs, Bad Bugs: A Modern Approach for Detecting Offensive Biological Weapons Research" (Center for Technology and National Policy, National Defense University, September, 2008) and in an article she wrote with V. G. Wells entitled, "Evolving Bioweapon Threats Require New Countermeasures." The article, published in the October 6, 2006 edition of *The Chronicle of Higher Education,* is reprinted in this volume of *Annual Editions: World Politics 11/12.* Another well-known work is a co-authored book entitled, *South Africa's Weapons of Mass Destruction,* published by Indiana University Press in 2005. She has published dozens of peer-review monographs and articles, along with serving as an expert for *60 Minutes* and other media forums.

Connect
Learn
Succeed™

ANNUAL EDITIONS: WORLD POLITICS, THIRTY-SECOND EDITION

Published by McGraw-Hill, a business unit of The McGraw-Hill Companies, Inc., 1221 Avenue
of the Americas, New York, NY 10020. Copyright © 2012 by The McGraw-Hill Companies, Inc.
All rights reserved. Previous editions © 2011, 2009, and 2008. No part of this publication may be
reproduced or distributed in any form or by any means, or stored in a database or retrieval system,
without the prior written consent of The McGraw-Hill Companies, Inc., including, but not limited
to, in any network or other electronic storage or transmission, or broadcast for distance learning.

Some ancillaries, including electronic and print components, may not be available to customers
outside the United States.

Annual Editions® is a registered trademark of The McGraw-Hill Companies, Inc.

Annual Editions is published by the **Contemporary Learning Series** group within the
McGraw-Hill Higher Education division.

1 2 3 4 5 6 7 8 9 0 QDB/QDB 1 0 9 8 7 6 5 4 3 2 1

ISBN 978-0-07-805093-0
MHID 0-07-805093-6
ISSN 1098-0300 (print)
ISSN 2159-0990 (online)

Managing Editor: *Larry Loeppke*
Developmental Editor: *Dave Welsh*
Permissions Coordinator: *DeAnna Dausener*
Marketing Specialist: *Alice Link*
Project Manager: *Robin A. Reed*
Design Coordinator: *Margarite Reynolds*
Buyer: *Susan K. Culbertson*
Media Project Manager: *Sridevi Palani*

Compositor: Laserwords Private Limited
Cover Image: DoD photo by Cherie Cullen/Released (inset): Andrew Ward/Life File/Getty Images
(background)

Editors/Academic Advisory Board

Members of the Academic Advisory Board are instrumental in the final selection of articles for each edition of ANNUAL EDITIONS. Their review of articles for content, level, and appropriateness provides critical direction to the editors and staff. We think that you will find their careful consideration well reflected in this volume.

ANNUAL EDITIONS: World Politics 11/12
32nd Edition

EDITOR

Helen E. Purkitt
United States Naval Academy

ACADEMIC ADVISORY BOARD MEMBERS

Preface

In publishing ANNUAL EDITIONS we recognize the enormous role played by the magazines, newspapers, and journals of the public press in providing current, first-rate educational information in a broad spectrum of interest areas. Many of these articles are appropriate for students, researchers, and professionals seeking accurate, current material to help bridge the gap between principles and theories and the real world. These articles, however, become more useful for study when those of lasting value are carefully collected, organized, indexed, and reproduced in a low-cost format, which provides easy and permanent access when the material is needed. That is the role played by ANNUAL EDITIONS.

*A*nnual Editions: World Politics 11/12 is aimed at filling a void in materials for learning about world politics and foreign policy. The articles are chosen for those who are new to the study of world politics. The goal is to help students learn more about international issues that often seem remote but may have profound consequences for a nation's well-being, security, and survival.

International relations can be viewed as a complex and dynamic system of actions and reactions by a diverse set of actors. The articles in this volume convey just how dynamic, interdependent, and complex the relations among different types of international actors are in contemporary international relations. Once, the international system was dominated by nation-states. Today's system looks more like a cobweb of nation-states, international governmental, non-governmental organizations (NGOs), and a host of legal and illicit transnational networks (e.g., terrorist and criminal groups) that span continents and are highly adaptive in terms of their bases of operations and modus operandi.

Increased globalization means that events in places as far away as Latin America, Asia, the Middle East, and Africa may effect the United States, just as America's actions—and inaction—have significant repercussions for other states. Interdependence also refers to the increased role of non-state actors such as multinational corporations, the United Nations, and a rich array of non-governmental actors such as the Cable News Network (CNN) and terrorist networks affiliated with or inspired by al-Qaeda.

The September 11, 2001, terrorist attack on the World Trade Towers and the Pentagon tragically underscored the reality that non-state actors increasingly influence the scope, nature, and pace of events worldwide. However, the U.S.-led military interventions in Afghanistan in 2002, the U.S. military invasion of Iraq in 2003, the increased tempo of fighting between U.S. troops and insurgents in Afghanistan while at the same time reducing U.S. military presence in Iraq, managing continuing tensions with nation-states, such as Iraq and North Korea, while also coping with other conflicts around the world, confirm that inter-state conflicts will also continue as a key feature of international relations. At the same time, the rapid spread of a SARS epidemic since 2004, the continuing spread of new HIV/AIDS infections and the H1N1 virus worldwide, the large number of deaths and devastation caused by floods in Pakistan and elsewhere in the world during 2010, man-made disasters such as the oil spill off the coast of Louisiana, and the continuing threat of a problems caused by global warming and other global climate trends remind us that natural disasters can also have wide-ranging effects on world politics as well. A report by 11 retired senior military officials to the Center for Naval Analysis (CNA) think tank in 2007 warning that climate change will affect all aspects of the United States' national security defense readiness was another indicator that global warming is continuing. The CNA report was also a timely reminder that there are global security threats that may increasingly threaten the security and well-being of citizens living in nation-states in both the developing and developed world.

While leaders of nation-states attempt to wrestle with traditional security and newly emerging ones, the continuing world slowdown reminds citizens worldwide of the downside of increased international interdependence. The current economic downturn has now spread worldwide to become the worse economic slowdown since the 1930 depression. The depth of the current financial, credit, and employment crises and the lack of signs that the recessionary part of the cycle is ending has surprised many foreign policy and economic experts. Today, a series of intertwined economic crises are forcing leaders in developed and developing countries to devise programs to attempt to help citizens cope while also scrambling to tap new sources of revenue as unemployment rises through national policies and increasingly in intergovernmental organizations and forums such as the G-20. The continuing adverse economic trends worldwide remind us of just how interdependent countries and citizens are in different parts of the world in a globalized system. Some international economists are warning that citizens living in developed societies may need to adjust to low or even negative growth rates while many developing countries, used to double-digit growth rates, must also adjust to lower growth rates and reduced public expenditures as part of a new international economic "normal." Whether citizens will be willing to peacefully scale back their expectations about a better life and standard of living for their children remains to be seen. There is little doubt, however, that recent international trends have heightened awareness of just how tightly coupled national security, human security, and collective security concerns have become in the 21st century.

International events proceed at such a rapid pace that what is said about international affairs today may be outdated by tomorrow, therefore it is important for readers to develop a mental framework or theory of the international system. The collection of articles in this volume about international events provides up-to-date information, commentaries about the current set of issues on the world agenda, and analyses of the significance of the issues and emerging trends for the structure and functioning of the post–Cold War international system. The articles in this volume can also be used to update readers' increasingly detailed and interconnected mental models of world affairs in long-term memory as a series of loosely connected and highly adaptive subsystems and networks.

While the United States remains the dominant military, political, and economic power in the post–Cold War system, indicators of an emerging multipolar system consisting of various types of subsystems and subnational, national, and transnational networks are everywhere. Complex trends in the current structure of the international system mean that we can no longer view international relations through a prism where the United States is considered the one lone superpower across all issue areas. Instead, subnational, national, regional, and transnational issues, actors, and linkages are increasingly important aspects of international relations in a multidimensional world system.

New to this edition are Learning Objectives, found at the beginning of each unit, as well as Assess Your Progress study questions found at the end of each article. Both additions will better aid students in their comprehension of what they have read.

I would like to thank Larry Loeppke, David Welsh, and their associates at McGraw-Hill Contemporary Learning Series for their help in putting this volume together. Many members of the Advisory Board and users of *Annual Editions: World Politics* took the time to contribute articles and comments on this collection of readings. I greatly appreciate these suggestions and the article evaluations. Please continue to provide feedback to guide the annual revision of this anthology by filling out the postage-paid *article rating form* on the last page of this book.

Helen Purkitt

Helen E. Purkitt
Editor

Contents

UNIT 1
The International System and Changing World Order of the Twenty-First Century

The concepts in bold italics are developed in the article. For further expansion, please refer to the Topic Guide.

UNIT 2
Managing Interstate Conflicts and the Proliferation of Weapons

The concepts in bold italics are developed in the article. For further expansion, please refer to the Topic Guide.

UNIT 3
Foreign Policy Decision Making

UNIT 4
Great Power Interstate Conflicts and Rivalries

The concepts in bold italics are developed in the article. For further expansion, please refer to the Topic Guide.

UNIT 5
North-South Interstate Conflicts and Rivalries

UNIT 6
Conflicts among Nation-States in the Global South, Sub-National Conflicts, and the Role of Non-State Actors in an Interdependent World

The concepts in bold italics are developed in the article. For further expansion, please refer to the Topic Guide.

UNIT 7
Asymmetric Conflicts: Trends in Terrorism and Counterterrorism

The concepts in bold italics are developed in the article. For further expansion, please refer to the Topic Guide.

UNIT 8
Contemporary Foreign Policy Debates

UNIT 9
International Organizations, International Law,
and Global Governance

The concepts in bold italics are developed in the article. For further expansion, please refer to the Topic Guide.

UNIT 10
The International Economic System

UNIT 11
Globalizing Issues

The concepts in bold italics are developed in the article. For further expansion, please refer to the Topic Guide.

Correlation Guide

The *Annual Editions* series provides students with convenient, inexpensive access to current, carefully selected articles from the public press. **Annual Editions: World Politics 11/12** is an easy-to-use reader that presents articles on important topics such as *World Politics, obesity and weight control, world hunger and malnutrition,* and many more. For more information on *Annual Editions* and other *McGraw-Hill Contemporary Learning Series* titles, visit www.mhhe.com/cls.

This convenient guide matches the units in **Annual Editions: World Politics 11/12** with the corresponding chapters in three of our best-selling McGraw-Hill Nutrition textbooks by Wardlaw/Smith and Schiff.

Annual Editions: World Politics 11/12	International Politics on the World Stage, Brief, 8/e by Rourke/Boyer
Unit 1: The International System and Changing World Order of the Twenty-First Century	**Chapter 2:** The Evolution of World Politics **Chapter 5:** Globalization: The Alternative Orientation **Chapter 12:** Preserving and Enhancing the Biosphere
Unit 2: Managing Interstate Conflicts and the Proliferation of Weapons	**Chapter 8:** International Law and Human Rights **Chapter 9:** Pursuing Security
Unit 3: Foreign Policy Decision Making	**Chapter 3:** Levels of Analysis and Foreign Policy **Chapter 5:** Globalization: The Alternative Orientation **Chapter 8:** International Law and Human Rights **Chapter 9:** Pursuing Security **Chapter 11:** International Economics: The Alternative Road
Unit 4: Great Power Interstate Conflicts and Rivalries	**Chapter 9:** Pursuing Security **Chapter 11:** International Economics: The Alternative Road
Unit 5: North-South Interstate Conflicts and Rivalries	**Chapter 2:** The Evolution of World Politics **Chapter 8:** International Law and Human Rights **Chapter 9:** Pursuing Security **Chapter 11:** International Economics: The Alternative Road
Unit 6: Conflicts among Nation-States in the Global South, Sub-National Conflicts, and the Role of Non-State Actors in an Interdependent World	**Chapter 2:** The Evolution of World Politics **Chapter 8:** International Law and Human Rights **Chapter 9:** Pursuing Security **Chapter 11:** International Economics: The Alternative Road
Unit 7: Asymmetric Conflicts: Trends in Terrorism and Counterterrorism	**Chapter 8:** International Law and Human Rights **Chapter 9:** Pursuing Security
Unit 8: Contemporary Foreign Policy Debates	**Chapter 1:** Thinking and Caring about World Politics **Chapter 2:** The Evolution of World Politics **Chapter 3:** Levels of Analysis and Foreign Policy
Unit 9: International Organizations, International Law, and Global Governance	**Chapter 7:** Intergovernmental Organizations: Alternative Governance **Chapter 8:** International Law and Human Rights **Chapter 11:** International Economics: The Alternative Road
Unit 10: The International Economic System	**Chapter 11:** International Economics: The Alternative Road
Unit 11: Globalizing Issues	**Chapter 5:** Globalization: The Alternative Orientation **Chapter 7:** Intergovernmental Organizations: Alternative Governance **Chapter 8:** International Law and Human Rights **Chapter 11:** International Economics: The Alternative Road **Chapter 12:** Preserving and Enhancing the Biosphere

Topic Guide

This topic guide suggests how the selections in this book relate to the subjects covered in your course. You may want to use the topics listed on these pages to search the Web more easily.

On the following pages a number of websites have been gathered specifically for this book. They are arranged to reflect the units of this Annual Editions reader. You can link to these sites by going to www.mhhe.com/cls

All the articles that relate to each topic are listed below the bold-faced term.

Internet References

The following Internet sites have been selected to support the articles found in this reader. These sites were available at the time of publication. However, because websites often change their structure and content, the information listed may no longer be available. We invite you to visit *www.mhhe.com/cls* for easy access to these sites.

Annual Editions: World Politics 11/12

General Sources

Central Intelligence Agency
www.odci.gov

Use this official home page to learn about many facets of the CIA and to get connections to other sites and resources, such as *The CIA Factbook,* which provides extensive statistical information about every country in the world.

CIA Factbook
www.cia.gov/cia/publications/factbook/index.html

This site provides information on various countries.

Country Indicators for Foreign Policy
www.carleton.ca/cifp

Statistical data on nation-states compiled by Carlton University, Canada.

Ilike2learn.com
www.ilike2learn.com/ilike2learn/geography.asp

Interactive geography quizzes to help learn the locations of the countries and capitals of the world, along with important bodies of water and mountain ranges in the world.

Social Science Information Gateway
http://sosig.esrc.bris.ac.uk

A project of the Economic and Social Research Council (ESRC), this is an online catalog of thousands of Internet resources relevant to political education and research.

World Wide Web Virtual Library: International Affairs Resources
www.etown.edu/vl

Surf this site and its links to learn about specific countries and regions, to research think tanks and organizations, and to study such vital topics as international law, development, the international economy, human rights, and peacekeeping.

Crisisweb: The International Crisis Group (ICG)
www.crisisweb.org/home/index.cfm

ICG is an organization "committed to strengthening the capacity of the international community to anticipate, understand, and act to prevent and contain conflict." Go to this site to view the latest reports and research concerning conflicts around the world.

IIMCR Institute for International Mediation and Conflict Resolution
www.iimcr.org

Programs, including training to become international mediators, publications, online resources related to conflicts, terrorism, and counterterrorism.

UNIT 1: The International System and Changing World Order of the Twenty-First Century

The Globalization Website
www.emory.edu/SOC/globalization

This site discusses globalization and is a guide to available sources on globalization.

Images of the Social and Political World
www-personal.umich.edu/~mejn/cartograms

Cartograms showing different aspects of world nation-states on the basis of population, GNP, HIV-AIDS, greenhouse gases, and more. Created by Mark Newman, Department of Physics and the Center for the Study of Complex Systems, University of Michigan.

National Security and the Threat of Climate Change
www.npr.org/documents/2007/apr/security_climate.pdf

Report issued by eleven retired senior military officials in 2007 to the Center for Naval Analysis warning that climate change will affect all aspects of the United States' defense readiness.

Population Reference Bureau
www.prb.org

This site provides data on the world population and census information.

Women in International Politics
www.guide2womenleaders.com

This site contains data on women who have served as political leaders.

Avalon Project at Yale Law School
www.yale.edu/lawweb/avalon/terrorism/terror.htm

The Avalon Project website features documents in the fields of law, history, economics, diplomacy, politics, government, and terrorism.

UNIT 2: Managing Interstate Conflicts and the Proliferation of Weapons

U.S. Department of State
www.state.gov/index.cfm

The site provides information organized by categories as well as "background notes" on specific countries and regions.

Belfer Center for Science and International Affairs (BCSIA)
www.ksg.harvard.edu/bcsia

BCSIA is a center for research, teaching, and training in international affairs.

FACTs
www.ploughshares.ca

Useful site for research on inter-state conflicts.

U.S.- Russia Developments
www.acronym.org.uk/start

This is a site maintained by Acronym Institute for Disarmament Diplomacy that provides information on U.S. and Russian disarmament activity.

The Bulletin of the Atomic Scientists
www.bullatomsci.org

This site allows you to read more about the Doomsday Clock and other issues as well as topics related to nuclear weaponry, arms control, and disarmament.

Federation of American Scientists
www.fas.org

This site provides useful information about, and links to, a variety of topics related to chemical and biological warfare, missiles, conventional arms, and terrorism.

Internet References

UNIT 3: Foreign Policy Decision Making

Carnegie Endowment for International Peace
www.ceip.org

One of the goals of this organization is to stimulate discussion and learning among experts and the public on a wide range of international issues. The site provides links to the journal *Foreign Policy* and to the Moscow Center.

The Heritage Foundation
www.heritage.org

This page offers discussion about, and links to, many sites of the Heritage Foundation and other organizations having to do with foreign policy and foreign affairs.

DOD Energy Blog
http://dodenergy.blogspot.com

U.S. Dept. of Defense–sponsored blog containing articles related to DOD's efforts to reduce energy needs.

Top SecretAmerica
http://projects.washingtonpost.com/top-secret-america

Supplemental materials related to a *Washington Post* special investigation of the interlocking system of government agencies and companies in the U.S. national security and intelligence system. The site includes video, social network connection map, list of private companies working for government security agencies, and other data.

UNIT 4: Great Power Interstate Conflicts and Rivalries

Archive of European Integration
http://aei.pitt.edu

The Archive of European Integration (AEI) is an electronic repository and archive for research materials on the topic of European integration and unification. The site contains official European Community/European Union documents and certain independently produced research materials.

ISN International Relations and Security Network
www.isn.ethz.ch

This site, maintained by the Center for Security Studies and Conflict Research, is a clearinghouse for extensive information on international relations and security policy.

The Henry L. Stimson Center—Peace Operations and Europe
www.stimson.org/fopo/?SN=FP20020610372

The Future of Peace Operations has begun to address specific areas concerning Europe and operations. The site links to useful UN, NATO, and EU documents, research pieces, and news sites.

Central Europe Online
www.centraleurope.com

This site contains daily updated information under headings such as news on the Web today, economics, trade, and currency.

Europa: European Union
http://europa.eu.int

This server site of the European Union will lead you to the history of the EU (and its predecessors); descriptions of EU policies, institutions, and goals; and documentation of treaties and other materials.

NATO Integrated Data Service
www.nato.int/structur/nids/nids.htm

Check out this website to review North Atlantic Treaty Organization documentation, to read *NATO Review,* and to explore key issues in the field of European security and transatlantic cooperation.

Russia Today
www.russiatoday.com

This site includes headline news, resources, government, politics, election results, and pressing issues.

Russian and East European Network Information Center, University of Texas at Austin
http://reenic.utexas.edu/reenic/index.html

This is *the* website for information on the former Soviet Union.

Inside China Today
www.insidechina.com

Part of the European Internet Network, this site leads you to information on all of China, including recent news, government, and related sites.

Japan Ministry of Foreign Affairs
www.mofa.go.jp

Visit this official site for Japanese foreign policy statements and press releases, archives, and discussions of regional and global relations.

UNIT 5: North-South Interstate Conflicts and Rivalries

National Defense University Website
www.ndu.edu

This contains information on current studies. This site also provides a look at the school where many senior marine and naval officers and senior civilians attend prior to assuming top-level positions.

The North American Institute
www.northamericaninstitute.org

NAMI, a trinational public-affairs organization, is concerned with the emerging "regional space" of Canada, the United States, and Mexico and the development of a North American community. It provides links for study of trade, the environment, and institutional developments.

Inter-American Dialogue
www.iadialog.org

This is the website for IAD, a premier U.S. center for policy analysis, communication, and exchange in Western Hemisphere affairs. The 100-member organization has helped to shape the agenda of issues and choices in hemispheric relations.

African Center for Strategic Studies (ACSS)
www.africacenter.org

The ACSS is a U.S. Dept. of Defense Initiative and component of the National Defense University established to promote security cooperation between the United States and African states. The Africa Center includes headlines drawn from media outlets around the globe that include the most important news affecting Africa today.

Observatory of Cultural Policies in Africa (OCPA)
http://ocpa.irmo.hr/resources/index-en.html

The OCPA Secretariat web page, Maputo, Mozambique contains links to African cultural politics and other relevant documentations, such as working papers, reports, and recommendations.

Internet References

United States Africa Command (AFRICOM)
www.africom.mil

Official site of AFRICOM, led by General William E. Ward. The site includes transcripts and documents, news articles, Africa-related links and frequently asked questions, including about employment with AFRICOM.

UNIT 6: Conflicts among Nation-States in the Global South, Sub-National Conflicts, and the Role of Non-State Actors in an Interdependent World

Pajhwok Afghan News
www.pajhwak.com

This site is Afghanistan's premier news agency offering the best on-the-ground coverage of economics, politics, and security by local reporters.

EI: Electronic Intifada
http://electronicintifada.net/new.shtml

EI is a major Palestinian portal for information about the Palestinian-Israeli conflict from a Palestinian perspective.

International Security Assistance Force (ISAF)
www.nato.int/ISAF

This is the web page of NATO/OTAN International Security Assistance Force in Afghanistan.

Not on Our Watch: The Mission to End Genocide in Darfur and Beyond
http://notonourwatchbook.enoughproject.org

A web page created by actor Don Cheadle and human rights activist John Prendergast that includes six strategies readers can implement to help stop genocide in Sudan. Videos and online resources are also provided.

The African Executive
www.africanexecutive.com

The African Executive offers a wide range of opinions and analyses on Africa's sociopolitical and economic development. It features analytical, issue-based coverage on subjects such as finance and banking, investment opportunities in Africa, technology, agriculture, governance, travel, and entertainment among others.

IslamiCity
http://islamicity.com

This is one of the largest Islamic sites on the web, reaching 50 million people a month. Based in California, it includes public opinion polls, links to television and radio broadcasts, and religious guidance.

Palestine-Israel—American Task Force on Palestine
www.americantaskforce.org

The American Task Force on Palestine (ATFP) is a non-partisan organization dedicated to bringing peace to the Middle East.

Private Military Companies (Mercenaries)
www.bicc.de/pmc/links.php

Website developed by the Bonn International Center for Conversion (BICC) Bonn, Germany to facilitate search for the most important (online) articles dealing with PMCs classified into a few key issues. It provides a wide range of information on all sectors concerning PMCs as well as a list of PMC websites. The list is arranged by the names of the articles, not the authors, because most of the contributions were found by the title.

Defense Web (South Africa)
www.defenceweb.co.za

African security and airlines events, in addition to military news from South Africa and throughout Africa (free daily newsletter, require sign on).

Douglas Farah's Blog
www.douglasfarah.com/presentations.shtml

Former *Washington Post* Bureau chief for West Africa and author of *Blood from Stones* and co-author of *Merchant of Death*. The blog provides information, analyses, and other materials about money laundering and other activities transnational illicit networks in Latin America, West Africa, and elsewhere in the developing world. Efforts to extradite the infamous arms dealer, Victor Bout, to the United States are also chronicled.

George Mason's Center for Global Policy
www.globalpolicy.gmu.edu

University research center that conducts research on conflict, terrorism, state-building, and specific policy issues. The Center also develops and serves as the home to several major cross-national data projects and resources for global policy. These include the *Polity IV* project of regime characteristics, the *Armed Conflict and Intervention* project, the U.S. Government's *Political Instability Task Force/State Failure* project, and the *Genocide/Politicide Project*. The Center publishes an annual Global Report on general system performance and state fragility.

George Mason's Terrorism, Transnational Crime, and Corruption Center (TraCCC)
www.policy-traccc.gmu.edu/abouttraccc/whoweare.html

A research center affiliated with the School of Public Policy at George Mason University that studies the links among terrorism, transnational crime, and corruption, and to teach, research, train, and help formulate policy on these critical issues.

Kubatana.net
www.kubatana.net

A vitual community of Zimbabwean activities who have formed the NGO Network Alliance Project. The project aims to improve the accessibility of human rights and civic information in Zimbabwe.

African News Services

AllAfrica.com
http://allafrica.com

News 24
http://news.24.com

African Resources

Global Footprint Network
footprints@footprintnetwork.org

This website has a link to *Africa Factbook 2009,* an electronic set of some of the most up-to-date charts and recent statistics about human and environmental trends in Africa. The *Factbook* is compiled by The Global Footprint Network, the Swiss Agency for Development, and other sponsors.

Columbia University Library Africa Studies Resources
www.cc.columbia.edu/cu/libraries/indiv/area/Africa

Indiana University African Studies Center
www.indiana.edu/~afrist

Northwestern University Program of African Studies
http://nuinfo.nwu.edu/african-studies

Internet References

Stanford University Guide to Internet Resources for Africa South of the Sahara
www-sul.stanford.edu/depts/ssrg/africa/guide.html

University of Illinois, Urbana-Champaign, African Studies Center
www.afrst.uiuc.edu

University of Pennsylvania African Studies Center
www.sas.upenn.edu/African_Studies/AS

University of Wisconsin, Madison, African Studies Center
www.wisc.edu/afr

UNIT 7: Asymmetric Conflicts: Trends in Terrorism and Counterterrorism

Columbia International Affairs Online
www.ciaonet.org/cbr/cbr00/video/cbr_v/cbr_v.html

At this site find excerpts from al-Qaeda's 2-hour videotape used to recruit young Muslims to fight in a holy war. The tape demonstates al-Qaeda's use of the Internet and media outlets for propaganda and persuasion purposes.

Combating Terrorism Center at West Point
http://ctc.usma.edu

This site offers original analyses, translations of al-Qaeda documents, and a gateway to other terrorism research and government sites (http://ctc.usma.edu/gateway.asp).

Stratfor Global Intelligence
www.stratfor.com/about_stratfor

STRATFOR is a private organization whose intelligence professionals provide brief situation analysis for free to email subscribers and more in-depth information about political, economic, and military developments.

SITE: The Search for International Terrorist Entities
www.siteinstitute.org/index.html

This is a site that includes background, current events, and websites about, or sponsored by, terrorist groups.

Terrorism Research Center
www.terrorism.com

The Terrorism Research Center features definitions and research on terrorism, counterterrorism documents, a comprehensive list of web links, and profiles of terrorist and counterterrorist groups.

United States Government Counterinsurgency Initiative
www.usgcoin.org

This site describes activities and papers from recent conference on U.S. counterinsurgency activities.

UNIT 8: Contemporary Foreign Policy Debates

Iraq Web Links
www.usip.org/library/regions/iraq.html

This is a special web page of the United States Institute of Peace that includes general resources, NBC weapons, government agencies and international organizations, maps and guides, and other resources.

Iraq Dispatches
http://dahrjamailiraq.com

Dahr Jamail, an "unembedded journalist," offers accounts of conditions in Iraq and provides an alternative view to reports by reporters who are embedded with U.S. troops in Iraq. Jamail's

dispatches are distributed through Alternet, a web-based independent media organization.

U.S. Central Command (Centcom)
www.centcom.mil

Official site of U.S. Central Command. Site includes announcements, new reports, pictures, and link to several conflict zones in area of responsibility (AOR), including Afghanistan.

ArabNet
www.arab.net

This page of ArabNet, the online resource for the Arab world in the Middle East and North Africa, presents links to 22 Arab countries. Each country page classifies information using a standardized system.

UNIT 9: International Organizations, International Law, and Global Governance

The Digital Library in International Conflict Management
www.usip.org/library/diglib.html

This link contains peace agreements and truth commissions from around the world.

InterAction
www.interaction.org

InterAction encourages grassroots action, engages policy makers on advocacy issues, and uses this site to inform people on its initiatives to expand international humanitarian relief and development assistance programs.

IRIN
www.irinnews.org

The UN Office for the Coordination of Humanitarian Affairs provides free analytical reports, fact sheets, interviews, daily country updates, and weekly summaries through this site and email distribution service. The site is a good source of news for crisis situations as they occur.

International Court of Justice (ICJ)
www.icj-cij.org

The International Court of Justice (commonly referred to as the World Court or ICJ) is the primary judicial organ of the United Nations. The ICJ acts to resolve matters of international law disputed by specific nations.

AfricanUnion
www.africa-union.org/root/au/index/index.htmAU

Official website for the African Union accessible in multiple languages, including Arabic, English, and French.

End Poverty 2015 Millennium Campaign
www.endpoverty2015.org/2010_mdg_review_summit

Website for a campaign to end poverty by 2015. The site is a good portal for background information, policy documents, and advice for persons interested in working to achieve the UN Millennium Development Goals (MDGs) by 2015. Site also includes information related to September 2010 UN Summit called to review progress toward achieving the MDGs and information about campaign to eradicate HIV/AIDS.

Genocide Watch Home Page
www.genocidewatch.org

Website for a non-government international campaign to end genocide.

International Criminal Court
www.icc-cpi.int/home.html&l=en

Internet References

The International Criminal Court is a permanent tribunal to prosecute individuals for genocide, crimes against humanity, war crimes, etc.

United Nations
http://untreaty.un.org

This site contains text on over 30,000 UN treaties.

United Nations Home Page
www.un.org

Here is the gateway to information about the United Nations. Also see www.undp.org/missions/usa/usna/htm for the U.S. Mission at the UN.

Human Rights Web
www.hrweb.org

This useful site offers ideas on how individuals can get involved in helping to protect human rights around the world.

United Nations Peacekeeping Home Page
www.un.org/Depts/dpko/dpko

This site summarizes past and current UN peacekeeping operations.

"A More Secure World: Our Shared Responsibility"
www.un.org/secureworld

Report delivered to Secretary General Kofi Annan in December 2004 that contains 101 recommendations regarding how to change the United Nations.

Global Policy Forum
www.globalpolicy.org

This site monitors several different United Nation policy initiatives and programs to evalue the effectiveness of such programs and to promote "accountability of global decisions." Visitors who know what types of material they are looking for will want to search through the headings which include such themes such as globalization, international justice, and UN reform. Each one of these sections contains a brief essay on their work, along with a smattering of reports, tables, and charts that highlight their analyses, past and present.

Amnesty International
www.amnesty.org

A non-governmental organization that is working to promote human rights and individual liberties worldwide.

UNIT 10: The International Economic System

Centre for Chinese Studies
www.ccs.org.za

The Centre for Chinese Studies (CCS) is the first institution devoted to the study of China in Sub-Saharan Africa. The Centre promotes the exchange of knowledge, ideas, and experiences between China and Africa and produces a regular, free China Monitor, detailing recent events and trends involving China and African countries.

Goldman Sachs/BRICs
www2.goldmansachs.com/ideas/brics/index.html

Dedicated web page of Goldman Sachs investment firm for stories about BRIC economies and investments.

The Earth Institute at Columbia University
www.earth.columbia.edu

The Earth Institute at Columbia University, led by Professor Jeffrey D. Sachs, is dedicated to addressing a number of complex issues related to sustainable development and the needs of the world's poor.

Graphs Comparing Countries
http://humandevelopment.bu.edu/use_existing_index/start_comp_graph.cfm

This site allows you to compare the statistics of various countries and nation-states using a visual tool.

International Monetary Fund
www.imf.org

This link brings you to the homepage for the International Monetary Fund.

Kiva
www.kiva.org

Kiva lets individuals make small loans for as little as $25 to specific entrepreneurs in the developing world so they can try to lift themselves out of poverty.

Peace Park Foundation
www.peaceparks.org

A private foundation to promote transfrontier conservation areas in southern Africa, including training Africans to become wildlife rangers. The organization works closely with the Southern African Development Organization (SADO) to help implement additional, or plan new, cross-border parks.

Transparency International
www.transparency.org

Transparency International is the global civil society organization leading the fight against corruption. TI publishes an annual International Corruption and International Bribery report that ranks nation-states in terms of the extent of corruption and bribery occurring in each country.

World Bank
www.worldbank.org

News (press releases, summaries of new projects, speeches) and coverage of numerous topics regarding development, countries, and regions are provided at this site. Go to the research and growth section of this site to access specific research and data regarding the world economy.

World Mapper Project
www.sasi.group.shef.ac.uk/worldmapper

This page offers a collection of world maps, where territories are sized to reflect basic data from as recently as 2006.

World Trade Organization
www.wto.org

The WTO is a place where member governments go, to try to sort out the trade problems they face with each other.

UNIT 11: Globalizing Issues

Human Security Report Project (HSRP)
www.hsrpgroup.org

The Security Report Project (HSRP) is an independent research centre affiliated with Simon Fraser University (SFU) in Vancouver, Canada. The HSRP tracks global and regional trends in organized violence, their causes and consequences. Research findings and analyses are published in the *Human Security Report, Human Security Brief* series, and the *miniAtlas of Human Security*.

Human Security Gateway
www.humansecuritygateway.com

The HSRP's Human Security Gateway contains over 30,000 entries that are free of charge on a broad range of global security

Internet References

issues accessible by region, country, or topic. Other linked but separately maintained web pages are the Afghanistan Conflict Monitor and Pakistan Conflict Monitor.

Stockholm International Water Institute
www.siwi.org

The Stockholm *International Water* Institute (SIWI) is a policy institute that seeks sustainable solutions to the world's escalating water crisis.

Worldometers—Real Time World Statistics
www.worldometers.info

Live world statistics on population, government and economics,and interesting statistics with *world population* clock about amount of forest loss this year, carbon dioxide, etc.

World Overpopulation Awareness (population)
www.overpopulation.org

A nonprofit organization that endeavors to make people aware of *population,* overpopulation, its impacts, etc.

World Water Council
www.worldwatercouncil.org/

International intergovernmental and NGO network dealing with *water* policy topics and issues at a high level, including transboundary issues.

Center for Naval Analysis "National Security and the Threat of Climate Change"
http://youtube.com/watch?v_RCfRGN0YIwQ

Link to video and attachments about climate change produced by a respected Washington, DC, think tank called Center for Naval Analysis (CAN).

The UN Millennium Project
www.unmillenniumproject.org

The Center for Naval Analysis (CNA) is a non-profit institution that conducts high-level, in-depth research and analysis to inform the important work of public sector decision makers.

The 11thHourAction.Com
www.11thhouraction.com

This is a web resource page based on the same topics as are covered in the movie. Page includes recent articles, information, blog, and action meetups based on a map, and forums focused on various environmental issues related to climate change.

CIA Report of the National Intelligence Council's 2020 Project
www.cia.gov/nic/NIC_ globaltrend2020.html

This link contains the full text of the most recent CIA-sponsored 2020 Project Report on future global trends.

Commonwealth Forum on Globalization and Health
www.ukglobalhealth.org

This website is sponsored by the Commonwealth Secretariat. Launched in April 2004, the Commonwealth Forum consists of a number of articles and excerpts on various facets of globalization and health.

Commission on Global Governance
www.sovereignty.net/p/gov/gganalysis.htm

This site provides access to *The Report of the Commission on Global Governance,* produced by an international group of leaders who want to find ways to help the global community to better manage its affairs.

Global Footprint Network
http://footprints@footprintnetwork.org

At Global Footprint Network our programs are designed to *influence* decision makers at all levels of society and to create a critical mass of powerful institutions using the Footprint to put an end to ecological *overshoot* and get our economies back into balance.

Global Trends 2005 Project
www.csis.org/gt2005/sumreport.html

The Center for Strategic and International Studies explores the coming global trends and challenges of the new millennium. Read their summary report at this website. Also access Enterprises for the Environment, Global Information Infrastructure Commission, and Americas at this site.

Greenpeace International
www.greenpeace.org/international

"Greenpeace exists because this fragile Earth deserves a voice. It needs solutions. It needs change. It needs actions." Website details recent environmental news related to climate changes and "greenpeace victories."

HIV/AIDS
www.unaids.org

This is a site giving information on the rising toll of HIV/AIDS.

RealClimate
www.realclimate.org

This site contains reports by climate scientists on recent events related to global warming and information about recent severe climate events.

UNIT 1

The International System and Changing World Order of the Twenty-First Century

Unit Selections

Learning Outcomes

- What are some of the characteristics of a nonpolarity international system?

- What types of connections contribute to America's power in the world?

- Which countries are likely to be the most dominant in a multipolar world?

- What are some of the characteristics that make Europe a "second great power?"

- Explain the factors that indicate that China is now a global leader.

- Which country, China or India, do you believe will become the dominant economic power in Asia? Why?

- Explain why regional powers such as Brazil have increasingly influential roles in international relations.

Student Website

www.mhhe.com/cls

Internet References

The Globalization Website
    www.emory.edu/SOC/globalization/
Images of the social and political world
    www.personal.umich.edu/~mejn/cartograms/
National Security and the Threat of Climate Change
    www.npr.org/documents/2007/apr/security_climate.pdf
Population Reference Bureau
    www.prb.org
Women in International Politics
    www.guide2womenleaders.com
Avalon Project at Yale Law School
    www.yale.edu/lawweb/avalon/terrorism/terror.htm

Since the end of the Cold War, the international system has evolved from a loose bipolar system to another state. Initially, analysts proclaimed the system to be a unipolar one dominated by the United States, but notions of a Pax Americana were quickly dashed once and for all by the September 11, 2001, terrorist attacks. More recent domestic economic crises have weakened the U.S. economy as well as the entire world economic system as the effects of the international slowdown evolved into the worse economic recession since the 1930s.

A great deal of U.S. economic resources and military might since 2001 has also been consumed fighting two overseas wars simultaneously. The initial military victories of the U.S.-led operation in Afghanistan were quickly eclipsed by the U.S. military invasion of Iraq. A United States military surge and shift to a counterinsurgency strategy that included working with certain local militias and some former Iraqi defense personnel helped turn the tide of the military struggle in Iraq's civil war after 2005. However, residual, lower-level sectarian fighting continued. The failure of the Shiite-dominated interim government led by Nouri al-Maliki to transition to a broad-based coalition reflecting the interests and concerns of all Iraqis left many apprehensive about the prospects for peace as the United States military presence was reduced during 2010. Simultaneous bombs exploded in most major urban centers across the country as United States combat troops withdrew during the summer. President Obama declared the American Combat Mission in Iraq to have ended by the early fall, once the main American combat force had left the country, but the future role of the United States remains undefined as nearly 50,000 United States troops remain in the country for an unspecified length of time.

As allied forces gained militarily in Iraq, there was a simultaneous worsening of the military situation in Afghanistan as additional jihadist foot soldiers and arms poured into the country. Despite Obama's campaign promises to end United States military involvement in both conflicts, the new United States president acted quickly on a military recommendation by former General McChrystal to send 40,000 additional troops to Afghanistan or face the prospect of a military loss to Taliban and al-Qaeda forces in the future. While approving a rapid buildup of United States forces, President Obama also established the summer of 2011 as a deadline when the effectiveness of the increased United States military presence in Afghanistan would be assessed. Although a majority of Americans supported the troop buildup initially, support declined rapidly as United States casualties mounted, the economic slowdown worsened, and unemployment levels rose to over 10 percent in many parts of the United States. Public support for the war eroded further as signs indicated that a military victory in Afghanistan would be neither, quick, decisive, nor possibly without a negotiated settlement between leaders of the United States-backed Karzai regime and at least some elements of the Taliban. Combined efforts by NATO and Pakistani forces in certain of Pakistan's border areas during 2010 failed to deny jihadist fighters their freedom to move between Afghanistan and Pakistan. Instead, tensions between the United States and Pakistan increased after a series of strikes by allied forces killed several members

of Pakistan's border force at a security post. To protest these strikes, the Pakistani government closed a vital supply route for United States and NATO forces in Afghanistan. U.S. officials scrambled to try to reopen vital supply routes that carry 80 percent of the war's materials and supplies. The incident underscored again the sometimes competing interests of Western and Pakistan allied forces in the Afghan war.

Against this international backdrop, the Obama Administration and a Democratic Party majority in the United States Congress entered the fall 2010 mid-term election season facing an increasingly unsupportive public at home for overseas counterinsurgency campaigns abroad. The United States military and allied forces, along with a new generation of Western political leaders, were relearning the painful lesson that earlier generations of counterinsurgency planners discovered in Afghanistan and Vietnam and elsewhere; to wit, that counterinsurgency campaigns are almost always "brutal, nasty, and long affairs."

As the United States and much of Europe were wrestling with increasingly unpopular overseas military campaigns and an expanding economic slowdown, much of the developing world, especially China and India, registered substantially higher growth rates after making rapid adjustments to their economies and focusing more on expanding demand in domestic and local markets. The swiftness of these adjustments surprised many experts. Some of these experts now predict that the growing global financial crisis and the high costs that the United States is paying to fund financial bailouts and for deficit spending will accelerate the establishment of a multipolar international system in which a several countries, including China, India, and regional powers such as Brazil and South Africa, will assume new influence, roles, and responsibilities in the international system.

During 2010, China replaced Japan as the world's second largest economy. China's state-directed development model is increasingly popular, especially among more socialist-inclined economic planners in developing countries. The Chinese military now routinely projects power well beyond China's traditional spheres of influence. The Chinese Navy patrols sea lands in the Pacific, Atlantic, and Indian Oceans long dominated by the United States Navy. China's new "far sea defense," strategy emphases building long-range capabilities as necessary in order to protect China's increasingly global commercial interests. For example, since 2006 the annual Africa–China summit meetings are one of the most important foreign policy events for resource-rich African countries. China's investments and political commitments in Latin America are also on the rise at the same time that regional powers, such as Brazil and Argentina, are asserting more independent foreign policies and diverse alliances that often do not include the United States.

The increased presence and commitments of China lead most analysts to classify the country as a global rather than a rising power. During 2010, China exercised her newfound power in some new ways. China temporarily cut off Japan's access to rare-earth minerals over a long-standing territorial dispute and ignored an earlier promise to let her currency value float on the open currency market despite a two-hour, private meeting with President Obama at the UN and increased calls for on Chinese imports in the United States Congress. In the United Nations, China shifted from her 2009 position of backing a limited number of sanctions against North Korea to shoring up this important but weak ally by opposing new sanctions. China also shifted from backing certain sanctions against Iran to opposing proposed new international sanctions that would hamper Iran's energy section from which China imports 12 percent of her total oil imports.

Some analysts warn that there are serious economic, political, and environmental cracks within the Chinese system and that more attention should be paid to other new powers such as India. However, the delays in building housing and other accommodations for the opening of the 2010 Commonwealth Games led many analysts to argue that India is still more like an adolescent than a fully matured world power. Still other analysts point to the growth of several major powers in every region of the world as signs that the world has already evolved to a multipolar system. These debates illustrate the lack of consensus about whether the world is more accurately portrayed as being in a state of "nonpolarity," where several nation-states play key roles depending on the nature of the issue or is now in a permanent "multipolar" system state.

Anne-Marie Slaughter in "America's Edge: Power in the Networked Century," takes the contrarian position that the United States is such a central node connecting so many key actors in the system that it will retain its dominant edge over others in the international system for years to come. Andrew Moravcsik in, "Europe, the Second Superpower," argues that the United States and Europe "will remain the only two global superpowers for the foreseeable future as they are the only nation-states able to project a full spectrum of 'smart power' internationally."

What role rising powers, such as China or India, or emerging powers such as Brazil, will play in the future is even more uncertain today than before the onset of the global economic crisis. This uncertainty is due largely to the fact that no one really knows what impact the current economic crisis will have on the existing distribution of economic and political power or whether governments will be able to work together to quickly resolve the intertwined and growing global crises. What is clear from recent trends is that major status quo powers, such as the United States, will have to undertake bold new initiatives in order to turn their countries' economies around. Current problems reflect deep-seated political conflicts and structural economic problems that will take decades to solve. The need for major initiatives in such areas as energy alternatives and the environment are why some economists, businessmen and politicians, including President Barak Obama, now call for a massive new "green initiative." If successful, government-supported research and development programs might be able to serve as a stimulus for new growth and modernization much like Eisenhower's interstate highway or FDR's new deal in earlier eras.

The articles in this section reflect the diversity of viewpoints evident among experts about the relative importance of specific nation-states, the likelihood that new nation-state powers or empires will arise, and even whether traditional rules of statescraft, national security, and power politics will prevail or be overtaken by human security needs, or larger, collective security issues, such a global warming.

The Age of Nonpolarity
What Will Follow U.S. Dominance?

RICHARD N. HAASS

The principal characteristic of twenty-first-century international relations is turning out to be nonpolarity: a world dominated not by one or two or even several states but rather by dozens of actors possessing and exercising various kinds of power. This represents a tectonic shift from the past.

The twentieth century started out distinctly multipolar. But after almost 50 years, two world wars, and many smaller conflicts, a bipolar system emerged. Then, with the end of the Cold War and the demise of the Soviet Union, bipolarity gave way to unipolarity—an international system dominated by one power, in this case the United States. But today power is diffuse, and the onset of nonpolarity raises a number of important questions. How does nonpolarity differ from other forms of international order? How and why did it materialize? What are its likely consequences? And how should the United States respond?

Newer World Order

In contrast to multipolarity—which involves several distinct poles or concentrations of power—a nonpolar international system is characterized by numerous centers with meaningful power.

In a multipolar system, no power dominates, or the system will become unipolar. Nor do concentrations of power revolve around two positions, or the system will become bipolar. Multipolar systems can be cooperative, even assuming the form of a concert of powers, in which a few major powers work together on setting the rules of the game and disciplining those who violate them. They can also be more competitive, revolving around a balance of power, or conflictual, when the balance breaks down.

At first glance, the world today may appear to be multipolar. The major powers—China, the European Union (EU), India, Japan, Russia, and the United States—contain just over half the world's people and account for 75 percent of global GDP and 80 percent of global defense spending. Appearances, however, can be deceiving. Today's world differs in a fundamental way from one of classic multipolarity: there are many more power centers, and quite a few of these poles are not nation-states. Indeed, one of the cardinal features of the contemporary international system is that nation-states have lost their monopoly on power and in some domains their preeminence as well. States are being challenged from above, by regional and global organizations; from below, by militias; and from the side, by a variety of nongovernmental organizations (NGOs) and corporations. Power is now found in many hands and in many places.

In addition to the six major world powers, there are numerous regional powers: Brazil and, arguably, Argentina, Chile, Mexico, and Venezuela in Latin America; Nigeria and South Africa in Africa; Egypt,

Iran, Israel, and Saudi Arabia in the Middle East; Pakistan in South Asia; Australia, Indonesia, and South Korea in East Asia and Oceania. A good many organizations would be on the list of power centers, including those that are global (the International Monetary Fund, the United Nations, the World Bank), those that are regional (the African Union, the Arab League, the Association of Southeast Asian Nations, the EU, the Organization of American States, the South Asian Association for Regional Cooperation), and those that are functional (the International Energy Agency, OPEC, the Shanghai Cooperation Organization, the World Health Organization). So, too, would states within nation-states, such as California and India's Uttar Pradesh, and cities, such as New York, São Paulo, and Shanghai. Then there are the large global companies, including those that dominate the worlds of energy, finance, and manufacturing. Other entities deserving inclusion would be global media outlets (al Jazeera, the BBC, CNN), militias (Hamas, Hezbollah, the Mahdi Army, the Taliban), political parties, religious institutions and movements, terrorist organizations (al Qaeda), drug cartels, and NGOs of a more benign sort (the Bill and Melinda Gates Foundation, Doctors Without Borders, Greenpeace). Today's world is increasingly one of distributed, rather than concentrated, power.

Today's world is increasingly one of distributed, rather than concentrated, power.

In this world, the United States is and will long remain the largest single aggregation of power. It spends more than $500 billion annually on its military—and more than $700 billion if the operations in Afghanistan and Iraq are included—and boasts land, air, and naval forces that are the world's most capable. Its economy, with a GDP of some $14 trillion, is the world's largest. The United States is also a major source of culture (through films and television), information, and innovation. But the reality of American strength should not mask the relative decline of the United States' position in the world—and with this relative decline in power an absolute decline in influence and independence. The U.S. share of global imports is already down to 15 percent. Although U.S. GDP accounts for over 25 percent of the world's total, this percentage is sure to decline over time given the actual and projected differential between the United States' growth rate and those of the Asian giants and many other countries, a large number of which are growing at more than two or three times the rate of the United States.

GDP growth is hardly the only indication of a move away from U.S. economic dominance. The rise of sovereign wealth funds—in countries such as China, Kuwait, Russia, Saudi Arabia, and the United Arab Emirates—is another. These government-controlled pools of wealth, mostly the result of oil and gas exports, now total some $3 trillion. They are growing at a projected rate of $1 trillion a year and are an increasingly important source of liquidity for U.S. firms. High energy prices, fueled mostly by the surge in Chinese and Indian demand, are here to stay for some time, meaning that the size and significance of these funds will continue to grow. Alternative stock exchanges are springing up and drawing away companies from the U.S. exchanges and even launching initial public offerings (IPOs). London, in particular, is competing with New York as the world's financial center and has already surpassed it in terms of the number of IPOs it hosts. The dollar has weakened against the euro and the British pound, and it is likely to decline in value relative to Asian currencies as well. A majority of the world's foreign exchange holdings are now in currencies other than the dollar, and a move to denominate oil in euros or a basket of currencies is possible, a step that would only leave the U.S. economy more vulnerable to inflation as well as currency crises.

U.S. primacy is also being challenged in other realms, such as military effectiveness and diplomacy. Measures of military spending are not the same as measures of military capacity. September 11 showed how a small investment by terrorists could cause extraordinary levels of human and physical damage. Many of the most costly pieces of modern weaponry are not particularly useful in modern conflicts in which traditional battlefields are replaced by urban combat zones. In such environments, large numbers of lightly armed soldiers can prove to be more than a match for smaller numbers of highly trained and better-armed U.S. troops.

Power and influence are less and less linked in an era of nonpolarity. U.S. calls for others to reform will tend to fall on deaf ears, U.S. assistance programs will buy less, and U.S.-led sanctions will accomplish less. After all, China proved to be the country best able to influence North Korea's nuclear program. Washington's ability to pressure Tehran has been strengthened by the participation of several western European countries—and weakened by the reluctance of China and Russia to sanction Iran. Both Beijing and Moscow have diluted international efforts to pressure the government in Sudan to end its war in Darfur. Pakistan, meanwhile, has repeatedly demonstrated an ability to resist U.S. entreaties, as have Iran, North Korea, Venezuela, and Zimbabwe.

The trend also extends to the worlds of culture and information. Bollywood produces more films every year than Hollywood. Alternatives to U.S.-produced and disseminated television are multiplying. websites and blogs from other countries provide further competition for U.S.-produced news and commentary. The proliferation of information is as much a cause of nonpolarity as is the proliferation of weaponry.

Farewell to Unipolarity

Charles Krauthammer was more correct than he realized when he wrote in these pages nearly two decades ago about what he termed "the unipolar moment." At the time, U.S. dominance was real. But it lasted for only 15 or 20 years. In historical terms, it was a moment. Traditional realist theory would have predicted the end of unipolarity and the dawn of a multipolar world. According to this line of reasoning, great powers, when they act as great powers are wont to do, stimulate competition from others that fear or resent them. Krauthammer, subscribing to just this theory, wrote, "No doubt, multipolarity will come in time. In perhaps another generation or so there will be great powers coequal with the United States, and the world will, in structure, resemble the pre-World War I era."

But this has not happened. Although anti-Americanism is widespread, no great-power rival or set of rivals has emerged to challenge the United States. In part, this is because the disparity between the power of the United States and that of any potential rivals is too great. Over time, countries such as China may come to possess GDPs comparable to that of the United States. But in the case of China, much of that wealth will necessarily be absorbed by providing for the country's enormous population (much of which remains poor) and will not be available to fund military development or external undertakings. Maintaining political stability during a period of such dynamic but uneven growth will be no easy feat. India faces many of the same demographic challenges and is further hampered by too much bureaucracy and too little infrastructure. The EU's GDP is now greater than that of the United States, but the EU does not act in the unified fashion of a nation-state, nor is it able or inclined to act in the assertive fashion of historic great powers. Japan, for its part, has a shrinking and aging population and lacks the political culture to play the role of a great power. Russia may be more inclined, but it still has a largely cash-crop economy and is saddled by a declining population and internal challenges to its cohesion.

The fact that classic great-power rivalry has not come to pass and is unlikely to arise anytime soon is also partly a result of the United States' behavior, which has not stimulated such a response. This is not to say that the United States under the leadership of George W. Bush has not alienated other nations; it surely has. But it has not, for the most part, acted in a manner that has led other states to conclude that the United States constitutes a threat to their vital national interests. Doubts about the wisdom and legitimacy of U.S. foreign policy are pervasive, but this has tended to lead more to denunciations (and an absence of cooperation) than outright resistance.

The transition to a nonpolar world will have mostly negative consequences for the United States.

A further constraint on the emergence of great-power rivals is that many of the other major powers are dependent on the international system for their economic welfare and political stability. They do not, accordingly, want to disrupt an order that serves their national interests. Those interests are closely tied to cross-border flows of goods, services, people, energy, investment, and technology—flows in which the United States plays a critical role. Integration into the modern world dampens great-power competition and conflict.

But even if great-power rivals have not emerged, unipolarity has ended. Three explanations for its demise stand out. The first is historical. States develop; they get better at generating and piecing together the human, financial, and technological resources that lead to productivity and prosperity. The same holds for corporations and other organizations. The rise of these new powers cannot be stopped. The result is an ever larger number of actors able to exert influence regionally or globally.

A second cause is U.S. policy. To paraphrase Walt Kelly's Pogo, the post-World War II comic hero, we have met the explanation and it is us. By both what it has done and what it has failed to do, the United States has accelerated the emergence of alternative power centers in the world and has weakened its own position relative to them. U.S. energy policy (or the lack thereof) is a driving force behind the end of unipolarity. Since the first oil shocks of the 1970s, U.S. consumption of oil has grown by approximately 20 percent, and, more important, U.S. imports of petroleum products have more than doubled in volume and nearly doubled as a percentage of consumption. This growth in demand for foreign oil has helped drive up the world price of oil from just over $20 a barrel to over $100 a barrel in less than a decade. The result is an enormous transfer of wealth and leverage to those states with energy reserves. In short, U.S. energy policy has helped bring about the emergence of oil and gas producers as major power centers.

U.S. economic policy has played a role as well. President Lyndon Johnson was widely criticized for simultaneously fighting a war in Vietnam and increasing domestic spending. President Bush has fought costly wars in Afghanistan and Iraq, allowed discretionary spending to increase by an annual rate of eight percent, and cut taxes. As a result, the United States' fiscal position declined from a surplus of over $100 billion in 2001 to an estimated deficit of approximately $250 billion in 2007. Perhaps more relevant is the ballooning current account deficit, which is now more than six percent of GDP. This places downward pressure on the dollar, stimulates inflation, and contributes to the accumulation of wealth and power elsewhere in the world. Poor regulation of the U.S. mortgage market and and the credit crisis it has spawned have exacerbated these problems.

The war in Iraq has also contributed to the dilution of the United States' position in the world. The war in Iraq has proved to be an expensive war of choice—militarily, economically, and diplomatically as well as in human terms. Years ago, the historian Paul Kennedy outlined his thesis about "imperial overstretch," which posited that the United States would eventually decline by overreaching, just as other great powers had in the past. Kennedy's theory turned out to apply most immediately to the Soviet Union, but the United States—for all its corrective mechanisms and dynamism—has not proved to be immune. It is not simply that the U.S. military will take a generation to recover from Iraq; it is also that the United States lacks sufficient military assets to continue doing what it is doing in Iraq, much less assume new burdens of any scale elsewhere.

Finally, today's nonpolar world is not simply a result of the rise of other states and organizations or of the failures and follies of U.S. policy. It is also an inevitable consequence of globalization. Globalization has increased the volume, velocity, and importance of cross-border flows of just about everything, from drugs, e-mails, greenhouse gases, manufactured goods, and people to television and radio signals, viruses (virtual and real), and weapons.

Globalization reinforces nonpolarity in two fundamental ways. First, many cross-border flows take place outside the control of governments and without their knowledge. As a result, globalization dilutes the influence of the major powers. Second, these same flows often strengthen the capacities of nonstate actors, such as energy exporters (who are experiencing a dramatic increase in wealth owing to transfers from importers), terrorists (who use the Internet to recruit and train, the international banking system to move resources, and the global transport system to move people), rogue states (who can exploit black and gray markets), and Fortune 500 firms (who quickly move personnel and investments). It is increasingly apparent that being the strongest state no longer means having a near monopoly on power. It is easier than ever before for individuals and groups to accumulate and project substantial power.

Nonpolar Disorder

The increasingly nonpolar world will have mostly negative consequences for the United States—and for much of the rest of the world as well. It will make it more difficult for Washington to lead on those occasions when it seeks to promote collective responses to regional and global challenges. One reason has to do with simple arithmetic. With so many more actors possessing meaningful power and trying to assert influence, it will be more difficult to build collective responses and make institutions work. Herding dozens is harder than herding a few. The inability to reach agreement in the Doha Round of global trade talks is a telling example.

Nonpolarity will also increase the number of threats and vulnerabilities facing a country such as the United States. These threats can take the form of rogue states, terrorist groups, energy producers that choose to reduce their output, or central banks whose action or inaction can create conditions that affect the role and strength of the U.S. dollar. The Federal Reserve might want to think twice before continuing to lower interest rates, lest it precipitate a further move away from the dollar. There can be worse things than a recession.

Iran is a case in point. Its effort to become a nuclear power is a result of nonpolarity. Thanks more than anything to the surge in oil prices, it has become another meaningful concentration of power, one able to exert influence in Iraq, Lebanon, Syria, the Palestinian territories, and beyond, as well as within OPEC. It has many sources of technology and finance and numerous markets for its energy exports. And due to nonpolarity, the United States cannot manage Iran alone. Rather, Washington is dependent on others to support political and economic sanctions or block Tehran's access to nuclear technology and materials. Nonpolarity begets nonpolarity.

Still, even if nonpolarity was inevitable, its character is not. To paraphrase the international relations theorist Hedley Bull, global politics at any point is a mixture of anarchy and society. The question is the balance and the trend. A great deal can and should be done to shape a nonpolar world. Order will not just emerge. To the contrary, left to its own devices, a nonpolar world will become messier over time. Entropy dictates that systems consisting of a large number of actors tend toward greater randomness and disorder in the absence of external intervention.

The United States can and should take steps to reduce the chances that a nonpolar world will become a cauldron of instability. This is not a call for unilateralism; it is a call for the United States to get its own house in order. Unipolarity is a thing of the past, but the United States still retains more capacity than any other actor to improve the quality of the international system. The question is whether it will continue to possess such capacity.

The United States no longer has the luxury of a "You're either with us or against us" foreign policy.

Energy is the most important issue. Current levels of U.S. consumption and imports (in addition to their adverse impact on the global climate) fuel nonpolarity by funneling vast financial resources to oil and gas producers. Reducing consumption would lessen the pressure on world prices, decrease U.S. vulnerability to market manipulation by oil suppliers, and slow the pace of climate change. The good news is that this can be done without hurting the U.S. economy.

Strengthening homeland security is also crucial. Terrorism, like disease, cannot be eradicated. There will always be people who cannot be integrated into societies and who pursue goals that cannot be realized through traditional politics. And sometimes, despite the best efforts of those entrusted with homeland security, terrorists will succeed. What is needed, then, are steps to make society more resilient, something that requires adequate funding and training of emergency responders and more flexible and durable infrastructure. The goal should be to reduce the impact of even successful attacks.

Resisting the further spread of nuclear weapons and unguarded nuclear materials, given their destructive potential, may be as important as any other set of undertakings. By establishing internationally managed enriched-uranium or spent-fuel banks that give countries access to sensitive nuclear materials, the international community could help countries use nuclear power to produce electricity rather than bombs. Security assurances and defensive systems can be provided to states that might otherwise feel compelled to develop nuclear programs of their own to counter those of their neighbors. Robust sanctions—on occasion backed by armed force—can also be introduced to influence the behavior of would-be nuclear states.

Even so, the question of using military force to destroy nuclear or biological weapons capabilities remains. Preemptive strikes—attacks that aim to stop an imminent threat—are widely accepted as a form of self-defense. Preventive strikes—attacks on capabilities when there is no indication of imminent use—are something else altogether. They should not be ruled out as a matter of principle, but nor should they be depended on. Beyond questions of feasibility, preventive strikes run the risk of making a nonpolar world less stable, both because they might actually encourage proliferation (governments could see developing or acquiring nuclear weapons as a deterrent) and because they would weaken the long-standing norm against the use of force for purposes other than self-defense.

Combating terrorism is also essential if the nonpolar era is not to turn into a modern Dark Ages. There are many ways to weaken existing terrorist organizations by using intelligence and law enforcement resources and military capabilities. But this is a loser's game unless something can be done to reduce recruitment. Parents, religious figures, and political leaders must delegitimize terrorism by shaming those who choose to embrace it. And more important, governments must find ways of integrating alienated young men and women into their societies, something that cannot occur in the absence of political and economic opportunity.

Trade can be a powerful tool of integration. It gives states a stake in avoiding conflict because instability interrupts beneficial commercial arrangements that provide greater wealth and strengthen the foundations of domestic political order. Trade also facilitates development, thereby decreasing the chance of state failure and alienation among citizens. The scope of the World Trade Organization must be extended through the negotiation of future global arrangements that further reduce subsidies and both tariff and nontariff barriers. Building domestic political support for such negotiations in developed countries will likely require the expansion of various safety nets, including portable health care and retirement accounts, education and training assistance, and wage insurance. These social policy reforms are costly and in some cases unwarranted (the cause of job loss is far more likely to be technological innovation than foreign competition), but they are worth providing nonetheless given the overall economic and political value of expanding the global trade regime.

A similar level of effort might be needed to ensure the continued flow of investment. The goal should be to create a World Investment Organization that would encourage capital flows across borders so as to minimize the chances that "investment protectionism" gets in the way of activities that, like trade, are economically beneficial and build political bulwarks against instability. A WIO could encourage transparency on the part of investors, determine when national security is a legitimate reason for prohibiting or limiting foreign investment, and establish a mechanism for resolving disputes.

Finally, the United States needs to enhance its capacity to prevent state failure and deal with its consequences. This will require building and maintaining a larger military, one with greater capacity to deal with the sort of threats faced in Afghanistan and Iraq. In addition, it will mean establishing a civilian counterpart to the military reserves that would provide a pool of human talent to assist with basic nation-building tasks. Continuing economic and military assistance will be vital in helping weak states meet their responsibilities to their citizens and their neighbors.

The Not-So-Lonely Superpower

Multilateralism will be essential in dealing with a nonpolar world. To succeed, though, it must be recast to include actors other than the great powers. The UN Security Council and the G-8 (the group of highly industrialized states) need to be reconstituted to reflect the world of today and not the post–World War II era. A recent meeting at the United Nations on how best to coordinate global responses to public health challenges provided a model. Representatives of governments, UN agencies, NGOs, pharmaceutical companies, foundations, think tanks, and universities were all in attendance. A similar range of participants attended the December 2007 Bali meeting on climate change. Multilateralism may have to be less formal and less comprehensive, at least in its initial phases. Networks will be needed alongside organizations. Getting everyone to agree on everything will be increasingly difficult; instead, the United States should consider signing accords with fewer parties and narrower goals. Trade is something of a model here, in that bilateral and regional accords are filling the vacuum created by a failure to conclude a global trade round. The same approach could work for climate change, where agreement on aspects of the problem (say, deforestation) or arrangements involving only some countries (the major carbon emitters, for example) may prove feasible, whereas an accord that involves every country and tries to resolve every issue may not. Multilateralism à la carte is likely to be the order of the day.

Nonpolarity complicates diplomacy. A nonpolar world not only involves more actors but also lacks the more predictable fixed structures and relationships that tend to define worlds of unipolarity, bipolarity, or multipolarity. Alliances, in particular, will lose much of their importance, if only because alliances require predictable threats, outlooks, and obligations, all of which are likely to be in short supply in a nonpolar world. Relationships will instead become more selective and situational. It will become harder to classify other countries as either allies or adversaries; they will cooperate on some issues and resist on others. There will be a premium on consultation and coalition building and on a diplomacy that encourages cooperation when possible and shields such cooperation from the fallout of inevitable disagreements. The United States will no longer have the luxury of a "You're either with us or against us" foreign policy.

Nonpolarity will be difficult and dangerous. But encouraging a greater degree of global integration will help promote stability. Establishing a core group of governments and others committed to cooperative multilateralism would be a great step forward. Call it "concerted nonpolarity." It would not eliminate nonpolarity, but it would help manage it and increase the odds that the international system will not deteriorate or disintegrate.

Critical Thinking

1. Use two recent current events to illustrate how different actors in the international system exercise different kinds of power.
2. Name three ways that the current international system state differs from the bi-polar structure in place during the Cold War.

RICHARD N. HAASS is President of the Council on Foreign Relations.

America's Edge
Power in the Networked Century

ANNE-MARIE SLAUGHTER

We live in a networked world. War is networked: the power of terrorists and the militaries that would defeat them depend on small, mobile groups of warriors connected to one another and to intelligence, communications, and support networks. Diplomacy is networked: managing international crises—from SARS to climate change—requires mobilizing international networks of public and private actors. Business is networked: every CEO advice manual published in the past decade has focused on the shift from the vertical world of hierarchy to the horizontal world of networks. Media are networked: online blogs and other forms of participatory media depend on contributions from readers to create a vast, networked conversation. Society is networked: the world of MySpace is creating a global world of "OurSpace," linking hundreds of millions of individuals across continents. Even religion is networked: as the pastor Rick Warren has argued, "The only thing big enough to solve the problems of spiritual emptiness, selfish leadership, poverty, disease, and ignorance is the network of millions of churches all around the world."

In this world, the measure of power is connectedness. Almost 30 years ago, the psychologist Carol Gilligan wrote about differences between the genders in their modes of thinking. She observed that men tend to see the world as made up of hierarchies of power and seek to get to the top, whereas women tend to see the world as containing webs of relationships and seek to move to the center. Gilligan's observations may be a function of nurture rather than nature; regardless, the two lenses she identified capture the differences between the twentieth-century and the twenty-first-century worlds.

The twentieth-century world was, at least in terms of geopolitics, a billiard-ball world, described by the political scientist Arnold Wolfers as a system of self-contained states colliding with one another. The results of these collisions were determined by military and economic power. This world still exists today: Russia invades Georgia, Iran seeks nuclear weapons, the United States strengthens its ties with India as a hedge against a rising China. This is what Fareed Zakaria, the editor of *Newsweek International,* has dubbed "the post-American world," in which the rise of new global powers inevitably means the relative decline of U.S. influence.

The emerging networked world of the twenty-first century, however, exists above the state, below the state, and through the state. In this world, the state with the most connections will be the central player, able to set the global agenda and unlock innovation and sustainable growth. Here, the United States has a clear and sustainable edge.

The Horizon of Hope

The United States' advantage is rooted in demography, geography, and culture. The United States has a relatively small population, only 20–30 percent of the size of China's or India's. Having fewer people will make it much easier for the United States to develop and profit from new energy technologies. At the same time, the heterogeneity of the U.S. population will allow Washington to extend its global reach. To this end, the United States should see its immigrants as living links back to their home countries and encourage a two-way flow of people, products, and ideas.

The United States is the anchor of the Atlantic hemisphere, a broadly defined area that includes Africa, the Americas, and Europe. The leading countries in the Atlantic hemisphere are more peaceful, stable, and economically diversified than those in the Asian hemisphere. At the same time, however, the United States is a pivotal power, able to profit simultaneously from its position in the Atlantic hemisphere and from its deep ties to the Asian hemisphere. The Atlantic and Pacific Oceans have long protected the United States from invasion and political interference. Soon, they will shield it from conflicts brought about by climate change, just as they are already reducing the amount of pollutants that head its way. The United States has a relatively horizontal social structure—albeit one that has become more hierarchical with the growth of income inequality—as well as a culture of entrepreneurship and innovation. These traits are great advantages in a global economy increasingly driven by networked clusters of the world's most creative people.

On January 20, 2009, Barack Obama will set about restoring the moral authority of the United States. The networked world provides a hopeful horizon. In this world, with the right policies, immigrants can be a source of jobs rather than a drain on resources, able to link their new home with markets and suppliers in their old homes. Businesses in the United States can orchestrate global networks of producers and suppliers. Consumers can buy locally, from revived local agricultural and customized small-business economies, and at the same time globally, from anywhere that can advertise online. The United States has the potential to be the most innovative and dynamic society anywhere in the world.

Life in a Networked World

In 2000, Procter and Gamble made a decision that reinvented how the company would do business in the twenty-first century. Instead of closely guarding its secret recipes for everything from soaps to potato chips, Procter and Gamble chose to open up its patent portfolio, making virtually all its formulas available to anyone willing to pay a licensing fee. At the same time, it asked its top managers to bring in half of their ideas for new products and services from outside the company. They now look to far-flung groups of inventors around the world and online, where innovators gather at sites such as InnoCentive, an auction website for ideas. Don Tapscott and Anthony Williams, the authors of *Wikinomics: How Mass Collaboration Changes Everything,* call businesses like InnoCentive "ideagoras," modern-day public squares that join people looking to sell their ideas with businesses seeking to buy them. In 2006, Samuel Palmisano, the head of IBM, predicted in these pages that corporations would move from being multinational, with small, self-replicated versions of themselves in every market, to being what he calls "globally integrated enterprises." Today, IBM funnels tasks to wherever they will be done best.

Consider the experience of Li and Fung, the world's largest and most successful export sourcing company. Its clients are retailers of virtually every kind of product known to man, or at least made by man. The job of Li and Fung is to identify suppliers from over 40 countries around the world and connect them in order to fill specific orders. The resulting networks must be fast, flexible, and able to work to a common high standard. According to William and Victor Fung, two of the current owners of the family business, the secret of sourcing is "orchestrating networks." It is the managerial equivalent of creating a system in which one can select a destination on a Paris metro map and see a possible route light up with a connecting web of differently colored lines—except, of course, that riders at each station might have their own ideas about how best to travel.

At first, these global webs may seem to be just the next generation of outsourcing. But something much deeper is going on. Outsourcing requires a central command that specifies precisely what and how much should be produced and then, through an established hierarchy, communicates those decisions to producers in multiple nations. In contrast, under a system of peer production, supply chains become "value webs," in which suppliers become partners and, instead of just supplying products, actually collaborate on their design. Boeing is a particularly striking example, given how it could be seen as the heart of old-style manufacturing. It has shifted from being simply an airplane manufacturer to being a "systems integrator," relying on a horizontal network of partners collaborating in real time. They share both risk and knowledge in order to achieve a higher level of performance. It is not simply a change in form but a change in culture. Hierarchy and control lose out to community, collaboration, and self-organization. At its core, a company can be quite small, often no more than a central node of leaders and manager-integrators.

But with the right networks, it can reach anywhere innovators, factories, and service providers can be found. In this world, as Tapscott and Williams write, "only the connected will survive."

Nongovernmental organizations (NGOs), too, have realized the power of connections. An early example was the International Campaign to Ban Landmines, which began in 1991 as a coalition of six NGOs from North America and Europe. It eventually grew to include over 1,100 groups in some 60 countries, and with this breadth came clout. After it won the Nobel Peace Prize in 1997, the network successfully pushed for a global treaty banning the use of land mines (although China, Russia, and the United States, among others, have refused to sign it). NGOs pursuing other causes have followed suit. In 1995, a small group of human rights organizations began calling for the creation of an international criminal court to try war criminals. They succeeded in convincing governments to establish a permanent court in 1998. Today, the Coalition for the International Criminal Court includes over 2,000 organizations from every corner of the world, which are now working to expand the court's jurisdiction. More recently, a global alliance of NGOs has been instrumental in pushing for action to stop the ongoing violence in Darfur.

In each of these cases, NGOs gained leverage over otherwise reluctant states. They formed transnational networks that multiplied their lobbying power and put their message on the agendas of international institutions. As Francis Sejersted, then chair of the Nobel Committee, noted when he recognized the land-mine campaign, "The mobilisation and focusing of broad popular involvement which we have witnessed bears promise that goes beyond the present issue. It appears to have established a pattern for how to realise political aims at the global level."

Governments have been slower to understand twenty-first-century challenges and to reform themselves accordingly, but they, too, are gradually moving toward a more networked structure. A report entitled *The Embassy of the Future,* issued by the Center for Strategic and International Studies in 2007, calls for U.S. diplomats to be "decentralized, flexible, and mobile," as well as "connected, responsive, and informed." U.S. embassy staff would have a more "distributed presence," both virtually and physically, if they worked at multiple locations and with a wide range of different groups in their host countries.

Similarly, Julie Gerberding, director of the Centers for Disease Control, realized after the anthrax scare in 2001 and the SARS crisis in 2002 that the CDC needed to create a network of public and private actors from around the world. Managing this network would, in turn, require a much more flexible and horizontal organization at the CDC's headquarters, in Atlanta. Gerberding was expected to get results but lacked the authority necessary to produce them. For Gerberding, the solution was to find partners around the world and to connect them in ways that would allow for the creation and sharing of knowledge during a crisis. Many judges and government regulators have had a similar insight. Bankruptcy judges, for example, now communicate with one another around the world, signing agreements to manage together the bankruptcies of multinational corporations. The current financial crisis could have been even worse if the world's central bankers had not already been connected and able to coordinate their actions.

Power can also flow from connections across different sectors. In his book *Superclass: The Global Power Elite and the World*

They Are Making, David Rothkopf explains how leaders connect across different power structures, from the worlds of business and finance to those of politics and the arts. "In fact," he writes, "such linkages are as distinguishing a characteristic of the superclass as wealth or individual position." In other words, it is connectivity, more than money or stature, that determines individual power. This dynamic can even extend to terrorist groups such as al Qaeda. John Robb, a former air force colonel and military strategist, has observed that Mohamed Atta was the leader of the 9/11 hijackers because, although no formal hierarchy existed in the group, "Atta had twenty-two connections to other people in the network, much more than any other, which gave him control of the operation."

The power that flows from this type of connectivity is not the power to impose outcomes. Networks are not directed and controlled as much as they are managed and orchestrated. Multiple players are integrated into a whole that is greater than the sum of its parts—an orchestra that plays differently according to the vision of its conductor and the talent of individual musicians. Obama's team-based campaign, with its relatively flat structure and emphasis on individual organizers, is a model of the twenty-first century's management style.

Most important, networked power flows from the ability to make the maximum number of valuable connections. The next requirement is to have the knowledge and skills to harness that power to achieve a common purpose. The United States is already following this model in a few specific ways. In combating terrorism, it has been able to stop planned attacks thanks to a dense global network of law enforcement officers, counterterrorism officials, and intelligence agencies. The U.S. government dramatically improved its standing in the Muslim world due to its swift and effective relief effort in Asia following the December 2004 tsunami. It coordinated an emergency-response strategy among government agencies and aid workers in Australia, India, Japan, and the United States itself. More recently, when the global financial crisis hit this past fall, the United States first reached out to central banks around the world to coordinate a monetary response and then reached out to central banks in key emerging markets to make sure their foreign currency needs were being met.

From this vantage point, predictions of an Asian century—such as those made by Kishore Mahbubani, a foreign policy scholar and dean of the Lee Kwan Yew School of Public Policy, in Singapore—seem premature. Even Zakaria's argument about "the rise of the rest" takes on a different significance. If, in a networked world, the issue is no longer relative power but centrality in an increasingly dense global web, then the explosion of innovation and entrepreneurship occurring today will provide that many more points of possible connection. The twenty-first century looks increasingly like another American century—although it will likely be a century of the Americas rather than of just America.

More People, More Problems

Demography is often cited as the chief factor behind the relative decline of the West. China and India make up over a third of the world's population, while Europe and Japan are actually shrinking and the United States is suddenly a relatively small nation of 300 million. This argument, however, rests largely on assumptions formed in the nineteenth and twentieth centuries. Throughout most of human history, territory and population translated into military and economic power. Military power depended on the number of soldiers a state could put into the field, the amount of territory an enemy had to cross to conquer it, and the economy's ability to supply the state's army. Population size mattered for economic power because without trade a state needed a domestic market large enough for manufacturers and merchants to thrive. With trade, however, small mercantile nations such as the Netherlands and Portugal were able to punch far above their weight. In the nineteenth century, to increase their power, small countries expanded their territory through colonization. But by the twentieth century, as political unrest in the colonial world grew, the advantages of trading rather than ruling became increasingly clear. Although the United States and the Soviet Union, two great continental powers, dominated the second half of the twentieth century, the countries that grew the richest were often the smallest. In 2007, the ten countries with the highest per capita GDPs all had populations smaller than that of New York City, with one notable exception: the United States.

In the twenty-first century, less is more. Domestic markets must be big enough to allow national firms to obtain a foothold so as to withstand international competition (although such markets can be obtained through free-trade areas and economic unions). But beyond this minimum, if trade barriers are low and transportation and communication are cheap, then size will be more of a burden than a benefit. When both markets and production are global, then productive members of every society will generate income across multiple societies. Business managers in one country can generate value by orchestrating a global and disparate network of researchers, designers, manufacturers, marketers, and distributors. It will remain the responsibility of government, however, to provide for the less productive members of society, namely, the elderly, the young, the disabled, and the unemployed—think of them as national overhead costs. From this perspective, the 300 million citizens in the United States look much more manageable than the more than a billion in China or India.

A shrinking population can actually act as a catalyst for innovation. In China, the answer to many problems is simply to throw people at them—both because people are the most available commodity and because the Chinese government needs to provide as many jobs as possible. In Japan, by contrast, the answer is to innovate. Nintendo, the Kyoto-based gaming giant, is bringing much of its manufacturing back to Japan from China and other parts of Asia. How can it possibly compete using high-cost Japanese labor? It will not have to—its new factories are almost entirely automated, with only a handful of highly skilled employees needed to run them. This approach uses less energy, costs less, and guarantees a higher standard of living for the Japanese population. As the priority shifts from economic growth to sustainable growth, the formula of fewer people plus better and greener technology will look increasingly attractive.

Finally, size carries its own set of political challenges. Over the past four centuries, the arrow of history has pointed in the direction of national self-determination. Empires and multiethnic countries have steadily divided and subdivided into smaller units so that nations, or dominant ethnic groups, could govern themselves. Ninety years after Woodrow Wilson laid out his vision of self-determination for the Balkan states, the process continues in Kosovo. In many ways, the breakup of the Soviet Union was another round of the decolonization and self-determination movement that began in the 1940s. It continues today with the conflicts over Abkhazia and South Ossetia, as well as with the potential for conflict on the Crimean Peninsula and in eastern Ukraine. Much of China's 5,000-year history has been a saga of the country's splitting apart and being welded back together. The Chinese government, like the Indian government, legitimately fears that current pockets of instability could quickly translate into multiple secessionist movements.

The United States faces no threats to its essential unity, which has been forged by a political and cultural ideology of unity amid diversity. The principal alternative to this ideology is the solution employed by the European Union and the Association of Southeast Asian Nations (ASEAN), in which individual states come together as larger economic and, gradually, quasi-political units. The most promising dimension of recent Chinese politics has been its adoption of a version of this solution with regard to Hong Kong and Macao—and one day Beijing may apply this model to Taiwan.

The United States benefits not only from its limited population but also from who makes up that population. It has long attracted the world's most entrepreneurial, creative, and determined individuals. A vast mixing of cultures has created an atmosphere for a fruitful cross-fertilization and innovation. These arguments still hold. In San Francisco, for instance, a new municipal telephone help line advertises that it can talk with callers in over 150 languages. This diversity, and the creativity that it produces, is visible everywhere: in Hollywood movies, in American music, and at U.S. universities. At Princeton University this past fall, five of the six student award winners for the highest grade point averages had come from abroad: from China, Germany, Moldova, Slovenia, and Turkey.

In the nineteenth- and twentieth-century era of nation-states, the United States absorbed its immigrants and molded them into Americans, thereby creating the national cohesion necessary to build military and economic strength. Today, diversity in the United States means something more. Immigrant communities flourish not only in large cities but also in smaller towns and rural areas. A mosaic has replaced the melting pot, and, more than ever, immigrants connect their new communities to their countries of origin. Along the southern border of the United States, for instance, immigration experts talk about "transnational communities," about clusters of families in the United States linked with the villages of Mexico and Central America. Now, where you are from means where you can, and do, go back to—and whom you know and trust enough to network with.

Consider, for example, how valuable the overseas Chinese community has been to China. Alan Wang, a former student of mine, was born in China, moved to Australia with his family at the age of 12, and went to college and law school there. He later came to the United States to pursue a graduate degree at Harvard. For a while, he practiced law with a large British firm in London, and then moved to its Shanghai office. When I asked him how he identified himself, he replied, "overseas Chinese." Millions of people similar to Wang have spread out from China throughout Southeast Asia, Australia, the United States, and Canada, creating trading and networking opportunities for people in all those places. Similarly, the United States must learn to think of its

ethnic communities as the source of future generations of "overseas Americans." Already, young Chinese Americans and Indian Americans are heading back to their parents' homelands to seek opportunity and make their fortunes. Soon, the children of U.S. immigrants from Africa, Asia, Latin America, and the Middle East will follow a similar path and return to their ethnic homelands, at least for a time. The key to succeeding in a networked economy is being able to harvest the best ideas and innovations from the widest array of sources. In this regard, the United States is plugged into all corners of the global brain.

Beyond its immigrant communities, the United States can also depend on a new generation to forge connections around the world. John Zogby, the influential pollster, calls Americans between the ages of 18 and 29 "the First Globals," a group he describes as "more networked and globally engaged than members of any similar age cohort in American history." More than half of the respondents aged 18 to 29 in a poll conducted in the United States in June 2007 by Zogby International said that they had friends or family living outside the United States, vastly more than any other U.S. age group. Other Zogby polls have shown that this generation holds passports in roughly the same proportion as other age groups but uses them far more frequently. A quarter of this group, according to Zogby's data, believes that they will "end up living for some significant period in a country other than America."

These young people spreading out around the world will be a huge asset to the United States. Children born abroad who acquire U.S. citizenship as a result of their parents' heritage or life decisions will add to this number. A college classmate of mine was born to Hungarian immigrants in Canada and later acquired U.S. citizenship. After graduation, he moved to China and then Japan, where he gained a Japanese residency permit while also applying for Hungarian citizenship. He now lives with his Chinese wife in Beijing, where his daughter was born. Not long after her birth, he took her to Tokyo so that she could register as a U.S. citizen and reenter China on a U.S. passport. These stories are legion in any large global city—couples from two different countries who are raising their children in a third or fourth or even fifth country. For many people who orbit in this floating cloud of nationalities, a U.S. passport, particularly now that the United States has relaxed its rules on dual citizenship, has become a new kind of reserve currency. With one, even the most venturesome and peripatetic have the guarantee of the political and cultural stability of the West. The United States must devise the incentives and conditions that will allow it to both encourage this phenomenon and profit from it.

The World Is Round Again

For most of modern history, the Eurocentric view of the world has placed North and South America in a hemisphere of their own—the Western Hemisphere. Today, the world is mapped in the round, with Asia in the East and Africa, the Americas, and Europe in the West. That, at least, is how some Asians increasingly think of themselves. In his recently published book, *The New Asian Hemisphere: The Irresistible Shift of Global Power to the East,* Mahbubani argues that the era of "Western domination of world history is over" and that the world is witnessing an "Asian march to modernity."

But if half of the world is now "the East," defined as the Asian hemisphere, then the other half is the Atlantic hemisphere, made up of Africa, the Americas, and Europe. It is quite a promising neighborhood, home to a wealth of human, economic, material, and natural resources. Politically, Europe and North America constitute a spreading community of liberal democracies that accounts for one-sixth of the world's population, almost 60 percent of global GDP, and the two primary global reserve currencies. More trade and direct investment pass over the Atlantic Ocean than any other part of the world—over $2 trillion in cumulative foreign direct investment alone. The potential for further integration of the hemisphere is enormous.

Even more important is the potential for deeper economic integration within the Americas. On energy questions, Canadian oil sands and Brazilian sugar cane are more promising than depending on Russian pipelines or Sudanese oil. Markets for renewable energy—such as from biomass, wind, geothermal technology, and other sources—are growing in Latin America. Miami is already a financial center for Latin America, and the steady growth of the Latino population in the United States will only deepen intra-American investment. The rise of Brazil and, to a somewhat lesser extent, Mexico will create an emerging counterbalance to the United States south of its border. But any initiative for strengthening economic ties must come from the United States itself. It first must address its immigration policy and then, similar to the economic and political assistance it provided to the European Union, offer support for an economic union in Central and South America. The result could be an integrated market and trading bloc of 800 million people, with tremendous natural resources, enormous opportunities for development and sustainable growth, and deep ties to Africa, Asia, and Europe.

That market would still have the protection of two wide oceans, and even in a networked world, there are benefits in being disconnected. Those oceans protect the United States against massive refugee flows, against other threats to security from civil and interstate wars, and, increasingly, from the effects of climate change. Researchers at Princeton University have found that rain over the Pacific Ocean washes out of the air substantial amounts of ozone and some other gases emitted in Asia before the air can ever get to the Americas. Most climate-change projections forecast rising waters overflowing the deltas of South and Southeast Asia, potentially threatening millions of lives in countries such as Bangladesh. Increasing desertification in northern Africa will force emigrants across the Mediterranean and into Europe; a similar process in northern China could push even greater numbers into Russia. Conflict is likely to follow these displaced peoples. New democracies, such as Indonesia, and one-party states, such as China and Vietnam, will find themselves economically and politically vulnerable. Of course, the Americas will not be fully protected from rising oceans, flooding, desertification, or the other nasty consequences of climate change. Still, both geography and demography—and the absence of hundreds of millions of people on the move—will insulate the New World from the afflictions of the Old.

A Culture of Creation

A nation's economic fate depends on its being able to maintain and nurture innovation. This past year, all the U.S. presidential candidates made repeated calls for a renewal of the conditions that had long made the United States the world leader in

innovative technology. In the twenty-first century, corporations, civic organizations, and government agencies will increasingly operate by collecting the best ideas from around the globe. In such an environment, it is critical not only to stimulate domestic innovation but also to foster networks that can produce collaborative innovations across the globe.

To this end, the United States needs to improve education and increase government investment in science and technology. But the most important U.S. edge in innovation is cultural. Fundamental flaws in China's political and economic systems will make it very difficult for China to move from being the world's factory to being the world's designer. The Chinese government is determined to develop innovation as if it were developing a fancy variety of soybeans, relying on industrial parks that mix equal parts technology, education, research, and recreation in self-described "talent highlands." The results can be extraordinary, as I saw last year at the Shanghai Zizhu Science-Based Industrial Park. The park, built in just five years, has enormous university campuses, research headquarters for over 20 Asian and Western firms, and a residential complex. The aim is to inspire innovation through a balance of nature, science, and ecology, or, as its planners suggest, to create the "building blocks" for a future Chinese society, just like the building blocks for a new generation of skyscrapers.

The park is awe-inspiring. "In China," our guide told us, "anything is possible." Looking at the pace, scale, and quality of the construction, it was quite possible to believe it. In the end, however, the Zizhu industrial park struck me as being similar to an aquacultural facility for manufacturing cultured pearls. But as all pearl lovers know, the richest innovations are created through unexpected and irregular irritations, not tightly controlled conditions. In 2003, the University of California alone generated more patents than either China or India. That same year, IBM generated five times as many patents as both countries combined. The problem is certainly not a lack of creativity on the part of Chinese or Indians; Silicon Valley is full of entrepreneurs from both groups. The issue is the surrounding culture, or what the urban studies theorist Richard Florida calls an "innovation ecosystem."

At the same time that China is seeking to maintain political tranquility, it depends on continued growth powered by innovation, which requires conflict—not violent conflict but positive, or constructive, conflict, the kind of conflict that produces non-zero-sum solutions. This is the kind of conflict found on American playing fields, in American courtrooms, and in the American political system. It is the conflict of structured competition, in which losers have a chance to win another day and everyone has a stake in continually improving the game. It is also the conflict of creative destruction, the process of destroying old business models to make way for new ones.

Most important, a culture of constructive conflict rewards challenging authority in every domain. Perhaps the best example is Google, a company in which hierarchy is almost nonexistent. Individuals are encouraged to go their own way, come up with their own ideas, and counter orthodoxies at every turn. In the United States, educational institutions have long emphasized critical thinking in ways that China and other countries are now trying to emulate. But a culture of innovation requires more than the ability to critique. It requires saying what you think, rather than what you believe your boss wants to hear, something many

Western managers struggle fruitlessly to encourage in China. A culture that requires a constant willingness to reimagine the world is not one that the Chinese Communist Party is likely to embrace. Indeed, a culture of innovation requires the encouragement of conflict within a larger culture of transparency and trust, placing a premium on cross-cultural competence. It is a culture for which Americans are ideally suited by both temperament and history.

The World of Wikis

Starting with Alexis de Tocqueville, nearly every observer of American culture has noted that Americans are inveterate joiners, volunteers, and debaters. Today, however, instead of sewing circles, debating societies, and charity bake sales, Americans have MySpace, blogs, and the Clinton Global Initiative. These qualities are evident in a growing number of collaborative enterprises, both online and off. In the world of wikis, perhaps best exemplified by Wikipedia, ideas are challenged, edited, and challenged again. The final product is the result of a different and gentler kind of adversarial process than that found in the U.S. legal system. But the premise is the same: multiple minds clashing and correcting one another in pursuit of the truth. The work of one contributor is open and available for others to use. Participants in this process are trusted to not take advantage of that openness but instead add their own contributions.

In a world that favors decentralization and positive conflict, the United States has an edge. Although trust and transparency are not unique to the United States, it is still one of the most open societies in the world. The Internet world, the wiki world, and the networked world all began in the United States and radiated outward. The characteristics of those worlds are the keys to innovation and problem solving in the twenty-first century.

In his book *Nonzero: The Logic of Human Destiny,* Robert Wright, a senior fellow at the New America Foundation, writes of human history as a steady process of increased exposure to complexity and the resulting ability to turn zero-sum problems into non-zero-sum solutions. The barbarian invasions that swept across Asia and Europe, for instance, were disastrous for many individual societies. Yet by adding new ideas and practices to the sum of human knowledge, the invaders spurred the process of innovation and problem solving. In other words, they brought progress. Today, the invaders are online rather than on horseback, and interaction is considerably more voluntary. The benefits will flow to those individuals and states that are most comfortable reaching across cultures. It will become increasingly necessary to appreciate and absorb contributions in any language and from any context.

Here, however, the conventional wisdom depicts Americans as woefully ignorant of foreign geography, languages, and cultures. Many Americans may still fit this description. But many others—immigrants and their children especially—negotiate cultural differences every day in their schools, in their workplaces, and on the street. From Boston to Los Angeles, recently immigrated Africans, Arabs, East Asians, Latinos, South Asians, and Southeast Asians all rub shoulders with members of more established communities, both black and white. At the elite level, the top graduate schools in the United States offer a similar education in multicultural competence; many of the cross-cultural couples

who are changing the face of global cities met at places such as Harvard and Stanford. Obama's parents may have been ahead of their time, but today far more young Americans than ever before are following their example. They are truly, as Zogby calls them, "the First Globals."

How to Get There from Here

At the moment, the United States' edge in this new world is more potential than actual. The country will face a vast amount of work in digging itself out of the many holes it has gotten itself into, both at home and abroad. In the process, the United States must adopt five policies and postures that will seize on its edge and sharpen it.

First, the United States must adopt comprehensive immigration reform that will make it easier for immigrants and guest workers to move across borders, regularize the status of the millions of illegal immigrants currently in the United States, and increase the number of visas for the world's most talented individuals. Part of changing U.S. attitudes toward immigration must include a recognition that because of their ties to their home countries, immigrants are potential engines of economic growth. New economic policies could offer subsidies or tax incentives to immigrants who create businesses based on connections they have cultivated to markets and talent in their home countries. Instead of a one-way, outgoing flow of remittances, the United States needs a two-way flow of goods, services, and people.

Second, as part of overhauling its educational system, the United States must come to see overseas study as an essential asset for all Americans. Indeed, organizations such as the Brown-Bell Foundation promote opportunities to study abroad for students at historically black colleges and universities, where such programs have traditionally been lacking. Just as important, the United States must see the children of immigrants who grow up learning Arabic, Hindi, Mandarin, Spanish, and other foreign languages as huge assets. Government programs and private initiatives should encourage them to study abroad in the countries of their parents or grandparents and, assuming they keep their U.S. passports, to gain dual citizenship.

A networked world requires a genuinely networked society, which means fostering economic and social equality. The United States has never been as egalitarian as it imagines itself to be, but this divide has worsened in the past decade, as the rich have become the superrich. Between the late 1950s and 2005, the income share of the wealthiest one percent of the U.S. population more than doubled. Even the Democratic Party is not immune: on the night that Obama accepted the nomination to be the Democratic presidential candidate, at Invesco Field in Denver, Colorado, his campaign blocked off an entire section of the stadium for big donors, stopping everyone else at the door. For a time, a culture in which money could buy status was a radically democratic and egalitarian idea. Instead of the European class system, in which breeding always trumped money, Americans could rely on education and employment for self-advancement. But this same culture becomes radically inegalitarian if only a relatively few have the chance to prosper financially. As the political scientist Larry Bartels argues, rising economic inequality is a political choice: Republican presidents have generally allowed inequality to expand, whereas Democratic presidents have not. If so, then the United States can choose to decrease inequality by making its society more horizontal, more democratic, and more integrated by class and race—and this is the third reform it should adopt. Doing so would add more potential circuits to the network.

Fourth, in foreign policy, the United States should put more effort toward engaging Latin America—not at the expense of its ties with Asia but in addition to the strong history of transpacific relations. Brazil, for example, defines its foreign policy in terms of concentric circles. It starts with Mercosur, the South American trading bloc, then continues to Latin America, the Americas, and then the rest of the world. Similarly, the United States should think in terms of the North American Free Trade Agreement and the Americas before turning to the rest of the world. The potential for growth and development in the Americas is enormous. Population links between the United States and Latin America are strong and growing stronger. Spanish is now taught in virtually every American public school from the early grades. Strengthening ties with Latin America also means cultivating links across the South Atlantic to Mediterranean countries such as Spain and Portugal, and also to France and Italy. Lastly, African blood runs in the veins of many North, Central, and South Americans. This fact is the legacy of a ghastly institution, but it means that many Americans have an African heritage that can allow them to reconnect with Africa today.

More generally, the United States must learn to see both itself and the world differently. If power is derived from connectivity, then the focus of leadership should be on making connections to solve shared problems. This approach is not only a different leadership style than that which has prevailed in the United States in recent years but also a fundamentally different concept of leadership. In contrast to the way it is in a hierarchy, in this concept of leadership a single leader cannot be directly in charge of everyone else. Different countries can mobilize diverse coalitions for specific purposes. Regional powers, for example, can address crises in their particular parts of the world: consider Australia's role in promoting stability in East Timor, ASEAN's ability to convince the Myanmar government to accept foreign aid after Cyclone Nargis, or Turkey's work in pushing for talks between Syria and Israel. The range and complexity of foreign policy challenges—and the speed with which a crisis can escalate—mean that knowing the right people to call and the right levers to pull in any corner of the world must be a key element of U.S. diplomacy.

Finally, the United States must recognize the necessity of orchestrating networks of public, private, and civic actors to address global problems. The era of government formulating and executing policy entirely on its own is over, even with a revitalized U.S. government that has a greater social and economic mandate. Outsourcing government functions to private and civic contractors is not the answer, however; government officials must instead learn to orchestrate networks of these actors and guide them toward collaborative solutions.

Sharpening the Edge

In this century, global power will increasingly be defined by connections—who is connected to whom and for what purposes. Of course, the world will still contain conflict. Networks can be as malign and deadly as they can be productive and beneficial. In addition, the gap between those who are connected to global networks and those who are excluded from them will sharply multiply existing inequities.

But on the whole, the positive effects of networks will greatly outweigh the negative. Imagine, for example, a U.S. economy powered by green technology and green infrastructure. Communities of American immigrants from Africa, Asia, Europe, Latin America, and the Middle East will share this new generation of products and services with villages and cities in their home countries. Innovation will flow in both directions. In the United States, universities will be able to offer courses in truly global classrooms, relying on their international students and faculty to connect with educational institutions abroad through travel, the Internet, and videoconferencing. Artists of all kinds will sit at the intersection of culture, learning, and creative energy. U.S. diplomats and other U.S. government officials will receive instant updates on events occurring around the world. They will be connected to their counterparts abroad, able to quickly coordinate preventive and problem-solving actions with a range of private and civic actors. The global landscape will resemble that of the Obama campaign, in which a vast network brought in millions of dollars in donations, motivated millions of volunteers, and mobilized millions of voters.

In a networked world, the United States has the potential to be the most connected country; it will also be connected to other power centers that are themselves widely connected. If it pursues the right policies, the United States has the capacity and the cultural capital to reinvent itself. It need not see itself as locked in a global struggle with other great powers; rather, it should view itself as a central player in an integrated world. In the twenty-first century, the United States' exceptional capacity for connection, rather than splendid isolation or hegemonic domination, will renew its power and restore its global purpose.

Critical Thinking

1. Give examples of three different types of connections that the United States has with other states or other actors in the world that contribute to its power.

2. Explain why you agree or disagree with Anne-Marie Slaughter's thesis that the United States inter-consecutiveness makes it the most powerful country in the world.

ANNE-MARIE SLAUGHTER is Dean of the Woodrow Wilson School of Public and International Affairs and Bert G. Kerstetter '66 University Professor of Politics and International Affairs at Princeton University.

Europe, the Second Superpower

"There are, and will remain for the foreseeable future, two global superpowers: the United States and Europe. Only these two actors are consistently able to project a full spectrum of 'smart power' internationally."

ANDREW MORAVCSIK

It has become fashionable to view the global system as dominated by the United States, China, and India. How often do we hear from leading politicians that "The most important relationship in the twenty-first century is that between Washington and Beijing"? Or that the "rise of the rest" is the great phenomenon of our time? Missing from this equation is Europe. The "Old Continent's" reputation for sluggish economic and demographic growth, political disunity, and weak militaries has convinced most foreign analysts that the future belongs to Asia and the United States.

Indeed, among scholars, commentators, and politicians alike, the conventional view is that the contemporary world is "unipolar," with the United States standing alone as a sole superpower. With the rise of China, India, and perhaps some other nations, the world may become—if it is not already—multipolar. But Europe's role in the geopolitical balance, according to this view, remains insignificant.

Such claims rest on economic, demographic, and military measures of power. European economic growth, it is said, is slow and getting slower. Meanwhile, a Brookings Institution study predicts that the median age in Europe will increase to 52.3 years in 2050 from 37.7 years in 2003 (whereas the median age for Americans will be only 35.4 years). This will have negative effects on Europe's productivity, growth, and fiscal stability. And as long as the United States spends twice as much of its national income on defense as Europe collectively does, it is suggested, the Europeans are condemned to second-tier status. From Beijing to Washington—and even in Brussels—the Old Continent is widely viewed as a spent geopolitical force.

These prognoses of European decline are misguided. In fact, the world today has two global superpowers. One is the United States—the other is Europe. Europe is the only region in the world, besides the United States, able to exert global influence across the full spectrum of power, from "hard" to "soft." Europe is the only region, besides the United States, that projects intercontinental military power. And European countries possess a range of effective civilian instruments for projecting international influence that is unmatched by any country, even the United States. These tools include European Union enlargement, neighborhood policy, trade, foreign aid, support for multilateral institutions and international law, and European values.

Since the end of the cold war, as the world system has become more interdependent, networked, democratic, and freer of overt ideological rivalry, Europe's distinctive instruments of influence have become relatively more effective, leading to a rise in European power. Over the next three or four generations, trends in the foundations of European power—high per capita income, sophisticated economic production, and patterns of global consensus—are also likely to be favorable. If we view power in this multidimensional way, Europe is clearly the second superpower in a bipolar world.

Realists versus Reality

From a theoretical perspective, the conclusion that Europe is in terminal decline as a force in great power politics rests on a traditional "realist" worldview. According to this view, sovereign nations engage in zero-sum competition by mobilizing coercive power resources. Such resources stem ultimately from gross demographic and economic power, which can be converted into relative military advantage.

According to this theory, Europe's global influence—its ability to get what it wants—will decline proportionately with its percentage of aggregate global power resources. Most realists believe the global system is already unipolar, with the United States as the sole superpower (though they differ about the precise consequences of this fact). They believe the system is trending toward one in which the largest sovereign states—the United States, China, and India—will dominate an increasingly multipolar system.

Immediately upon the collapse of the Soviet Union nearly 20 years ago, realists such as John Mearsheimer, Kenneth Waltz, Stephen Walt, and Charles Kupchan began predicting that the decline of an immediate, common Soviet threat would undermine transatlantic cooperation, sow discord among Western powers, weaken NATO, and hurt European cooperation. The Iraq crisis, with its illusion of "soft balancing" against the United States, seemed to confirm this prognosis.

For slightly different reasons, having to do with new challenges coming from autocracies like Russia and China, as well as from Islamic radicals, neoconservatives have predicted disorder, believing, in Robert Kagan's words, that "the twenty-first century will look like the nineteenth." Neoconservatives like Kagan share the realist view that greater military power projection capability is the key for Europe to be taken seriously in the contemporary world. For Europe to reestablish itself as a major global force, or simply to hedge against a wayward America, many have argued that meaningful European defense cooperation and a European defense buildup would be required.

Few short-term predictions in social science are as clear as these—and few have been, thus far, so unambiguously disconfirmed. Over the past two decades, Europeans, both among themselves and in the transatlantic relationship, have experienced extraordinary amity, cooperation, and policy success. The continent has been pacified. The EU has enjoyed an astonishingly successful run: It completed the single market; established a single currency; created a zone without internal frontiers ("Schengen"); launched common defense, foreign, and internal security policies; promulgated a constitutional treaty; and, most importantly, expanded from 12 to 27 multicultural members, with a half dozen more states on the list to join eventually.

Far from falling into disarray, the EU has emerged as the most ambitious and successful international organization of all time, pioneering institutional practices far in advance of anything seen elsewhere. At the same time, despite its lack of any military buildup, Europe has established itself unambiguously as the world's "second" military power, with combat troops active across the globe.

The EU has emerged as the most ambitious and successful international organization of all time.

Its military operations, moreover, are conducted almost exclusively in close cooperation with the United States. No Euro-Chinese "balancing" alliance has emerged. Instead, America and Europe have drawn closer together (the Iraq crisis constituting the single major exception). Meanwhile, the EU's distinctive tools of civilian influence have gained in utility vis-à-vis hard military power. The EU's enlargement may well be the single most cost-effective instrument to spread peace and security that the West has deployed over the past 20 years.

To understand why realist predictions were so wrong, we need to turn away from realism to a liberal theory of international relations. "Liberal" does not refer here to a theory that stresses the role of international law and institutions, nor left-of-center or utopian ideals, nor unbounded belief in *laissez faire* economics. What is meant instead is a theoretical approach to analyzing international relations that emphasizes the varied underlying national interests—"state preferences"—that governments bring to world politics, and which are transmitted from society to decision makers via domestic politics, societal interdependence, and globalization.

In the liberal view, these varied social pressures are the most fundamental cause of foreign policy behavior. Zero-sum security rivalry, military force, and power balancing are not ubiquitous conditions. They are only a few among a number of possible circumstances—in fact, they are rather rare. Increasingly, international interactions are positive-sum, such that the rise of more than one country or region can be complementary.

Liberals argue that the realist view of power, whereby global influence is grounded in population and aggregate national income, which feed into military mobilization and spending, may not be entirely irrelevant, but it is no longer central to most issues in world politics—if indeed it ever was. Instead, most global

influence today rests on various forms of "civilian" power: high per capita income; a central position in networks of trade, investment, and migration; an important role in international institutions; and the attractiveness of social and political values. All of these are areas in which Europe is and will remain preeminent for the foreseeable future.

Venus and Mars Too

Europe's comparative advantage lies in its projection of influence via economic and civilian instruments. But Europe is also a far more formidable military power than most observers acknowledge. The reason is that a major military force is, in the modern world, a luxury that can be mustered only by countries with a high per capita income, technological sophistication, and a long legacy of military spending. Europe enjoys unique advantages in these areas.

Many observers write off European military power entirely. Kagan's catchphrase, "Americans are from Mars, Europeans are from Venus," is often believed, even in Europe. Yet Europe accounts for 21 percent of the world's military spending—a good deal less than America's 43 percent, to be sure, but still considerably more than China's 5 percent, Russia's 3 percent, India's 2 percent, and Brazil's 1.5 percent.

Europeans, moreover, do not just equip forces; they use them. European states have had 50,000 to 100,000 troops stationed in combat roles outside their home countries for most of the past decade. They provide the bulk of non-US troops in global operations. Listening to criticism of Europeans for their failure to do more in Iraq and Afghanistan might give one the impression that only Americans are engaged there. In fact, 24 allied countries, of which 21 are European, are involved in Afghanistan. Military interventions and peacekeeping operations, if they are not led by the United States, tend to be led by Europeans—as in Sierra Leone, Lebanon, and Chad.

Arguably, European interventions in low-intensity situations are more effective than those of the United States. Certainly no region or country, save America, possesses a portfolio of military capabilities and a willingness to use them comparable to Europe's—nor is any likely to challenge European preeminence soon. China's military remains a largely landlocked, labor-intensive force still focused on Taiwan and internal security. Russia, with far greater military assets than China's, does little more than project power into renegade provinces like Chechnya, or a few hundred miles over the border into the former Soviet republic of Georgia.

The Power of Attraction

Its considerable hard power notwithstanding, Europe is, in contrast to the United States, a "quiet" superpower. It specializes in the use of economic influence, international law, "soft power" (the capacity to attract others to your way of thinking), and "smart power" (matching military with civilian forms of influence). In fact, Europe today is more effective at projecting civilian power globally than any other state or non-state actor. And Europeans have demonstrated, contra realist claims, that such instruments of power can be extremely influential. Some of these tools are wielded by a unified Europe, some by European governments acting in loose coordination, and some by European governments acting unilaterally.

Europe today is more effective at projecting civilian power globally than any other state or non-state actor.

Accession to the EU is the single most powerful policy instrument Europe possesses. Since 1989, Europe's "power of attraction" has helped stabilize the polities and economies of over a dozen neighboring countries. Enlargement has created a focal point and a set of incentives around which moderate domestic forces have organized. And the effects are visible well beyond the 12 members that have joined most recently, with European influence powerful in Croatia, Serbia, Montenegro, Albania, Macedonia, and even Turkey. EU enlargement has almost certainly had far more impact—and in a less provocative way—than NATO enlargement. The United States, China, India, Japan, and other major powers enjoy no comparable instruments for projecting regional influence.

In addition, Europe pursues an active "neighborhood policy," intervening diplomatically to resolve conflicts and promote political and economic reform in its neighborhood, backed by Europe's economic, financial, legal, and military might. The EU has signed association and free trade arrangements with many countries in the broader region. Europeans have taken the lead in recent successful diplomatic initiatives—and not just with states that are candidates for EU membership. Even where membership is only a distant possibility, as with Ukraine, Moldova, or Albania, or an essentially nonexistent possibility, as with Morocco, Libya, and Israel, there is evidence that EU initiatives have had an impact. For example, quiet EU diplomacy toward Morocco—backed by trade, immigration, security, and human rights ties—has been credited with encouraging political and economic reform in that country.

More fundamentally, European governments are the strongest and most consistent supporters of international law and institutions across the board. The EU is the single largest financial contributor to the UN system. Europeans fund 38 percent of the UN's regular budget, more than two-fifths of UN peacekeeping operations, and about one-half of all UN member states' contributions to UN funds and programs. EU member states are also signatories to almost all international treaties currently in force.

Europeans are overrepresented compared to their population in many international organizations. Those who favor institutional reform of highly symbolic elite international leadership bodies such as the UN Security Council and the G-groups, presumably with the aim of integrating and socializing some larger developing countries into responsible statecraft, have been critical of European obstruction. Yet Europeans did not block the Group of Eight's evolution into the G-20, and they have favored integration of developing countries like China into functional organizations such as the World Trade Organization (WTO). Many believe that, with US cooperation in recent years, a deal would have been possible on Security Council reform as well.

A Global Economic Force

In trade and investment affairs, Europe is a global economic superpower larger than the United States and far ahead of countries such as China or India. And in some respects, Europe is institutionally better able to exploit its economic position. What motivates countries outside the EU to participate in its enlargement or neighborhood policies, after all, is not primarily an idealistic desire to be part of "Europe," but rather a desire to enjoy the enormous economic benefits of membership in (or association with) the EU. Europe dominates its neighborhood economically, trading more with each Middle Eastern country (except Jordan), and nearly all African countries, than any other single trading partner.

Europe's continuing economic influence extends to the global level. Even excluding intra-regional trade, the EU is the largest exporter and importer in the world. Of the top nine exporting countries in the world, five are European: Germany, France, Italy, the United Kingdom, and the Netherlands. Germany alone exports roughly as much as China every year, and its goods have far more value added. Europe trades more with China than the United States does, and its bilateral balance of trade is stronger. Yet trade statistics actually understate the importance of European centrality in the world economy.

If we measure intra-firm trade, investment, and research and development—increasingly the true drivers of modern international economic activity—then Europe remains an order of magnitude more important than China or India. Often, trade statistics are cited in the United States to illustrate a shift from Atlantic to Pacific economic activity. But if we look not at trade but at investment, US affiliate sales, foreign assets, and R&D—which are more profound measures of modern economic activity—transatlantic economic exchange is far more robust than transpacific exchange. Europe accounted for over 57 percent of total US foreign direct investment from 2000 to 2008, while total US investment in China, India, Russia, and Brazil *combined* was only 14 percent. In this same period, US firms invested $26.4 billion in China—less than half of US investment in Ireland alone. And Europe is still far and away the most important global R&D destination for US companies.

The EU's common currency, the euro, is the only serious alternative to the dollar as a global reserve currency. Although the euro will not supplant the dollar any time soon, in part because of the greater depth of American capital markets, it has established an important secondary position. At the end of 2008, some 45 percent of international debt securities were denominated in dollars, compared to 32 percent in euros.

European policy on tariffs and other basic trade issues is unified, due to the EU's status as a customs union. The EU negotiates as a bloc at the WTO. While it is true that developing countries are playing a stronger role today, and the trading world is slowly growing more multipolar, the EU and the United States remain dominant forces within the WTO. China, by contrast, has accommodated itself to Western terms in order to enter the trading system.

Meanwhile, even with a recent increase in US aid, EU member states and the European Commission together dispense about 50 percent of the world's foreign aid, while the US share amounts to about 20 percent. Europe is second to none at delivering development services. And, contrary to popular belief, the EU even exceeds the United States in disbursement of private aid.

Europe's political and social values are certainly no less important a support for its global influence. Both polling and practice suggest that European social and political models are more attractive worldwide than US alternatives. Apparently publics around the world favor generous social welfare and health policies, parliamentary government, adherence to international human rights standards, and a smaller role for money in politics—all associated with Europe. Very few countries in the so-called third wave of democracies have copied major elements of the US Constitution.

Taken together with its military activities, Europe's civilian capabilities, economic importance, and political attractiveness render it a full-spectrum power, wielding a wide range of instruments for regional and global influence.

Europe's Future

Of course Europe's civilian as well as its military power derives ultimately from a highly productive economy. Policies like EU enlargement and association agreements with neighboring states are attractive to others because of the massive pull of the European economy. Aid, education, trade, the European social model, and other aspects of Europe's foreign policy portfolio must be funded. Moreover, the informational, educational, and legal sophistication of European policies are byproducts of highly developed economies.

This has led many to ask whether sluggish demographic and economic growth rates will undermine Europe's role in the world. A 2008 assessment by the US National Intelligence Council (NIC) is typical. The NIC suggested:

> The drop-off in working-age population will prove a severe test for Europe's social welfare model, a foundation stone of Western Europe's political cohesion since World War II. Progress on economic liberalization is likely to continue only in gradual steps until aging populations or prolonged economic stagnation force more dramatic changes. There are no easy fixes for Europe's demographic deficits except likely cutbacks in health and retirement benefits. Defense expenditures are likely to be cut further to stave off the need for serious restructuring of social benefits programs. The challenge of integrating immigrant, especially Muslim, communities will become acute if citizens faced with a sudden lowering of expectations resort to more narrow nationalism and concentrate on parochial interests, as happened in the past. Europe's strategic perspective is likely to remain narrower than Washington's. Divergent threat perceptions within Europe and the likelihood that defense spending will remain uncoordinated suggest the EU will not be a major military power by 2025.

There are three main reasons why this sort of conventional pessimism about Europe's future is misguided. First, demographic and economic estimates of European decline are greatly exaggerated. Europe constitutes a bloc of countries that, whether or not they are explicitly coordinated, generally take similar positions. And the size of Europe's population, as a whole, is quite significant in relation to that of other great powers. It will remain so for generations.

The European share of global economic activity has been stable over time. Even evaluated by the traditional measures of aggregate population and GDP, Europe's relative slice is declining only very slowly. Analysts often overlook that even the direst prognoses project Europe's share of global GDP declining from 22 percent to 17 percent over the next generation—hardly catastrophic. And these scenarios rest on the historically unprecedented assumption that Asian growth rates will continue at around 10 percent for over 30 years—an unlikely scenario given demographic, environmental, and political hurdles facing Asian societies.

The second reason that the conventional view of European decline is misleading is that aggregate population and GDP are the wrong measures of power. The linear relationship between global power and gross population and GDP is an analytical anachronism of the nineteenth and twentieth centuries. Liberal theory is highly suspicious of any such simple relationship, in part because the extent of underlying conflicts of interest among states is a variable rather than a constant: Rivalries can occur, but the zero-sum situations assumed by realism are relatively rare.

When most governments had few social welfare demands, could reliably control colonial territory, and planned for wartime mass mobilization, as during World Wars I and II or the cold war, population and aggregate GDP were perhaps plausible determinants of great power geopolitical influence. Yet today the primary imperative for most governments—not least those in Beijing, New Delhi, Brasília, and other major emerging country capitals—is to maintain legitimacy by providing adequate economic growth, social mobility, and public services. Interstate war of any kind, let alone total war decided by the total commitment of population and thus aggregate GDP or demographics, has become exceedingly rare among great powers.

Indeed, for poor countries, a large population can be as much a burden as a benefit. Consider China. One often reads alarming statistics about the sheer size of the Chinese population, economy, or military. But China would be far more capable internationally without the political imperative of caring for 700 million poor Chinese in the hinterland—the welfare of whom constitutes the paramount political issue for any Chinese leader. Were this not enough of a headache, Chinese and Indian leaders face opposition from unruly national minorities across their vast multicultural spaces. The need to devote resources to internal priorities imposes a fundamental constraint on military spending and foreign policy adventurism.

This is not to deny that Europe may face difficulties allocating resources in the future, or that the relative size of the United States, China, and Europe counts for something. But crude demographic and economic size is less important than high *per capita* income—and in this area the long-term structural trends still greatly favor Europe.

Per capita income not only measures the existence of a surplus that can be used to fund international power projection. It also indicates (in non–resource-based economies) the complexity and modernization of a society aiming to support sophisticated civilian power instruments. Effective forms of global influence these days—not just advanced military technology, but also education, sophisticated legal mechanisms of cooperation, foreign aid, complex trade and investment arrangements, advanced political institutions, effective diplomatic engagement, and inward immigration—all suppose high per capita income.

High per capita income, moreover, generates cultural influence. Again, consider China. Certainly Chinese economic influence is growing in East Asia, and with it the number of people speaking Chinese, studying in China, and perhaps even appreciating things Chinese. But China and its culture do not have nearly the preponderant weight that Japanese or Korean culture enjoys in the region—let alone the extraordinary impact that EU legal norms have had in "Europeanizing" the other end of Eurasia, or that Anglophone language and culture enjoy across the globe.

17

The Cooperative Giant

The third and most important reason that the conventional view of European demographic and economic decline is misleading is that governments increasingly interact on the basis of reciprocity—peaceful, negotiated exchange of concessions—unrelated to traditional material coercive capabilities of any kind. Europe is well placed to take advantage of this shift, because underlying material and ideological conflict between Europe and other great powers is decreasing. The cold war is over. Fundamental ideological alternatives to regulated capitalism are disappearing. Democracy is spreading. Nationalist conflicts are disappearing, particularly in the immediate proximity of Europe. As most global relations become more positive-sum, and great power war becomes rarer, the value of Europe's portfolio of civilian power instruments will be multiplied.

This prediction is consistent with liberal international relations theory. Liberal theory treats the level of convergence of and conflict between nations' underlying social interests as a variable that shapes international relations. Contrary to realist predictions, Europe and the EU have been *rising* in regional and global influence over the past 20 years. And this is not only because, as we have seen, Europe's civilian instruments of power projection have become more appropriate. It is also because the extent to which any given nation can project influence depends on the extent to which its interests converge with those of other, particularly neighboring, great powers. The greater the level of consensus, the greater the slack resources available to a state. Where underlying preferences converge due to trade, democracy, and ideological convergence—the trends we have observed over the past two decades—we should expect to see widespread opportunities for cooperation with interdependent, democratic, modern states, such as those of Europe.

Looking to the future, three specific types of converging international interests are likely to be particularly advantageous for Europe, augmenting its relative global influence. First, Europe is increasingly *a quiet region.* European countries face an ever-smaller number of security threats within their region. Now that Balkan security threats have died down, the closest live threats are in the Caucasus, in the Middle East, or perhaps across the Mediterranean. This permits European governments to focus efforts "out of area." By contrast, Asian powers face a far more hostile immediate environment. One player's rapid ascent in that region is more likely to provoke alarm among its closest neighbors. So, even if Asian powers were to increase their military power in the future, it is less likely that they would be able to project it globally.

A second advantage enjoyed by Europe is a felicitous shift in the preferences of major governments around the world. Most European policy goals involve efforts to encourage ongoing long-term reform of countries in the direction of democracy, economic development, and cooperative international relations. Most great powers—most notably China and Russia, for all their problems—have made enormous strides in this direction since the end of the cold war. This reduces the useful range of (American) high-intensity military capabilities, while increasing the utility of European civilian power instruments. As more countries become market-oriented, democratic, and free of expansionist ideological claims, we should expect European policies to be better suited to advancing the regional and global interests of European countries. European preferences on major global issues are increasingly compatible with median views of the global community. Europe should find itself closer to the consensus point of global bargains.

Finally, Europe's relationship with the United States, whatever tensions there may be, contains less conflict than at any time in recent memory. This is even true in the area where realists and neoconservatives alike have predicted the least agreement, namely military intervention "out of area." Far from being a source of greater transatlantic conflict compared to during the cold war, military intervention today is a matter of near total Euro-American consensus.

There is of course the fact that coalitions of Europeans and Americans are fighting together in the periphery, including forces from a much broader range of countries (such as Germany, as well as the Eastern bloc countries) than ever were involved during the cold war. Even more striking is the high level of current transatlantic consensus about the proper purposes of such interventions. Since the end of the cold war, a period that has seen well over a dozen major military interventions by Western powers, fundamental disagreement has arisen in *only one case:* Iraq in 1998–2003. (I set aside tactical disagreements over the timing and mode of Balkans interventions, which were in any case eventually resolved.)

The "war of choice" in Iraq is truly an exception that proves the rule, since it is now widely viewed in retrospect as a policy error—of a sort that would be unsustainable as an instrument of US policy more than once in a generation. Post–cold war transatlantic consensus with regard to the use of force contrasts strikingly with relations during the last 25 years of the cold war, during which the United States and Europe disagreed on almost every major unilateral military intervention after Korea. In many cases Europeans voted against their US allies in the UN or even funded US enemies, as in Latin America.

Liberal theory's emphasis on the convergence of state preferences as a precondition for cooperation, rather than the realist focus on power balancing, leads to the prediction that US-EU cooperation is likely to persist.

Decentralization Works

Europe, it is often argued, must unify in order to become a superpower. Proposals to achieve this include an expansion of majority voting, a centralized spokesperson, mandatory common policies, a common European military force, a European defense industry policy, and so on. Centralization is often taken to be the measure of effectiveness. If centralizing reforms fail, European defense and foreign policies fail as well.

In fact, Europe has centralized a number of important policies: on trade, enlargement, regulation, UN issues, and many more. But many EU policies, particularly the more "political-military" ones, remain essentially decentralized. Is Europe destined to remain, as Henry Kissinger once said of Germany, an "economic giant and a political dwarf"?

Not as much as it may seem. Europe often functions very effectively as a rather decentralized network of governments—at times more effectively than it would if it were more centralized. During the cold war, European security policy was dominated by the task of establishing a collective deterrent against potential Soviet intimidation or attack. This task required extremely credible common positions. The result was a centralized institutional and ideological apparatus. Considerable pressure was placed on any government that strayed from common NATO policy.

Post–cold war security challenges, by contrast, do not generally involve direct and immediate security threats to Europe, beyond homeland security concerns. The challenge is rather to encourage a subset of countries to deploy a modest force against a smaller enemy in pursuit of a secondary security concern. It is unrealistic to expect the EU or any international organization to "pre-commit" governments to act in such circumstances. And needless to say, governments in Europe are unlikely to relinquish sovereignty to form a common European army. They did not do so during the cold war, when the threat was more serious than it is today. Given the smaller scale and less imperative nature of current operations, it is often unnecessary, even counterproductive, for all nations to be involved in any given action. The more decentralized, "coalition-of-the-willing" form of Europe today may thus be more effective because it is more flexible. Particularly in conditions of incomplete consensus, decentralized institutions may be better suited to the challenges facing the continent.

The Treaty of Lisbon, the compromise conclusion of the European Constitution, though much maligned, in fact has done a good deal to improve the European balance of centralization and flexibility. It has created a European "foreign minister" figure who can set the agenda for EU decision making, represent the EU abroad, and reduce competition among EU institutions. But the treaty also facilitates the use of EU institutions for military activities by subgroups ("coalitions of the willing") among EU countries. In any case, it is unnecessary for Europe to unify or centralize far beyond what it has already done in order to reap the benefits of its power.

Rising in Tandem

The world today is bipolar. There are, and will remain for the foreseeable future, two global superpowers: the United States and Europe. Only these two actors are consistently able to project a full spectrum of "smart power" internationally. And European states possess an unmatched range and depth of civilian instruments for international influence. Because the post–cold war world is continuously becoming a more hospitable place for the exercise of forms of power that are, in practice, distinctively European, Europe's influence has increased accordingly. There is every reason to believe this trend will continue.

This is not to deny that a number of other great powers—the United States, China, and India among them—are also on the rise. This may seem contradictory: How can most great powers be "rising" at once? In fact, this is a puzzle only for realists, who assume that the aims of governments conflict in a zero-sum fashion. From a liberal perspective, the notion that more than one country gains influence at the same time is quite natural, as long as the

environment is essentially positive-sum and the countries' aims are compatible.

> **How can most great powers be "rising" at once? This is a puzzle only for realists, who assume that the aims of governments conflict.**

The rise of other powers—the economic success of China, the military prowess of America, the emergence of new partners on Europe's borders—has not undermined Europe's rise; it has enhanced it.

Nevertheless, in Washington, Europe is still widely viewed as a declining region, barely able to take care of its own geopolitical interests, and increasingly irrelevant unless it centralizes its policy making. It is ironic that this should be so at a time when high US officials have unanimously embraced the need for more "smart power"—backing up military power with civilian initiatives—yet the American political system seems consistently unable or unwilling to generate the resources for such an effort.

Rather than discussing the obvious possibilities for complementarity, the transatlantic debate remains mired, as it was 10, 20, and 40 years ago, in discussions of military burden-sharing—today in the form of questions about who is providing troops to Afghanistan for a counterinsurgency mission that US and European analysts agree will fail without a massive civilian surge. This is a failure to learn lessons not simply from history, but from international relations theory.

Critical Thinking

1. List two other characteristics that the Europe and the United States have in common that make each powerful besides their ability to project intercontinental military power.

2. Give an example from recent current events where the European Community seems to have an edge on theUnited States and one where the US seems to have an advantage over European countries whose national economies and institutions are increasingly integrated with each other.

ANDREW MORAVCSIK is a professor of politics and international affairs at Princeton University and the director of the university's European Union program.

From *Current History*, March 2010, pp. 91–98. Copyright © 2010 by Current History, Inc. Reprinted by permission.

Is Beijing Ready for Global Leadership?

"Beijing has been largely working within—indeed, deftly leveraging—the current international system to advance its foreign policy objectives."

Evan S. Medeiros

The global financial crisis has been a heady time for China's leaders. Among elites in China, a tinge of triumphalism is in the air. The world media are awash in speculation about a historical tipping point from the United States to China. All the major Western economies have been wounded. Their financial institutions, once seen as the white knights of global capitalism, have fallen—some fatally. China now boasts the three largest banks in the world, positions recently held by American behemoths like Citigroup and Bank of America.

The Group of Eight, meanwhile, has become anachronistic as a concept almost overnight. The Group of 20 has emerged as its de facto successor, with China as a leading member. The first two summits of G-20 heads of state, held in Washington and London, the Mecca and Medina of the Western financial system, were pregnant with opportunity for China. What was China—now the world's third-largest economy and trading power—going to do? Would it assume the mantle of global leadership?

In fact, Beijing's actions were far from what the clairvoyants of the new discipline of "geo-economics" had been predicting. At the Washington G-20 summit in November 2008, China's initial response to the financial crisis was to say, in essence, "we will help the world by helping ourselves." China's "contribution" was a 4 trillion renminbi ($590 billion) domestic stimulus package, some of which was already in the pipeline. During the London summit in April 2009, China lobbied for a greater voice in the International Monetary Fund (IMF) but was reluctant to commit funds to recapitalizing it. Even more telling was the US-China bargaining at the summit. During the negotiation of parallel press statements, there was much agreement on the severity of the economic crisis and the need for coordinated action. Yet Chinese diplomats made sure one word was eliminated from their statement: leadership.

China's behavior in Washington and London was instructive. China has become a truly global actor. There are few global problems for which Beijing is not a necessary part of the solution. Simply by changing itself, China affects the world. China's policy makers and its people enthusiastically accept the attention and deference resulting from China's position as a rising power that the world increasingly needs. However, for China, there are also limits. China's policy makers regularly point out that their foreign policy serves domestic goals of reform and development. Chinese leaders fear that taking on too many responsibilities would divert their attention and drain their nation's resources.

The result is an emerging tension between the international community and China: The world wants China to do more while Beijing gingerly gropes its way forward with its new-found status, influence, responsibilities, expectations, and constraints. While China may be a global actor, it does not yet see itself as a global power—even less a global leader. And Chinese leaders want to keep it that way, at least for now.

While China may be a global actor, it does not yet see itself as a global power.

A Window of Opportunity

Understanding China's view of its role in the world begins with an understanding of its past experiences. Chinese policy makers and scholars look at the world through three historically determined lenses that color and shade their perceptions of China's position.

First, China is in the process of *reclaiming* its status as a major regional power and, eventually, as a great power—although the latter goal is not well defined or articulated. Chinese policy makers and analysts refer to China's rise as a "*re*vitalization" and a "*re*juvenation." Second, many Chinese see themselves as victims of "100 years of shame and humiliation" at the hands of Western and other foreign powers, especially Japan. The government's promotion of this victimization narrative over the past 60 years has fostered an acute sensitivity to coercion by foreign powers and especially infringements (real or perceived) on its sovereignty. Last, China has a defensive security outlook that stems from fears (based on historical experience) that foreign powers will exploit its internal weaknesses in order to constrain or coerce it.

These views inform more tangible perceptions of China's current external environment. There is now a widely held belief that China's success is inextricably linked to the rest of the world, more so than ever before. In the words of China's 2008 national defense white paper, "the future and destiny of China have been increasingly closely connected with the international community. China cannot develop in isolation from the rest of the world, nor can the world enjoy prosperity and stability without China." At the same time, a pervasive uncertainty persists among elites about the range and severity of threats to China's economic and security interests. For some, China has never been so secure; for others, the number and types of security threats are growing, which motivates deep insecurity about the future.

On balance, China's top leaders have concluded that their external environment is favorable and that the next 15 to 20 years represent a "strategic window of opportunity" (*zhanlue jiyuqi*) for China to achieve its ultimate objective of national revitalization through continued economic, social, and military development. Chinese policy makers seek, to the extent possible, to extend this window of opportunity through diplomacy.

Coherent Strategy

China's perceptions of its interests and place in the world have produced a distinct set of foreign policy objectives and policies. These collectively comprise a relatively coherent (but not always consistent) international strategy.

First, as Chinese policy makers have articulated for decades, China seeks to maintain a stable international environment to facilitate continued reform and development at home. This domestic focus entails a growing variety of external requirements: China actively uses its diplomacy to expand access to markets, capital, technology, and natural resources. Second, China seeks to reassure the international community that its growing capabilities will not undermine other states' economic and security interests, particularly those of China's Asian neighbors and countries it sees as "major powers."

Third, Chinese diplomacy, especially in Asia, seeks to reduce the ability or willingness of other nations, singularly or collectively, to contain, constrain, or otherwise hinder China's revitalization. Fourth, China is striving to diversify its access to energy and other natural resources, with a focus on Africa, the Middle East, and Latin America. Energy security encompasses diversifying both suppliers and supply routes. Fifth, China seeks to reduce Taiwan's international space and limit other nations' ability to confer legitimacy on Taiwan. Manifestations of this goal have moderated in the past year following improvements in cross-strait relations, but the objective remains a core one.

China has developed a bevy of new and effective ways to pursue these five objectives. Beijing has established "strategic partnerships" with developed and developing countries alike and has initiated high-level "strategic dialogues" with several major powers. It has embraced multilateral institutions, in every region and on several functional issues. China's expansion of its role in existing organizations and its formation of new organizations have become staples of its regional diplomacy.

China's use of economic diplomacy is robust and multifaceted; it includes not only bilateral trade but also outward direct investment, financial arrangements, development aid, and free trade agreements to advance both economic and political objectives. China's military diplomacy now incorporates extensive participation in United Nations peacekeeping operations, high-level defense exchanges, joint exercises, and joint training and education; reassurance is a major goal of these enhanced efforts.

What does this all mean for China's role in the world?

China has been largely working within—indeed, deftly leveraging—the current international system to advance its foreign policy objectives. It sees more opportunities than constraints in using the current system to promote its interests. China's international behavior is not ideologically driven. Beijing has not pursued a revolutionary foreign policy that seeks primarily to acquire new territory, forge balancing coalitions, or advance alternative models of economic development or global security.

China, in sum, is not trying to tear down or radically revise the current constellation of global rules, norms, and institutions on economic and security affairs. Rather, it has been seeking to master them to advance its interests—an approach that, to date, has proved quite productive for Beijing.

To be sure, China has been dissatisfied with certain attributes of the current status quo, such as the undetermined status of Taiwan and US global predominance in security and, more recently, in economic affairs. Beijing's response has been to leverage the system to address its concerns. This strategy has included attempts to reduce the relative power and influence of the United States, such as questioning the US dollar's role as the world's reserve currency. But China does not currently seek to confront the United States to erect a new international order, nor does it have the capability to do so.

China's overall approach has been geared more toward attracting and binding others to it, rather than directly challenging their interests: It is more gravitational than confrontational. It seeks to create an environment in Asia, and globally, in which states are drawn to, become reliant on, and thereby are deferential to Beijing. It sees this as a way to reduce vulnerabilities, minimize constraints, and thus maximize freedom of action.

Reluctant to Lead

China's worldview and its international strategy produce a unique reluctance to be a global leader. China wants the status and influence associated with global activism but it fears the burdens of leadership. Chinese leaders still approach their international behavior from the vantage point of domestic affairs: using foreign policy to assist the increasingly complex tasks of economic and social development at home. As such, China's policy makers worry their country lacks the expertise to be effective as a global leader and that trying to play such a role would divert political and economic resources away from national development.

This disposition has a strong basis in Communist Party doctrine—a significant, though not insurmountable, barrier to change in a Leninist political system. Two decades ago, Deng Xiaoping cautioned Chinese leaders "not to fly their flag" (*bu kang qi*) and "not to stick their head above the fray" (*bu dang tou*); perhaps most famously (and inscrutably), Deng also counseled them "to hide their capabilities and bide their time" (*tao guang yang hui*). These ideas continue to influence internal debates, especially on controversial foreign policy issues that require a break from past practice. Given the prominence of Deng's judgments in Communist Party orthodoxy, these ideas can constrain—and have constrained—high-profile international activities.

Policy manifestations of China's reluctance to lead abound, in the past and today. It took almost a decade before Beijing was willing to support UN Security Council action against North Korea and Iran's nuclear weapons programs, preferring to support its developing-nation brethren and their skepticism regarding nonproliferation. For the past several years, China has quietly rejected entreaties to join the G-8, arguing in part that it had not reached that level of development. Meanwhile, President Hu Jintao specifically termed his external strategy in the most benign manner possible: "peaceful development." He did so to signal explicitly a desire to avoid the experiences of past rising powers (for example, Nazi Germany and Imperial Japan) that prominently staked claims to global leadership by challenging the dominant powers at the time.

More recently, China's top diplomats were quick to reject any notion of a US-China "G-2" strategic condominium because they feared it would needlessly thrust China into the global spotlight at the very time it needed to tackle the immodest task of reengineering its national growth strategy. (Privately, Chinese elites relished the idea that the United States and China would be treated as the two most powerful countries in the world.)

As a further indication of a reluctance to lead, China continues to be adept at free-riding off the progress of other states and institutions. China's leaders, for example, reiterate that they will fully participate in international climate change and arms control negotiations, but only *after* the major powers responsible for originally creating these problems have made binding and costly commitments.

Capacity Constraints

China's role as a global leader is limited not only by the country's reluctance to take on such a responsibility but also by capacity constraints. Beijing's foreign aid bureaucracy, for example, suffers from serious communication and coordination problems. No single organization sets policy on foreign assistance or harmonizes the provision of development and humanitarian aid with the much larger category of government-supported overseas investment. Indeed, Beijing does not even publish a single figure for how much official development assistance and state-subsidized investment China dispenses each year. A major reason that China has long resisted conducting a regular dialogue on foreign aid policies with US agencies is precisely that Beijing cannot decide who will lead China's delegation.

This lack of coordination results in behavior that has undermined China's image and its economic and political interests,

especially in Africa. It has even put China at cross purposes with international financial institutions such as the IMF. Contributing to this problem is the fact that China's Foreign Ministry has no effective economic component, which could coordinate the country's diplomatic, trade, and investment goals. Some of China's main economic agencies, such as the Finance Ministry, are politically weak institutions and have little authority to make international economic policy. These limitations will only become more glaring as China's activities in global economic institutions become more complex and prominent.

China has twice tried and failed to produce a Ministry of Energy to coordinate both internal energy policies and their external manifestations. As Erica Downs of the Brookings Institution has argued, China's national-level energy bureaucracy is understaffed, underfunded, and lacking in political authority vis-à-vis the increasingly influential state-owned energy companies, which are well staffed, well funded, and in possession of substantial political clout.

These imbalances have had major consequences for China's foreign policy. The equity investments of Chinese energy firms have had undue influence in shaping China's policies toward Sudan, the Middle East, Russia, and Central Asia. Where corporate interests diverge from national interests, the former have tended to dominate in recent years. President Hu and Prime Minister Wen Jiabao are notably trying to address this issue.

China's national security bureaucracy is plagued with problems arising from excessive secrecy; from divisions among the civilian, intelligence, and military decision-making structures; and from a lack of means to coordinate between civilian and military organizations. These problems have resulted in slow and haphazard responses to crises with international dimensions. Prominent examples of these weaknesses include China's delayed and inadequate response to the SARS epidemic, the prominence of the military's narrative in the April 2001 incident involving a downed US surveillance aircraft, and the tardy and vague explanation of China's January 2007 test of a direct-ascent anti-satellite weapon.

Weaknesses of this sort will become more problematic for China's foreign relations as the military improves its force projection capabilities and conducts operations beyond China's immediate periphery. Some military activities, such as submarine patrols, are already raising concerns among China's neighbors.

Greater Expectations

Internal and external pressures for China to play a more prominent, if not leading, role in international affairs are growing. The external requirements for ensuring continued economic and social development at home are intensifying and have assumed new dimensions. For China, acting locally now requires that it think globally.

For China, acting locally now requires that it think globally.

Thus domestic pressures such as urbanization and increased energy consumption have led China, within the past decade, to expand significantly its trade and investment with Latin America and the Middle East, regions once of marginal interest. Trade with these regions is now the fastest growing aspect of China's global trade and will be critical to sustaining a modest level of exports in a global recession. Importantly, China's growth requirements have thrust energy security onto its foreign policy agenda and, in doing so, have given considerable influence to state-owned oil companies in the formulation and execution of China's foreign policy.

One of the newest and most influential internal pressures for a greater global role is the Chinese people. They are tuned into China's policies and practices on global affairs, and they voice their views. Chinese "netizens" in the spring of 2005 initiated an online petition to derail Japan's bid to become a permanent member of the UN Security Council, sparking a few days of violent anti-Japan protests in Shanghai. Anti-Japanese sentiment among the public has consistently constrained the leadership's ability to put China-Japan relations on a stable footing.

Of even greater significance, Chinese citizens now are traveling and living abroad more than ever before. According to Chinese data, 32 million Chinese citizens traveled abroad in 2006; 7,000 Chinese companies were operating or investing abroad; and 670,000 citizens studied or worked abroad, with about 100,000 in Africa alone. As China's international footprint expands, the Chinese people expect their government to do more to protect both their investments and their physical security. Between 2004 and 2007, according to Chinese data, 27 Chinese citizens were killed abroad (in Ethiopia, Pakistan, and Afghanistan), 45 were kidnapped (in Pakistan, Nigeria, and Iraq), and some 911 were evacuated from crises in Lebanon, East Timor, Tonga, and the Solomon Islands.

The international community expects more of China as well. Many nations now want China, as the greatest current producer of greenhouse gases, to accept binding quantitative limits on these pollutants; at a minimum the international community agrees that, for any climate change solution to be meaningful, China must participate. Most Asian policy makers see China as the key to coercing North Korea to give up its nuclear weapons program, even if this provokes some instability on China's northeastern border. An important external motivation for China to expand its international reach came in 2004 and 2005 during the tsunami disaster in Southeast Asia. China was embarrassed and frustrated that it could not provide much humanitarian aid due to the military's limited airlift and sealift capabilities and its lack of experience providing crisis assistance.

In the current global recession, the world looks longingly to China as one of the only large economies that continues to grow. Although China's economy is less than a third the size of America's or the European Union's (at market exchange rates), China's importance to global growth is increasing.

The IMF estimates that China will account for as much as 60 percent of global growth during the current downturn, and that by 2014 China's gross domestic product could be 50 percent as large as America's. As China shifts to a more consumption-oriented growth model, its domestic market may play a bigger role in the economic growth of its Asian neighbors (assuming they adjust their growth models accordingly). In 2008, in fact, China exceeded Japan, for a second consecutive year, as the largest retail market in Asia.

A Bigger Comfort Zone

These internal and external pressures have induced a variety of new behaviors that reflect China's recognition that it can and should do more. Beijing increasingly sees the need and opportunity to be more active, even assertive, globally. China, for example, has moved far away from its original reluctance to be heavily involved in the North Korean and Iranian nuclear crises. In both of these cases, China within the past five years has supported multiple UN Security Council resolutions— including imposition of UN Chapter 7 economic sanctions, penalties it had long abjured. As the convener of the six-party talks on North Korea's nuclear program, China has assumed de facto leadership in managing that crisis.

China is moving away from a strict interpretation and application of the principle of noninterference in the internal affairs of states, which has long circumscribed its foreign policy. Beijing's involvement, albeit limited, in managing the political crises in Sudan and Myanmar offers some evidence of this. As China's political and economic investments in such countries have grown and China has become more comfortable with using its influence to effect change, Beijing has come to recognize the net value of promoting political stability and reducing violence in these regions.

> **China is moving away from a strict interpretation and application of the principle of noninterference in the internal affairs of states.**

One of the most interesting, if perhaps ominous, shifts has been in China's military doctrine and operations. Chinese military strategists now state that the People's Liberation Army (PLA) is transitioning from an exclusive focus on the defense of "Chinese territory" to a new and additional focus on the protection of "Chinese interests." China's latest defense white paper highlighted that the PLA now sees "military operations other than war (MOOTW)" as a new mission—a concept that, for US strategists, includes maritime interdiction, peace operations, protection of sea lanes, noncombatant evacuation, and many other tasks.

Recent forays into this new world of MOOTW include China's deployment of naval vessels to the Gulf of Aden off Somalia's coast to participate in a UN-sanctioned counter-piracy operation. This was a first for the PLA. The military also just commissioned its first hospital ship (the "Peace Ark") and other large naval vessels that will allow it to contribute to humanitarian relief operations far from China's borders.

These new missions and capabilities reflect China's desire to be seen as contributing to global "public goods" in a manner consistent with China's stated policy of acting like a "responsible major power." They could also be the harbinger of improved power projection capabilities that could be used to enforce maritime territorial claims or to secure access to resources.

A Place at the Table

Yet another important force is motivating China to play a leading role in international affairs: Chinese policy makers want to participate in shaping global rules, norms, and institutions. In part for reasons of status and in part for tangible influence over these processes, China wants more "voice opportunities." This has been most evident in Beijing's multilateral diplomacy: China has created new organizations (for example, the Shanghai Cooperation Organization and the China-Africa Cooperation Forum) and expanded its participation in existing ones (for example, the Association of Southeast Asian Nations Regional Forum).

China's role as an agenda- and rule-setter will only become a more prominent feature of its diplomacy in the future. Experience in these realms will also push China to think about the cost-benefit ratios associated with leadership.

To date, however, China's actual track record in the shaping of international rules and institutions has been limited and episodic. Far more instances exist of China gradually accepting international rules than of objecting to and trying to revise them (and succeeding). Globally, China has adopted numerous, complex trade and weapons nonproliferation commitments, albeit with a mixed compliance record. Even in East Asia, China's strategic backyard, Beijing backed down after overplaying its hand trying to influence the membership and agenda of the East Asia Summit. Although China took charge of the six-party process on North Korea, it did so only after it began to fear that the situation would escalate beyond its control; Beijing has subsequently sought to calibrate its role so that it is not held solely responsible if the process fails.

In Southeast Asia, Beijing appears, so far, to have accepted regional norms on conflict resolution and has made pledges about peacefully resolving maritime territorial disputes in the South China Sea. Although the nature of China's ultimate behavior in these territorial disputes is still being determined (and that behavior includes some provocative activities), Beijing's initial commitments indicate, importantly, a degree of self-binding for the sake of reassurance.

The limits of China's rule-making potential are particularly evident in the recent Chinese proposal challenging the US dollar as the world's reserve currency. China's head banker, Zhou Xiaochuan, in the spring of 2009 called for increasing the use of a specialized IMF monetary instrument, called special drawing rights, to reduce the US dollar's global prevalence. This proposal reflected China's anxiety over its deep vulnerability to the dollar's value and to the overall health of the US economy. It also reflected the impotence of the renminbi (because of China's closed capital account) to present any kind of alternative.

Yet few other IMF members endorsed China's proposal. Indeed, some senior *Chinese* officials publicly backed away from it, noting that it was meant to mollify domestic critics of China's lackluster investments in US equities. In sum, China's reserve currency initiative was—by design—far more symbolic than substantive. It allowed the government to appear responsive to domestic frustrations, but, given the proposal's lack of feasibility and domestic or international appeal, there was no intention of pursuing it.

As with institutions, China's success at shaping other countries' policies and preferences has been limited. Despite China's growing international presence and its interactions with countries and institutions all over the world, the instances of China using its diplomacy to change the behavior of other states are very few.

China has been somewhat successful in shaping others' policies on issues of particular sensitivity to Beijing, such as Taiwan and Tibet. In these instances, the costs to the target state of accommodating China were often low and the benefits were substantial. China has been most effective at raising its profile among countries in Asia, Africa, and Latin America. States in these regions are now more aware of Chinese views and interests, resulting in some accommodation of Beijing's views but also some rejection as well.

The Stakeholder Paradox

So, is China ready for global leadership? The short answer is: not any time soon. But this conclusion requires constant reassessment.

Multiple forces tug China in different directions. Its default position, ingrained in the current generation of policy makers, is to avoid international leadership while focusing on domestic development. This tendency will persist for the foreseeable future. The opposite forces, those pushing China to be more globally involved, are diverse and growing stronger as well. As a result, China will be more prominent and effective in using its diplomacy to meet its domestic needs, and it will look for opportunities to contribute to maintaining the global commons.

In pursuing both goals, China will seek a greater voice in international rule-making. These imperatives have already led China to become an international actor of major consequence and occasionally to assume *a leading role*—at times grudgingly—with other major powers in managing regional and global problems.

But these activities are not global leadership. They are more about working within an existing consensus than about generating a new one and then leading the charge. Moreover, evidence suggesting that other nations would be willing to follow China's lead on a major international issue is scant. Thus, while China is willing occasionally to assume a leading role in concert with other states, it remains far from being a global leader in terms of either its mindset or its capabilities.

Analyzing China's leadership potential brings to light a tension at the center of US policy toward China. I call this the "stakeholder paradox." On one hand, Washington is encouraging China to define broadly its national interests; it is trying to empower Beijing to contribute to global problem solving and, ultimately, to the maintenance of the current international system. This was the thrust of former US Deputy Secretary of State

Robert Zoellick's policy of challenging China to be a "responsible stakeholder," the essential logic of which persists today.

On the other hand, many American and international strategists worry that this policy may broaden China's global ambitions while improving its capabilities to pursue them—including in ways that may not buttress global rules, norms, and institutions.

The ability of US policy makers to balance these concerns will be critical to the success of America's China policy. The arguments in this essay suggest that this balance is decidedly manageable for the foreseeable future. As China's capabilities grow, the internal constraints and external restraints on a revisionist turn in China's foreign and defense policies remain substantial, and some of them will increase.

China's current and next generations of leaders are resistant to assuming too many responsibilities and commitments. They are acutely aware of China's myriad domestic challenges—many of which will grow. They remain mindful of the miscalculations of past rising powers.

Externally, China lives in a tough neighborhood, much unlike the United States at the beginning of the twentieth century. China shares borders with 14 nations, some of which it has gone to war with. China's neighbors, especially Russia, Japan, and India, are monitoring China's behavior and will check its advances. As China's global interactions grow, the costs of becoming a revisionist state will increase exponentially, if not geometrically.

A critical element of US policy responses to China's rise is to maintain America's material and moral strengths while ensuring the credibility of US commitments. These goals begin with restoring America's economic health and well-being, both to ensure the foundations of US power and as a sign of American self-discipline. Internationally, Washington needs to take a broad view of its global responsibilities and its participation in international institutions, including an acceptance that restraint can be a powerful source of legitimacy and influence—especially for a superpower. These actions would help ensure that the United States is well positioned to deal with a more economically vibrant and geopolitically influential China in the years ahead.

Critical Thinking

1. Provide an example of a recent international problem where China, along with other major powers, played an important role in attempting to solve the problem.

2. Provide an example of a recent international problem where China did not play an important role in attempting to solve an international problem.

EVAN S. MEDEIROS in August became director for China, Taiwan, and Mongolia affairs at the National Security Council. He completed this essay while still a senior political scientist at the RAND Corporation. The article reflects his personal views and not those of the US government, the National Security Council, or the Obama administration.

From *Current History,* September 2009, pp. 250–256. Copyright © 2009 by Current History, Inc. Reprinted by permission.

The Elephant in the Room

The biggest pain in Asia isn't the country you'd think.

BARBARA CROSSETTE

Think for a moment about which countries cause the most global consternation. Afghanistan. Iran. Venezuela. North Korea. Pakistan. Perhaps rising China. But India? Surely not. In the popular imagination, the world's largest democracy evokes Gandhi, Bollywood, and chicken tikka. In reality, however, it's India that often gives global governance the biggest headache.

Of course, India gets marvelous press. Feature stories from there typically bring to life Internet entrepreneurs, hospitality industry pioneers, and gurus keeping spiritual traditions alive while lovingly bridging Eastern and Western cultures.

But something is left out of the cheery picture. For all its business acumen and the extraordinary creativity unleashed in the service of growth, today's India is an international adolescent, a country of outsize ambition but anemic influence. India's colorful, stubborn loquaciousness, so enchanting on a personal level, turns out to be anything but when it comes to the country's international relations. On crucial matters of global concern, from climate change to multilateral trade, India all too often just says no.

India, first and foremost, believes that the world's rules don't apply to it. Bucking an international trend since the Cold War, successive Indian governments have refused to sign nuclear testing and nonproliferation agreements—accelerating a nuclear arms race in South Asia. (India's second nuclear tests in 1998 led to Pakistan's decision to detonate its own nuclear weapons.)

Once the pious proponent of a nuclear-free world, New Delhi today maintains an attitude of "not now, not ever" when it comes to the 1968 Nuclear Non-Proliferation Treaty and the 1996 Comprehensive Test Ban Treaty. As defense analyst Matthew Hoey recently wrote in the *Bulletin of the Atomic Scientists,* "India's behavior has been comparable to other defiant nuclear states [and] will undoubtedly contribute to a deteriorating security environment in Asia."

Not only does India reject existing treaties, but it also deep-sixes international efforts to develop new ones. In 2008, India single-handedly foiled the last Doha round of global trade talks, an effort to nail together a global deal that almost nobody loved, but one that would have benefited developing countries most. "I reject everything," declared Kamal Nath, then the Indian commerce and industry minister, after grueling days and sleepless nights of negotiations in Geneva in the summer of 2008.

On climate change, India has been no less intransigent. In July, India's environment minister, Jairam Ramesh, pre-emptively told U.S. Secretary of State Hillary Clinton five months before the U.N. climate summit in Copenhagen that India, a fast-growing producer of greenhouse gases, would flat-out not accept binding carbon emissions targets.

India happily attacks individuals, as well as institutions and treaty talks. As ex-World Bank staffers have revealed in interviews with Indian media, India worked behind the scenes to help push Paul Wolfowitz out of the World Bank presidency, not because his relationship with a female official caused a public furor, but because he had turned his attention to Indian corruption and fraud in the diversion of bank funds.

By the time a broad investigation had ended—and Robert Zoellick had become the new World Bank president—a whopping $600 million had been diverted, as the *Wall Street Journal* reported, from projects that would have served the Indian poor through malaria, tuberculosis, HIV/AIDS, and drug-quality improvement programs. Calling the level of fraud "unacceptable," Zoellick later sent a flock of officials to New Delhi to work with the Indian government in investigating the accounts. In a 2009 interview with the weekly *India Abroad,* former bank employee Steve Berkman said the level of corruption among Indian officials was "no different than what I've seen in Africa and other places."

India certainly affords its citizens more freedoms than China, but it is hardly a liberal democratic paradise. India limits outside assistance to nongovernmental organizations and most educational institutions. It restricts the work of foreign scholars (and sometimes journalists) and bans books. Last fall, India refused to allow Bangladeshi and Sri Lankan journalists to attend a workshop on environmental journalism.

India also regularly refuses visas for international rights advocates. In 2003, India denied a visa to the head of Amnesty International, Irene Khan. Although no official reason was given, it was likely a punishment for Amnesty's critical stance on the government's handling of Hindu attacks that killed as many as 2,000 Muslims in Gujarat the previous year.

Most recently, a delegation from the U.S. Commission on International Religious Freedom, a congressionally mandated body, was denied Indian visas. In the past, the commission had called attention to attacks on both Muslims and Christians in India.

Nor does New Delhi stand up for freedom abroad. In the U.N. General Assembly and the U.N. Human Rights Council, India votes regularly with human rights offenders, international scofflaws, and enemies of democracy. Just last year, after Sri Lanka had pounded civilians held hostage by the Tamil Tigers and then rounded up survivors of the carnage and put them in holding camps that have drawn universal opprobrium, India joined China and Russia in subverting a human rights resolution suggesting a war crimes investigation and instead backed a move that seemed to congratulate the Sri Lankans.

India votes regularly with human rights offenders, international scofflaws, and enemies of democracy.

David Malone, Canada's high commissioner in New Delhi from 2006 to 2008 and author of a forthcoming book, *Does the Elephant Dance? Contemporary Indian Foreign Policy,* says that, when it comes to global negotiations, "There's a certain style of Indian diplomacy that alienates debating partners, allies, and opponents." And looking forward? India craves a permanent seat on the U.N. Security Council, seeking greater authority in shaping the global agenda. But not a small number of other countries wonder what India would do with that power. Its petulant track record is the elephant in the room.

Critical Thinking

1. Use the Internet to determine what India's foreign policy has been in recent years in one issue area such as climate change or multilateral trade. After doing this research, do you agree or disagree with Barbara Crossette's assessment that India" too often just says.

BARBARA CROSSETTE, a former New Delhi bureau chief for the *New York Times,* is author of *So Close to Heaven: The Vanishing Buddhist Kingdoms of the Himalayas.*

UNIT 2

Managing Interstate Conflicts and the Proliferation of Weapons

Unit Selections

Learning Outcomes

- Given recent political tensions, why is economic integration between Russia and the European Union proceeding?
- Describe the five future possible scenarios that might lead to conflict on the Korean Peninsula.
- Which of the five scenarios for future possible conflict on the Korean Peninsula is the most likely to occur? Why?
- Identify the most important provisions of the new START treaty.
- Why is substantial more progress in negotiating additional multilateral arms agreements unlikely?
- Explain why you agree or disagree with the view that the United States will be able to mitigate the consequences of Iran 'going nuclear'?
- Why is it impossible today to control the dissemination of biological weapon equipment, supplies, or knowledge?
- Explain why you believe that biological weapons are or is not a serious security threat.
- Which actor in the International System—e.g., nation-states, terrorists, disgruntled individuals—is most likely to use biological weapons in the future as a weapon of mass terror?
- What additional homeland defense measures should be taken to prepare for a future nuclear, biological, chemical, or radiation (NBCR) attack in the United States?

Student Website

www.mhhe.com/cls

Internet References

United States Defense Department, Cyber Command, Cyber Security
www.defense.gov/home/features/2010/0410_cybersec/

United States Department of State
www.state.gov/index.cfm

Belfer Center for Science and International Affairs (BCSIA)
www.ksg.harvard.edu/bcsia/

FACTs
www.ploughshares.ca

United States-Russia Developments
www.acronym.org.uk/start

Nuclear Threat Initiative (NTI) homepage
www.nti.org/index.php

The Bulletin of the Atomic Scientists
www.bullatomsci.org

Federation of American Scientists
www.fas.org

The Russian military intervention into disputed areas of Georgia in 2008 and the first Russian military operation since the invasion of Afghanistan in 1979 underscored the enduring nature of power politics and the fact that nation-states will resort to military means to protect their national interests. While the invasion surprised some, realists were quick to claim that the incursions were part of a long-term goal of Russia that had only temporarily been suspended in the years immediately following the collapse of the Soviet Union. The immediate goal was to prevent Georgia from joining NATO, but the longer-term implementations of the invasion are likely to be felt throughout Europe, Asia, and the Middle East for years to come.

Unlike the motivational approach favored by realists, social scientists who analyze international relations are more likely to stress the multi-causal and complex nature of relations among international actors and the fact that all nation-states have several, sometimes conflicting, interests. This perspective can also be illustrated by examples from recent Russian foreign policy trends. While Russia opposes efforts by the Baltic states to join the European Community and possibly also NATO, Russian policymakers are also encouraging policies designed to deepen economic integration among countries surrounding Europe, including Russia. The downturn in the growth of the Russian economy and the wider global slowdown is forcing many countries to look for new markets at home, within their immediate geographic neighborhood and throughout the world.

Periodic cycles of escalating tensions between North and South Korea have been a constant feature of international relations on the Korean Peninsula since a negotiated peace ended the Korean War. A long-running but uneasy status quo followed. Recent events triggered another round of escalating threats and military mobilizations after strong evidence surfaced that a torpedoed South Korean warship and killed 40 sailors was the work of the North Korean military. South Korea quickly closed sea lanes to shipping from North Korea and blasted propaganda over loudspeakers across the border. The North Koreans responded by threatening to shoot out the loudspeakers and use nuclear weapons as a response to joint United States-South Korean military maneuvers. By the fall of 2010, United States efforts to relaunch a new round of more effective peace talks had stalled. The promotion of Kim Jong Un, the youngest son of North Korean leader Kim Jong II, to the position of a four-star general from a non-military position and his prominent role in a Workers' Party convention at the end of September 2010 suggests that an authoritarian regime will remain even after the death of Kim Jong II unless the regime collapses. David Sanger outlines five possible future scenarios that could lead to future conflict, an incident at sea, the shelling of the DMZ, a power struggle or coup in the North, an internal collapse, or a nuclear provocation. Sanger concludes that the "biggest worry is that North Korea could decide that teaching others how to build nuclear weapons would be the fastest, stealthiest way to defy a new American President who has declared that stopping proliferation is Job No. 1."

In pursuit of a long-term goal of complete nuclear disarmament, President Obama initiated a new Nuclear Posture Review,

© www.defenseimagery.mil/imagery.html#a=search&s=Weapons_tanks&chk=6cf
e0&p=3&guid=e84b47557b708766a59d25659e396523a9450627

the New START Treaty negotiation process and held a Nuclear Security Summit in Washington. While neither domestic nor international factors favor reaching this long-term goal anytime soon, the United States and Russia did reach agreement on the New START Treaty in March 2010 after a difficult and protracted negotiation process. The new treaty builds upon two decades of nuclear arms negotiations and several prior treaties between the United States and Russia since the end of the Cold War that reduced the nuclear arsenal of the two nations by 80 percent. While the New START Treaty only makes modest reductions to the number of deployed strategic nuclear weapons from past treaties, it replaces the set of counting rules, definitions, and verification measures that were provided by the START I Treaty until it expired at the end of 2009. The Obama Administration hailed the treaty as a significant milestone treaty and set to work to win ratification of the new treaty in the United States Congress. To bolster support for the treaty among congressional opponents and on the advice of experts, President Obama also sent to Congress a request to spend $180 billion over the next decade to modernize the current United States nuclear stockpile.

It remains uncertain whether the Obama Administration will be able to win ratification of the New START treaty or achieve additional breakthroughs in multilateral arms control any time soon. One key issue area complicating the Obama's nuclear non-proliferation agenda is what to do about Iran's continued progress toward achieving operational nuclear weapons. There is an intense, long-running debate occurring behind the scenes within United States policy and intelligence circles as to whether it is desirable or even feasible to knock out Iran's dispersed nuclear weapons research and development (R&D) facilities. An equally intense debate continues within the United States government about whether it would be best if the United States restrained Israel from making a preemptive military strike and sought to contain and mitigate the consequences of Iran's "going nuclear" through diplomatic means.

In 2009, the Obama Administration released previously classified information confirming a heretofore secret nuclear reactor built inside a mountain near the holy city of Qom south of the capital in Iran. Faced with increased international pressure, Iran's President Mahmoud Ahmadinejad agreed to let International Atomic Energy Agency (IAEA) inspectors visit the recently disclosed facilities. However, Iran refused to sign a UN-draft agreement to send nuclear fuel out of the country for enrichment. Subsequent U.S-led diplomatic efforts in the UN and elsewhere to build a coalition to support additional sanctions against Iran by the permanent members of the UN have been unsuccessful as well. While acknowledging that a nuclear armed Iran may destabilize Middle East politics further, James M. Lindsay and Ray Takeyh in "After Iran Gets the Bomb" articulate the increasingly popular position that the United States will "still be able to contain and mitigate the consequences of Iran's nuclear defiance . . . from becoming a catastrophic one." These authors, however, are silent about what to do about the two dozen or so other countries, including possibly close allies such as South Korea who moved to start recycling spent nuclear fuel in 2010, who may be pursuing covert nuclear weapons R&D programs.

Recent events in Afghanistan and Pakistan also fuel worries about nuclear terrorism. There have been attacks on Pakistan's nuclear sites in the past, and many now worry about the prospect of one or more individuals working in nuclear facilities in Pakistan with access to nuclear weapons might be willing to transfer nuclear weapons components or expertise to terrorists living in Pakistan. Such threats seems plausible given the precedent of A.Q. Khan, the former head of Pakistan's nuclear weapons program, who led a covert network that sold WMD expertise and components throughout the world after he retired from government service. While the extent of proliferation damage caused by the A.Q. Kahn network remains unknown, it is clear that several nation-states, including North Korea and Libya, could not have progressed so fast toward developing sophisticated nuclear weapons without the expertise and components supplied by A.Q. Kahn's network. Such amorphous, highly adaptive, and underground transnational criminal networks may increasingly pose the greatest nuclear proliferatin threat to nation-states and the collective security of citizens in several countries.

Scholars and practitioners tend to disagree whether nation-states, terrorists, or lone deviants are most likely to use chemical or biological agents as weapons of terror against civilians in the future. There is even less agreement now than in past years about whether it is possible to deter or counter the use of chemical or biological weapons. It took seven years for the FBI to announce that the former United States Army microbiologist Bruce Ivies was implicated in the United States anthrax letter attacks in 2001. The resulting skepticism that Ivies was the sole perpetrator of the attacks, even though he killed himself prior to being arrested, illustrates just how difficult it can be to determine who is the attacker in a single or series of biological incidents.

The difficulties determining the extent of sophistication of several past covert chemical-biological weapons programs in such varied places as South Africa, Iraq, and Libya further illustrate why it is probably impossible to apply the same type of control strategies to deny would-be nuclear proliferators access to nuclear energy or to control the proliferation of equipment, supplies, or expertise needed to build chemical or biological weapons. These difficulties are compounded by the fact many countries throughout the developing and developed world are attempting to develop high-tech biotechnology, nanotechnology, and information technologies economic sectors that can mask covert chemical-biological weapons research and development, especially if the goal is mass disruption rather than mass destruction. In "Evolving Bioweapon Threats Require New Countermeasures," Helen Purkitt and Virgen Wells discuss why it is impossible to control the equipment, supplies, and knowledge needed to develop sophisticated or naturally occurring biological agents as weapons. Instead of instituting control strategies, Purkitt and Wells advocate designing public policies that will promote new transparency norms among nation-states and citizens throughout the world.

Europe and Russia: Up from the Abyss?

Andrew C. Kuchins

The past year was the most contentious in Russia-Europe relations since the collapse of the Soviet Union. From differences over Kosovo's status, NATO enlargement, and missile defense in the spring, to the Georgia war in August, to another natural gas dispute between Russia and Ukraine that began at the end of the year, tensions and differences dominated 2008. And on many issues Europeans could not agree among themselves, or with the Bush administration, about how best to engage Vladimir Putin's recently resurgent Russia.

Yet, while political relations worsened, economic integration between Russia and the European Union continued to deepen and widen, as trade and investment volumes reached all-time highs. In the summer the Russian Ministry of Economic Development and Trade published a long report detailing Russia's economic goals through the year 2020. The most striking finding in that report is that Europeans especially, and the West more broadly, would be far and away the most important partners in helping Russia to achieve its best-case growth scenarios in the coming decade.

This combination of trends—deepening economic integration amid worsening political relations—did not seem sustainable in the summer of 2008, and now after the war in Georgia and the impact of the global economic crisis, it seems even less so. The question is: Will political relations between Europe and Russia continue to deteriorate?

Dmitri Medvedev was inaugurated as Russia's president in May 2008. Later in that month the Russian stock market hit its all-time high. And in July oil prices peaked at $147 per barrel. The Russian government had more money than it knew what to do with, as foreign currency reserves peaked at nearly $600 billion, with another $200 billion put aside in a formal "stabilization fund." The Russian GDP (in nominal dollar terms) had increased by a factor of six in less than a decade. The Ministry of Economic Development and Trade report on strategic economic goals through 2020 called for similar growth levels that would ultimately make Russia the fifth-largest economy in the world and larger than any in Europe. Kremlin officials talked about Russia possibly being a "safe haven" or "island of stability" as the impact of the U.S. mortgage crisis widened to the world economy.

But how quickly things change. Russia's economic hubris has been smashed as its economy in the past few months has been perhaps the hardest hit of large emerging markets. By January 2009 the Russian stock market had lost about 80 percent of its value, the ruble had lost more than 30 percent, and reserves had fallen by one-third, with additional tens of billions promised in various bail-out and stimulus measures. Most prognoses for economic performance have predicted zero or negative growth for 2009.

All national economies are struggling to adjust to the deepest global slump in recent times, but the change in momentum for policy makers in Moscow is especially stark and challenging. Since so many millions of Russians have benefited from the prosperity of the past decade, the impact of the current crisis affects a far greater percentage of the population than the last economic crisis, in 1998. Prime Minister Putin's approach to governance, the so-called "vertical of power," will be tested like never before as prospects for social unrest and even bankruptcy become possible, especially if the slump endures for more than 12 to 18 months.

> **Lower oil price environments correlate with a more accommodating and moderate foreign policy from Moscow.**

New Dynamics

What does this turnabout suggest for relations with Europe? Historically, since the first oil crisis in the early 1970s, there has been a powerful correlation between a high oil price environment and a more assertive and aggressive Soviet or Russian foreign policy. This dynamic corresponds to the later Brezhnev years and the Putin period, especially since 2003. Lower oil price environments, as during the Gorbachev and Yeltsin years, correlate with a more accommodating and moderate foreign policy from Moscow.

Also relevant to Europe's ties with Russia is this reality: In a world of higher oil and gas prices, Moscow, like other states that rely a great deal on hydrocarbon revenues, can make decisions about production, allocation, and distribution of energy resources on more political and less commercial terms. Not surprisingly, given the mountains of money coming into Kremlin coffers in recent years from oil and gas sales, Russians have engaged in a variety of intimidating behaviors that have particularly tended to put their neighbors in "New Europe" on edge.

At least in the short term, or however long this global recession lasts, the Russians will feel far more economically constrained than in the recent halcyon years. Even when global demand begins to recover, Russia will be competing for investment with all economies whose assets have dramatically declined in value—as opposed to 10 years ago, when Russia was more unusual as a large emerging market with undervalued assets.

A second major difference the Russians will face is that, for the near and middle term, prospects for growth in domestic production of oil and gas resources are grim. After the country's financial crash in 1998, Russian domestic oil companies, led by Yukos at the time, achieved remarkably rapid growth in production with the application of modern technologies to old Soviet wells. That feat cannot be repeated, and new production will have to come in geologically and climatically challenging conditions from greenfield projects that will be the most expensive and complicated of their kind in history.

Finally, there is another important new factor in the equation: the election of Barack Obama and the end of the George W. Bush era in the United States. While we must beware of excessive expectations regarding the new president, the Bush administration had unprecedentedly strained relations with much of Europe as well as with the Russians. Bush's deep unpopularity at home as well as abroad gave Moscow more leverage to split America's European allies, most notably over the Iraq War.

The Obama administration will bring a new dynamic to relations among the United States, Europe, and Russia. Some of the most neuralgic issues in Russia-West relations will be defused somewhat. For example, Kosovo's declaration of independence is past. Missile defense will be pursued more circumspectly. And NATO enlargement to include Ukraine and Georgia will also slow down—partly because key European allies are skeptical, and partly because a new administration in Washington will not be racing against the clock to cement its legacy.

Rebalancing Relations

The Georgia war, although it has been overshadowed by the global financial crisis, was a watershed event that confirmed, nearly 20 years after the fall of the Berlin Wall and the end of the cold war, that we have not yet succeeded in making Europe "whole, free, and secure." There is increasing evidence, however, that Europeans are ready to take more initiative, despite their cleavages regarding Russia, and rebalance responsibilities on security issues with Washington. The EU's decision to take the lead in mediating a ceasefire agreement between Georgia and Russia under the auspices of French President Nicolas Sarkozy testifies to this.

Likewise, the compromise last year on Georgia and Ukraine's requests for NATO membership action plans—essentially postponing the plans while reassuring the countries that they can eventually join the alliance—was reached by European initiative, prompted by German and other European objections to the Bush administration's approach. This too suggested a rebalancing between Europe and the United States in managing relations with Russia.

While it would be wrong to get irrationally exuberant about a new golden age in Russia-Europe relations and Russia-West relations more broadly, the coalescence of an economic downturn and a new political environment suggests that the structural environment for the relationship may be conducive to greater cooperation and less conflict than has been the case in the recent past. Hopefully we will be able to regard 2008 as the bottom of an abyss in Russia-West relations.

Critical Thinking

1. When did the Russian economy begin to slow down?

2. Did the economic slowdown in Russia coincide with an increase in cooperation with European countries?

3. Provide an example from recent international relations when Russia cooperated with the European Union in a policy area where they had no cooperation in the past.

ANDREW C. KUCHINS is a senior fellow and director of the Russia and Eurasia Program at the Center for Strategic and International Studies.

From *Current History,* March, 2009, pp. 138–139. Copyright © 2009 by Current History, Inc. Reprinted by permission.

In the Koreas, Five Possible Ways to War

David E. Sanger

Usually, there is a familiar cycle to Korea crises. Like a street gang showing off its power to run amok in a well-heeled neighborhood, the North Koreans launch a missile over Japan or set off a nuclear test or stage an attack—as strong evidence indicates they did in March, when a South Korean warship was torpedoed. Expressions of outrage follow. So do vows that this time, the North Koreans will pay a steep price.

In time, though, the United States and *North Korea's* neighbors—China, Japan, *South Korea* and Russia—remind one another that they have nothing to gain from a prolonged confrontation, much less a war. Gradually, sanctions get watered down. Negotiations reconvene. Soon the North hints it can be enticed or bribed into giving up a slice of its nuclear program. Eventually, the cycle repeats.

The White House betting is that the latest crisis, stemming from the March attack, will also abate without much escalation. But there is more than a tinge of doubt. The big risk, as always, is what happens if the North Koreans make a major miscalculation. (It wouldn't be their first. Sixty years ago, Mr. Kim's father, Kim Il-sung, thought the West wouldn't fight when he invaded the South. The result was the Korean War.)

What's more, the dynamic does feel different from recent crises. The South has a hardline government whose first instinct was to cut off aid to the North, not offer it new bribes. At the same time, the North is going through a murky, ill-understood succession crisis.

And *President Obama* has made it clear he intends to break the old cycle. "We're out of the inducements game," one senior administration official, who would not discuss internal policy discussions on the record, said last week. "For 15 years at least, the North Koreans have been in the extortion business, and the U.S. has largely played along. That's over."

That may change the North's behavior, but it could backfire. "There's an argument that in these circumstances, the North Koreans may perceive that their best strategy is to escalate," says Joel Wit, a former State Department official who now runs a website that follows North Korean diplomacy.

The encouraging thought is the history of cooler heads prevailing in every crisis since the Korean War. There was no retaliation after a 1968 raid on South Korea's presidential palace; or when the North seized the American spy ship Pueblo days later; or in 1983 when much of the South Korean cabinet was killed in a bomb explosion in Rangoon, Burma; or in 1987 when a South Korean airliner was blown up by North Korean agents, killing all 115 people on board.

So what if this time is different? Here are five situations in which good sense might not prevail.

An Incident at Sea

Ever since an armistice ended the Korean War, the two sides have argued over—and from time to time skirmished over—the precise location of the "Northern Limit Line," which divides their territorial waters. That was where the naval patrol ship *Cheonan* was sunk in March. So first on the Obama administration's list of concerns is another incident at sea that might turn into a prolonged firefight. Any heavy engagement could draw in the United States, South Korea's chief ally, which is responsible for taking command if a major conflict breaks out.

What worries some officials is the chance of an intelligence failure in which the West misreads North Korea's willingness and ability to escalate. The failure would not be unprecedented. Until a five-nation investigation concluded that the *Cheonan* had been torpedoed, South Korea and its allies did not think the North's mini-submarine fleet was powerful enough to sink a fully armed South Korean warship.

Shelling the DMZ

American and South Korean war planners still work each day to refine how they would react if North Korea's 1.2 million-man army poured over the Demilitarized Zone, 1950s-style. Few really expect that to happen—the South Koreans build and sell expensive condos between Seoul and the DMZ—but that doesn't mean the planning is unjustified.

In one retaliatory measure last week, South Korea threatened to resume propaganda broadcasts from loudspeakers at the DMZ. In past years, such blaring denunciations, of *Kim Jong-il*'s economic failures, were heard only by North Korean guards and the wildlife that now occupies the no-man's land. Still, the threat was enough to drive the North's leadership to threaten to shell the loudspeakers. That, in turn, could lead to tit-for-tat exchanges of fire, and to a threat from the North to fire on Seoul, which is within easy reach of mortars. If that happened, thousands could die in frenzied flight from the city, and investors in South Korea's economy would almost certainly panic.

American officials believe the South is now rethinking the wisdom of turning on the loudspeakers.

A Power Struggle or Coup

Ask American intelligence analysts what could escalate this or a future crisis, and they name a 27-year-old *Kim Jong-un,* the youngest of Kim Jong-il's three sons, and the father's choice to succeed him. Little is known about him, but his main qualifications for the job may be that he is considered less corrupt or despised than his two older brothers.

One senior American intelligence official described the succession crisis this way: "We can't think of a bigger nightmare than a third generation of the Kim family" running the country with an iron hand, throwing opponents into the country's gulags, and mismanaging an economy that leaves millions starving.

It is possible that on the issue of succession, many in the North Korean elite, including in the military, agree with the American intelligence official. According to some reports, they view Kim Jong-un as untested, and perhaps unworthy.

"We're seeing considerable signs of stress inside the North Korean system," another official reported.

And that raises the possibility of more provocations—and potential miscalculations—ahead.

One line of analysis is that the younger Kim has to put a few notches in his belt by ordering some attacks on the South, the way his father once built up a little credibility. Another possibility is that internal fighting over the succession could bring wide-scale violence inside North Korea, tempting outside powers to intervene to stop the bloodshed.

Curiously, when Kim Jong-il took the train to China a few weeks ago, his heir apparent did not travel with him. Some experts read that as a sign that the Kim dynasty might fear a coup if both were out of the country—or that it might not be wise to put father and son on the same track at the same time, because accidents do happen.

An Internal Collapse

America's most enduring North Korea strategy isn't a strategy at all; it's a prayer for the country's collapse. *Harry Truman, Dwight Eisenhower* and *John F. Kennedy* hoped for it. *Dick Cheney* tried to speed it.

The regime has survived them all.

But could the North collapse in the midst of the power struggle? Sure.

And that is the one scenario that most terrifies the Chinese. It also explains why they keep pumping money into a neighbor they can barely stand.

For China, a collapse would mean a flood of millions of hungry refugees (who couldn't flee south; there they are blocked by the minefield of the DMZ); it would also mean the possibility of having South Korea's military, and its American allies, nervously contending with the Chinese over who would occupy the territory of a fallen regime in order to stabilize the territory. China is deeply interested in North Korea's minerals; the South Koreans may be as interested in North Korea's small nuclear arsenal.

A Nuclear Provocation

With tensions high, American spy satellites are looking for evidence that the North Koreans are getting ready to test another nuclear weapon—just as they did in 2006 and 2009—or shoot off some more long-range missiles. It is a sure way to grab headlines and rattle the neighborhood. In the past, such tests have ratcheted up tension, and could do so again. But they are not the Obama administration's biggest worry. As one of Mr. Obama's top aides said months ago, there is reason to hope that the North will shoot off "a nuclear test every week," since they are thought to have enough fuel for only eight to twelve.

Far more worrisome would be a decision by Pyongyang to export its nuclear technology and a failure by Americans to notice.

For years, American intelligence agencies missed evidence that the North was building a reactor in the Syrian desert, near the Iraq border. The Israelis found it, and wiped it out in an air attack in 2007. Now, the search is on to find out if other countries are buying up North Korean technology or, worse yet, bomb fuel. (There are worries about Myanmar.)

In short, the biggest worry is that North Korea could decide that teaching others how to build nuclear weapons would be the fastest, stealthiest way to defy a new American president who has declared that stopping proliferation is Job No. 1.

It is unclear whether the American intelligence community would pick up the signals that it missed in Syria. And if it did, a crisis might not be contained in the Korean Peninsula; it could spread to the Middle East or Southeast Asia, or wherever else North Korea found its customers.

Critical Thinking

1. Which of the five scenarios outlined in "In the Koreas, Five Possible Ways to War" do you believe is most likely to lead to armed conflict between North and South Korea? Be sure you can explain your reasoning and reasons for this prediction.
2. Why does David Sanger conclude that the "biggest worry is that North Korea could decide that teaching others how to build nuclear weapons would be the fastest, stealthiest way to defy the Obama administration?"

Obama's Nuclear Policy: Limited Change

The change in US nuclear policy as announced by President Obama in his Prague speech finds reflection in the Nuclear Posture Review, the New START Treaty, and the Nuclear Security Summit held in Washington. Obama has succeeded in reintroducing nuclear disarmament to the international agenda, but domestic factors, alliance policy, and strategic considerations limit the scope for major turns in US policy. Neither a sustainable reinforcement of the non-proliferation regime nor substantial progress in multilateral arms control are in the offing.

DANIEL MOCKLI

U S nuclear policy is undergoing change. President Barack Obama defined the conceptual framework for this transformation in his Prague speech on 5 April 2009. At the time, he declared his support for the idea of a world free of nuclear weapons and outlined an ambitious disarmament agenda. He also emphasised the goal of strengthening the non-proliferation regime. What is more, he identified nuclear terrorism as "the most immediate and extreme threat to global security" and announced an initiative for securing all nuclear material worldwide within four years.

One year on, Obama's policies have yielded some first practical results. On the doctrinal level, the Nuclear Posture Review (NPR) published on 6 April 2010 assumes a reduced importance of US nuclear weapons within the overall national security strategy. Two days later, Obama and Russian President Dmitry Medvedev signed the New START Treaty on the reduction of strategic offensive arms. Finally, on 12 and 13 April 2010, Obama received more than 40 heads of state and government for a summit on nuclear security in Washington, D.C. that produced a timetable for implementation of Obama's four-year target.

Although all these measures demonstrate Obama's determination to create new impetus in US nuclear policy, a closer look reveals that the scope for change is limited in some areas. This is due to divergent assessments on nuclear strategy within the US political establishment, alliance policy considerations, and the stances adopted by other nuclear states. Accordingly, Obama's approach of pushing nuclear disarmament to garner international support for strengthening the non-proliferation regime and effective measures against Iran and North Korea may only deliver limited results. This is also because the nexus between proliferation issues and the state of disarmament is weaker than is often claimed.

The link between nuclear disarmament and non-proliferation should not be overestimated.

New Nuclear Doctrine

The review of the US nuclear posture was accompanied by intense controversies within the Obama administration. As a result, the NPR was only published after several months' delay. The document features some substantial changes compared to the previous version. In accordance with the changing threat picture, there is a modified hierarchy of strategic priorities. Non-proliferation and nuclear security are moving to the centre of nuclear policy—although the US continues to attribute great importance to traditional challenges of nuclear deterrence and strategic stability vis-à-vis Russia and China.

Also, nuclear weapons are assigned a more limited role. The "fundamental role" of US nuclear arms is now defined as deterring a nuclear attack on the US or its allies. Thus, the deployment scenario in case of biological or chemical weapons attacks, as envisaged under the previous Bush administration, has been abolished. By confirming that the US will not use or threaten to use nuclear weapons against those countries that are members of the Non-Proliferation Treaty (NPT) and meet their respective obligations, the Obama administration is expanding its negative security assurance. The new NPR justifies this measure by pointing to the changed strategic situation, advances in missile defense, and the huge conventional superiority of US forces that greatly reduces the importance of nuclear weapons for deterring non-nuclear attacks.

Overall, however, the changes in the NPR are more limited than had previously been speculated. Many had hoped that Obama would define deterrence of a nuclear attack as the "sole purpose" of the US nuclear arsenal. The new nuclear doctrine explicitly disclaims this formula and argues that scenarios involving nuclear deterrence of non-nuclear attacks are still conceivable in cases of nuclear powers and of non-nuclear states that fail to meet their non-proliferation obligations. This accommodates both the wishes of allies such as South Korea and the concerns voiced in the Department of Defense, not to mention the deep ranks of the Republican Party. The new US stance is further qualified by the caveat that the negative security assurance could be reconsidered should the threat of biological weapons increase. Moreover, the NPR does not commit the US to a policy of no first use of nuclear arms as some had hoped.

The changes in the Nuclear Posture Review are more limited than many had hoped.

As far as the structure and operability of the US nuclear arsenal is concerned, the NPR follows established patterns. The US government continues to adhere to the Cold War strategic nuclear triad of land-based intercontinental ballistic missiles, submarine-based missiles, and strategic bombers. Neither has it heeded calls to modify the alert posture of its nuclear weapons ("de-alerting"). Concerning the modernisation of its nuclear arsenal, it does exclude the development of new warheads. The stated spectrum of measures for extending the lifetime of warheads does however admit the option of significantly modifying them. Furthermore, it is remarkable that Obama has promised to spend $80 billion over ten years to maintain and modernise the US nuclear arsenal. All of these decisions should at least partially be understood as domestic concessions to disarmament skeptics.

Regarding the sensitive issue of the future role of tactical nuclear weapons that the US still keeps in several European NATO states, the NPR includes no decision. Some NATO members are urging for these weapons to be withdrawn, arguing that their two original purposes—preventing a nuclearisation of Germany and facilitating a flexible, gradual escalation in case of a conflict—are obsolete today. They also consider the principle of nuclear sharing that is linked to these weapons to be inconsistent with Obama's disarmament stance. The NPR, on the other hand, emphasises the importance of tactical nuclear weapons for transatlantic cohesion and as reassurance for the Europeans. This view is shared in particular by some Eastern European states, which point to Russia's 3'000 tactical nuclear weapons. According to the NPR, the allies are to reach a consensual agreement in the process of elaborating a new strategic concept for NATO—which means that continuation of the status quo is a likely outcome.

Back to the START

The significance of the so-called New START Treaty is mainly political. It represents an essential foundation for the improvement of bilateral relations between the US and Russia. At the same time, it instills new life to the long-neglected issue of disarmament. Unlike the Strategic Offensive Reduction Treaty concluded by the Bush administration in Moscow in 2002, the new treaty contains verification mechanisms. These are indispensable elements of a credible arms control policy. In this way, New START is a follow-up to the START I treaty of 1991, which expired in December 2009. The fact that implementation of this core pillar of Obama's nuclear policy was delayed by several months, despite early targets set by himself and Medvedev, indicates the enormous complexity of nuclear disarmament.

From a strategic perspective, New START is very modest on substance. While the new ceiling of 1.550 deployed strategic warheads is 74 per cent less than the specifications in START I, and 30 per cent less than those of the Moscow Treaty, the US and Russia will hardly have to reduce the actual number of their respective warheads relative to current levels, due to a new counting methodology. Although bombers can carry up to 20 warheads, the new equation is "1 bomber = 1 warhead". Even if bombers constitute the least important element of the strategic triad today, the new counting method reduces the impact of New START. This is compounded by the fact that the treaty does not demand the destruction of warheads, but only stipulates that they be removed from delivery systems. Also, reserve warheads in storage are not covered by the agreement. As far as deployed strategic delivery systems are concerned, the new upper limit of 700 amounts to approximately a halving compared to START I. But even here, the US and Russia will only have to undertake modest steps in arms reduction compared to current levels.

Missile defense is not explicitly covered in the treaty. The exclusion of this contentious issue was an important success for Washington. However, already now, Medvedev is interpreting the reference to the correlation between offensive and strategic arms in the (legally non-binding) preamble of the treaty as a proviso allowing Russia to withdraw from New START should it feel threatened by a missile defense system. From the Russian point of view, therefore, New START certainly constitutes a lever to be used against US plans for missile defense. The conflict will only be defused if the ideas of a shared missile defense shield of NATO and Russia should become more concrete.

The ratification of the New START Treaty, both in Russia and in the US, is a hurdle that should not be underestimated. In Russia, where a simple parliamentary majority is required, both the lack of an explicit reference to missile defense and the new counting system are criticised as unilaterally favoring the US. In the US, on the other hand, New START offers little real grounds for criticism, as the Obama administration ensured that its substance is modest due to domestic political considerations. Nevertheless, gaining the necessary two-thirds Senate majority will be a challenge for Obama.

Further Disarmament Steps?

Obama's stated intention to push for further nuclear disarmament based on New START is unlikely to be successful in the foreseeable future. This is for three reasons: First, as Russia has vastly inferior conventional forces compared to the US, it has no interest in further reducing its nuclear arsenal to below the level of what it can finance in the medium term. Second, other nuclear states such as China remain skeptical towards the prospect of being involved in any multilateral disarmament negotiations. Third, with the US Congressional midterm elections approaching, the domestic support for any drastic cutbacks to the US nuclear arsenal may reduce even further.

Obama has indefinitely postponed his stated intention to pursue ratification of the Comprehensive Nuclear Test Ban Treaty (CTBT) "immediately and aggressively", as announced in Prague in 2009. Some concerns about the verifiability of the treaty's provisions, which had caused ratification to be withheld in the US Senate in 1999, can today be alleviated due to technical progress. Still, considerable domestic skepticism remains when it comes to treaty-based restrictions on freedom of action in nuclear policy. Even though 151 of the 182 signatory states have so far ratified the treaty, it cannot come into force until it has been ratified by the specifically mentioned 44 states that have nuclear technology. It is questionable whether the US, by ratifying the treaty, can also compel states such as China, India, Iran, Pakistan, and North Korea to follow suit.

Obama gained a minor success when agreement was reached on taking up negotiations over a ban on producing fissile material for nuclear weapons in the framework of the UN disarmament conference in May 2009. This agreement was mainly due to a change of course that he initiated when the US accepted verification measures as part of a Fissile Material Cutoff Treaty (FMCT). The brief euphoria after years of stalled negotiations has, however, already dissipated, as Pakistan is preventing implementation of the work program in protest against broad support for India's nuclear program. In terms of substance, the 65 participating countries have greatly diverging views on the specifics of a verification system, as well as on the matter of including already available fissile material. Even if negotiations should be taken up at some point, a breakthrough is not to be expected in the foreseeable future.

The NPT Review Conference

From the very start, Obama's disarmament efforts were presented in the context of his non-proliferation efforts. Thus, the NPR leaves no doubt that the US ultimately regards both New START and its CTBT and FMCT policies as a means of gaining international support for strengthening the non-proliferation regime. In this way, Washington hopes to head off critics who regard the non-compliance of nuclear NPT states with their disarmament obligations as the main cause of increasing proliferation tendencies among non-nuclear NPT states. The increased transparency of the US nuclear arsenal (as announced at the NPT Review Conference in May 2010) should also be seen in this context.

In view of the ambiguous interim results, it remains questionable whether Obama's disarmament policy will have a positive impact on his non-proliferation objectives beyond an improved atmosphere at the NPT Review Conference. But irrespective of the specifics of his disarmament balance sheet, the question remains how strong the nexus between the growing problem of proliferation and the state of NPT states' disarmament efforts really is. There is much to indicate that states that refuse to support measures such as enhanced IAEA verification options, predefined sanctions in case of treaty violations, and the multilateralisation of the fuel cycle only point their finger at insufficient disarmament to deviate attention from their real motives, such as concerns over sovereignty and the desire to leave a loophole for a nuclear option of their own. Against this background and with regard to the US efforts to put into place new sanctions against Iran, the NPT Review Conference is faced with a very difficult task.

Nuclear Safety

Since the attacks in the US on 11 September 2001, the proliferation issue is increasingly also framed within the specter of proliferation to non-state actors. The US in particular has undertaken numerous measures to ensure worldwide safeguards of fissile material. At the Washington summit, Obama appealed to the responsibility of all states to enforce nuclear safety. This involves not only weapons-grade uranium and plutonium, but also radioactive material that can be combined with conventional explosives to create a radiological weapon ("dirty bomb").

However, some states regard the threat of nuclear terrorism as being less acute than the Obama administration claims it to be. They think that an attack using a nuclear device is an unlikely prospect, since fissile material is well guarded in most countries and terrorist groups hardly have the know-how needed for such an undertaking. They believe that the problem is limited to a handful of states. The main focus here is on Pakistan, which faces political instability and a growing activity of Islamist militants and has been regarded as a potential hub for nuclear smuggling ever since the disclosure of the network of A.Q. Khan.

There is agreement, however, on the danger of radiological weapons. Still, only the follow-up conference to the Washington summit, to be held in South Korea in 2012, will show to what extent the participating states will really enhance safeguards for their nuclear and radiological material. Due to a number of unilateral measures already announced in Washington, Obama was able to claim some success at least at the opening summit. But it is unlikely that he will be able to meet his four-year-objective.

Critical Thinking

1. Describe some of the ways that the Obama Administration is attempting to change U.S. nuclear policies.

2. Why does Daniel Mockli conclude that the Obama Administration will not be able to make substantial progress in multilateral arms control negotiations?

From *Center for Security Studies (CSS)*, no. 74, May 2010, pp. 1–3. Copyright © 2010 by CSS ETH Zurich. Reprinted by permission.

After Iran Gets the Bomb
Containment and Its Complications

JAMES M. LINDSAY AND RAY TAKEYH

The Islamic Republic of Iran is determined to become the world's tenth nuclear power. It is defying its international obligations and resisting concerted diplomatic pressure to stop it from enriching uranium. It has flouted several UN Security Council resolutions directing it to suspend enrichment and has refused to fully explain its nuclear activities to the International Atomic Energy Agency. Even a successful military strike against Iran's nuclear facilities would delay Iran's program by only a few years, and it would almost certainly harden Tehran's determination to go nuclear. The ongoing political unrest in Iran could topple the regime, leading to fundamental changes in Tehran's foreign policy and ending its pursuit of nuclear weapons. But that is an outcome that cannot be assumed. If Iran's nuclear program continues to progress at its current rate, Tehran could have the nuclear material needed to build a bomb before U.S. President Barack Obama's current term in office expires.

The dangers of Iran's entry into the nuclear club are well known: emboldened by this development, Tehran might multiply its attempts at subverting its neighbors and encouraging terrorism against the United States and Israel; the risk of both conventional and nuclear war in the Middle East would escalate; more states in the region might also want to become nuclear powers; the geopolitical balance in the Middle East would be reordered; and broader efforts to stop the spread of nuclear weapons would be undermined. The advent of a nuclear Iran—even one that is satisfied with having only the materials and infrastructure necessary to assemble a bomb on short notice rather than a nuclear arsenal—would be seen as a major diplomatic defeat for the United States. Friends and foes would openly question the U.S. government's power and resolve to shape events in the Middle East. Friends would respond by distancing themselves from Washington; foes would challenge U.S. policies more aggressively.

Such a scenario can be avoided, however. Even if Washington fails to prevent Iran from going nuclear, it can contain and mitigate the consequences of Iran's nuclear defiance. It should make clear to Tehran that acquiring the bomb will not produce the benefits it anticipates but isolate and weaken the regime.

Washington will need to lay down clear "redlines" defining what it considers to be unacceptable behavior—and be willing to use military force if Tehran crosses them. It will also need to reassure its friends and allies in the Middle East that it remains firmly committed to preserving the balance of power in the region.

Containing a nuclear Iran would not be easy. It would require considerable diplomatic skill and political will on the part of the United States. And it could fail. A nuclear Iran may choose to flex its muscles and test U.S. resolve. Even under the best circumstances, the opaque nature of decision-making in Tehran could complicate Washington's efforts to deter it. Thus, it would be far preferable if Iran stopped—or were stopped—before it became a nuclear power. Current efforts to limit Iran's nuclear program must be pursued with vigor. Economic pressure on Tehran must be maintained. Military options to prevent Iran from going nuclear must not be taken off the table.

But these steps may not be enough. If Iran's recalcitrant mullahs cross the nuclear threshold, the challenge for the United States will be to make sure that an abhorrent outcome does not become a catastrophic one. This will require understanding how a nuclear Iran is likely to behave, how its neighbors are likely to respond, and what Washington can do to shape the perceptions and actions of all these players.

Messianic and Pragmatic

IRAN IS a peculiarity: it is a modern-day theocracy that pursues revolutionary ideals while safeguarding its practical interests. After three decades of experimentation, Iran has not outgrown its ideological compunctions. The founder of the Islamic Republic, Ayatollah Ruhollah Khomeini, bequeathed to his successors a clerical cosmology that divides the world between oppressors and oppressed and invests Iran with the mission of redeeming the Middle East for the forces of righteousness. But the political imperative of staying in power has pulled Iran's leaders in a different direction, too: they have had to manage Iran's economy, meet the demands of the country's growing population, and advance Iran's interests in a turbulent region. The clerical rulers have been forced to strike agreements with their rivals and their enemies, occasionally softening the hard edges of their creed. The task of governing has required them to make concessions to often unpalatable realities and has sapped their revolutionary energies. Often, the clash of ideology and pragmatism has put Iran in the paradoxical position of having to secure its objectives within a regional order that it has pledged to undermine.

To satisfy their revolutionary impulses, Iran's leaders have turned anti-Americanism and a strident opposition to Israel into pillars of the state. Tehran supports extremist groups, such as Hamas, Hezbollah, and the Islamist militias opposing U.S. forces in Iraq. The mullahs have sporadically attempted to subvert the U.S.-allied sheikdoms of the Persian Gulf. But the regime has survived because its rulers have recognized the limits of their power and have thus mixed revolutionary agitation with pragmatic adjustment. Although it has denounced the United States as the Great Satan and called for Israel's obliteration, Iran has avoided direct military confrontation with either state. It has vociferously defended the Palestinians, but it has stood by as the Russians have slaughtered Chechens and the Chinese have suppressed Muslim Uighurs. Ideological purity, it seems, has been less important leaders would not be deposed. But regime security and power projection are two very different propositions. It is difficult to imagine Sunni regimes yielding to a resurgent Shiite state, nuclear or not; more likely, the Persian Gulf states would take even more refuge under the U.S. security umbrella. Paradoxically, a weapon that was designed to ensure Iran's regional preeminence could further alienate it from its neighbors and prolong indefinitely the presence of U.S. troops on its periphery. In other words, nuclear empowerment could well thwart Iran's hegemonic ambitions. Like other nuclear aspirants before them, the guardians of the theocracy might discover that nuclear bombs are simply not good for diplomatic leverage or strategic aggrandizement.

Likewise, although the protection of a nuclear Iran might allow Hamas, Hezbollah, and other militant groups in the Middle East to become both more strident in their demands and bolder in their actions, Israel's nuclear arsenal and considerable conventional military power, as well as the United States' support for Israel, would keep those actors in check. To be sure, Tehran will rattle its sabers and pledge its solidarity with Hamas and Hezbollah, but it will not risk a nuclear confrontation with Israel to assist these groups' activities. Hamas and Hezbollah learned from their recent confrontations with Israel that waging war against the Jewish state is a lonely struggle.

The prospect that Iran might transfer a crude nuclear device to its terrorist protégés is another danger, but it, too, is unlikely. Such a move would place Tehran squarely in the cross hairs of the United States and Israel. Despite its messianic pretensions, Iran has observed clear limits when supporting militias and terrorist organizations in the Middle East. Iran has not provided Hezbollah with chemical or biological weapons or Iraqi militias with the means to shoot down U.S. aircraft. Iran's rulers understand that such provocative actions could imperil their rule by inviting retaliation. On the other hand, by coupling strident rhetoric with only limited support in practice, the clerical establishment is able to at once garner popular acclaim for defying the West and oppose the United States and Israel without exposing itself to severe retribution. A nuclear Iran would likely act no differently, at least given the possibility of robust U.S. retaliation. Nor is it likely that Iran would become the new Pakistan, selling nuclear fuel and materials to other states. The prospects of additional sanctions and a military confrontation with the United States are likely to deter Iran from acting impetuously.

A nuclear Iran would undeniably pose new dangers in the Middle East, especially at first, when it would likely be at its most reckless. It might thrash about the Middle East, as it tried to press the presumed advantages of its newfound capability, and it might test the United States' limits. But the mullahs will find it difficult to translate Iran's nuclear status into a tangible political advantage.

And if Washington makes clear that rash actions on their part will come at a high cost, they will be far less likely to take any.

The Ripples in the Region

IN ASSESSING the consequences of Iran's nuclearization, it is important to consider not only how Iran is likely to act but also how other states will react to this outcome—and what the United States could do to influence their responses. Iran's nuclearization would not reduce Washington to passively observing events in the region. Washington would retain considerable ability to shape what Iran's neighbors do and do not do.

The nightmare scenario that could be unleashed by Iran's nuclearization is easy to sketch. Israel would go on a hair-trigger alert—ready to launch a nuclear weapon at a moment's notice—putting both countries minutes away from annihilation. Egypt, Saudi Arabia, and Turkey would scramble to join the nuclear club. The Nonproliferation Treaty (NPT) would collapse, unleashing a wave of nuclear proliferation around the globe.

Such a doomsday scenario could pan out. Whether it did would depend greatly on how the United States and others, starting with Israel, responded to Iran's nuclearization. Whether Israeli Prime Minister Benjamin Netanyahu forgoes a preventive strike against Iran's nuclear facilities or opts for launching an attack and it fails, the Israeli government will continue to regard the Iranian regime as an existential threat to Israel that must be countered by any means possible, including the use of nuclear weapons. Given Israel's unique history and Ahmadinejad's contemptible denials of the Holocaust, no Israeli prime minister can afford to think otherwise.

The riskiness of a nuclear standoff between Israel and Iran would vary with the nature and size of Tehran's nuclear arsenal. An Iran with only the capability to build a nuclear weapon would pose a far less immediate threat to Israel than an Iran that possessed an actual weapon. Iran's possession of a bomb would create an inherently unstable situation, in which both parties would have an incentive to strike first: Iran, to avoid losing its arsenal, and Israel, to keep Tehran from using it. The Israeli government's calculations about Iran would depend on its assessment of the United States' willingness and ability to deter Iran. Israel's decision-making would be shaped by a number of factors: the United States' long-standing support for Israel, Israel's doubts about U.S. leadership after Washington's failure to stop Iran from going nuclear, and Washington's response to Iran's nuclearization.

Another danger that would have to be countered would be nuclear proliferation in the Middle East. Iran's regional rivals might try to catch up with it. History suggests, however, that states go nuclear for reasons beyond tit for tat; many hold back even when their enemies get nuclear weapons. China's pursuit of the bomb in the 1960s prompted fears that Japan would follow, but nearly half a century later, Japan remains nonnuclear. Although Israel has more than 200 nuclear weapons, neither its neighbors—not even Egypt, which fought and lost four wars with Israel—nor regional powers, such as Saudi Arabia or Turkey, have followed its lead.

An Iranian nuclear bomb could change these calculations. The U.S. National Intelligence Council concluded in a 2008 report that "Iran's growing nuclear capabilities are already partly responsible for the surge of interest in nuclear energy in the Middle East." And nuclear energy programs can serve as the foundation for drives for nuclear weapons. But it would not be easy for countries in the region to get nuclear weapons. Many lack the infrastructure to develop their own weapons and the missiles needed to deliver them. Egypt and Turkey might blanch at the expense of building a nuclear arsenal. The Pakistanis were willing to "eat grass" for the privilege of joining the nuclear club, as the Pakistani leader Zulfikar Ali Bhutto once famously put it, but not everyone is.

Cost considerations aside, it would take years for nuclear aspirants to develop indigenous nuclear capabilities. They would need to build nuclear reactors, acquire nuclear fuel, master enrichment or reprocessing technologies, and build weapons and the means to deliver them. While they tried, the United States and other states would have ample opportunity to increase the costs of proliferation. Indeed, the economic and security interests of Egypt, Saudi Arabia, and Turkey, unlike those of Iran, are tied to the United States and the broader global economy, and developing nuclear weapons would put those interests at risk. Egypt would jeopardize the $1.5 billion in economic and military aid that it receives from Washington each year; Saudi Arabia, its implicit U.S. security guarantee; and Turkey, its place in NATO. Given their extensive investments in and business ties to the United States and Europe, all three countries would be far more vulnerable than Iran is to any economic sanctions that U.S. law imposed, or could impose, on nuclear proliferators.

States seeking nuclear weapons might try to sidestep these technological and political hurdles by buying, rather than making, the weapons. Saudi Arabia's clandestine acquisition of medium-range ballistic missiles from China in the 1980s suggests that even countries that depend on U.S. security guarantees might be tempted to buy their way into the nuclear club. Although neither the five acknowledged nuclear powers nor India would be likely to sell nuclear weapons to another state, Pakistan and North Korea could be another matter. Both countries have a history of abetting proliferation, and Pakistan has warm ties with its fellow Muslim-majority countries. But selling complete nuclear weapons would come at great political cost. Pakistan might forfeit U.S. foreign assistance and drive the United States into closer cooperation with India, Pakistan's mortal enemy. North Korea would endanger the economic aid it gets from China, which the regime needs to stay in power.

If a buyer did manage to find a seller, it would have to avoid a preventive strike by Israel—which would be likely if the sale became known before the weapon was activated—and then handle the inevitable international political and economic fallout. (In 1988, Saudi Arabia avoided a major rift with Washington over its missile deal with China only by finally agreeing to sign and abide by the NPT.) Furthermore, any country that bought a nuclear weapon would have to worry about whether it would actually work; in global politics, as in everyday life, swindles are possible. Obtaining a nuclear weapon could thus put a country in the worst of all worlds: owning a worthless weapon that is a magnet for an attack.

If Iran's neighbors decided against trying to get nuclear weapons, they could pursue the opposite approach and try to appease Tehran. The temptation would be greatest for small Persian Gulf states, such as Bahrain and Kuwait, which sit uncomfortably close to Iran and have large Shiite populations. Such a tilt toward Iran would damage U.S. interests in the region. The U.S. Fifth Fleet is based in Bahrain, and U.S. military bases in Bahrain, Kuwait, and the United Arab Emirates are crucial to projecting U.S. power

and reassuring U.S. allies in the region. But as long as these governments believe that Washington is committed to their security, appeasement will be unappealing. Pursuing that strategy would mean casting aside U.S. help and betting on the mercy of Tehran. In the absence of a U.S. security guarantee, however, Iran would be free to conduct in those countries the very subversive activities that their governments' appeasement was intended to prevent.

Although Iran's nuclearization would probably not spell the end of efforts to halt proliferation in other parts of the world, it would undeniably deal the nonproliferation regime a setback, by demonstrating that the great powers are unable or unwilling to act collectively to stop proliferators. On the other hand, most states adhere to the NPT because they have compelling national reasons to do so. They may not feel threatened by a nuclear power; they may be covered by the nuclear umbrella of another state; they may lack the financial or technological wherewithal to build a bomb. Iran's success in developing a nuclear weapon would not change these calculations. Nor would it prevent Washington from pushing ahead with its efforts to strengthen the Proliferation Security Initiative (a U.S.-led multinational effort launched by the Bush administration that seeks to stop trafficking in weapons of mass destruction), impose a cutoff on the further production of fissile material, tighten global rules on trade in nuclear materials, and otherwise make it more difficult for nuclear technologies to spread.

Iran's acquisition of a nuclear bomb could have disastrous consequences in the Middle East. But Washington would have considerable opportunities to influence, and constrain, how Iran's neighbors reacted to its new status. It would matter whether Washington reassured Israel or fueled its fears. It would matter whether Washington confronted regional proliferation efforts or turned a blind eye, as it did with Pakistan in the 1980s. It would matter whether Washington pushed ahead with efforts to strengthen the NPT regime or threw in the towel. To keep the nightmare scenario at bay, the United States will need to think carefully about how to maximize its leverage in the region.

I Say No, No, No

TEHRAN is an adversary that speaks in ideological terms, wants to become a dominant regional power, and is capable of acting recklessly. But it is also an adversary that recognizes its limitations, wants to preserve its hold on power, and operates among wary neighbors. Its acquiring a nuclear bomb, or the capacity to make a nuclear bomb, need not remake the Middle East—at least not if the United States acts confidently and wisely to exploit Iran's weaknesses.

Tehran's acquiring a nuclear bomb need not remake the Middle East—if Washington wisely exploits Tehran's weaknesses.

Any strategy to contain Iran must begin with the recognition that this effort will have to be different from that to contain the Soviet Union. Iran poses a different threat. During the early years of the Cold War, U.S. policymakers tried to protect like-minded countries against a Soviet invasion that would have imposed communist rule, or against widespread economic dislocation, which could have produced a communist takeover from within. Their strategy was to turn to the NATO alliance and launch the Marshall Plan. The United States' containment strategy toward Iran must reflect different realities today. Iran does not seek to invade its neighbors, and its ideological appeal does not rest on promises of economic justice. It seeks to establish itself as the dominant power in the region while preserving political control at home.

Deterrence would by necessity be the cornerstone of a U.S. strategy to contain a nuclear Iran. Success is by no means guaranteed. Deterrence can fail: it nearly did during the Cuban missile crisis, in 1962, and at several other critical junctures of the Cold War. Iran's revisionist aims and paranoia about U.S. power may appear to make the country uniquely difficult to deter. But that conclusion conveniently—and mistakenly—recasts the history of U.S. confrontations with emerging nuclear powers in a gentler light than is deserved. At the start of the Cold War, U.S. officials hardly saw the Soviet Union as a status quo power. In the 1960s, China looked like the ultimate rogue regime: it had intervened in Korea and gone to war with India, and it repressed its own people. Mao boasted that although nuclear war might kill half the world's population, it would also mean that "imperialism would be razed to the ground and the whole world would become socialist."

Today, the challenge for U.S. policymakers devising a deterrence strategy toward Iran will be to unambiguously identify what behavior they seek to deter—and what they are willing to do about it. When Washington publicly presents its policy on how to contain a nuclear Iran, it should be explicit: no initiation of conventional warfare against other countries; no use or transfer of nuclear weapons, materials, or technologies; and no stepped-up support for terrorist or subversive activities. It should also make clear that the price of Iran's violating these three prohibitions could be U.S. military retaliation by any and all means necessary, up to and including nuclear weapons.

The pledge to deter a conventional attack would be the easiest of the three prohibitions to enforce. Iran's ability to project sustained military power outside its borders is limited. And it is unlikely to grow substantially anytime soon: even more arms embargoes would likely be imposed on Iran if it crossed the nuclear threshold. At their current level, U.S. troops in the region are more than sufficient to deter Iran from undertaking incursions into Iraq or amphibious operations across the Persian Gulf—or to stop them if they occurred.

Deterring Iran from using or threatening to use nuclear weapons would present a different set of challenges. So long as Iran lacks the ability to strike the United States with a nuclear-tipped missile, the United States can credibly threaten to retaliate militarily if Iran uses or threatens to use a nuclear bomb against anyone. But that could change if Iran developed long-range missiles. Tehran might also try to deter the United States by threatening to attack Europe, which would raise well-known concerns about the viability of so-called extended deterrence, the ability of one state to deter an attack on another. These possibilities highlight the importance of developing robust, multilayered ballistic missile defenses. The Obama administration's decision to reorient U.S. missile defenses in Europe to protect against shorter-range missiles while continuing to develop defenses against longer-range missiles is just the right approach.

A tougher challenge would be to ensure stable deterrence between Iran and Israel. With regard to this issue, too, the Iranian nuclear program's ultimate degree of development would

be pivotal: an Iran armed with nuclear weapons would present a significantly more dangerous threat than one that merely had the capacity to build them. It is thus essential that Washington continue to apply diplomatic and economic pressure to keep Tehran, should it manage to complete the nuclear fuel cycle, from taking the final step. The United States should also publicly pledge to retaliate by any means it chooses if Iran uses nuclear weapons against Israel; this would in effect supplement whatever second-strike capability Israel has. If the Israelis need a formal commitment to be more reassured, this pledge could be made in an executive agreement or a treaty. As a tangible expression of its commitment, Washington should also be prepared to deploy U.S. troops on Israeli soil as a tripwire, which would show that the United States would be inextricably bound to Israel in the event of any Iranian attack.

Washington should also inform Tehran that it would strike preemptively, with whatever means it deemed necessary, if Iran ever placed its nuclear forces on alert. And it should bring both Israel and Israel's Arab neighbors fully under its missile defense umbrella. The more aggressive Iran is, the more inclined its neighbors will be to work with Washington to construct missile defenses on their territories.

Deterring Iran from transferring nuclear weapons, materials, and technologies to state and nonstate actors would require another set of measures. For the most part, Iran has reasons not to pursue such perilous activities, but it could be tempted to exploit the difficulty of tracking the clandestine trade in nuclear materials. The United States and its allies would need to act decisively to prevent Tehran from seeking to profit in the international nuclear bazaar, for example, through the Proliferation Security Initiative and through UN resolutions that imposed additional sanctions on Iran and its potential business partners. To impress on Iran's ruling mullahs that it is singularly important for them to control whatever nuclear arsenal they may develop or obtain, Washington should hold Tehran responsible for any nuclear transfer, whether authorized or not; Tehran cannot be allowed to escape punishment or retaliation by pleading loss of control. Increased investments in monitoring and spying on Iran would be critical. The United States must improve its ability to track nuclear weapons, materials, and debris and prove and publicize whether they came from Iran (or any other country, for that matter). Such nuclear forensics is crucial to determining who is responsible for nuclear transfers and would be crucial to building support for any U.S. retaliation against Iran, if it were the culprit.

Deterring Iranian support for terrorist and subversive groups—the third redline prohibition that the United States should impose—would be difficult. Such activities take place secretly, making it hard to establish precisely who is complicit. That complication places a premium on improving the ability of the U.S. intelligence community, acting alone and in concert with its counterparts abroad, to track Iran's clandestine activities.

Whats and What Nots

IN ADDITION to holding Iran accountable for violating any of the three nos, the United States' containment strategy should seek to influence and, where necessary, constrain Iran's friends in the Middle East. An energetic diplomacy that softened the disagreements between Israel and its neighbors would undermine Iran's efforts to exploit anger in the region. A concerted push, diplomatic and economic, to improve the lives of the Palestinians would limit Iran's appeal among them. Drawing Syria into a comprehensive Israeli-Palestinian peace process could not only attenuate Tehran's links with Damascus but also stem Iran's ability to supply weapons to Hezbollah. Washington should seek to further limit Iran's strategic reach by strengthening the institutional and military capabilities of Afghanistan and Iraq. It should reassure the Persian Gulf states that it is committed to preserving the existing balance of power, which would require expanding trade agreements, enhancing their security and intelligence apparatuses, and developing a more integrated approach to defense planning in the region. At the same time, the United States will need to dissuade these governments from further suppressing their Shiite minorities, a practice that inadvertently aids Tehran. And it should work assiduously to prevent more countries in the Middle East from going nuclear; the United States cannot look the other way again, as it did with Pakistan during the 1980s.

Tone and conviction will matter. Washington must keep in mind that Iran's entry into the nuclear club would be read by Israel and Arab states as a failure of the United States' political will and a demonstration of the limits of U.S. power. Washington cannot afford to compound its credibility problem by hesitating or vacillating. An indecisive U.S. response would undermine the efforts both to deter Iran and to reassure U.S. friends and allies in the region.

Washington should also push other major powers to contain the Iranian threat. The five permanent members of the UN Security Council have sponsored numerous resolutions demanding that Iran cease its nuclear activities and cooperate with the International Atomic Energy Agency. They should have a vested interest in punishing Iran, an original signatory to the NPT, if it reneges on its decades-old pledge to remain a nonnuclear power. Doing nothing would substantially undermine the UN Security Council's authority and with it their status as permanent members of the council. Europe should be pressed to commit troops and naval vessels to preserve the free flow of traffic through the Persian Gulf. Russia should cease its nuclear cooperation with and its conventional arms sales to Iran. China should be pressed to curtail its investment in Iran's energy sector, which does so much to fuel Iran's belligerence. The United States would have to do much of the heavy lifting in containing a nuclear Iran, but any concerted containment strategy must have not just regional support but also an international complexion.

Just as important as what Washington should do to contain Iran is what it should not do. If Iran gets a nuclear bomb, the United States might be tempted to respond by substantially expanding the presence of U.S. troops in the Middle East. But this would not appreciably increase Washington's ability to deter Iran from launching a nuclear or conventional attack; there are already enough U.S. forces in the region for that. It could, however, play into the hands of Tehran's proxies by inflaming anti-American sentiment and fanning civil unrest in the Persian Gulf.

Washington might also be tempted to seek to further undermine Iran's economy by imposing broad-based economic sanctions, an idea that enjoys considerable support on Capitol Hill. But such measures would wind up punishing only Iran's disenfranchised citizenry (which is why Iranian opposition leaders have strenuously opposed them). The wiser course of action would be to strengthen and better monitor existing export controls, in order to make certain that Iran's nuclear and defense industries do not have access to dual-use technologies, and to reinforce targeted sanctions against the Iranian leadership and the business enterprises controlled by the Revolutionary Guards. Washington should push, both inside and outside the UN, for travel bans on Iranian leaders and measures denying Iran access to capital markets, for example. It should also find ways to penalize foreign businesses that invest in Iran's dilapidated oil industry. Smart sanctions of this kind would punish Iran's leaders but spare ordinary Iranians, who have no say over the regime's actions.

The United States should refrain from greatly expanding the range of weaponry it sells to the Persian Gulf states, which see the United States as a military guarantor and their chief arms supplier. To some extent, increasing arms sales will be necessary: the Arab governments of the region would regard such sales as a tangible sign of the strength of Washington's commitment to their defense, and if Washington holds back, these governments will look for weapons elsewhere. On the other hand, throwing the doors of the armory wide open would do little to secure the buyers and might even increase instability in the region. A smart U.S. arms sales policy would focus on offering weapons systems that are designed to deter or help counter an Iranian attack, such as missile defense systems and command-and-control systems, which would provide advance notice of Iranian actions.

Finally, Washington should resist any urge to sign mutual security treaties with Arab countries in the Middle East. (Israel, whose relations with Iran are fundamentally different from those of every other power in the region, is a special case.) Such efforts would do little to enhance deterrence and could do a lot to undermine it. Many members of the U.S. Senate, which would have to vote on any alliance treaty, would question whether the United States should further tie itself to authoritarian regimes that many Americans find odious. The spectacle of that debate would exacerbate doubts in the Middle East about the depth of the United States' commitment. Efforts to construct formal alliances might also lead Iran to believe that any country left out of these agreements is fair game for intimidation or attack. Washington should be mindful not to invite a replay of North Korea's calculation in 1950 that South Korea lay outside the U.S. defense perimeter.

Instead, the U.S. government should encourage the formation of a regional alliance network that would marshal Arab states into a more cohesive defense grouping. The network could be organized along the lines of the Middle East Treaty Organization (then the Central Treaty Organization), a security arrangement among Iran, Pakistan, Turkey, the United Kingdom, and, for a time, Iraq (with the United States participating in the organization's military and security committees) that existed from 1955 to 1979. An alliance of this kind would secure all the benefits of a regionwide commitment to deterrence without exposing the United States and its allies to the complexities of formal bilateral or multilateral security treaties.

Dangerous Times

IRAN'S NUCLEARIZATION would make the Middle East a more dangerous place: it would heighten tensions, reduce the margin for error, and raise the prospect of mass catastrophe. The international community should not let up on its efforts to stop Iran's progress. But given the mullahs' seeming indifference to the benefits of engagement, U.S. policymakers must consider now what to do if Iran does get the bomb.

Containment would be neither a perfect nor a foolproof policy. The task of foiling Iran's support for Hamas and Hezbollah would be difficult, as would countering Iran's support for terrorist and subversive groups in the region. The need to gain favor with Arab dictatorships would likely tempt Washington to shelve its calls for domestic political reforms in those countries—even though such reforms could diminish Iran's ability to meddle there by improving the lot of local minority Shiites who might otherwise be susceptible to Tehran's influence. Maintaining great-power support for pressure on Iran could require overlooking objectionable Chinese and Russian behavior on other matters. Containment would not be a substitute for the use of force. To the contrary, its very success would depend on the willingness of the United States to use force against Iran or threaten to do so should Tehran cross Washington's redlines. Applying pressure without a commitment to punishing infractions is a recipe for failure—and for a more violent and dangerous Middle East.

Containment could buy Washington time to persuade the Iranian ruling class that the revisionist game it has been playing is simply not worth the candle. Thus, even as Washington pushes to counter Iran, it should be open to the possibility that Tehran's calculations might change. To press Tehran in the right direction, Washington should signal that it seeks to create an order in the Middle East that is peaceful and self-sustaining. The United States will remain part of the region's security architecture for the foreseeable future, but it need not maintain an antagonistic posture toward Iran. An Islamic Republic that abandoned its nuclear ambitions, accepted prevailing international norms, and respected the sovereignty of its neighbors would discover that the United States is willing to work with, rather than against, Iran's legitimate national aspirations.

Critical Thinking

1. What are some ways the United States, with or without the help of other nuclear powers, might be able to contain threats related to Iran obtaining nuclear weapons in the future?

2. What are some ways the United States, with or without the help of other nuclear powers, might be able to mitigate future behavior by Iran once the country has "gone nuclear?"

James M. Lindsay is Senior Vice President, Director of Studies, and Maurice R. Greenberg Chair at the Council on Foreign Relations. **Ray Takeyh** is a Senior Fellow at the Council on Foreign Relations and the author of *Guardians of the Revolution: Iran and the World in the Age of the Ayatollahs.* For an annotated guide to this topic, see "What to Read on Iranian Politics" at www.foreignaffairs.com/readinglists/iran and "What to Read on Nuclear Proliferation" at www.foreignaffairs.com/readinglists/nuclear-proliferation.

From *Foreign Affairs,* 89:2, March/April 2010, pp. 33–49. Copyright © 2010 by Council on Foreign Relations, Inc. Reprinted by permission of Foreign Affairs. www.ForeignAffairs.com

Evolving Bioweapon Threats Require New Countermeasures

HELEN PURKITT AND VIRGEN WELLS

To better understand possible development and uses of biological weapons by nations and terrorist groups, we have studied past covert government programs in South Africa and Iraq, and recent trends in civilian biotechnology in South Africa.

U.S. monitoring of bioweapon threats is geared primarily toward uncovering large-scale, highly sophisticated programs, like that of the former Soviet Union during the cold war. But covert bioweapon development has become more diffuse, and many potential actors have far different goals than they did then. We think the United States needs to work with other nations to build new norms of transparency and greater international cooperation in regulating the operation of civilian-biotechnology laboratories and the dispersal of relevant data that may have military applications. Only through such global cooperation can we effectively monitor trends in potential bioweapon research and look for early-warning signs of covert biowarfare-weapons development by nation-states or by terrorists and other nonstate actors.

Our research indicates that terrorists are likely to use biological weapons not to inflict mass destruction but to commit blackmail or fuel political discontent, panic, or economic disruption. That's important because the development of biological weapons of mass disruption no longer requires large capital investment, great expertise, vast infrastructure, and sophisticated delivery devices like medium- or long-range missiles. Policy analysts and some policy makers have made similar points, but many of the United States' biosecurity priorities and policies do not reflect the new realities.

In the 1960s and 70s, a common pattern for developing countries was to send the "best and brightest" of their young scientists abroad for advanced study or training. Many of those scientists went on to work in their countries' covert bioweapons programs. For instance, Rihab Rashid Taha al-Azzawi al-Tikriti, a microbiologist (nicknamed "Dr. Germ" by U.N. weapons inspectors) who headed Iraq's bacterial program at al-Hakim for several years, earned a doctorate from the University of East Anglia, in England, where she studied plant disease. Huda Salih Mahdi Ammash, who was dubbed "Mrs. Anthrax" by U.S. intelligence services for her work reconstructing Iraq's biological weapons facilities after the 1991 Persian Gulf war, studied for a master-of-science degree in microbiology at Texas Woman's University, in Denton, and later earned a doctorate in microbiology at the University of Missouri at Columbia. Also, biowarfare scientists recruited to work on covert programs in developing countries were often trained in fields other than biology. For example, South Africa's former covert bioweapons program, Project Coast, recruited many of its first researchers from among veterinarians with advanced degrees in at least two scientific fields. Some Iraqi and South African researchers participated in American or English training exercises at military and government installations, and in scientific exchanges. But the United States closed down a defensive bioweapons-research program in the 1970s, and as concerns grew about Iraqi and South African politics and development of weapons of mass destruction, it became, by the late 1980s, more difficult for scientists from those countries to travel abroad.

The United States further reduced foreign students' and scientists' access to American universities after the terrorist attacks of September 11, 2001, and the still-unsolved anthrax-letter incidents the following month. Unfortunately, the belief that students and scientists from developing countries must obtain their higher education in the West in order to acquire the skills needed to work with and weaponize biological agents is misguided and out-of-date. Today there are premier research universities throughout the world.

Visa restrictions and the rising cost of an American education have led many graduate students and scientists in the biological and physical sciences, especially from Middle Eastern countries, to study or work in countries in their own region or in Europe, Asia, or Africa. Moreover, the online availability of the information necessary to produce many biological pathogens, including step-by-step protocols, means that terrorists can obtain the requisite knowledge and even academic credentials while living almost anywhere.

If information is easy to come by, so are pathogens or potential pathogens. Before they shifted to genetic-modification techniques, both South African and Iraqi biowarfare scientists explored the feasibility of using naturally occurring pathogens. In their initial efforts, Iraqi scientists studied fungal toxins (for instance, mycotoxins and aflatoxins), anthrax spores, and a variety of other toxins, bacteria, and viruses, including those that cause botulism, cholera, polio, and influenza. Other early research involved creating deadly compounds from wheat and castor beans. Similarly, early South African experiments allegedly involved having military forces use biological agents to poison wells and putting cholera in some rivers in southern Africa. Project Coast scientists explored common viruses and bacteria and worked extensively with anthrax, which occurs naturally throughout southern Africa.

Those projects strongly suggest that covert-biowarfare scientists and terrorists are likely to use readily available, naturally occurring pathogens in initial attempts to create bioweapons. So thought the vast majority of the 43 scientists and researchers we interviewed in South Africa during 2003. Several of them noted that hundreds of different fungi found on the diverse plants and trees in rural areas throughout the world could easily be processed to form new biowarfare pathogens.

Some government officials are becoming alert to the prospect that natural pathogens could be used as a fast and easy way to acquire a seed stock for immediate use or further research on creating pathogenicity. To try to counter this emerging threat, 39 nations and the European Commission—all participants at the 2004 plenary session of the Australia Group—agreed to add five plant pathogens to its list of restricted items, the first expansion of the list since 1993. (The Australia Group is an informal network of countries that seeks to harmonize national export-licensing measures to stem the proliferation of chemical and biological weapons.)

Cloning techniques are another underestimated source of potential small-scale biological weapons. In 2003 three researchers in South Africa used an "in house" protocol for cloning that required minimal equipment and expertise to produce the first African cloned cow at a remote research station. Once scientists identify a gene that can cause disease, other scientists or terrorists can clone the gene and introduce it into common host bacteria by using a cloning kit readily available in catalogs of lab equipment.

Although cloning is a relatively common process that does not require a complex lab, safely conducting research on many viruses does demand a Biosafety Level 3 facility. Work with the most serious viruses—infectious diseases that are transmitted through the air and for which there is no known cure—require a BSL-4 laboratory. In BSL-3 labs, researchers wear protective gear to work in negative-pressure environments with transmissible infectious agents like tuberculosis. BSL-4 labs are highly secure areas for the study of the most infectious diseases, like the Ebola virus, and have multiple locked chambers, with constant monitoring of directed air flow. Scientists at those facilities wear suits with their own air supplies and work on infectious agents in special cabinets, also with their own air. The BSL-4 facilities require very careful construction, with holes for electrical, plumbing, piping, and camera outlets embedded ahead of time in their concrete walls.

Those needs have long been thought to limit the activities of scientists or terrorists working in poor countries. Recent technological advances, however, make it possible to set up a modular mobile BSL-3 lab within days, even in a remote location. As far as we know, all such facilities now are in the hands of agencies such as the U.S. Centers for Disease Control and Prevention. But recent changes in the Australia Group's export-control list reflect concern about smaller and more mobile equipment that could be used for covert biowarfare. In 2002, for instance, the group passed new export restrictions on small fermenters that could be used in the production of bacteria. But that type of equipment is already available for sale on the Internet, and if it hasn't already, it could soon fall into the wrong hands.

A great deal of public attention has focused on the use or genetic modification of extremely dangerous diseases such as Ebola or smallpox. A large portion of the money committed to date in contracts for the United States' Project BioShield ($877-million out of $5.6-billion) is for a program to buy 75 million doses of anthrax vaccine from a single company, VaxGen, even though the plan to inoculate all military personnel has run into legal, scientific, and production delays. The public concerns and large government efforts to counter those pathogens are understandable in the aftermath of the 2001 anthrax letters and public discussion of future terrorist scenarios involving Ebola, smallpox, or highly refined anthrax. However, any government or terrorist group would probably find it simpler to use common pathogens such as E. coli and salmonella, which are easier and cheaper to purchase, reproduce, and use.

Despite a flurry of recent research focused on the potential use of civilian biotechnology as a weapon, there have been remarkably few empirical studies of biotech trends in developing countries, especially African ones.

The online availability of the information necessary to produce many biological pathogens means that terrorists can obtain the requisite knowledge while living almost anywhere.

That lack of interest is unfortunate because nearly every country in the developing world is seeking to create the scientific and industrial capacity needed to compete in the biotech revolution. Even Zimbabwe, a failing state, recently passed a national biotechnology plan. Most such efforts focus on civilian biotechnology, which is widely viewed as a way to develop new high-value, high-tech products and processes for export, creating new jobs. Several countries in the developing world have also formed special-purpose transnational networks, like the Developing Country Vaccine Manufacturers Network, with a common focus like producing generic drugs for common infectious diseases. But terrorist groups interested in acquiring biotechnology expertise and products have also been reported to be forming transnational networks.

Public and private laboratories in the developing world are also gaining access to sophisticated bioinformatics-computing facilities and gene, tissue, and protein libraries. For example, the South African National Bioinformatics Institute has the long-term goal of connecting researchers at various sites in a transnational network. It will eventually permit scientists across the continent to access a common bioinformatics computer architecture, the power of the one high-speed Cray computer in South Africa, shared access to gene and protein libraries, and the computational tools necessary to conduct sophisticated bioinformatics research on shared problems.

Those trends suggest that before long the world may simultaneously face biological-weapons threats from naturally occurring pathogens and genetically modified organisms. Governments need to develop new approaches to monitor and manage this still poorly understood class of threats.

Traditional control strategies are unlikely to prevent the development of covert bioweapons by either nations or terrorists. The last major effort to ensure compliance with the 1975 Biological and Toxin Weapons Convention was in 2001–2 when a draft protocol was presented to member nations for a vote. The United States rejected it on the grounds that it was an ineffective arms-control approach, would compromise national-security and confidential business information, and would benefit would-be proliferators. But the failure to find evidence of any active WMD programs in Iraq and the suspected Iraqi mobile labs that are now believed to have been hydrogen-production units for weather balloons underscore how difficult it is to verify the existence of a covert biological-weapons program in the absence of sustained, intrusive inspections by neutral outside observers.

Many experts argue that the nature of biotech research is such that greater transparency and cooperation among nations and corporations may be the only way to monitor it. While the U.S. government worries about roughly three dozen countries that may have covert biowarfare programs, the number of possible bioterrorism threats seems limitless. One approach that might help would be to categorize possible threats emanating from different types of countries, and tailor monitoring and security efforts to each category.

Most biotechnology research and development is currently located in the United States, Europe, Japan, and Australia. However, India and China have many public and private biotech companies that are nearing the cutting edge.

A second tier of countries fosters a much smaller scale of biotech research. For example, Argentina and Brazil are significant producers of biotech agricultural crops and rank second and third, behind the United States, in the number of hectares devoted to such crops. Countries as diverse as Cuba, Egypt, Israel, South Africa, and South Korea play host to private and public biotech R&D activities. Much of that consists of civilian efforts to find a niche market in arenas dominated by large multinational businesses or to invent a unique product or process that could be sold to a multinational business. The governments of those countries share a commitment to help stimulate further biotech R&D, for which there is a modest amount of capital available from local or foreign sources. Despite their similarities, however, the countries differ in their degree of foreign collaboration, the extent of engagement in the global economy, and whether the government is a member of the biological-weapons convention.

Before long the world may simultaneously face biological-weapons threats from naturally occurring pathogens and genetically modified organisms.

A third tier consists of most other countries, which have limited civilian biotech research and little chance of closing the economic and technological gap between themselves and Tiers 1 and 2. These countries—such as Dubai, Kenya, Thailand, and the United Arab Emirates—primarily function as junior partners, labor reserves, or off-shore tax shelters for multinational biotech companies.

A final tier are countries that have no functioning central government (like Somalia) or have large ungoverned and lawless spaces (like Colombia). In those nation-states the large, lawless areas can serve as attractive locations for terrorist activities.

Given that range, greater transparency seems to be a better approach than traditional control strategies. For example, Western governments should focus more attention on standardizing Good Laboratory Practice (GLP) and safety standards at public and private laboratories. GLP guidelines include inspections of active laboratories, university labs, foreign labs, and inactive labs. Those inspections are focused on standard practices and safety—for example, accountability for reagents and equipment certifications, maintenance of laboratory records, and specimen and sample tracking. The guidelines may help to control access to reagents and equipment, or to monitor illegal labs in remote areas or suburban-kitchen labs operated by terrorists or lone dissidents. But they might also, in the long term, promote greater transparency in biotechnology research and further the development of new international norms about what constitutes public and proprietary information and activities.

We need new regulations for the publication and other dissemination of peer-reviewed research that has possible biowarfare uses. Of course, creating such regulations would involve thorny, fundamental issues regarding the scientific process and the free press. On March 4, 2004, the Bush administration announced the creation of a new federal advisory board designed to help ensure that terrorists cannot make use of federally supported biological research. The new 25-member National Science Advisory Board for Biosecurity is intended to advise federal departments and agencies that conduct or support research of interest to terrorists on how best to keep it out of their hands. The creation of the board was one recommendation of a recent National Academies' National Research Council report (known as the Fink report) that focused on how to keep genetically engineered viruses and other works from being used in bioterrorism. Of course, the board's mandate does not cover research that receives no federal funds or that is conducted abroad, so there is an enormous security gap waiting to be filled.

Most of the scientists we interviewed cautioned that if handled clumsily, efforts to regulate the dissemination of federally supported biological research could damage the United States' position as a research leader. In a global world of science, American and foreign researchers working in the life sciences in America today have many options, including: opting out of research programs related to biosecurity, relying on private or foreign funds for research, or pursuing their research in other countries.

Many of the scientists also conveyed serious concerns about new restrictions on travel for graduate students. Some foreign students who left the United States to visit their home countries have had trouble returning to their American labs. The scientists were also concerned that many talented foreign graduate students who had been accepted into their programs were experiencing difficulties obtaining U.S. visas. Although entry restrictions have eased somewhat, continuing limits and bureaucratic obstacles have led many foreigners to go elsewhere for their education or advanced research. Such restrictions have been imposed in the name of security, but in the long run, they may become one of America's most serious security problems as they gradually erode our centrality in biotech innovation.

We support a significant easing of restrictions on foreigners seeking advanced scientific education or jobs in the West, but also the establishment of an enhanced monitoring system that would include more reliable procedures to ensure that all visa applicants undergo background investigations and checks. And we recommend a new reporting system that would allow the government to better track the whereabouts of foreign graduate students and scientists during their stays in the United States. We also recommend that more attention be given by relevant U.S. agencies to tracking the activities of foreign scientists and students after they have completed their work or studies and have left the United States. Perhaps if such a reporting requirement was incorporated as a condition for the initial visa it would be less controversial.

None of our suggestions would solve the host of problems created by the proliferation of biological expertise, equipment, and supplies. However, an important first step in improving security is to recognize that we face a range of biological threats from many different types of perpetrators, and that although we can monitor and reduce the dangers, we can never fully guard ourselves against attack. Enhancing our national security while also keeping American biotech research at the cutting edge are complementary goals. We can make progress toward both if we strive for greater international norms and transparency, while gauging threats in a more thoughtful and case-specific manner.

Critical Thinking

1. Explain why control strategies will probably fail to prevent committed deviants (e.g., individuals, groups, nation-states) from making or obtaining biological weapons?

2. Which type of secret biological weapons programs do you believe jihadist terrorists are likely to be conducting research and development currently or in the future?

3. Explain why you agree or disagree with the authors' call for promoting a new transparency norm as the most effective way to deal with future bioweapon threats.

HELEN PURKITT is a professor of political science at the U.S. Naval Academy. **VIRGEN WELLS,** a microbiologist, is a former fellow at the American Association for the Advancement of Science. Their research cited here was supported by the Advanced Systems and Concepts Office of the Defense Threat Reduction Agency, the Institute for National Security Studies at the U.S. Air Force Academy, and the U.S. Naval Academy. However, the views expressed here are those of the authors and not those of the U.S. government.

UNIT 3

Foreign Policy Decision Making

Unit Selections

Learning Objectives

- What are some of the ways that the foreign policies of the Obama Administration are similar to and different to those of the Bush Administration?

- Why does every U.S. president fail to carry out at least some of his or her campaign promises?

- What is the meaning of national security, human security, and collective security?

- What are some policy areas where two or more of these security concerns overlap?

- Who are the key actors in the national security establishment?

- Was former President Eisenhower correct to warn about the rising power of the military-industrial complex?

- Describe some current and future technologies that may help DOD save energy.

- What other added advantages will the United States gain if the DOD manages to reap cost savings from more effective technologies designed to reduce energy needs?

Student Website
www.mhhe.com/cls

Internet References

STRATFOR
www.stratfor.com
Center for a New American Security
www.cnas.org
Carnegie Endowment for International Peace
www.ceip.org
The Heritage Foundation
www.heritage.org
Top Secret America
www.projects.washingtonpost.com/top-secret-america/
DOD Energy Blog
www.dodenergy.blogspot.com

Mid-way into George W. Bush's second term in office, his administration's policy on the preventive use of force was being revised to emphasize other instruments of foreign policy and greater reliance on multilateral diplomacy. Consequently, it is not surprising that some of Obama's foreign policies, such as the timetable for the withdrawal of U.S. troops from Iraq and relations with European powers, Russia, and China, are consistent with the policies of the Bush Administration. In other areas such as arms control, the Obama Administration has launched significantly different proposals and positions than those of his predecessor. The deteriorating security situation in Afghanistan forced the Obama Administration to adopt policies that were very different from his campaign promises. In "Obama's Foreign Policy: The End of the Beginning," George Friedman describes how the Obama regime has shifted "from a purely defensive posture to a mixed posture of selective offense and defense." Friedman concludes that this shift is hardly surprising since all United States presidents operate in a world of constraints with limited options. Friedman concludes that "like all good Presidents, Obama is leaving behind certain campaign promises to govern."

A focus on how to maximize a nation-states vital, important, and secondary interests have been the mainstay of a nation-state's foreign policy decision makers' calculus since the formation of the nation-state system. However, as the size of the world's population and the number of people lacking the most basic needs in terms of food, water, shelter, and personal security grow exponentially, there has been a greater recognition that traditional national security interests increasingly intersect with policies designed to improve human security in the developing world. The nexus between traditional and human security concerns became more salient to United States foreign policy decision makers and military leaders as they had to modify war strategies to achieve more successful counterinsurgency operations in Iraq. A growing recognition that the two types of security are intertwined was also a core consideration on the minds of the architects who established a new unified military command, AFRICOM, for the African continent in the fall of 2008. Similar reorganization policies have occurred in the United States military command SOUTHCOM, which has operational responsibility for Latin America and the Caribbean, and by the newly created NORTHCOM. SOUTHCOM has adopted a similar core mission to that of AFRICOM. Both commands are integrated, interagency organizations that are attempting to promote security while also providing help where feasible to promote economic development by working with representatives of other United States national agencies in countries within the region. While the increased involvement of United States military stationed abroad in nontraditional military missions is still controversial, most United States decision makers and analysts stress that these new organizational changes merely reflect budgetary realities and realities on the ground. The United States military often is the only agency with the operational capacity to help in emergency and non-emergency situations.

A generalized recognition that a third type of threat, collective security threats that might harm all of humankind may be

© Royalty-Free/CORBIS

growing has led many policy makers and analysts to stress the future impact of collective security threats that may occur from such worldwide phenomenon as global warming and the spread of new, incurable infectious diseases. The potential threat to world civilizations in the event of a nuclear war was always present during the Cold War. However, today there is a greater possibility that national and human security issues will coincide with global collective security. Today, the United States, much like other nation-state, faces a host of novel challenges related to longer-term, sustainable security approach.

Prior to World War II, many realist analysts in the West assumed that foreign policy decision makers used the same maximizing logic worldwide to identify their country's important national interests. Thus, classical realists such as Hans Morgenthau talked about the vital and important interests of nation-states in universal terms. However, as recent debates over whether the United States should continue its special relationship with Israel illustrates, there is rarely a consensus on the definition of vital or important national interests within the national homeland. There are debates about what constitutes a nation-state's vital national interest, especially within democracies, because what constitutes states most important interests is not an objective or universal set of values. Thus, the questions of how best to maximize a country's national interests are always a topic of political debates.

Such debates often cast the key actors as nation-states. However, since the Eisenhower Administration, a modern military industrial-complex has expanded and serves to constrain and influence the formulation of foreign policy options and the way that foreign policies are implemented. This system became even larger and more complex after the terrorist attacks of September 11, 2001. Despite a different rhetoric and renewed commitment to multilateral diplomacy, the Obama Administration has continued to expand the largely secret United States war against al-Qaeda and other radical groups using covert military capabilities controlled by the military and several civilian intelligence agencies. According to a series of special reports in the *Washington Post* published in 2010, United States Special Operation forces have grown in size and in terms of their budget and are now deployed in 75 countries, compared to about 60 in 2009. The increase in Special Operations deployments, along with intensified CIA drone attacks in Pakistan, Somalia, and elsewhere reflects the increased use of covert operations by the Obama Administration much like the former Bush Administration. No one really knows how large this covert foreign policy decision-making apparatus actually is today. As Dana Priest and William M. Arkin detail in "A Hidden World, Growing beyond Control," the expanded "top-secret world the government . . . has become so large, so unwieldy and so secretive that no one knows how much money it costs, how many people it employs."

During the same period that the United States secret military-industrial complex grew, the Defense Department was attempting to save money and fight more efficiently in the future by financing research on alternative fuels and fuel efficiencies while also reducing the military's carbon footprint. Armory B. Lovins in "DOD's Energy Challenge as Strategic Opportunity" describes some of the current, near-term, and emerging efficiency technologies that are designed to save energy costs for land, sea and air platforms. Lovins stresses that future energy solutions will require a focus on increasing endurance and resilience capabilities, details. These approaches involve many of the same things that are required in other areas of national security, climate change, increasing jobs and United States competitiveness.

Obama's Foreign Policy: The End of the Beginning

GEORGE FRIEDMAN

As August draws to a close, so does the first phase of the Obama presidency. The first months of any U.S. presidency are spent filling key positions and learning the levers of foreign and national security policy. There are also the first rounds of visits with foreign leaders and the first tentative forays into foreign policy. The first summer sees the leaders of the Northern Hemisphere take their annual vacations, and barring a crisis or war, little happens in the foreign policy arena. Then September comes and the world gets back in motion, and the first phase of the president's foreign policy ends. The president is no longer thinking about what sort of foreign policy he will have; he now has a foreign policy that he is carrying out.

We therefore are at a good point to stop and consider not what U.S. President Barack Obama will do in the realm of foreign policy, but what he has done and is doing. As we have mentioned before, the single most remarkable thing about Obama's foreign policy is how consistent it is with the policies of former President George W. Bush. This is not surprising. Presidents operate in the world of constraints; their options are limited. Still, it is worth pausing to note how little Obama has deviated from the Bush foreign policy.

During the 2008 U.S. presidential campaign, particularly in its early stages, Obama ran against the Iraq war. The centerpiece of his early position was that the war was a mistake, and that he would end it. Obama argued that Bush's policies—and more important, his style—alienated U.S. allies. He charged Bush with pursuing a unilateral foreign policy, alienating allies by failing to act in concert with them. In doing so, he maintained that the war in Iraq destroyed the international coalition the United States needs to execute any war successfully. Obama further argued that Iraq was a distraction and that the major effort should be in Afghanistan. He added that the United States would need its NATO allies' support in Afghanistan. He said an Obama administration would reach out to the Europeans, rebuild U.S. ties there and win greater support from them.

Though around 40 countries cooperated with the United States in Iraq, albeit many with only symbolic contributions, the major continental European powers—particularly France and Germany—refused to participate. When Obama spoke of alienating allies, he clearly meant these two countries, as well as smaller European powers that had belonged to the U.S. Cold War coalition but were unwilling to participate in Iraq and were now actively hostile to U.S. policy.

A European Rebuff

Early in his administration, Obama made two strategic decisions. First, instead of ordering an immediate withdrawal from Iraq, he adopted the Bush administration's policy of a staged withdrawal keyed to political stabilization and the development of Iraqi security forces. While he tweaked the timeline on the withdrawal, the basic strategy remained intact. Indeed, he retained Bush's defense secretary, Robert Gates, to oversee the withdrawal.

Second, he increased the number of U.S. troops in Afghanistan. The Bush administration had committed itself to Afghanistan from 9/11 onward. But it had remained in a defensive posture in the belief that given the forces available, enemy capabilities and the historic record, that was the best that could be done, especially as the Pentagon was almost immediately reoriented and refocused on the invasion and subsequent occupation of Iraq. Toward the end, the Bush administration began exploring—under the influence of Gen. David Petraeus, who designed the strategy in Iraq—the possibility of some sort of political accommodation in Afghanistan.

Obama has shifted his strategy in Afghanistan to this extent: He has moved from a purely defensive posture to a mixed posture of selective offense and defense, and has placed more forces into Afghanistan (although the United States still has nowhere near the number of troops the Soviets had when they lost their Afghan war). Therefore, the core structure of Obama's policy remains the same as Bush's except for the introduction of limited offensives. In a major shift since Obama took office, the Pakistanis have taken a more aggressive stance (or at least want to appear more aggressive) toward the Taliban and al Qaeda, at least within their own borders. But even so, Obama's basic strategy remains the same as Bush's: hold in Afghanistan until the political situation evolves to the point that a political settlement is possible.

Most interesting is how little success Obama has had with the French and the Germans. Bush had given up asking for assistance in Afghanistan, but Obama tried again. He received the same answer Bush did: no. Except for some minor, short-term assistance, the French and Germans were unwilling to commit forces to Obama's major foreign policy effort, something that stands out.

Given the degree to which the Europeans disliked Bush and were eager to have a president who would revert the U.S.-European relationship to what it once was (at least in their view), one would have thought the French and Germans would be eager to make some substantial gesture rewarding the United States for selecting a pro-European president. Certainly, it was in their interest to strengthen Obama. That they proved unwilling to make that gesture suggests that the French and German relationship with the United States is much less important to Paris and Berlin than it would appear. Obama, a pro-European president, was emphasizing a war France and Germany approved of over a war they disapproved of and asked for their help, but virtually none was forthcoming.

The Russian Non-Reset

Obama's desire to reset European relations was matched by his desire to reset U.S.-Russian relations. Ever since the Orange Revolution in the Ukraine in late 2004 and early 2005, U.S.-Russian relations had deteriorated dramatically, with Moscow charging Washington with interfering in the internal affairs of former Soviet republics with the aim of weakening Russia. This culminated in the Russo-Georgian war last August. The Obama administration has since suggested a "reset" in relations, with Secretary of State Hillary Clinton actually carrying a box labeled "reset button" to her spring meeting with the Russians.

The problem, of course, was that the last thing the Russians wanted was to reset relations with the United States. They did not want to go back to the period after the Orange Revolution, nor did they want to go back to the period between the collapse of the Soviet Union and the Orange Revolution. The Obama administration's call for a reset showed the distance between the Russians and the Americans: The Russians regard the latter period as an economic and geopolitical disaster, while the Americans regard it as quite satisfactory. Both views are completely understandable.

The Obama administration was signaling that it intends to continue the Bush administration's Russia policy. That policy was that Russia had no legitimate right to claim priority in the former Soviet Union, and that the United States had the right to develop bilateral relations with any country and expand NATO as it wished. But the Bush administration saw the Russian leadership as unwilling to follow the basic architecture of relations that had developed after 1991, and as unreasonably redefining what the Americans thought of as a stable and desirable relationship. The Russian response was that an entirely new relationship was needed between the two countries, or the Russians would pursue an independent foreign policy matching U.S. hostility with Russian hostility. Highlighting the continuity in U.S.-Russian relations, plans for the prospective ballistic missile defense installation in Poland, a symbol of antagonistic U.S.-Russian relations, remain unchanged.

The underlying problem is that the Cold War generation of U.S.-Russian experts has been supplanted by the post-Cold War generation, now grown to maturity and authority. If the Cold warriors were forged in the 1960s, the post-Cold warriors are forever caught in the 1990s. They believed that the 1990s represented a stable platform from which to reform Russia, and that the grumbling of Russians plunged into poverty and international irrelevancy at that time is simply part of the post-Cold War order. They believe that without economic power, Russia cannot hope to be an important player on the international stage. That Russia has never been an economic power even at the height of its influence but has frequently been a military power doesn't register. Therefore, they are constantly expecting Russia to revert to its 1990s patterns, and

believe that if Moscow doesn't, it will collapse—which explains U.S. Vice President Joe Biden's interview in *The Wall Street Journal* where he discussed Russia's decline in terms of its economic and demographic challenges. Obama's key advisers come from the Clinton administration, and their view of Russia—like that of the Bush administration—was forged in the 1990s.

Foreign Policy Continuity Elsewhere

When we look at U.S.-China policy, we see very similar patterns with the Bush administration. The United States under Obama has the same interest in maintaining economic ties and avoiding political complications as the Bush administration did. Indeed, Hillary Clinton explicitly refused to involve herself in human rights issues during her visit to China. Campaign talk of engaging China on human rights issues is gone. Given the interests of both countries, this makes sense, but it is also noteworthy given the ample opportunity to speak to China on this front (and fulfill campaign promises) that has arisen since Obama took office (such as the Uighur riots).

Of great interest, of course, were the three great openings of the early Obama administration, to Cuba, to Iran, and to the Islamic world in general through his Cairo speech. The Cubans and Iranians rebuffed his opening, whereas the net result of the speech to the Islamic world remains unclear. With Iran we see the most important continuity. Obama continues to demand an end to Tehran's nuclear program, and has promised further sanctions unless Iran agrees to enter into serious talks by late September.

On Israel, the United States has merely shifted the atmospherics. Both the Bush and Obama administrations demanded that the Israelis halt settlements, as have many other administrations. The Israelis have usually responded by agreeing to something small while ignoring the larger issue. The Obama administration seemed ready to make a major issue of this, but instead continued to maintain security collaboration with the Israelis on Iran and Lebanon (and we assume intelligence collaboration). Like the Bush administration, the Obama administration has not allowed the settlements to get in the way of fundamental strategic interests.

This is not a criticism of Obama. Presidents—all presidents—run on a platform that will win. If they are good presidents, they will leave behind these promises to govern as they must. This is what Obama has done. He ran for president as the antithesis of Bush. He has conducted his foreign policy as if he were Bush. This is because Bush's foreign policy was shaped by necessity, and Obama's foreign policy is shaped by the same necessity. Presidents who believe they can govern independent of reality are failures. Obama doesn't intend to fail.

Critical Thinking

1. Pick one of the following policy areas and use the Internet to determine whether George Friedman's thesis that U.S. foreign policies under President George Bush and Barak Obama were remarkably similar: U.S. withdrawal from Iraq; U.S.-European security relations; U.S. foreign policy towards Russia; or U.S. foreign policy towards China.

2. Identify two campaign promises related to foreign policy that President Obama had to abandon or modify. Why?

In Search of Sustainable Security
Linking National Security, Human Security, and Collective Security to Protect America and Our World

Gayle E. Smith

Introduction and Summary

Not long ago I conducted an informal survey during a trip to East Africa, asking everyone I met how they view America. My interlocutors were from Africa, the Middle East, and Asia. They were, in the main, educated and working in the private sector, the policy world, or government. Many of them hold dual passports.

Their answers were strikingly similar. Most of them said in one way or another that the "idea" of America has changed for the worse, and most asserted that they are less interested in traveling to, working in, or working with the United States now than in the past. But most disconcerting was the hope, expressed with striking consistency, that China would soon attain its full power so that American hegemony could be brought in check.

This was not for any love of China's ideology or even the aggressive aid and investment strategies Beijing is deploying in the developing world. It was, as a young woman attorney explained, because "America used to be the champion for all of us, and now it is the champion only for itself."

That much of the world has lost faith in America bodes ill for our national security because our role in the world is secured not simply by our military power or economic clout, but also by our ability to compel other nations to follow our lead. The next president will have the opportunity to craft a modern national security strategy that can equip the United States to lead a majority of capable, democratic states in pursuit of a global common good—a strategy that can guide a secure America that is the world's "champion for all of us."

But positioning America to lead in a 21st century world will take more than extending a hand to our allies, fixing a long list of misdirected policies, or crafting a new national security strategy that is tough but also smart. With globalization providing the immutable backdrop to our foreign policy, America is today competing on a global playing field that is more complex, dynamic, and interdependent and thus far less certain than in the past.

Leading in this new world will require a fundamental shift from our outdated notion of national security to a more modern concept of sustainable security—that is, our security as defined by the contours of a world gone global and shaped by our common humanity. Sustainable security combines three approaches:

- *National* security, or the safety of the United States
- *Human* security, or the well-being and safety of people
- *Collective* security, or the shared interests of the entire world

Sustainable security, in short, can shape our continued ability to simultaneously prevent or defend against real-time threats to America, reduce the sweeping human insecurity around the world, and manage long term threats to our collective, global security. This new approach takes into account the many (and ongoing) changes that have swept our planet since the end of the Cold War and the fall of the Soviet Union. To understand the efficacy of this new doctrine, though, requires a quick look at this new global landscape.

The New Realities of the 21st Century

During his presidency, Bill Clinton spoke often and passionately about our global interdependence and of positioning America to cross a "bridge to the 21st century." Once across, however, the Bush administration took a sharp right turn. In the wake of the September 11 terrorist attacks on the United States, the administration narrowly defined the quest for America's security, distinct from and uninformed by the interests of the larger world we inhabit.

The challenge before us, President Bush asserted, was the struggle between good and evil, our strategy was to wage his so called "war on terror," and our goal was to shape a "world without tyranny." Our primary tool was a strong military backed by the resolve to use force without seeking a "permission slip" from the international community. And our object was the "axis of evil," and the rest of the world was either "with us or against us." Anyone who suggested that it might not be quite that simple was quickly and effectively discounted as "soft on terrorism."

Despite ambitious rhetoric about the promotion of our core values—of leading "the long march to freedom" and pursuing the "non-negotiable demands of human dignity"—the Bush administration has culled its allies not from among those countries most committed to democracy, but from among those who have oil. The Bush administration had to leverage all of its diplomatic and economic clout to persuade the so-called "Coalition of the Willing" to participate at all in the invasion of Iraq. Then, the administration offered up not the shining example of an America where human and civil rights prevail, but an America where Guantanamo, Abu Gharaib, and illegal wire-tapping are justified by an elusive, greater purpose.

The United States has for the last five years defined America's role in the world with near exclusive reference to the invasion of Iraq. The deaths of 4,000[1] American soldiers, maiming of tens of thousands more, and the expenditure of well over $400 billion,[2] has failed to lay the foundations for either stability or democracy. And as defined by the Bush administration, the "War on Terror" has fared no better: Al Qaeda has not been defeated, and Osama bin Laden, its leader and the mastermind of the September 11 attacks, has yet to be captured.

Our losses, however, extend far beyond the edges of a failed Iraq policy or the shortcomings of an ill-defined "war on terror." We have also lost precious time, and are well behind the curve in our now tardy efforts to tackle the global challenges that are already shaping our future—climate change, energy insecurity, growing resource scarcity, the proliferation of illegal syndicates moving people, arms, and money—all of them global challenges that have been steadfastly ignored and in some cases denied by an ideologically driven Bush administration lodged firmly in its own distinct version of the here and now.

Perhaps most damaging, however, is this: We have lost our moral standing in the eyes of many who now believe that the United States has only its own national interests at heart, and has little understanding of or regard for either global security or our common humanity. Just as potent as the unsustainable federal budget deficit George W. Bush will leave in his wake is the unsustainable national security deficit that he will pass on to his successor. Whoever prevails in November will face a daunting list of real-time national security imperatives, among them:

- A spiraling crisis in Iraq
- Afghanistan's steady implosion
- A fragile Pakistan
- An emboldened Iran
- A raging genocide in Sudan
- The growing insecurity of our oil supplies
- A nuclear North Korea
- An increasingly dangerous Arab–Israeli conflict

Just to name a few. But the next president will also face looming and less tangible threats to our national security in a world where power has grown more diffuse and threats more potent—a world in which our security depends not only on the behavior of states, but also on a host of transnational threats that transcend national borders, such as terrorism, pandemics, money laundering, and the drug trade.

And finally, the next president will be confronted by the more subtle but potent threats and moral challenges arising from sweeping human insecurity in a world divided by sharp disparities between rich and poor, between those nations actively engaged in fast-paced globalization and those left behind, and between people who have tangible reasons to believe in a secure and prosperous world and those who daily confront the evidence that violence is a more potent tool for change than is hope.

Sustainable Security Is the Answer

The world has changed profoundly during the last 50 years, but our concept of national security has not. The concept of national security came into being after World War II, and has had as its primary focus a world dominated by the nation state. In this new era of globalization, we continue to rely upon the narrow definition offered by George Kennan, who in 1948 described our national security as "the continued ability of the country to pursue the development of its internal life without serious interference, or threat of interference, from foreign powers."[3] While Kennan's definition might have been relevant to the era of containment, it is insufficient in today's integrated and interdependent world.

A modern concept of national security demands more than an ability to protect and defend the United States. It requires that we expand our goal to include the attainment of *sustainable* security.

A modern concept of national security demands more than an ability to protect and defend the United States.

The pursuit of sustainable security requires more than a reliance on our conventional power to deflect threats to the United States, but also that we maintain the moral authority to lead a global effort to overcome threats to our common security. With its global scope, sustainable security demands that we focus not only on the security of nation states, but also of people, on *human* security. An emerging concept borne of multidisciplinary analyses of international affairs, economics, development, and conflict, human security targets the fundamental freedoms—from want and from fear—that define human dignity.

National security and human security are compatible but distinct. National security focuses on the security of the state, and governments are its primary clients, while human security is centered on the security of individuals and thus on a diverse array of stakeholders. National security aims to ensure the ability of states to protect their citizens from external aggression; human security focuses on the management of threats and challenges that affect people everywhere—inside, outside, and across state borders.

A national security strategy is commonly crafted in real time and focused on tangible, proximate threats, while a human security strategy aimed at improving the human condition assumes a longer-term horizon. Sustainable security combines the two, thus allowing for a focus on the twin challenges of protecting the United States while also championing our global humanity—not simply because it is the right thing to do, but also because our security demands it.

For a majority of the world's people, security is defined in the very personal terms of survival. The primary threats to this *human* security have far less to do with terrorism than with poverty and conflict, with governments that cannot deliver or turn on their own citizens, and with a global economy that offers differentiated access and opportunities to the powerful and the powerless. For literally billions of the world's people, weapons of mass destruction are not nuclear bombs in the hands of Iran, but the proliferation of small arms. For them, freedom is not defined simply by the demise of dictators, but also by the rise of economic opportunity.

Ensuring our security in today's world, however, also requires a focus on collective security. Among the major challenges that the United States will face over the coming decades are climate change, water scarcity, food insecurity, and environmental degradation. These are challenges that will threaten the economic well-being and security of all countries on earth, and by dint of their global nature, their effects cannot be overcome unless we adopt a global perspective and strategy.

Take the example of the world food crisis that emerged in the spring of 2008. No single cause triggered the near doubling of world food prices. Indeed, the causes included the skyrocketing price of oil, the growth of the middle class in the developing world (and thus rising demand in China and India), droughts in Australia and Ukraine, a weak dollar, and the expansion of biofuels production in the United States and Europe.

The consequent rise in food prices triggered riots or protests in Europe, Mexico, Egypt, Afghanistan, and several other countries, and plunged millions in the developing world into abject poverty. In the United States, the number of Americans seeking assistance from food banks rose 20 percent to 25 percent.

Or consider "transnational threats," such as money laundering, terrorism, and international drug and crime syndicates, all of which transcend state borders. These are threats that pose risks to the United States, but also to the well-being of our allies, to global stability, and to the world economy.

A national security approach seeks to prevent or reduce the effects of these trends and threats to the United States; a collective security approach, in contrast, assumes that the United States must act globally—in partnership with allies and in coordination with international institutions—to prevent or manage them.

Sustainable Security in Practice

Crafting a sustainable security strategy requires three fundamental steps. The first is to prioritize, integrate, and coordinate the global development policies and programs pursued by the United States. While our military power provides a critical and effective tool for managing our security, our support for the well-being of the world's people will not only provide us with a moral foundation from which to lead but will also enhance our ability to manage effectively the range of threats and trends that shape the modern world.

Second, we must modernize our foreign aid system in order to allow the United States to make strategic investments in global economic development that can help us to build capable states, open societies, and a global economy that benefits the world's majority. Third, we must re-enter the international arena, stepping up to the plate to lead the reform of international institutions that have not kept pace, and to create new institutions that are needed to manage our collective security.

In the pages that follow, this paper will present the challenges that threaten our national, human, and collective security in order to show just how important it is for the next president to embrace

these sustainable security policies. As this report will demonstrate, changing course will be difficult, but changing course is imperative to secure the future prosperity of humanity— an original and time-tested American value.

Human Security under Threat

In today's world, human security is elusive. There are six billion people in the world. Nearly half of them live on less than two dollars per day, and over one billion people survive on half that amount.[4] These are not people waiting idly for a hand-out from the international community. The vast majority of them are working men and women who earn for their daily labors less than it costs to rent a DVD, and who annually take home to their families less than half of what the average American will spend on a summer vacation this year.

Women and children are the hardest hit. According to the United Nations, 70 percent of the world's poor and two-thirds of the world's illiterate are women, and though they provide the backbone for rural economies, women own only one percent of the world's titled land and control only a small percentage of rural capital.[5] Over ten million children die before their fifth birthday each year, mostly from preventable diseases,[6] while roughly a quarter of all children in the developing world do not finish primary school.[7]

More than a billion people do not have safe supplies of water,[8] and more than twice as many have no access to basic sanitation.[9] Only one-third of the world's people enjoy the kind of access to energy that we take for granted, another third have only intermittent access, and the remaining third—some two billion people— live without modern energy supplies.[10] This means that they don't have lights to read by, or refrigerators to preserve vaccines, or trucks to get their goods to market.

The antidote to economic decline is increased borrowing. Developing world debt increased to almost 3 trillion dollars early in this decade, meaning that developing countries spend on average $13 on debt repayment—to wealthy countries and private creditors in the developed world—for every one dollar they receive in grants.[11] The international debt relief supported by the current and past administrations may have staunched the bleeding, but it has not closed the wound for the poor, who remain dangerously vulnerable to external shocks because they have little or nothing to fall back on.

For this reason, shocks to already fragile societies, such as climate change, have a greater effect on the poor than on other, wealthier communities. According to the United Nations Development Program, over 250 million people were affected by climate disasters annually from 2000 to 2004, and over 98 percent of them were in the developing world. In the world's developed countries, one in 1,500 people was affected by climate disaster; in the world's poorest countries, it was one in 19.[12]

Similarly, the rising price of oil is an enormous shock to the world's poor. The fiscal gains of a majority of countries that have received debt relief through the Heavily Indebted Poor Countries Initiative, for example, had by last year been wiped out by the increase in the world price of oil. Those same countries now face a near doubling in the world market price of basic food commodities. Theirs is a losing game of catch up, and the consequences of the vicious cycle of poverty are clear—more than 50 countries are poorer today than they were in 1990.[13]

A Vicious Cycle and Downward Spiral

This stunning privation feeds on itself, in part because poverty increases the risk of war. War is development in reverse—a civil war reduces a country's growth rate by 2.3 percent, a typical seven-year war leaves a country 15 percent poorer,[14] and wars speed both the "brain drain" and the flow and volume of capital flight. The costs of conflict are also borne by citizens—largely as a consequence of war, one in every 120 people on earth is either internally displaced or a refugee.[15]

It is estimated that Africa is losing $18 billion per year to conflict, or almost twice what the continent spends on health and education.[16] Or consider Sri Lanka, where a long-running civil war has cost the country over two years of GDP. Defense expenditures average four percent to six percent of GDP while those for health and education combined run just four percent to five percent.[17] Meanwhile one quarter of Sri Lankans live in poverty.

Finally, the world's donor countries incur tremendous costs over many years. Conflict drives U.S. spending on humanitarian assistance to levels that well exceed expenditures on economic development and conflict prevention. Recent wars, most of them in the developing world, triggered the authorization of 26 new UN peacekeeping missions between 1988 and 1995.[18] Today, the UN is leading 17 peacekeeping operations, and providing support to three more.[19] Each of these missions is expensive, especially to the United States, which bears almost one quarter of the cost, and several have ended in failure.

Finally, the recovery costs are enormous. According to a study by the Center for Global Development, it takes the world's donors between 15 to 27 years to exit from a conflict country because it takes that long for post-war economies to generate sufficient internal revenues to reduce the need for the external assistance that is provided by the United Nations, the United States, and other donors.[20] As the costs of war mount, neither the victims nor the world's donors can realistically keep up.

Against this backdrop, sweeping demographic changes are altering the contours of the global socioeconomic landscape, and providing new fuel for the cycle of poverty and new triggers for instability. While the developed world is now incurring the economic burdens of an aging population, over 100 countries are grappling with an expanding youth bulge. Today, 85 percent of young people between the ages of 15 and 24 live in developing countries,[21] where educational and job opportunities are few. This means that millions of young women are denied opportunities for economic independence and that millions of young men face a future devoid of either hope or prosperity.

Urban populations have grown fourfold over the last 50 years,[22] and by 2025, 60 percent of the world's population will live in cities.[23] Many of them—Cairo, Lagos, Nairobi, and Mumbai—are ill-equipped to provide the jobs, housing, and services that this expanded urban population will require. These vast demographic convulsions will exert increased pressure on already over-stretched natural resources and exacerbate growing poverty.

As the future hurtles towards us, we will see even greater threats to human security borne of our ecological interdependence. The world is facing a threefold increase in energy use by 2050.[24]

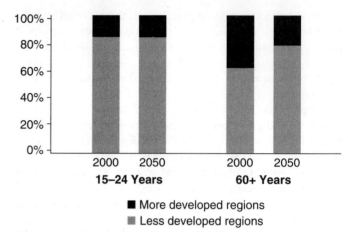

The proportions of youth and older persons in the total world population, 2000 and 2050.

Source: United Nations, *World Population Prospects: The 2002 Revisions: Volume II: Sex and Age* (Sales No. 03. XII.7).

World demand for fresh water has doubled over the last 50 years,[25] and the number of people living in water-stressed countries is expected to increase to 3 billion by 2025.[26] As global production, consumption, and population expand, so too will the competition for increasingly scarce resources. At the same time, the worst effects of climate change will reverberate in the world's poorest countries, which bear the least responsibility for global warming and have the least capacity to manage its impact.

A Different Take on "Us" and "Them"

Sweeping human insecurity also widens the gap between the world's rich and poor, a gap that might be more accurately described as a gulf. Although they constitute only 14 percent of the world's population, the world's ten wealthiest countries account for 75 percent of global GDP, and are 75 times richer than the ten poorest.[27] With the expansion of the Internet and satellite television, globalization is making this disparity more visible, including to those on the bottom.

Even with significant expansion, meanwhile, global trade has yet to yield sustainable benefits or to narrow this gap. Only two-thirds of the world's countries are engaged effectively in globalization. Low-income countries account for only three cents of every dollar generated through exports in the international trading system,[28] and the world's poorest region—sub-Saharan Africa—receives less than one percent of the total global flow of foreign direct investment.[29]

Global trade talks aimed at addressing this imbalance under the banner of the "Doha Development Round" have failed to deliver. Instead, these negotiations have all but collapsed under the weight of sharp disagreement between the world's rich and poor countries over the high subsidies paid out by the European Union and the United States to their agricultural producers.

What's worse, low- and middle-income countries bear 90 percent of the global disease burden yet they benefit least from global gains in treatment.[30] According to the Worldwatch Institute, only one percent of the over 1,200 new drugs that reached the global marketplace between 1975 and 1997 were applicable to the infectious tropical diseases that account for the most deaths around the world.[31] This is a human security problem of potentially immense proportions.

Total Youth Unemployment, 1995, 2004, and 2005

	Youth Unemployment (thousands)			
	1995	**2004**	**2005**	**% Change 1995–2005**
World	74,302	84,546	85,278	14.8
Developed Economies and European Union	10,281	8,997	8,481	−17.5
Central and Eastern Europe (non-EU) and CIS	5,962	5,724	5,900	−1.0
East Asia	13,149	11,840	12,076	−8.2
South East Asia and the Pacific	5,242	9,687	9,727	85.5
South Asia	11,765	13,561	13,662	16.1
Latin America and the Caribbean	7,722	9,263	9,495	23.0
Middle East and North Africa	7,209	8,380	8,525	18.2
Sub-Saharan Africa	12,972	17,095	17,414	34.2

Source: ILO, 2006:16.

Challenges to Our Collective Security

Democracy is making great gains, but so, too, are its opponents. Since 1974, some 90 countries have embraced democracy,[32] a positive gain to be sure, but one that is yet to be locked in. Many of the world's new democracies remain exceedingly fragile as their governments and citizens grapple simultaneously with profound political transitions, the legacies of war and repression, and the strains of poverty. Seemingly stable democracies in Kenya, Cote d'Ivoire, Georgia, and Thailand have proven to be vulnerable, while in many countries, structural poverty and corruption have precluded the delivery of a tangible democracy dividend.

In many countries, meanwhile, the failure of rulers to deliver economically or politically is speeding the rise of extremism. Across much of the Middle East, Africa, and Asia, extremism is forging a new political construct shaped by Islam, and with it the rise of a hostile, transnational political identity. In some regions, extremism takes the form of predatory movements, such as northern Uganda's Lord's Resistance Army, that prey on civilians and particularly on children.

In struggling democracies such as the Democratic Republic of the Congo, the echoes of the Rwandan genocide and the legacy of colonialism and post-colonial mis-rule reverberate in the form of militia wars, skyrocketing death rates, and rampant rape. Violence continues to threaten democratic gains in Nepal, Turkey, Sri Lanka, and the Philippines. And at the far worst and still-too-common end of the spectrum, genocide continues to rear its ugly head in places such as Darfur where, five years on, people still await a meaningful response from the international community.

The Power of Weak States

Both economic development and democracy are under further strain from the fact that a billion people live in states that do not deliver for their citizens. A recent study by the Brookings Institution notes that of the world's 193 countries, 28 qualify as weak and another 28 are critically weak or failed. Eighty-five percent of these countries have experienced conflict in the past 15 years, and the United Nations—and in some cases the United States—has had to deploy peacekeepers or observers to half of them.[33]

Governments in these countries lack the will or capacity to provide basic security or control their borders, cannot or do not meet the basic human needs of their citizens, and fail to provide either legitimate or effective governance. They are unable to adapt to the technological innovations that drive economic progress, establish the institutional foundations that are required for democratic stability, or function as reliable members of the international community.

They are equally incapable of meeting the challenges posed by environmental degradation, are more vulnerable to transnational threats than their more capable counterparts, and are unable to provide barriers to the spread of these threats across borders. Most important, they are unable (or unwilling) to offer their people economic opportunity, political freedom, or hope.

These weak and failing states include countries such as the Democratic Republic of the Congo, which by dint of the unresolved conflict in its eastern Kivu region is winning a fierce global competition for the worst humanitarian crisis on earth. They include Nigeria, where vast oil reserves have led not to prosperity but to sweeping systemic corruption, and to the rise of a pernicious insurgency in the Niger Delta. And they include Myanmar, where an authoritarian regime has not only failed to protect its citizens in the wake of a devastating cyclone, but has also prevented the world from aiding them.

These are countries often consigned to the bottom of our foreign policy priority list, but countries where unchecked instability and limited capacity risk the lives of millions. State weakness in these countries not only portends hopelessness for many of their citizens. It also poses a threat to global peace and security. Though viewed by many as of lesser import than countries in the Middle East or Asia, these African countries matter—Nigeria provides more than eight percent of our imported oil, and resource-rich Congo has, among other assets, uranium. Their security matters—to their people, and also to us.

Our Shared Interests

Americans are right to ask their government why they should add the costly charge of promoting human security and collective security to the already heavy burden of the spiraling federal budget deficit, rising gas and food prices, a home mortgage crisis, and multiple security challenges already on our national plate. The first reason is simple: It is the right thing to do. By championing the cause of the world's least powerful, the United States can build a stronger moral foundation from which to lead and a compelling example for the world to follow.

There is precedent on which to build, as both security imperatives and moral convictions have led the United States to help improve the lives of the world's poor throughout our modern history. In his inaugural address in 1961, President John F. Kennedy highlighted this commitment of the American people:

> "To those peoples in the huts and villages across the globe struggling to break the bonds of mass misery, we pledge our best efforts to help them help themselves, for whatever period is required—not because the Communists may be doing it, not because we seek their votes, but because it is right. If a free society cannot help the many who are poor, it cannot save the few who are rich."[34]

Almost 50 years later, General Anthony Zinni (USMC-ret.) and Admiral Leighton Smith Jr. (USN-ret.) put it this way:

> "It is time to repair our relationship with the world and begin to take it to the next level—a level defined not only by our military strength but also by the lives we save and the opportunities we create for the people of other nations . . . today our enemies are often conditions—poverty, infectious disease, political instability and corruption, global warming—which generate the biggest threats. By addressing them in meaningful ways, we can forestall crises."[35]

The second reason is more pragmatic but just as compelling. If we fail to act now, we will be forced to pay later, both financially and with our own national security. Human insecurity feeds on itself, laying the ground for conflict and the extreme vulnerability that causes people to fall over the economic edge when weather, wars, or world market prices disrupt their fragile, subsistence economies.

The United States leads the world in responding to the humanitarian crises that arise out of this acute vulnerability. Today, we spend more on emergency relief to treat the symptoms of these crises than we do to promote the development that might prevent them. The United States, for example, spends far more on food aid than it invests in agricultural development, and with food prices surging globally, we have had to increase spending on emergency food aid to forestall famine and food riots in the world's poorest countries.

Experts predict that our humanitarian and military expenditures will increase further unless the vulnerability of the world's poor to climate change is substantially reduced. A 2007 report by 11 former U.S. generals and admirals found that "Climate change can act as a threat multiplier for instability in some of the most volatile regions of the world, and it presents significant national security challenges for the United States."[36] When these new crises arise, the United States will be expected to respond.

We also pay for our failure to address our collective security. Globalization has spawned an interconnected world where capital, goods, people, and threats move freely across borders. These potent transnational threats affect the lives of ordinary Americans, whether in the form of the West Nile virus or a spike in oil prices triggered by the sabotage of oil pipelines by Nigerians desperate for fuel they cannot afford.

Moreover, threats to our collective security—the money laundering that fuels terrorist networks, crime syndicates and the drug trade, uranium smuggling and illegal weapons shipments—can be neither contained nor controlled by the United States alone. We need competent, capable partners, in all corners of the globe.

Shifting to Sustainable Security

America's power is unmatched. We account for roughly half of all global defense spending, and generate 20 percent of all global output. But in an interdependent world where power has grown more diffuse and threats more diverse, our military and economic superpower status is not enough to provide for sustainable security for us or the world we live in.

If our goal is simply to protect and defend America against external interference, then reliance on military force and a wall on the border with Mexico might suffice. But if our aim is to ensure the sustainable security of the United States in a fast-moving, rapidly-changing world driven by complex, global threats and challenges, we need to bring to bear all of the tools we can muster.

Offered up by academia and Washington's think tanks, the concepts of "soft power," "integrated power," and "smart power" bear in common the counsel that America must recalibrate its foreign policy to rely less on military power and more on other tools that can foster change and enhance our security. One of these is enhanced and robust diplomacy; the other is development.

A statement endorsed by eight former Secretaries of State, five former Secretaries of Defense, and four former National Security Advisors, put it this way: "Our increasingly interconnected world requires strong U.S. leadership to strengthen democratic governance, harness economic potential, alleviate global poverty and improve human conditions. American investments in these goals will reaffirm America's tradition of moral leadership, reduce our vulnerability to threats from destabilizing forces and improve America's image abroad."[37]

Secretary of Defense Robert Gates, meanwhile, recently called for the development of "a permanent, sizeable cadre of immediately deployable experts with disparate skills,"[38] and for beefing up our capacity to promote global development. Clearly, there is growing recognition that our sustainable security requires that we beef up our diplomatic capabilities and also strengthen our capacity to promote the development of capable, democratic states and healthy societies.

But when it comes to development, we've got it half right and upside down. Development dollars are up, but we have neither a development policy nor a development strategy. Our foreign aid system is chaotic, but instead of fixing it we are appending to it multiple new tools that, though necessary, risk complicating it further. And instead of balancing our military power with civilian-led capabilities to support development, we are giving the development lead to the Department of Defense.

> When it comes to development, we've got it half right and upside down. The dollars are up, but we have neither a policy nor a strategy.

Development Earns Widespread Support

On the positive side of the ledger, we have seen during the last eight years a dramatic increase in development funding legislated with strong bipartisan support. A new milestone was set this year when 186 members of Congress—from both sides of the aisle—wrote to President Bush urging him to increase next year's (fiscal year 2009) International Affairs Budget consistent with the 2006 National Security Strategy, which states that, "Development reinforces diplomacy and defense, reducing long-term threats to our national security by helping to build stable, prosperous, and peaceful societies."[39] President Bush responded by increasing the fiscal year 2009 budget for international affairs to $39.5 billion, a 16 percent increase over the previous year.[40]

Support for two major Bush administration initiatives has also been strong. In January 2004, the United States established and pledged $4.8 billion to the Millennium Challenge Corporation (MCC), a grant-making government agency targeted to countries that are performing well against set economic and political criteria. By the end of fiscal year 2007, 14 countries had signed MCC compacts and 14 more were on the "threshold," making efforts to adhere to the social, judicial, and political reform indicators set forth under the program.[41]

The MCC has been the object of budget battles and the target of criticism for the significant gap between the Bush administration's stated ambitions and the agency's actual implementation, but it has garnered support from both Republicans and Democrats. Bipartisan support for PEPFAR—the President's Emergency Program for AIDS Relief—is even more robust, with both parties in Congress supporting both initial outlays as well as President Bush's 2008 call to double program funding.

Moreover, there is today a growing constituency for action. Driven largely by young people and faith-based communities and elevated to media visibility by celebrities, major campaigns focused on global poverty and Darfur, for example, have caught the attention of the public, Capitol Hill, and the White House. Support for development initiatives such as these was once a predominantly liberal cause, but today it stretches across the political spectrum, and is increasingly prominent among conservatives.

Among young evangelicals, for example, global poverty and human trafficking are gradually overtaking abortion and gay marriage as top priorities. The leading champions for Darfur on Capitol Hill, meanwhile, are Senator Sam Brownback (R-KS) and Representative Donald Payne (D-NJ), two men who disagree on a host of issues but are firmly united in their conviction that America has a moral obligation to end the suffering in Sudan.

Most Americans also want their leaders to do more. A 2007 Gallup poll found that 56 percent of Americans were "dissatisfied" with the current role of the United States in global affairs.[42] Another poll showed that 65 percent of Americans—and the majority of both Republicans and Democrats—support increasing global poverty reduction expenditure to 0.7 percent of GDP.[43] Doing more to improve the lives of the poor is one way in which Americans believe they can restore our global image—and a key way, they believe, for the next president to be an effective and representative global leader.

But Development Gets Short Shrift

On the negative side of the ledger, development remains the poor stepchild of defense and diplomacy. Even with substantial increases in our foreign aid budget, 95 percent of the total outlays for national security in the fiscal year 2007 federal budget were for defense, compared with 3.5 percent for development.[44] Nearly half of that development allocation goes to ten countries, including Egypt, Colombia, Pakistan and Jordan, while the world's poorest receive only six percent.[45] And where foreign aid allocations are at their highest, short-term security imperatives dominate and development comes last.

Consider the case of Pakistan, a country where the United States has used aid to enhance the security of the Pakistani state, with only brief interruptions, since the 1980s. Despite the $24 billion invested by the United States in Pakistan over the last 25 years, we now face a more dangerous mixture of political instability, entrenched poverty, and extremism than existed in the early 1980s—all in a country that possesses nuclear weapons.

According to an August 2007 report from the Center for Strategic and International Studies, the bulk of the $10.5 billion in assistance provided by the U.S. to Pakistan since 9/11 "has not been directed to Pakistan's underlying fault lines, but to specific short-term counterterrorism objectives."[46] Only 10 percent of overall funding has gone for development or for meeting humanitarian needs,[47] and in the Federally Administered Tribal Areas along the country's north-western border with Afghanistan, development assistance comprises only one percent of our total aid package.[48]

In part because development has not been a priority, our heavy financial investment in Pakistan has neither reduced the security threats that Pakistan poses nor earned us the allegiance of the Pakistani people. Our consistent disregard for human security has borne a high cost. Deaths from internal terrorist attacks have skyrocketed since 2001, from 189 in 2003 to 648 in 2005 and 3,599 in 2007.[49] But as a recent Stanley Foundation report highlighted, "most Pakistanis are much more likely to suffer a premature death as a result of poverty or non-existent medical services as they are from an Islamist attack."[50]

Thirty-five percent of Pakistanis live in abject poverty. According to the World Food Program, food insecurity is on the rise, with 60 million people unable to secure an adequate nutritional intake, and an additional 18 million affected by the recent surge in global food prices.[51] Agricultural livelihoods are further threatened by untended environmental changes as the Indus River, upon which a majority of Pakistan's rural population depends for both drinking water and irrigation, begins to go dry.

Nearly half of all Pakistanis are illiterate, literacy rates for women stand at 30 percent, and only three percent of people in Federally Administered Tribal Areas—where some believe Osama bin Laden is hiding—can read or write.[52] Of the billions of dollars in aid provided by the United States since 2001, aid allocated to education represents at most 4.2 percent of the total package—an average of less than $2 per Pakistani child per year.[53] Unable to read, with few job prospects, and angered by U.S. military action within Pakistani borders, the strong financial incentives offered by extremist groups[54] are increasingly a welcome alternative. A recent public opinion poll, meanwhile, found that 72 percent of Pakistanis have unfavorable views of the United States, and only 38 percent of Pakistanis have a favorable view of our ally, President Pervez Musharraf. The same poll showed that free elections, a free press, and an independent judiciary are the most important long-term priority for a majority of Pakistanis.[55] Each of these remains elusive and none of them is a priority in our $10 billion aid package.

Even if there was sufficient political will to elevate development alongside defense and diplomacy, it would be practically impossible because our foreign aid system is irretrievably broken. In 2007, the bipartisan HELP Commission, appointed by Congress and mandated to review U.S. foreign aid, reported that of over 100 government officials (both civilian and military), aid practitioners, foreign policy experts, academics, and private-sector representatives consulted, "not one person appeared before this Commission to defend the status quo."[56]

The System Is Broken

America's ability to invest in global development is seriously constrained. The United States has neither a global development policy nor a strategy. The legislation governing foreign aid was written in 1961, and has since been amended to include 33 goals, 247 directives, and 75 priorities,[57] rendering it so cumbersome that it provides neither coherent guidance to the executive branch nor a roadmap for oversight to the legislative branch. In the absence of a policy, strategy, or effective guiding legislation, aid programming is driven in the main by congressional earmarks, presidential directives, and reaction.

Development programming was once the purview of the U.S. Agency for International Development (USAID), an agency that had a permanent staff of 15,000 during Vietnam but just 3,000 today, and is therefore compelled to rely heavily on expensive outside contractors to manage programs in over 150 countries.[58] Presently, over half of all aid programs are administered by agencies other than USAID, and development funding is arrayed across more than 20[59] government agencies, departments, and initiatives, each with its own goals, priorities, and procedures. No single individual or agency has the authority or the responsibility to oversee or coordinate these myriad programs.

The colossal failure of reconstruction efforts in Iraq and Afghanistan, meanwhile, has rightly focused Washington's attention on crisis management, and has led to the creation of even more instruments and initiatives. In 2004, Congress authorized funds to create an Office of Reconstruction and Stabilization in the State Department, and last year the House and Senate introduced legislation calling for the creation of an expert civilian response capability to carry out our reconstruction and stabilization activities.

The Department of Defense has established a Commanders' Emergency Response Program to meet emergency and reconstruction needs in Iraq and Afghanistan, and the 2006 National Defense Authorization Act created the "1206" fund to assist countries engaged in counter-terrorism and stability operations.

The Pentagon is now seeking to make these temporary crisis management authorities permanent through the "Building Global Partnerships Act."

President Bush deserves credit for dramatic increases in U.S. aid levels and global leadership in the fight against HIV/AIDS. But the changes the U.S. foreign aid system has undergone over the last several years have exacerbated rather than repaired the flaws in the system. These changes have also set far-reaching and potentially detrimental precedents.

The State Department's 2006 "Transformational Diplomacy" plan, for example, established a new Deputy Undersecretary for Foreign Aid in the State Department as a means of achieving greater coordination and policy coherence within the Executive Branch. But the pretense of coordination is more potent than is its practice. Although "Transformational Diplomacy" consolidated some aid accounts, the new Deputy Undersecretary has no jurisdiction over the growing development aid budget managed by the military, and provides guidance to but does not have authority over either the Millennium Challenge Corporation or the anti-AIDs program PEPFAR.

The continued lack of coordination not only leads to inefficiencies in the management of taxpayer funds, but it also places an enormous burden on international development partners who are forced to deal with multiple agencies, requirements, and procedures. It also fosters policy incoherence. Research conducted by the HELP Commission, for example, found that the United States collects more in tariffs from countries eligible for funding from the Millennium Challenge Account than is provided in aid. This fact was news to senior policymakers, who missed it for the simple reason that there is no coordination between our trade agencies and our aid agencies.

Moreover, the administration has launched robust, discrete initiatives without benefit of an overarching policy or strategy, and thus allowed significant gaps to emerge. For example, although agriculture represents almost 40 percent of GDP, 35 percent of exports, and 70 percent of employment in developing countries, less than two percent of the proposed fiscal year 2009 development budget targets agricultural development.

Robust funding to fight the HIV/AIDS pandemic, meanwhile, has not been matched by parallel investments in other sectors. Clearly, global health issues like HIV/AIDS are of paramount importance, but so too are education, agricultural development, institution-building, and job creation.

Consider the case of Kenya, a country that serves as the economic anchor for east and central Africa and has for over two decades functioned—at least in the eyes of the outside world—as an island of stability in a sea of turmoil. Kenya has for years provided staging and overflight rights for U.S. military operations, is the hub for emergency relief efforts throughout the region, regularly contributes troops to U.N. peacekeeping efforts, and has been a staunch ally of the United States in our campaign against global terrorist networks since the U.S. embassy there was bombed by Al Qaeda in 1998.

Close elections late last year brought Kenya's internal contradictions to the surface, however, as the country exploded in a wave of stunning violence that led to the deaths of over 1000 people and economic losses estimated to be in the range of $3 billion.[60]

The most effective tool on hand for the United States to foster stability and functional democracy in Kenya is foreign aid, and the goal of U.S. development efforts in Kenya is in fact to build an economically prosperous country. But of the over $700 million that Kenya now receives annually, over $500 million is earmarked for HIV/ AIDS, over $120 million goes for food aid, and most of the balance is for security and counter-terrorism programs. The net result is that there is little or no funding available to counter the economic or political conditions that gave rise to Kenya's destabilizing post-electoral crisis or to consolidate the fragile peace achieved by the recent formation of a unity government.

A broken, incoherent, and understaffed foreign aid system has allowed for the emergence of some isolated successes, but has also created a vacuum. The United States has neither the policies nor the people it needs to make development an effective foreign policy tool. What may prove to be the most far-reaching of the Bush administration's efforts in the development sphere is its decision to give the lead in filling this vacuum to the Department of Defense.

The Pentagon Steps up to the Plate

Traditionally, the role of the Department of Defense (DoD) in development has been restricted to three key areas: support for humanitarian operations; engagement in small-scale community development projects linked to training missions and site visits; and, with the Department of State, "train and equip" programs for foreign militaries. But major deployments in Iraq, Afghanistan, and the Horn of Africa have taught the Pentagon three lessons.

First, from Iraq and Afghanistan it became clear that the fragile peace that can be won with military force cannot be sustained without a tangible peace dividend alongside a robust stabilization effort linked to long-term, sustainable development. The second lesson came from the deployment of U.S. forces to Djibouti under the banner of the Combined Joint Task Force-Horn of Africa, where the military has been mandated to conduct counter-terrorism operations and support the efforts of regional governments to contain and prevent the spread of terrorist networks.

It soon became clear that poor countries with weak governments cannot protect or defend their borders without also providing essential services to and securing the allegiance of the citizens who live in the vast, ungoverned spaces that are most vulnerable to terrorist infiltration. The third lesson was that with USAID's staffing eroded to bare bones levels, and with the State Department both non-operational and otherwise occupied, no government agency except the Department of Defense has the personnel or the proclivity to fill these gaps.

The Defense Department is responding, reflecting the observation of Defense Secretary Gates that "the non-military instruments of America's national power need to be rebuilt, modernized, and committed to the fight."[61] The Pentagon's development budget has soared from 5.6 percent of the executive branch total in 2002 to 21.7 percent, or $5.5 billion, in 2005,[62] and is slated to increase further. New authorities have been secured, new programs have been initiated, and with DoD Directive 3000.05, the U.S. military is now mandated to treat stability operations as a core mission on par with combat operations.[63]

But the Department's expanding role goes further than stability operations. In 2007, the Pentagon launched AFRICOM, a unified military headquarters for Africa that is focused on "war prevention," and is designed to "better enable the Department of Defense and other elements of the U.S. government to work in concert and with partners to achieve a more stable environment in which political and economic growth can take place." AFRICOM not only gives a regional military command a development mandate, it also operates with an integrated interagency staff, and thus provides the platform for the coordination of other U.S. government agencies.

The plan for AFRICOM's forward deployment in Africa, however, was poorly received by most African governments, which were not widely consulted in advance of its unveiling, and by civic groups across the continent, which opposed what they viewed as a permanent U.S. military presence in Africa. AFRICOM is thus slated to remain in Germany for the time being, but the AFRICOM model is spreading to other regional commands. SOUTHCOM's latest strategy document, for example, proposes that the command coordinate all relevant government agencies, including civilian, to address the full range of regional challenges in Latin America and the Caribbean.

There are those who believe that DoD's expanded role in development is a sign of the Department's intention to militarize foreign aid. The more plausible explanation is that the Pentagon is stepping in to fill a vacuum that has been left wanting by USAID's dire circumstances, and by the State Department's lack of intent. In much the same way that she ceded control over the Iraq war to the Pentagon during her tenure as National Security Advisor in the early years of the Bush administration, Secretary of State Condoleezza Rice has posed no visible or effective opposition to the Pentagon's expanded role in areas traditionally considered the purview of civilian agencies.

DoD's role has also grown more prominent because it is operational and capable. In contrast, the State Department is not operational, and a weakened USAID no longer has the capacity to tackle all of the development challenges the United States faces. Congress, therefore, is more inclined to allocate aid dollars to the Pentagon than to its weaker and less capable counterparts.

The greatest peril lies not in the fact that the Defense Department has stepped in to fill the development vacuum and pick up the slack on inter-agency coordination, or even that the Pentagon has no expertise or experience in the field of development. The hazard lies in the fact that the frontal face of America's support for development in the poorest corners of the world is our military, and not our civilian agencies. As the lukewarm reception to AFRICOM has made clear, this places our interest in human security squarely in the frame of our national security and, in particular, the war on terrorism—and not, as it should be, in the context of our shared commitment to the global common good.

Three Steps toward Sustainable Security

Adapting to today's world and achieving sustainable security requires that we pursue not only our national security, but also global and human security. This more modern approach can afford us the ability to deal simultaneously with short-term, nation-state based threats and with the global challenges that transcend state borders. Importantly, this sustainable security approach allows us to lead from a position of moral strength. But getting there requires three core elements:

- An organizing principle that can unite a majority of the world's people
- The elevation and strategic utilization of the full range of our foreign policy tool
- A revitalized international system that reflects not just the challenges that existed when it was created in the wake of World War II, but also the realities of today

It also requires that the next president establish the predicate for change, and speak truth to the American people. Over the course of two terms, the Bush administration has posited that the combination of its moral certitude and America's military might are sufficient to secure our national interests, and has treated threats to our global security—whether climate change or energy security—as electives rather than imperatives.

The next president instead must update and advise the American people, making clear that our ability to lead on the world stage demands not only awesome power but also moral authority, and that our interests are best served when we act in pursuit of our global security and common humanity.

The shift toward a sustainable security approach will take time, and the next president will face a daunting list of immediate challenges. But there are several steps that can be taken in 2009 to lay the ground for an increased and practical focus on the profound moral challenges of our world, to modernize our foreign aid system, and to lay the ground for the increased international cooperation that is necessary going forward. Specifically, the next president should:

- Add a third and powerful tool to our foreign policy apparatus, in addition to defense and diplomacy, by elevating, integrating, and coordinating U.S. global development policies and programs.
- Take immediate steps to modernize our foreign aid system so that a new administration can move nimbly and effectively to invest in building capable states, open societies, and a global marketplace that serves the world's majority.
- Move swiftly to re-engage on the international stage by signaling America's willingness to lead in the reform of international institutions and the creation of new mechanisms for managing our shared global interests.

The shift toward a sustainable security approach will take time, and the next president will face a daunting list of immediate challenges.

These three steps, in turn, require detailed action to ensure success. All three of these overarching policy proposals, when examined in detail, would elevate sustainable security to an active policy of global engagement within the first term of the next administration.

Prioritize, Integrate, and Coordinate Development

It will take presidential leadership to elevate development, a strong hand to integrate the concept of human security across the range of our foreign policy agencies, and high-level action to coordinate the myriad foreign aid agencies, instruments, and initiatives now spread across the executive branch. There are four key steps that the next president can take to lay the ground for progress in all three areas.

First, the president should use the administration's first National Security Strategy to lay the ground for a sustainable security approach by focusing on traditional national security, collective security, and human security. Though required by law, National Security Strategies are often boilerplate documents that provide little other than a narrative list of foreign policy priorities. The next president should use his first NSS as a tool for pivoting to sustainable security.

Second, the president should appoint a third Deputy National Security Advisor (NSA) for long-term strategic planning. In a White House facing the pressures of competing global and domestic crises, 24-hour news coverage, and a four-year election cycle, there is little time for thinking about and planning for the long term. A designated Deputy NSA mandated to think and plan ahead will not only allow the administration to make up for the time lost by the Bush administration on issues like climate change, but will also allow an administration to get out ahead of future threats like resource scarcity and new global pandemics.

Third, as the first step toward formulating a government-wide policy on development and crafting a whole-of-government development strategy, the president should issue a Presidential Directive providing initial guidance to the multiple agencies, departments, and offices that are now pursuing their own individual agendas. The guidance should neither be so vague—by pointing to, for example, "reducing global poverty"—as to be meaningless, nor so prescriptive that it undercuts the ability of professionals on the ground to make informed decisions.

Instead, it should focus on the priorities that serve our national interests and reflect a global common good, for example by building the capacity of governments and civil society; reducing the vulnerability of the poor; laying the ground for improved resource management; and enhancing the access of poor communities and low-income countries to capital and markets.

Fourth, the president should create a directorate, led jointly by the National Security Council and National Economic Council, to initiate and oversee the coordination of all foreign aid agencies, initiatives, departments, and programs. Given the growing role of non-governmental organizations, philanthropic groups, and corporations in humanitarian and development efforts overseas, the directorate should also ensure that the U.S. government is in regular consultation with these prominent partners.

Modernize Our Foreign Aid System

There is an urgent need to reform the structure, operations, and staffing of our foreign aid system, and an equally important need to coordinate a sweeping reform process with the Congress. Reform will likely require new legislation to replace the almost 50-year old Foreign Assistance Act, as well as an overhaul of critical internal procedures ranging from evaluation to procurement.

A growing number of development experts, NGOs, corporate leaders, and foreign-policy specialists are lending support to the creation of an independent, cabinet-level development agency, similar to Britain's Department for International Development, which was created by former Prime Minister Tony Blair and has been given an even more prominent role by his successor, Gordon Brown. The rationale is that because development is a field distinct from either defense or diplomacy, it warrants its own department and leadership, and a seat at the foreign policy-making table.

There is also a need, advocates argue, to bring our various foreign aid agencies under one roof. As well, there is growing recognition of the need to insulate the development portion of our foreign aid budget from the pressure of short-term security imperatives, and instead focus on long-term development objectives across the span of successive administrations.

The proposal is that military aid, including "train and equip" programs for foreign militaries, peacekeeping funds, and economic security funds, or ESF, would remain under the jurisdiction of the Departments of Defense and State. Humanitarian and development aid—including PEPFAR and the MCA—would be centralized under a new, professionally staffed department, insulated from short-term imperatives and focused on long-term goals.

Critics argue that the development portfolio should remain within State and be made a priority by the secretary. They point to the problems incurred by the creation of the Department of Homeland Security as evidence that a new independent agency will not work, and argue that an independent development agency will inevitably be sidelined. Further, there is concern that the creation of a separate development department would weaken and compete with the Department of State.

The "uber State Department" is clearly the easier option, but given the experience of USAID over the years, and the structural flaws in the State Department's "Transformational Diplomacy," it is also the least likely to bring about a fundamental change to the status quo. First of all, the State Department is not operational and is thus not equipped to manage the development portfolio. Second, the independent agency proposal entails uniting agencies and departments with common mandates, and not, as was the case with the Department of Homeland Security, creating a department that combines multiple operational agencies with distinct and varied mandates.

And third, a cabinet-level development agency reinforced by the Executive Office of the President and backed by the development budget is no more likely to be marginalized than is an office housed within the State Department. What's more, concerns about weakening the State Department overlook two salient facts.

First, development and diplomacy are two entirely different tasks that are undertaken on the basis of different time horizons, require distinct expertise and different capabilities, and entail separate and contrasting approaches. Past policy has been hindered by the assumption that development requires little expertise other than an understanding of international affairs and a concern for the plight of the poor, and that the development aspect of a given policy can thus be easily handled by either the Department of State or the Department of Defense. The dangers of this flawed assumption are now evident, however, in Iraq,

Afghanistan, Pakistan, Egypt, and countless other cases where we have failed to bring a development perspective to bear.

Second, this concern misdiagnoses the current weakness of the State Department, which has less to do with its authority over foreign aid and more to do with its failure to craft and act on a modern diplomatic agenda and its willingness to concede influence to the Department of Defense.

In the next administration, the State Department must take the foreign policy lead, including on reforming the international institutions that make up our global architecture and on crafting and implementing the policies that can enable the U.S. to manage a host of global threats and challenges. State's strength will and should derive from its leadership in formulating these and other policies that guide the use of all of our foreign policy tools—diplomacy, defense, and development.

But the next president needs to hear views forged from each of these perspectives. Just as the State and Defense Departments craft their own unique strategies, oversee their own budgets, and bring their own specific expertise and distinct perspectives to the decision-making table in the White House, so too should a department for development.

The next president, however, cannot create a new department without extensive internal deliberation or consultation with Congress. Fortunately, leading members of Congress have already taken on the cause of modernizing our foreign aid system.

The next president should immediately engage with this ongoing congressional process and appoint, during the transition, a high-level White House official to consult within and outside of government and develop options for rationalizing and modernizing our foreign aid system during his first term. Because traditional institutional imperatives may cause a new Secretary of State to oppose an independent cabinet-level agency, the president should also secure the support of the new secretary to consider the full range of options.

Re-Enter the International Arena

The next president has the opportunity to re-engage the international community and reposition America to lead. But this will take clear signals from the White House that the new administration is ready and willing to engage, and recognition that just as our own foreign policy architecture is out of date, so too is the international architecture in urgent need of reform. The next president can move on both fronts by taking four steps.

The next president has the opportunity to re-engage the international community and reposition America to lead.

First, he should work with Congress to ensure that the United States can fully cover its U.N. arrears within the first year of a new administration. As happened during the 1990s, the failure of the United States to pay its dues both hinders U.N. operations in critical areas such as peacekeeping, but also undermines our ability to make the case for, or demand, critical reforms.

Second, in an effort to begin reconciling our national interests and our global security, the next president should work with Congress, across the whole of government, and with allies from the developed and developing worlds to craft a strategy for global food security. The worldwide crisis that erupted when food prices nearly doubled exposed the need to harmonize policies in an interconnected world, and has affected consumers in every country in the world. In some cases, the crisis has triggered riots and instability, in others it has pushed millions over the edge from subsistence to hunger, and in the United States it has fostered economic hardship and a spike in demand for food stamps and other nutritional programs.

By the time the next president is sworn in, the Doha "Development Round" of trade talks will likely be dead on the mantle of disagreement between the world's rich and poor countries on agricultural policies. And barring some radical and unforeseen change, the global food market will still be volatile. Rationalizing America's agricultural policies to conform to a new global environment will take heavy political lifting, but the opportunity and indeed imperative created by collapsed trade talks and the global food crisis provide a window for starting the discussion.

Third, the next president should initiate the next phase of PEPFAR. While giving full credit to President Bush for launching and robustly funding the initiative, the next president should provide a larger share of HIV/AIDS funding through the Global Fund for AIDS, Tuberculosis, and Malaria, signaling our willingness to work collectively to address the global challenge that these diseases represent. A new and improved PEPFAR should also invest more resources in capacity-building and the ability of the world's poorest countries to manage future epidemics and health crises.

Fourth and finally, the next president should make Darfur—and indeed the issue of crimes against humanity across the globe—a top priority. There is little chance that the Darfur crisis will be resolved by next January, but there are plenty of other places where crimes against humanity are going untended by the world.

The Darfur genocide is now entering its sixth year, and cries of "never again" and pledges of "not on my watch" ring hollow. The next president needs to dedicate his time, and that of the secretary of state, to show the world that America is ready to stand up to the worst of all threats to human security, genocide, so that America's claim to global leadership will be shaped not only by the actions we take but also by those that we do not.

Conclusion

Few would envy the task of handling the long list of first priorities that awaits the next president. But while protecting and defending America's national security will be first on the list, so too should be adapting to the modern concept of sustainable security.

At the dawn of the 21st century, in a world seized by far-reaching and tumultuous change, President Bush dedicated eight years to waging a "war on terror" and reminding the rest of the world of what America is *against*. It is time for our next president to remind the rest of the world that we stand *for* the sustainable security of our shared world. To do otherwise would be to diminish our collective security and abandon our common humanity.

Notes

1. Iraq Coalition Casualty Count, available at http://www.icasualties.org/oif/ (last accessed May 2008).

2. Amy Belasco, "The Cost of Iraq, Afghanistan, and Other Global War on Terror Operations Since 9/11" (Washington: Congressional Research Service, 2008), available at http://www.fas.org/sgp/crs/natsec/RL33110.pdf (last accessed May 2008) p. 16.

3. George F. Kennan, "Comments on the General Trend of U.S. Foreign Policy" (Princeton: George F. Kennan Papers, August 20, 1948).

4. The United States Commission on Helping to Enhance the Livelihood of People around the Globe, "Beyond Assistance: The HELP Commission Report of Foreign Assistance Reform" (2007). p. 10.

5. Dr. Fareda Banda, "Project on a Mechanism to Address Laws that Discriminate Against Women" (The United Nations' Office of the High Commissioner for Human Rights, March 6 2008), available at http://www.reliefweb.int/rw/lib.nsf/db900sid/PANA-7DHGQM/$file/ohchr_mar2008.pdf?openelement (last accessed May 2008).

6. The United States Commission on Helping to Enhance the Livelihood of People around the Globe, "Beyond Assistance: The HELP Commission Report of Foreign Assistance Reform" (2007) p. 12.

7. William Easterly, *The White Man's Burden: Why the West's Efforts to Aid the Rest Have Done So Much Ill and So Little Good* (New York: Penguin Books, 2006) p. 8.

8. The Millennium Project of the World Federation of UN Associations, "Water: How Can Everyone Have Sufficient Clean Water Without Conflict?" available at http://www.millennium-project.org/millennium/Global_Challenges/chall-02.html (last accessed May 2008).

9. The World Health Organization, "Statement from WHO's Director General" (2008), available at http://www.who.int/water_sanitation_health/hygiene/iys/about/en/index.html (last accessed May 2008).

10. Energy Future Coalition, "Challenge and Opportunity: Charting a New Energy Future," available at http://www.energyfuturecoalition.org/pubs/EFCReport.pdf (last accessed May 2008) p. 36.

11. The United Nations, "Poverty Briefing," available at http://www.un.org/Pubs/CyberSchoolBus//briefing/poverty/poverty.pdf last accessed May 2008).

12. The United Nations Development Programme, "Human Development Report 2007/2008, Fighting Climate Change: Human Solidarity in a Divided World," (New York: The United Nations, 2007), available at http://hdr.undp.org/en/media/hdr_20072008_en_complete.pdf (last accessed May 2008) p. 8.

13. The United Nations Development Programme, "Human Development Report 2003: Millenium Development Goals: A Compact Among Nations to End Human Poverty," (New York: Oxford University Press, 2003), available at http://hdr.undp.org/en/media/hdr03_complete.pdf (last accessed May 2008) p. 34.

14. Paul Collier, *The Bottom Billion: Why the Poorest Countries are Failing and What Can Be Done About It,* (New York: Oxford University Press, 2007) p. 27.

15. Robert Muggah and Martin Griffiths, "Reconsidering the Tools of War: Small Arms and Humanitarian Action" (Humanitarian Practice Network, 2002) p. 13.

16. Oxfam, Saferworld, and International Action Network on Small Arms, "Africa's Missing Billions: International Arms Flows and the Costs of Conflict" (October 2007), available at http://www.oxfam.org/en/files/bp107_africas_missing_billions_0710.pdf/download (last accessed May 2008) p. 9.

17. The World Bank, "Sri Lanka: Recapturing Missed Opportunities," Report No: 20430-CE, (June 16, 2000), available at http:// siteresources.worldbank.org/SRILANKAEXTN/Resources/Missed-opportunities/full_report.pdf (last accessed June 2008).

18. Larry Minear and Ian Smillie, *The Charity of Nations: Humanitarian Action in a Calculating World,* (Connecticut: Kumarian Press, 2004) p. 10.

19. The United Nations, "United Nations Peacekeeping Operations" (March 2008), available at http://www.un.org/Depts/dpko/dpko/bnote.htm (last accessed May 2008).

20. Satish Chand and Ruth Coffman, "How Soon Can Donors Exit From Post-Conflict States?" (Center for Global Development, Working Paper Number 141, February 2008), available at http://www.cgdev.org/content/publications/detail/15464 (last accessed May 2008).

21. The United Nations, "World Youth Report 2005: Young people Today, and in 2015,*"* (2005), available at http://www.un.org/esa/socdev/unyin/documents/wyr05book.pdf (last accessed May 2008).

22. Dapo Oyewole, "Participation of Youth As Partners in Peace and Development in Africa: An Overview of Issues and Challenge" (Paper presented at the Expert Group Meeting on Youth in Africa: Participation of Youth as Partners in Peace and Development in Post-Conflict Countries, Windhoek, Namibia, November 14–16, 2006), available at http://www.un.org/esa/socdev/unyin/documents/namibia_overview.pdf (last accessed May 2008).

23. The United Nations, "The State of World Population: Population Change and Peoples Choice" (1999), available at http://www.unfpa.org/swp/1999/chapter2d.htm (last accessed May 2008).

24. The World Business Council for Sustainable Development, "Facts and Trends to 2050: Energy and Climate Change" (2004), available at http://www.wbcsd.org/DocRoot/FjSOTYajhk3cIRxCbijT/Basic-Facts-Trends-2050.pdf (last accessed May 2008) p. 1.

25. Lester Brown, "How Water Scarcity Will Shape the New Century" (Keynote speech presented at Stockhold Water Conference, August, 14, 2000), available at http://www.earth-policy.org/Transcripts/Transcript1.htm (last accessed May 2008).

26. The United Nations Environment Programme, "Water-Two Billion People Are Dying for It" (2003), available at http://www.unep.org/wed/2003/keyfacts.htm (last accessed May 2008).

27. Oxfam International, "Rigged Rules and Double Standards: Trade, Globalization, and the Fight Against Poverty" (2002), available at http://www.oxfam.org.uk/resources/papers/downloads/trade_report.pdf (last accessed May 2008) p. 7.

28. Ibid, p. 9–10.

29. Ibid, p. 177.

30. Phillip Stevens, "Diseases of Poverty and the 10/90 Gap" (International Policy Network: London, 2004), available at http:// www.fightingdiseases.org/pdf/Diseases_of_Poverty_FINAL.pdf (last accessed May 2008) p. 3.

31. Worldwatch Institute, "Vital Signs: The Trends that are Shaping our Future" (London: W.W. Norton Company, 2001), available at http://www.worldwatch.org/system/files/EVS103.pdf (last accessed May 2008) p. 21.

32. Larry Diamond, "The Democratic Rollback" *Foreign Affairs,* March/April 2008.

33. Stewart Patrick and Susan E. Rice, "Index of State Weakness in the Developing World" (Washington: The Brookings Institution, 2008) p. 17.

34. President John F. Kennedy, "Inaugural Address" (January 20, 1961), available at http://www.bartleby.com/124/pres56.html (last accessed May 2008).

35. Leighton W. Smith Jr. and Anthony C. Zinni, "A Smarter Weapon: Why Two Retired Military Officers Believe It's Essential that the Next President Use Outreach, Good Deeds and a Strong Military to Make the United States Safer" *USA Today,* March 27, 2008, available at http://www.usatoday.com/printedition/news/20080327/oplede_wednesday.art.htm (last accessed May 2008).

36. The CNA Corporation, "National Security and the Threat of Climate Change" (2007), available at http://securityandclimate.cna.org/report/National%20Security%20and%20the%20Threat%20of%20Climate%20Change.pdf (last accessed May 2008).

37. Center for U.S. Global Engagement, "A 21st Century Vision of U.S. Global Leadership: Building a Better Safer World" (2007), available at http://www.usglobalengagement.org/SignonStatement/tabid/890/Default.asp#Signatories (last accessed May 2008).

38. Robert M. Gates, "Landon Lecture, Kansas State University" (November 26, 2007), available at http://www.defenselink.mil/speeches/speech.aspx?speechid=1199 (last access May 2008).

39. The White House, "The National Security Strategy of the United States of America" (March 2006), available at http://www.whitehouse.gov/nsc/nss/2006/nss2006.pdf (last accessed May 2008) p. 33.

40. The United States Department of State, "Summary and Highlights: International Affairs Function 150, Fiscal Year 2009 Budget Request" (2008), available at http://www.state.gov/documents/organization/100014.pdf (last accessed May 2008) p. 6.

41. The United States of America Millennium Challenge Corporation, "Changing Lives: 2007 Annual Report," available at http://www.mcc.gov/documents/mcc-2007-annualreport.pdf (last accessed May 2008) p. 6.

42. WorldPublicOpinion.org, "US Role in the World," available at http://www.americans-world.org/digest/overview/us_role/general_principles.cfm (last accessed May 2008).

43. Program on International Policy Attitudes and Knowledge Networks, "Americans on Addressing World Poverty" (June 30, 2005), available at http://www.pipa.org/OnlineReports/ForeignAid/WorldPoverty_Jun05/WorldPoverty_Jun05_rpt.pdf (last accessed May 2008).

44. Oxfam America, "Smart Development: Why US Foreign Aid Demands Major Reform" (Oxfam America Inc. 2008), available at http://www.oxfamamerica.org/newsandpublications/publications/briefing_papers/smart-development/smart-development-may2008.pdf (last accessed May 2008) p. 5–6.

45. Ibid.

46. Craig Cohen, "A Perilous Course: U.S. Strategy and Assistance to Pakistan" (Washington: Center for Strategic and International Studies, August 2007), available at http://www.csis.org/media/csis/pubs/071214_pakistan.pdf (last accessed May 2008) pg. viii.

47. Ibid, p. 26.

48. United States Government Accountability Office, "Combating Terrorism: The United States Lacks Comprehensive Plan to Destroy the Terrorist Threat to Close the Safe Haven in Pakistan's Federally Administered Tribal Areas" (April 2008), available at http://www.gao.gov/new.items/d08622.pdf (last accessed May 2008) p. 12.

49. South Asia Intelligence Review, "Casualties of Terrorist Violence in Pakistan," available at http://satp.org/satporgtp/countries/pakistan/database/casualties.htm (last accessed May 2008).

50. Owen Bennett-Jones, "US Policy Options Toward Pakistan: A Principled and Realistic Approach" (Iowa: The Stanley Foundation, February 2008) p. 4.

51. "Half of Pakistan's population is 'food insecure'; WFP," *The News-International,* April 23, 2008, available at http://www.thenews.com.pk/daily_detail.asp?id=108337 (last accessed May 2008).

52. Craig Cohen, "A Perilous Course: U.S. Strategy and Assistance to Pakistan" (Washington: Center for Strategic and International Studies, August 2007), available at http://www.csis.org/media/csis/pubs/071214_pakistan.pdf (last accessed May 2008) p. 27.

53. Ibid, p. 26.

54. The United States Institute of Peace, "Islamic Extremists: How Do They Mobilize Support?" (July 2002, Special Report 89), available at http://www.usip.org/pubs/specialreports/sr89.pdf (last accessed May 2008) p. 4.

55. Terror Free Tomorrow, "Pakistanis Reject US Military Action against Al Qaeda; More Support bin Laden than President Musharraf: Results of a New Nationwide Public Opinion Survey of Pakistan" (2007) available at http://www.terrorfreetomorrow.org/upimagestft/Pakistan%20Poll%20Report.pdf (last accessed May 2008).

56. The United States Commission on Helping to Enhance the Livelihood of People around the Globe, "Beyond Assistance: The HELP Commission Report of Foreign Assistance Reform" (2007) p. 1.

57. Steven Radelet, "Foreign Assistance Reforms: Successes, Failures, and Next Steps" (Testimony for the Senate Foreign Relations Subcommittee on International Development, Foreign Assistance, Economic Affairs, and International Environmental Protection, June 12, 2007), available at http://www.senate.gov/~foreign/testimony/2007/RadeletTestimony070612.pdf (last accessed May 2008).

58. Robert M. Gates, "Landon Lecture, Kansas State University" (November 26, 2007), available at http://www.defenselink.mil/speeches/speech.aspx?speechid=1199 (last access May 2008).

59. The United States Commission on Helping to Enhance the Livelihood of People around the Globe, "Beyond Assistance: The HELP Commission Report of Foreign Assistance Reform" (2007) p. 63.

60. Cathy Majtenyi, "Economic Impact of Election Violence on Display in Western Kenyan City," *Voice of America,* March 4, 2008, available at http://www.voanews.com/english/archive/2008-03/2008-03-04-voa29.cfm (last accessed May 2008).

61. Robert M. Gates, "Address to the Marine Corps Association" (July 18, 2007), available at http://smallwarsjournal.com/blog/2007/07/secretary-gates-addresses-the/ (last accessed May 2008).

62. Kaysie Brown and Stewart Patrick, "The Pentagon and Global Development: Making Sense of the DoD's Expanding Role" (Washington: The Center for Global Development Working Paper Number 131, November 2007), available at http://www.cgdev.org/content/publications/detail/14815/ (last accessed May 2008).

63. United States Department of Defense, "Directive 3000.05" (November 28, 2005), available at http://www.dtic.mil/whs/directives/corres/pdf/300005p.pdf (last accessed May 2008) p. 2.

Critical Thinking

1. What are the three different types of security interests that Gayle Smith argues should be taken into account in understanding U.S. long-term interests using the concept of 'sustainable security.'

2. Provide examples of U.S. security interests in the three different types of security discussed by Galye Smith.

3. Explain why you agree or disagree that with Gale Smith's thesis that national, human, and collective security interests must be promoted to promote the United States' longer term 'sustainable security' interests. Be sure to provide specific examples to support your position.

From *Center for American Progress,* June 2008. Copyright © 2008 by Center for American Progress. Reprinted by permission.

A Hidden World, Growing beyond Control

Dana Priest and William M. Arkin

The top-secret world the government created in response to the terrorist attacks of Sept. 11, 2001, has become so large, so unwieldy and so secretive that no one knows how much money it costs, how many people it employs, how many programs exist within it or exactly how many agencies do the same work.

These are some of the findings of a two-year investigation by The Washington Post that discovered what amounts to an alternative geography of the United States, a Top Secret America hidden from public view and lacking in thorough oversight. After nine years of unprecedented spending and growth, the result is that the system put in place to keep the United States safe is so massive that its effectiveness is impossible to determine.

The investigation's other findings include:

- Some 1,271 government organizations and 1,931 private companies work on programs related to counterterrorism, homeland security and intelligence in about 10,000 locations across the United States.
- An estimated 854,000 people, nearly 1.5 times as many people as live in Washington, D.C., hold top-secret security clearances.
- In Washington and the surrounding area, 33 building complexes for top-secret intelligence work are under construction or have been built since September 2001. Together they occupy the equivalent of almost three Pentagons or 22 U.S. Capitol buildings—about 17 million square feet of space.
- Many security and intelligence agencies do the same work, creating redundancy and waste. For example, 51 federal organizations and military commands, operating in 15 U.S. cities, track the flow of money to and from terrorist networks.
- Analysts who make sense of documents and conversations obtained by foreign and domestic spying share their judgment by publishing 50,000 intelligence reports each year—a volume so large that many are routinely ignored.

An Alternative Geography

Since Sept. 11, 2001, the top-secret world created to respond to the terrorist attacks has grown into an unwieldy enterprise spread over 10,000 U.S. locations.

These are not academic issues; lack of focus, not lack of resources, was at the heart of the Fort Hood shooting that left 13 dead, as well as the Christmas Day bomb attempt thwarted not by the thousands of analysts employed to find lone terrorists but by an alert airline passenger who saw smoke coming from his seatmate.

They are also issues that greatly concern some of the people in charge of the nation's security.

"There has been so much growth since 9/11 that getting your arms around that—not just for the CIA, for the secretary of defense—is a challenge," Defense Secretary Robert M. Gates said in an interview with The Post last week.

In the Department of Defense, where more than two-thirds of the intelligence programs reside, only a handful of senior officials—called Super Users—have the ability to even know about all the department's activities. But as two of the Super Users indicated in interviews, there is simply no way they can keep up with the nation's most sensitive work.

"I'm not going to live long enough to be briefed on everything" was how one Super User put it. The other recounted that for his initial briefing, he was escorted into a tiny, dark room, seated at a small table and told he couldn't take notes. Program after program began flashing on a screen, he said, until he yelled "Stop!" in frustration.

"I wasn't remembering any of it," he said.

Underscoring the seriousness of these issues are the conclusions of retired Army Lt. Gen. John R. Vines, who was asked last year to review the method for tracking the Defense Department's most sensitive programs. Vines, who once commanded 145,000 troops in Iraq and is familiar with complex problems, was stunned by what he discovered.

"I'm not aware of any agency with the authority, responsibility or a process in place to coordinate all these interagency and commercial activities," he said in an interview. "The complexity of this system defies description."

The result, he added, is that it's impossible to tell whether the country is safer because of all this spending and all these activities. "Because it lacks a synchronizing process, it inevitably results in message dissonance, reduced effectiveness and waste," Vines said. "We consequently can't effectively assess whether it is making us more safe."

The Post's investigation is based on government documents and contracts, job descriptions, property records, corporate and social networking Web sites, additional records, and hundreds of interviews with intelligence, military and corporate officials and former officials. Most requested anonymity either because they are prohibited from speaking publicly or because, they said, they feared retaliation at work for describing their concerns.

The Post's online database of government organizations and private companies was built entirely on public records. The investigation focused on top-secret work because the amount classified at the secret level is too large to accurately track.

Today's article describes the government's role in this expanding enterprise. Tuesday's article describes the government's dependence on private contractors. Wednesday's is a portrait of one Top Secret America community. On the Web, an extensive, searchable database built by The Post about Top Secret America is available at washingtonpost.com/topsecretamerica.

Defense Secretary Gates, in his interview with The Post, said that he does not believe the system has become too big to manage but that getting precise data is sometimes difficult. Singling out the growth of intelligence units in the Defense Department, he said he intends to review those programs for waste. "Nine years after 9/11, it makes a lot of sense to sort of take a look at this and say, 'Okay, we've built tremendous capability, but do we have more than we need?' " he said.

CIA Director Leon Panetta, who was also interviewed by The Post last week, said he's begun mapping out a five-year plan for his agency because the levels of spending since 9/11 are not sustainable. "Particularly with these deficits, we're going to hit the wall. I want to be prepared for that," he said. "Frankly, I think everyone in intelligence ought to be doing that."

In an interview before he resigned as the director of national intelligence in May, retired Adm. Dennis C. Blair said he did not believe there was overlap and redundancy in the intelligence world. "Much of what appears to be redundancy is, in fact, providing tailored intelligence for many different customers," he said.

Blair also expressed confidence that subordinates told him what he needed to know. "I have visibility on all the important intelligence programs across the community, and there are processes in place to ensure the different intelligence capabilities are working together where they need to," he said.

Weeks later, as he sat in the corner of a ballroom at the Willard Hotel waiting to give a speech, he mused about The Post's findings. "After 9/11, when we decided to attack violent extremism, we did as we so often do in this country," he said. "The attitude was, if it's worth doing, it's probably worth overdoing."

Outside a gated subdivision of mansions in McLean, a line of cars idles every weekday morning as a new day in Top Secret America gets underway. The drivers wait patiently to turn left, then crawl up a hill and around a bend to a destination that is not on any public map and not announced by any street sign.

Liberty Crossing tries hard to hide from view. But in the winter, leafless trees can't conceal a mountain of cement and windows the size of five Wal-Mart stores stacked on top of one another rising behind a grassy berm. One step too close without the right badge, and men in black jump out of nowhere, guns at the ready.

Past the armed guards and the hydraulic steel barriers, at least 1,700 federal employees and 1,200 private contractors work at Liberty Crossing, the nickname for the two headquarters of the Office of the Director of National Intelligence and its National Counterterrorism Center. The two share a police force, a canine unit and thousands of parking spaces.

Liberty Crossing is at the center of the collection of U.S. government agencies and corporate contractors that mushroomed after the 2001 attacks. But it is not nearly the biggest, the most costly or even the most secretive part of the 9/11 enterprise.

In an Arlington County office building, the lobby directory doesn't include the Air Force's mysteriously named XOIWS unit, but there's a big "Welcome!" sign in the hallway greeting visitors who know to step off the elevator on the third floor. In Elkridge, Md., a clandestine program hides in a tall concrete structure fitted with false windows to look like a normal office building. In Arnold, Mo., the location is across the street from a Target and a Home Depot. In St. Petersburg, Fla., it's in a modest brick bungalow in a run-down business park.

Every day across the United States, 854,000 civil servants, military personnel and private contractors with top-secret security clearances are scanned into offices protected by electromagnetic locks, retinal cameras and fortified walls that eavesdropping equipment cannot penetrate.

This is not exactly President Dwight D. Eisenhower's "military-industrial complex," which emerged with the Cold War and centered on building nuclear weapons to deter the Soviet Union. This is a national security enterprise with a more amorphous mission: defeating transnational violent extremists.

Much of the information about this mission is classified. That is the reason it is so difficult to gauge the success and identify the problems of Top Secret America, including whether money is being spent wisely. The U.S. intelligence budget is vast, publicly announced last year as $75 billion, 2½ times the size it was on Sept. 10, 2001. But the figure doesn't include many military activities or domestic counterterrorism programs.

At least 20 percent of the government organizations that exist to fend off terrorist threats were established or refashioned in the wake of 9/11. Many that existed before the attacks grew to historic proportions as the Bush administration and Congress gave agencies more money than they were capable of responsibly spending.

The Pentagon's *Defense Intelligence Agency,* for example, has gone from 7,500 employees in 2002 to 16,500 today. The budget of the National Security Agency, which conducts electronic eavesdropping, doubled. Thirty-five FBI Joint Terrorism Task Forces became 106. It was phenomenal growth that began almost as soon as the Sept. 11 attacks ended.

Nine days after the attacks, Congress committed $40 billion beyond what was in the federal budget to fortify domestic defenses and to launch a global offensive against al-Qaeda. It followed that up with an additional $36.5 billion in 2002 and $44 billion in 2003. That was only a beginning.

With the quick infusion of money, military and intelligence agencies multiplied. Twenty-four organizations were created by the end of 2001, including the Office of Homeland Security and the Foreign Terrorist Asset Tracking Task Force. In 2002, 37 more were created to track weapons of mass destruction, collect threat tips and coordinate the new focus on counterterrorism. That was followed the next year by 36 new organizations; and 26 after that; and 31 more; and 32 more; and 20 or more each in 2007, 2008 and 2009.

In all, at least 263 organizations have been created or reorganized as a response to 9/11. Each has required more people, and those people have required more administrative and logistic support: phone operators, secretaries, librarians, architects, carpenters, construction workers, air-conditioning mechanics and, because of where they work, even janitors with top-secret clearances.

With so many more employees, units and organizations, the lines of responsibility began to blur. To remedy this, at the recommendation of the bipartisan 9/11 Commission, the George W. Bush administration and Congress decided to create an agency in 2004 with overarching responsibilities called the Office of the Director of National Intelligence (ODNI) to bring the colossal effort under control.

While that was the idea, Washington has its own ways.

The first problem was that the law passed by Congress did not give the director clear legal or budgetary authority over intelligence matters, which meant he wouldn't have power over the individual agencies he was supposed to control.

The second problem: Even before the first director, Ambassador John D. Negroponte, was on the job, the turf battles began. The Defense Department shifted billions of dollars out of one budget and into another so that the ODNI could not touch it, according to two senior officials who watched the process. The CIA reclassified some of its most sensitive information at a higher level so the National Counterterrorism Center staff, part of the ODNI, would not be allowed to see it, said former intelligence officers involved.

And then came a problem that continues to this day, which has to do with the ODNI's rapid expansion.

When it opened in the spring of 2005, Negroponte's office was all of 11 people stuffed into a secure vault with closet-size rooms a block from the *White House.* A year later, the budding agency moved to two floors of another building. In April 2008, it moved into its huge permanent home, Liberty Crossing.

Critical Thinking

1. Provide an educated guess of how many people work in the U.S. national security system and explain why it is nearly impossible to arrive at a precise figure.

2. Identify two key actors in the national security establishment that are not official units of the U.S. government.

DOD's Energy Challenge as Strategic Opportunity

AMORY B. LOVINS

Energy is the lifeblood of modern societies and a pillar of America's prowess and prosperity. Yet energy is also a major source of global instability, conflict, pollution, and risk. Many of the gravest threats to national security are intimately intertwined with energy, including oil supply interruptions, oil-funded terrorism, oil-fed conflict and instability, nuclear proliferation, domestic critical infrastructure vulnerabilities, and climate change (which changes everything).[1]

Every combatant command has significant and increasing energy-related missions. Energy has become such a "master key"—it is so pervasive in its tangled linkages to nearly every other security issue—that no national security strategy or doctrine can succeed without a broad and sharp focus on how the United States and the world get and use energy. For the first time, 37 years after the 1973 oil embargo, the 2010 Quadrennial Defense Review is expected to recognize energy's centrality to the mission of the Department of Defense (DOD), and to suggest how DOD can turn energy from a major risk into a source of breakthrough advantage.

DOD faces its own internal energy challenges. The heavy steel forces that defeated the Axis "floated to victory on a sea of oil," six-sevenths of which came from Texas. Today, Texas is a net importer of oil, and warfighting is about 16 times more energy-intensive: its oil intensity per warfighter rose 2.6 percent annually for the past 40 years and is projected to rise another 1.5 percent annually through 2017 due to greater mechanization, remote expeditionary conflict, rugged terrain, and irregular operations.[2] Fuel price volatility also buffets defense budgets: each $10 per barrel (bbl) rise in oil price costs DOD over $1.3 billion per year. But of immediate concern, DOD's mission is at risk (as recent wargaming confirms), and the Department is paying a huge cost in lives, dollars, and compromised warfighting capability for two reasons:

- pervasively inefficient use of energy in the battlespace
- ~99 percent dependence of fixed-facility critical missions on the vulnerable electricity grid.

This discussion of both issues draws heavily on the Defense Science Board's (DSB's) 2008 report *More Fight—Less Fuel*.[3] That analysis, building on and reinforcing its largely overlooked 2001 predecessor, found that solutions are available to turn these handicaps into revolutionary gains in warfighting capability, at comparable or lower capital cost and at far lower operating cost, without tradeoff or compromise. The prize is great. As the Logistics Management Institute stated, "Aggressively developing and applying energy-saving technologies to military applications would potentially do more to solve the most pressing long-term challenges facing DOD and our national security than any other single investment area."[4]

Fuel Logistics: DOD's Soft Underbelly

Fuel has long been peripheral to DOD's focus ("We don't *do* fuel—we *buy* fuel"), but turbulent oil markets and geopolitics have lately led some to question the Department's long-term access to mobility fuel. Echoing the International Energy Agency's chief economist, Fatih Birol—"We must leave oil before it leaves us"—some analysts assert world oil output capability has peaked or soon will. They overlook recent evidence that "peak oil" is more clearly imminent in demand than in supply. U.S. gasoline use—an eighth of world oil—is probably in permanent decline.[5] So may be Organisation for Economic Co-operation and Development countries' oil use, which has been falling since early 2005.[6] Deutsche Bank projects world oil use to peak in 2016, then be cut by electric cars to ~40 percent below the consensus forecast or ~8 percent below current levels by 2030.[7] This assumes China's new cars will be 26 percent electrified by 2020 (China's target is 80 percent), and omits lightweight and low-drag cars, superefficient trucks and planes, and other important oil savings well under way. Oil, as predicted for two decades, is becoming uncompetitive even at low prices before it becomes unavailable even at high prices.

Nobody knows how much oil is in the ground: governments, which often do not know or will not transparently reveal what they have, hold about 94 percent of reserves. But DOD, like the United States, has three compelling reasons to get off oil regardless: security, climate, and cost. Long-term oil availability concerns for DOD are misdirected; even more so, as we will see, are proposals to create a defense synthetic fuel industry. Indeed, DOD is probably the world's largest institutional oil buyer, consuming in fiscal year (FY) 2008 120 million barrels costing $16 billion—93 percent of all U.S. Government oil use. But oil is a largely fungible commodity in a global market; the Department uses only 0.4 percent of the world's oil output (about what two good-sized Gulf of Mexico platforms produce); and in a crisis, DOD has oil-buying priority. Rather, the issue is that DOD's unnecessarily inefficient use of oil makes it move huge quantities of fuel from purchase to use, imposing high costs in blood, treasure, and combat effectiveness.

Nobody knows how much oil is in the ground: governments, which often do not know or will not transparently reveal what they have, hold about 94 percent of reserves.

Logistics uses roughly half the Department's personnel and a third of its budget. One-fifth of DOD's oil—at least 90 million gallons each month—supports Iraq and Afghanistan operations that have increased forward bases' oil use tenfold.[8] Of the tonnage moved when the Army deploys, roughly half is fuel.[9] A typical Marine combat brigade needs more than a half-million gallons per day. *Desert Storm*'s flanking maneuver burned 70,000 tons of fuel in 5 days.[10] Delivering that quantity is a huge job for brigades of logistics personnel and for the personnel and assets needed to maintain and protect the logistics chain.

Despite extensive land and air forces trying to guard them—a "huge burden on the combat forces"[11]—fuel convoys are attractive and vulnerable targets, making them one of the Marine Corps Commandant's most pressing casualty risks in Afghanistan.[12] In FY07, attacks on fuel convoys cost the U.S. Army 132 casualties in Iraq (.026/ convoy) and 38 in Afghanistan (.034/convoy).[13] About 12 percent of *total* FY07 U.S. casualties in Iraq and 35 percent in Afghanistan were Army losses—including contractors but not other Services or coalition partners—associated with convoys.[14] Their constrained routes expose them to improvised explosive devices (IEDs), which probably caused the majority of U.S. fatalities in Afghanistan in 2009. Should that conflict follow an Iraq-like profile, its casualty rates could rise 17.5 percent annually.[15] Just the dollar cost of protecting fuel convoys can be "upward of 15 times the actual purchase cost of fuel, . . . [increasing] exponentially as the delivery cost increases or when force protection is provided from air."[16]

Thus, attacks on fuel assets and other serious hazards to fuel convoys increase mission risk, while fuel logistics and protection divert combat effort and hammer oil-strained budgets. Yet the need for most of the fuel delivered at such high cost could have been avoided by far more efficient use. Efficiency lags because when requiring, designing, and acquiring the fuel-using devices, DOD has systematically assumed that fuel logistics is free and invulnerable—so much so that wargames did not and often could not model it. Instead of analyzing fuel logistics' burden on effectiveness and signaling it by price, DOD valued fuel at its wholesale price delivered in bulk to a secure major base (around $1–$3 per gallon), rather than at its fully burdened cost delivered to the platform in theater in wartime (usually tens and sometimes hundreds of dollars per gallon). Lacking requirements, instructions, shadow prices, rationales, or rewards for saving fuel, hardly anyone considered the military value of achieving, nor strove to achieve, high fuel efficiency.

As consequences became obvious in theater and began to emerge in wargames, the Department in 2007 started changing its policy to value-energy savings at the "Fully Burdened Cost of Fuel" (FBCF, in dollars per gallon), including force protection, *delivered* to its end-user in theater. The 2009 National Defense Authorization Act (NDAA) codified both FBCF and new energy Key Performance Parameters (KPPs, in gallons per day or mission). Those are to receive similar weight to traditional KPPs like lethality, protection, and reliability that encapsulate the Department's pursuit of capability. In principle, both FBCF and energy KPPs will guide requirements writing, analyses of alternatives, choices in the acquisition tradespace, and the focus of DOD's science and technology (S&T) investments. In practice, energy KPPs have not yet been applied (their "selective use" is allowed but not yet launched), and much work must be organized and resourced to get the FBCF numbers right and apply them systematically.[17]

The FBCFs initially in use are incomplete. Current guidance still appears to omit support pyramids, multipliers to rotational force strength, actual (not book) depreciation lives, full headcounts including borrowed and perhaps contractor personnel, theft and attrition adjustments,[18] and uncounted Air Force and Navy lift costs to and from theater. All should be included: FBCF should count all assets and activities—at their end-to-end, lifecycle, fully burdened total cost

of ownership—that will no longer be needed, or can be realigned, if a given gallon need no longer be delivered. Thus, if fielded fuel supply needs shrink, so do its garrison costs for related training and maintenance. Conversely, garrison costs should be additive to FBCF, not dilutive: some analysts average peacetime with wartime costs to water down FBCF, or even assume a peacetime operating tempo, but as the 2008 task force stated, "FBCF is a wartime capability planning factor, not a peacetime cost estimate."[19]

If fielded fuel supply needs shrink, so do its garrison costs for related training and maintenance.

Even before these conservatisms are made realistic, initial FBCF estimates value saved fuel often *one to two orders of magnitude* higher than previously. If these new metrics gain momentum and top-level focus, they could drive strategic shifts and innovations that could revolutionize military capability and effectiveness.

More Fight—Less Fuel mapped a detailed military energy reform agenda, broadly backed by DOD's 2008 Energy Security Task Force. DSB offered specific solutions for its key findings: that DOD lacks the strategy, policies, metrics, information, and governance structure to properly manage its energy risks; that technologies are available to make DOD systems more energy-efficient, but they are undervalued, slowing implementation and resulting in inadequate S&T investments; and that there are many opportunities to reduce energy demand by changing wasteful operational practices and procedures.

The 2009 NDAA codified reforms on the lines recommended by DSB, to be led by a new DOD Director of Operational Energy. As of December 1, 2009, that critical post remained vacant, but some encouraging Service adoption initiatives had begun, such as the *Army Energy Security Implementation Strategy* and Navy Secretary Ray Mabus's invigorating energy goals. But the DSB task force, not stopping with bureaucratic fixes, had added the even more incisive finding that "DOD's energy problems [are] sufficiently critical to add two new strategic vectors"—an older term for "succinct descriptions of capabilities that would make a big difference in military operations"[20]—to complement the four historic ones: "speed, stealth, precision, and networking."

In today's more familiar language, Endurance and Resilience are new capabilities that drive *and* apply new operational requirements. An Endurance capability will create transformational strategies and tactics that both tell the requirements writer to make a new platform fuel-efficient *and* inspire the force planner to exploit its increased range and agility. Today's DOD habits would instead tend to make it heavier with the same range—much as Detroit's engine improvements since the 1970s, rather than saving one-third of civilian cars' fuel, only made them more muscular. The need to change entrenched habits in force planning and operational requirements makes big new capabilities both vital and hard. Driving them deeply into doctrine, strategy, organizational structures, cultures, training, reward systems, and behaviors requires strong, consistent, persistent senior leadership. But once so embedded, new capabilities disruptively and profoundly improve military effectiveness and cost-effectiveness.

The Endurance Capability

Endurance traditionally means "ability to sustain operations for an extended time without support or replenishment."[21] The DSB task force elaborated: "Endurance exploits improved energy efficiency and

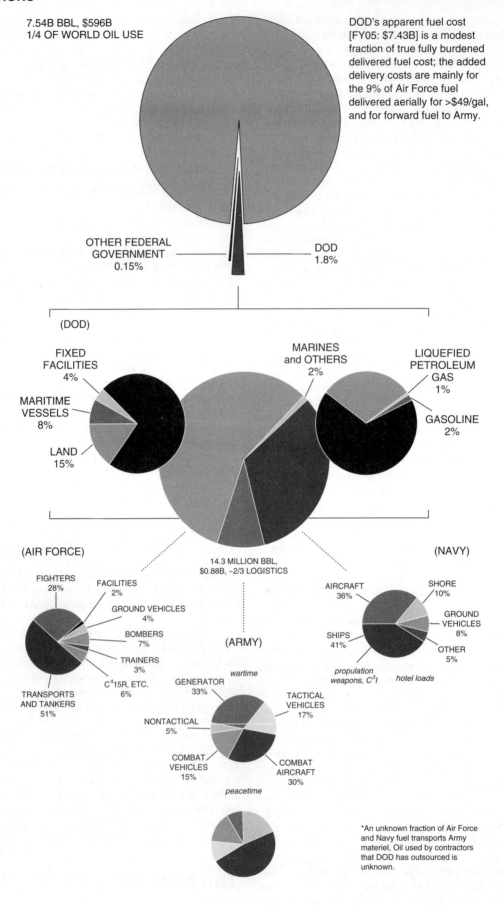

7.54B BBL, $596B
1/4 OF WORLD OIL USE

DOD's apparent fuel cost [FY05: $7.43B] is a modest fraction of true fully burdened delivered fuel cost; the added delivery costs are mainly for the 9% of Air Force fuel delivered aerially for >$49/gal, and for forward fuel to Army.

OTHER FEDERAL GOVERNMENT
0.15%

DOD
1.8%

(DOD)

FIXED FACILITIES
4%

MARITIME VESSELS
8%

LAND
15%

MARINES and OTHERS
2%

LIQUEFIED PETROLEUM GAS
1%

GASOLINE
2%

(AIR FORCE)

14.3 MILLION BBL,
$0.88B, ~2/3 LOGISTICS

(NAVY)

FIGHTERS
28%

FACILITIES
2%

GROUND VEHICLES
4%

BOMBERS
7%

TRAINERS
3%

$C^4$15R, ETC.
6%

TRANSPORTS AND TANKERS
51%

AIRCRAFT
36%

SHORE
10%

GROUND VEHICLES
8%

OTHER
5%

SHIPS
41%

propulsion weapons, C^3I

hotel loads

(ARMY)

wartime

GENERATOR
33%

TACTICAL VEHICLES
17%

NONTACTICAL
5%

COMBAT VEHICLES
15%

COMBAT AIRCRAFT
30%

peacetime

*An unknown fraction of Air Force and Navy fuel transports Army materiel. Oil used by contractors that DOD has outsourced is unknown.

autonomous energy supply to extend range and dwell—recognizing the need for affordable dominance, requiring little or no fuel logistics, in persistent, dispersed, and remote operations, while enhancing overmatch in more traditional operations."[22]

A lean or zero fuel logistics tail also increases mobility, maneuver, tactical and operational flexibility, versatility, and reliability—all required to combat asymmetrical, adaptive, demassed, elusive, faraway adversaries. Endurance is needed in every "platform" using energy in the battlespace, from mobility platforms to expeditionary base power to battery-powered land-warrior electronics. Endurance is even more valuable in stability operations, which often need even more persistence, dispersion, and affordability than the combat operations with which they now enjoy comparable priority.[23]

The DSB report found "enormous technical potential to cost effectively become more fuel efficient and by so doing to significantly enhance operational effectiveness."[24] Current, near-term, and emerging efficiency technologies offer major fuel savings in land, sea, and air platforms,[25] with better warfighting capability (not one of 143 briefs disclosed a trade-off), and with generally excellent economics and operational characteristics.

Early adoption has begun at a modest scale. For example, field commanders in Iraq noticed that:

> Fuel that is transported at great risk, great cost in lives and money, and substantial diversion of combat assets for convoy protection, is burned in generator sets to produce electricity that is, in turn, used to air condition un-insulated and even unoccupied tents. . . . One recently analyzed FOB [forward operating base] used about 95% of its genset [engine-generator set] electricity for this purpose, and about one-third of the Army's total wartime fuel use is for running gensets.[26]

Current, near-term, and emerging efficiency technologies offer major fuel savings in land, sea, and air platforms.

A single typical 60-kilowatt genset burns 4 to 5 gallons per hour, or $0.7 million per year at a typical Afghanistan FBCF of $17.44/gal. Fueling one FOB's gensets might cost $34 million per year—plus, at the FY07 casualty rate, nearly one casualty.[27]

In response, DOD is spraying over 17 million square feet of insulating foam onto temporary structures in theater, saving over half their air-conditioning energy. This $146 million investment should repay its cost in 67 to 74 days at the estimated Iraq $13.80 per gallon FBCF—10 times faster than under the old assumption of undelivered and unprotected fuel. The first $22 million worth should save more than $65 million each year—and more than one convoy casualty.[28] Next steps include far more efficient gensets and air conditioners, encompassing emerging concepts for cooling without electricity.

Lieutenant General James Mattis's 2003 challenge to "unleash us from the tether of fuel" and Major General Richard Zilmer's 2006 operational request from Anbar Province for a "self-sustainable energy solution" stimulated the Army's Rapid Equipping Force to develop a portable renewable/hybrid energy supply system, demonstrated at the National Training Center but not yet fielded. In theater, at the fully burdened cost of fuel, it would probably have been paid back in months[29]—faster if credited for avoided casualties and enhanced combat capability. The Marines have pledged resources for such work.

Over several decades, concerted adoption of identified energy efficiency technologies holds the estimated potential to cut total DOD mobility-fuel requirements by about two-thirds, perhaps even three-fourths. The fattest targets vary according to intent:

- The most gallons can be saved in aircraft, which use 73 percent of DOD fuel. Saving 35 percent of aircraft fuel would free up as much fuel as all DOD land and maritime vehicles plus facilities use. New heavy fixed-wing platforms can save at least 50 percent and new rotary-wing platforms 80 percent, since those fleets use designs that are, respectively, 50 to 60 and 30 to 50 years old.

- The biggest gains in combat effectiveness will come from fuel-efficient ground forces (land and vertical-lift platforms, land warriors, FOBs). For example, Soldiers carry an average of 2 kilograms of batteries per mission-day.

- Savings downstream in a long logistics chain save more fuel: delivering 1 gallon to the Army speartip consumes about 1.4 extra gallons in logistics.

- Savings in aerially refueled aircraft and forward-deployed ground forces save the most delivery cost and thus realignable support assets.

Reset, such as the tens of billions of dollars slated for Humvee replacement, offers a ripe opportunity for leap-ahead performance if, for example, a breakthrough light tactical vehicle already substantially developed can get the "intensive development, design and competitive prototyping" recommended by the 2008 DSB task force. A vehicle as protective and lethal as a 23- to 29-ton mine resistant ambush protected (MRAP) vehicle, but with acceleration, agility, and stability similar to a top-of-the-line pickup truck—and fuel economy, weight, and cost better than a 5- to 6-ton up-armored Humvee—sounds more promising than a Humvee or MRAP. Yet the innovative competitor's prototyping remains stalled, and Office of the Secretary of Defense policy bars using reset funds for innovative platforms.

Both DSB task forces recommended changes in DOD doctrine, structure, business processes, and other activities—emphasizing design and acquisition—to capture these opportunities aggressively and exploit five major military energy efficiency benefits:

- *Force protector,* with far fewer vulnerable fuel convoys.
- *Force multiplier,* freeing up convoy guards for combat tasks—turning fuel-guarders into trigger-pullers.
- *Force enabler,* equipping warfighters with the greatly enhanced dwell, reach, agility, and flexibility that can affordably dominate in both dispersed and focused combat.
- *Key to transformational realignment* from tail to tooth—shifts totaling multi-divisional size, worth many tens of billions of dollars per year.
- *Catalyst for leap-ahead fuel savings in the civilian sector,* which uses more than 50 times as much fuel as DOD. Valuing saved military fuel at FBCF will drive astonishing innovations that accelerate civilian vehicle efficiency, much as past military S&T investment yielded the Internet, Global Positioning System, and jet engine and microchip industries.

DSB's 2008 report summarized: "Unnecessarily high and growing battlespace fuel demand compromises operational capability and mission success; requires an excessive support force structure at the expense of operational forces; creates more risk for support operations than necessary; and increases life-cycle operations and support costs."[30] Yet radically boosting platforms' energy efficiency and combat effectiveness at reasonable or reduced up-front cost can turn each of these energy risks into major warfighting gains. Requiring and exploiting Endurance can give DOD more effective forces *and* a more stable world, at reduced cost and risk. This better-than-free opportunity must become a cornerstone of military doctrine.

Radically boosting platforms' energy efficiency and combat effectiveness at reasonable or reduced up-front cost can turn each of these energy risks into major warfighting gains.

This shift will not be easy. It requires fundamentally redesigning military energy flows to support fast-changing strategic, operational, and tactical requirements. It demands new DOD planning processes that recognize Endurance's operational value so it becomes a requirement in platforms now in development, and appreciate that delivering an operational effect within a fixed energy budget is itself an important capability. A new system's energy budget is an important requirement—as important as any other—and should be analytically based on the size of the logistics tail the system demands and the burden that assuring successful delivery of that logistics tail imposes on the force. Severalfold greater platform fuel efficiency comes from rapidly adopting and fielding advances in ultra-light and ultra-strong materials, fluid dynamics, actuators, and propulsion, all synergistic with alternative fuel and power supplies. It also depends on transformational approaches, incentivized by FBCF and potentially required by energy KPPs but unfamiliar to most DOD contractors, that use integrative design to achieve expanding, not diminishing, returns to investments in energy efficiency—yielding major energy savings at *lower* capital cost without trading off nonenergy KPPs. Basic innovation in design and acquisition requires taking intelligent risks and rewarding those who do so. All this will require senior leadership to tackle head-on the issue that a previous DSB report described thus: "Often the very technology that can provide the United States with a disruptive advantage is itself disruptive to DOD's culture . . . and antibodies rapidly and reflexively form to reject it."[31] Yet such disruptive concepts can be so clearly beneficial that masterful and resolute leadership breaks through hesitancy and resistance. This is the Department's imperative today.

Fuel and power autonomy
Very efficient energy use stretches fuel and power made in theater from wastes, opportunistically acquired feedstocks, or renewable energy flows. Fedex and Virgin Airways plan to fuel 30 percent and 100 percent of their respective fleets with biofuels by 2020. Domestically produced biofuels from centralized, specialized plants do little for DOD's expeditionary needs, but much cutting-edge research emphasizes portable biofuel converters akin to an "opportunistic foraging herbivore."[32] The 2008 DSB task force favored promising expeditionary biofuel and synfuel technologies, and the Services are examining some.

In contrast, the DSB task force expressed "strong concerns" about the coal-to-liquids synfuels favored by the Air Force and Navy (but illegally carbon-intensive under a 2007 law), finding they "do not contribute to [solving] DOD's most critical fuel problem—delivering fuel to deployed forces," "do not appear to have a viable market future or contribute to reducing battlespace fuel demand," and do not appear to address a real problem. Fuel interdiction risk in theater is best countered by efficient use, diversified fuels and supply chains, and greater or more secure local stockpiling. If the concern is long-term fuel availability, military and civilian end-use efficiency is by

far the cheapest choice. In 2005, Wal-Mart's giant Class 8 truck fleet launched gallon perton-mile savings that reached 38 percent in 2008 and are targeted to reach 50 percent in 2015. General U.S. adoption of those doubled-efficiency civilian trucks will save 6 percent of U.S. oil—triple DOD's total use. The Secretary of Defense's JASON science advisors, whose energy report also pointedly failed to endorse coal-to-liquids, suggested saving oil by redesigning the Postal Service's delivery fleet.[33]

Nuclear power is sometimes suggested for land installations or even expeditionary forces,[34] typically without discussing cost (grossly uncompetitive), modern renewables (typically much cheaper), operational reliability (usually needing 100 percent backup), or security. For these and other reasons, the 2008 DSB and JASON task forces did not endorse this option. After vast investment in hardware and a unique technical culture, nuclear propulsion has proven its merit in submarines and aircraft carriers. In 2006–2009, congressional enthusiasts announced supposed Naval Sea Systems Command (NAVSEA) findings that nuclear propulsion in new medium surface combatants could beat $70/bbl oil. However, the 2008 DSB task force discovered that NAVSEA's actual finding ($75–$225/bbl) had improperly assumed a zero real discount rate. A 3 percent annual real discount rate yielded a $132–$345/bbl breakeven oil price; NAVSEA did not respond to requests to test the 7 percent annual real discount rate that the Office of Management and Budget probably mandates. Presumably, the Secretary of Defense will reject this option and focus resources on making ships optimally efficient.

The 2008 DSB and JASON studies are redirecting military energy conversation from exotic, speculative, and often inappropriate supplies to efficient use, which makes autonomous in-theater supply important and often cost-effective. But all such choices depend on a further fundamental reform in DOD's metrics and procedures.

Studies are redirecting military energy conversation from exotic, speculative, and often inappropriate supplies to efficient use.

Gross versus net capability. A change that would boost operational capability by greatly increasing tooth-to-tail ratios was identified in a little-noticed but "important observation of the [2008 DSB] Task Force":

[W]hat [the Joint Capabilities Integration Development System][35] currently calls "capability" is actually the theoretical performance of a platform or system unconstrained by the logistics tail required for its operation. But tail takes money, people, and materiel that detract from tooth. True net capability, constrained by sustainment, is thus the gross capability (performance) of a platform or system times its "effectiveness factor"—its ratio of effect to effort:

Effectiveness Factor = Tooth/(Tooth + Tail)

Also, in an actual budget, Tooth = (Resources − Tail), so

Effectiveness Factor = (Resources − Tail)/Resources.

Effectiveness factor ranges from zero (with infinite tail) to one (with zero tail). If tail > 0, true net capability is always less than theoretical (tail-less) performance, but DOD consistently confuses these two metrics, and so misallocates resources. Buying more tooth that comes with more (but invisible) tail may achieve little, no, or negative net gain in true capability. While the Department recognizes the need to reduce tail, the analytical tools needed to inform decisions on how to do so are not in place. Focusing on reducing tail can create revolutionary capability gains and free up support personnel, equipment, and budget for realignment. The task force recommendations are intended to build the analytical and policy foundation to begin introducing this way of thinking into the requirements, acquisition and budget forecasting processes.[36]

To summarize, current force planning does not and cannot predict or compare competing options' needed tail size or their net capability, so after decades, the "tail is eating the tooth." Reversing this impairment needs five missing steps: (1) an Endurance capability to drive and exploit operational requirements for radical efficiency, (2) enforced by energy KPPs, (3) valued at FBCF, (4) competed on *net* capability, and (5) tested with wargaming and campaign-modeling tools revised so they "play fuel" and reveal the full operational value of lean fuel logistics. All five together will help drive DOD toward ultimately breeding, where possible, a Manx force—one with no tail. Efficient and passively or renewably cooled tents in the desert can mean no gensets, no fuel convoys, no problem. Such a thrust toward efficiency in every use of fuel and electricity also strongly supports the second proposed new key capability—Resilience.

The Resilience Capability

Resilience "combines efficient energy use with more diverse, dispersed, renewable supply—turning the loss of critical missions from energy supply failures (by accident or malice) from inevitable to near-impossible."[37] This capability is vital because the:

> [a]lmost complete dependence of military installations on a fragile and vulnerable commercial power grid and other critical national infrastructure places critical military and Homeland defense missions at an unacceptably high risk of extended disruption. . . . [Backup generators and their fuel supplies at military installations are generally sized] for only short-term commercial outages and seldom properly prioritized to critical loads because those are often not wired separately from non-essential loads. DOD's approach to providing power to installations is based on assumptions that commercial power is highly reliable, subject to infrequent and short term outages, and backups can meet demands. [These assumptions are] . . . no longer valid and DOD must take a more rigorous risk-based approach to assuring adequate power to its critical missions.[38]

The 2008 DSB Task Force found that the confluence of many risks to electric supply—grid overloads, natural disasters, sabotage or terrorism via physical or cyberattacks on the electric grid, and many kinds of interruptions to generating plants—hazards electricity-dependent hydrocarbon delivery, the national economy, social stability, and DOD's mission continuity.

The U.S. electric grid was named by the National Academy of Engineering as the top engineering achievement of the 20th century. It is very capital-intensive, complex, technologically unforgiving, usually reliable, but inherently brittle. It is responsible for ~ 98–99 percent of U.S. power failures, and occasionally blacking out large areas within seconds—because the grid requires exact synchrony across subcontinental areas and relies on components taking years to build in just a few factories or one (often abroad), and can be interrupted by a lightning bolt, rifle bullet, malicious computer program, untrimmed branch, or errant squirrel. Grid vulnerabilities are serious, inherent, and not amenable to quick fixes; current Federal investments in the

"smart grid" do not even require simple mitigations. Indeed, the policy reflex to add more and bigger power plants and power lines after each regional blackout may make the next blackout more likely and severe, much as suppressing forest fires can accumulate fuel loadings that turn the next unsuppressed fire into an uncontrollable conflagration.

The U.S. electric grid can be interrupted by a lightning bolt, rifle bullet, malicious computer program, untrimmed branch, or errant squirrel.

Power-system vulnerabilities are even worse in-theater, where infrastructure and the capacity to repair it are often marginal: "attacks on the grid are one of the most common and effective tactics of insurgents in Iraq, and are increasingly seen in Afghanistan."[39] Thus *electric,* not oil, vulnerabilities now hazard national and theater energy security. Simple exploitation of domestic electric vulnerabilities could take down DOD's basic operating ability and the whole economy, while oil supply is only a gathering storm.

The DSB Task Force took electrical threats so seriously that it advised DOD—following prior but unimplemented DOD policy[40]—to replace grid reliance, for critical missions at U.S. bases, with onsite (preferably renewable) power supplies in netted, islandable[41] microgrids. The Department of Energy's Pacific Northwest National Laboratory found ~ 90 percent of those bases could actually meet those critical power needs from onsite or nearby and mainly renewable sources, and often more cheaply. This could achieve zero daily net energy need for facilities, operations, and ground vehicles; full independence in hunker-down mode (no grid); and increased ability to help serve surrounding communities and nucleate blackstart of the failed commercial grid.

Implementing these sensible policies merits high priority: probably only DOD can move as decisively as the threat to national security warrants. And as with the Endurance capability, exploiting Resilience—building on DOD's position as the world's leading director-indirect buyer of renewable energy—would provide leadership, market expansion, delivery refinement, and training that would accelerate civilian adoption. Already, the 2008 NDAA requires DOD to establish a goal to make or buy at least 25 percent of its electricity from renewables by 2020, and study solar and windpower feasibility for expeditionary forces. Under 2007 Executive Order 13423's Government-wide mandate, DOD must also reduce energy intensity by FY15 to 30 percent below FY03. The Resilience capability would focus all these efforts on robust architectures and implementation paths, ensuring that bases' onsite renewables deliver reliable power to critical loads whether or not the commercial grid is working—a goal not achieved by today's focus on compliance with renewables quotas.

Resilience is even more vital and valuable abroad, in fixed installations and especially in FOBs (whose expeditionary character emphasizes the Endurance logic of Fully Burdened Cost of Electricity). Foreign grids are often less reliable and secure than U.S. grids; protection and social stability may be worse; logistics are riskier and costlier in more remote and austere sites; and civilian populations may be more helped and influenced. Field commanders strongly correlate reliable electricity supplies with political stability. In Sadr City, Army Reserve Major General Jeffrey Talley's Task Force Gold proved in 2008–2009 that *making* electricity reliable, and thus underpinning systematic infrastructure-building, is an effective cornerstone of counterinsurgency.

Reconstruction in Iraq and Afghanistan is starting to define and capture this opportunity to build civic cohesion and dampen insurgency, while reducing attacks' disruption and attractiveness. A resilient, distributed electrical architecture can bring important economic and social side-benefits, as with Afghan microhydropower programs for rural development. Cuba lately showed, too, that aggressively integrating end-use efficiency with micropower can cut national blackouts—caused by decrepit infrastructure, not attacks—by one to two orders of magnitude in a year.

At home, DOD efficiency and micro-power echo new domestic energy policy and startling developments in the marketplace. In 2006, micropower[42] delivered one-sixth of the world's electricity, one-third of its new electricity, and 16 to 52 percent of all electricity in a dozen industrialized countries (the United States lagged with 7 percent). In 2008, for the first time in about a century, the world invested more in renewable than in fossil-fueled power supplies; renewables (excluding big hydroelectric dams) added 40 billion watts of global capacity and got $100 billion of private investment. Their competitive and falling costs, short lead times, and low financial risks attract private capital. Shifting to these more resilient energy solutions goes with the market's flow.

Expanding DOD's Energy Voice

Endurance and Resilience offer synergistic national security benefits far beyond those internal to the Department's mission effectiveness. As a dozen retired flag officers concluded, "We can say, with certainty, that we need not exchange benefits in one dimension for harm in another; in fact, we have found that the best approaches to energy, climate change, and national security may be one and the same."[43] Moreover, whether we care most about national security, climate change, or jobs and competitiveness, we should do exactly the same things about energy. Thus, focusing on our energy actions' attributes and outcomes, not motives, could build broad consensus.

Whether we care most about national security, climate change, or jobs and competitiveness, we should do exactly the same things about energy.

The resulting benefits could be enlarged by bringing DOD's perspective and expertise more vigorously into national energy policy-making. A common critique holds that past Federal energy policy has constituted the most comprehensive threat to national energy security by:

- perpetuating America's expanding oil dependence
- strongly favoring overcentralized energy system architectures inherently vulnerable to disruption
- creating attractive new terrorist targets
- aiming to increase and prolong reliance on the most vulnerable domestic infrastructure
- promoting technologies that encourage proliferation.

Now that national energy policy is shifting—often for additional reasons such as economic recovery, competitive advantage, and climate protection—DOD's knowledge of energy-related security risks needs to inform the councils of government more systematically. If past national security outcomes are not what DOD wants, it is the duty

of military professionals to say so. Their guidance, and increasingly their achievements, can help the Department of Defense build a stronger America and a richer, fairer, cooler, and safer world.

The United States can and must make oil obsolete as a strategic commodity—just as refrigeration did to salt (once so vital a preservative that countries fought over salt mines)[44]—and electric power a boon unshadowed by threat. DOD's leadership in adopting and exploiting the two new capabilities proposed here would dramatically speed that journey toward a world beyond oil—with "negamissions" in the Persian Gulf, Mission Unnecessary—and indeed beyond all energy vulnerabilities. Fighting for Endurance and Resilience in Pentagon decisions today can eliminate the need to fight for oil on the battlefield tomorrow.

Notes

1. Center for Naval Analyses, *National Security and the Threat of Climate Change, 2007;* Gwynne Dyer, *Climate Wars* (Toronto: Random House of Canada, 2008); Thomas Fingar, unclassified summary of *National Intelligence Assessment on the National Security Implications of Global Climate Change to 2030,* June 25, 2008, testimony to the U.S. House of Representatives.

2. Deloitte, *Energy Security: America's Best Defense* (Washington, DC: Deloitte, November 9, 2009), available at www.deloitte.com/assets/Dcom-UnitedStates/Local%20Assets/Documents/us_ad_energy%20security.pdf.

3. Defense Science Board (DSB), *"More Fight—Less Fuel": Report of the Defense Science Board Task Force on DOD Energy Strategy* (Washington, DC: Department of Defense, February 2008), available at www.acq.osd.mil/dsb/reports/ADA477619.pdf.

4. D. Berkey et al., *Energy Independence Assessment: Draft Final Briefing for Office of Force Transformation* (Washington, DC: LMI, January 12, 2005).

5. Russell Gold and Ana Campoy, "Oil Industry Braces for Drop in U.S. Thirst for Gasoline," *The Wall Street Journal,* April 13, 2009.

6. Cambridge Energy Research Associates, "Peak Oil Demand in the Developed World: It's Here," September 29, 2009.

7. Paul Sankey et al., "The Peak Oil Market," *Deutsche Bank Global Markets Research,* October 4, 2009.

8. Deloitte, 15.

9. Army Environmental Policy Institute, "Sustain the Mission Project: Energy and Water Costing Methodology and Decision Support Tools," July 2008.

10. Marvin Baker Schaffer and like Chang, "Mobile Nuclear Power for Future Land Combat," *Joint Force Quarterly* 52 (1st Quarter 2009), 51.

11. Ashton Carter, 2009 congressional testimony, quoted in Deloitte, 15.

12. Ibid.

13. Army Environmental Policy Institute, "Sustain the Mission Project: Casualty Factors for Fuel and Water Resupply Convoys," September 2009.

14. Deloitte; total U.S. casualty data available at http://icasualties.org.

15. Ibid., 18.

16. Ibid., 19.

17. Andrew Bochman, "Measure, Manage, Win: The Case for Operational Energy Metrics," *Joint Force Quarterly* 55 (4th Quarter 2009), 113–119.

18. Deloitte also notes that attacks are far from the only hazard: bad weather, traffic accidents, and pilferage lost DOD some 44 trucks and 220,000 gallons of fuel in June 2008 alone (15).

19. DSB, 31.

20. DSB, *Defense Science Board 2006 Summer Study Report on 21st Century Strategic Technology Vectors,* vol. 1, Main Report (February 2007), x–xi, available at www.acq.osd.mil/dsb/reports/ADA463361.pdf.

21. DSB, *"More Fight—Less Fuel,"* 25.

22. Ibid., 35.

23. DOD Instruction 3000.05, "Stability Operations," September 16, 2009, §4.1, available at www.dtic.mil/whs/directives/corres/pdf/300005p.pdf.

24. Ibid., 37.

25. DSB, *"More Fight—Less Fuel."* Innovation was encouraging on the supply side in the recent Wearable Power Prize Competition but seems to lag in efficient use.

26. Ibid., 29–30.

27. Army Environmental Policy Institute, "Sustain the Mission Project: Casualty Factors for Fuel and Water Resupply Convoys," September 2009; for genset and FOB data, G.D. Kuntz, "Renewable Energy Systems: Viable Options for Contingency Operations," *Environmental Practice* 9 (2007), 157–161.

28. Troy Wilke and Bradley Frounfelker, "Tent Foam Insulation Cost Benefit Analysis," 48th Annual Army Operations Research Symposium, Fort Lee, VA, October 14–15, 2009; personal communications from Troy Wilke and John Spiller (November 29–December 1, 2009).

29. DSB, *"More Fight—Less Fuel,"* 45.

30. Ibid., 3.

31. DSB, *Defense Science Board 2006 Summer Study Report,* xviii.

32. Amory B. Lovins and James Newcomb, "Bioconversion: What's the Right Size?" February 20, 2008, brief to National Research Council Panel on Alternative Liquid Transportation Fuels.

33. JASON, The MITRE Corporation, *Reducing DoD Fossil-Fuel Dependence,* JSR-06-135 (McLean, VA: MITRE, September 2006), available at www.fas.org/irp/agency/dod/jason/fossil.pdf.

34. Schaffer and Chang.

35. *Manual for the Operation of the Joint Capabilities Integration and Development System,* July 31, 2009, available at https://acc.dau.mil/Community-Browser.aspx?id=267116&lang=en-US.

36. DSB, *"More Fight—Less Fuel,"* 28–29.

37. As of FY97, Defense Science Board Summer 1998 Study Task Force, *DOD Logistics Transformation,* Annotated Briefing Slides, slide 7, which also shows that "Active duty combat forces [were then] half [the] size of active logistics forces." One estimate of DOD's FY09 logistics and sustainment cost is $270 billion—over half the base budget (35).

38. Ibid., 3 and 53.

39. DSB, *"More Fight—Less Fuel,"* 55.

40. Ibid., 59–60; DOD Instruction 1470.11 §5.2.3.

41. *Islandable* describes onsite supplies that can continuously serve the base and neighboring communities whether or not the commercial grid is operating.

42. Defined here as cogeneration plus renewables minus big (>10 megawatt electrical) hydro. RMI maintains a global database.

43. Center for Naval Analyses Military Advisory Board, *Powering America's Defense: Energy and the Risks to National Security,* May 2009.

44. R. James Woolsey and Anne Korin, "Turning Oil into Salt," *National Review,* September 25, 2007.

Critical Thinking

1. Explain why you agree or disagree with President Eisenhower's warning at the end of his term in the late 1950s that the military-industrial complex was likely to continue to grow and be difficult to control.

2. Surf the net and identify at least one new technology either already in production or being researched that may help the U.S. Defense Department save energy on land, sea, or in the air.

3. Next, determine whether the technology you have identified may also be useful for addressing problems related to climate change.

AMORY B. LOVINS is Chairman and Chief Scientist of Rocky Mountain Institute.

UNIT 4

Great Power Interstate Conflicts and Rivalries

Unit Selections

Learning Objectives

- Explain the role played by the Organization for Security and Co-operation in Europe (OSCE) in stopping the civil strife in Kyrgyzstan in 2010.

- What should the United States and European countries do to improve relations and stimulate more economic integration within the European Union?

- Describe China's former military strategy and how this doctrine has changed in recent years.

- Explain the concept of an "economic exclusive zone (EEZ)" and why different definitions of an EEZ may led to tensions between the United States and China in the future.

- Explain what Aaron David Miller means when he says that the United States support for the Middle East peace process has become a religious doctrine.

Student Website
www.mhhe.com/cls

Internet References

Archive of European Integration
http://aei.pitt.edu
ISN International Relations and Security Network
www.isn.ethz.ch
The Henry L. Stimson Center—Peace Operations and Europe
www.stimson.org/fopo/?SN = FP20020610372
Central Europe Online
www.centraleurope.com
Europa: European Union
http://europa.eu.int
NATO Integrated Data Service
www.nato.int/structur/nids/nids.htm.
Russia Today
www.russiatoday.com

Russian and East European Network Information Center, University of Texas at Austin
http://reenic.utexas.edu/reenic/index.html
DOD Energy Blog
http://dodenergy.blogspot.com
Inside China Today
www.insidechina.com
Japan Ministry of Foreign Affairs
www.mofa.go.jp
EI: Electronic Intifada
http://electronicintifada.net/new.shtml
Palestine-Israel-American Task Force on Palestine
www.americantaskforce.org

As power relations among nation-states change in a world transitioning toward a multipolar world, there are gradual shifts in the roles of different nation-states and other actors, as well as new alignments and allocations of responsibilities. Such a shift is occurring in Europe as the region moves from being dominated in security matters by one hegemonic power, the United States, toward a system in which several European states through the collective weight of the European Community and other European-dominated institutions assume more importance. During the Cold War, the North Atlantic Treaty Organization (NATO) was the most important international security organization in Europe. However, other European-dominated organizations are now playing increasingly more important roles in maintaining peace and security throughout Europe. This trend was demonstrated in 2010 when the Organization for Security and Co-operation in Europe (OSCE), led by Kazakhstan leaders, along with help from the Uinited States and Russia, prevented civil strife in Kyrgyzstan from becoming an all-out civil war.

Another important shift in the power arrangements among major powers has been the increased importance of China. The need for the EU countries, the United States, Russia, and China to cooperate in order to maintain peace and prosperity were apparent during the fall of 2009 as the three countries sent representatives to a UN-sponsored meeting to try to dissuade Iran from pursing nuclear enrichment and storage at home. In a similar cooperative fashion, these same major powers worked together in the Indian Ocean to protect shipping lanes from Somali-based pirates.

The rise of new powers also causes new sources for conflicts. Edward Wong, in "Chinese Military Seeks to Extend Its Naval Power," describes how China's expanding naval power "well beyond the Chinese coast," to the Middle East, Africa, and "the Pacific where the United States Navy has long reigned as the dominant force," as well as "extending its operational reach beyond the South China Sea and Philippines, is a sharp break from the traditional doctrine of preparing for war" with Taiwan or defending the Chinese coast. The United States and China have already clashed due to different definitions of "exclusive economic zones." As China deploys new Jin-class submarines, some analysts predict China's naval rise may in the future diminish the U.S. throughout the world.

China is also increasingly flexing its new military capabilities and economic might to prevail in long-running territorial disputes. In 2010, Japan arrested the captain of a Chinese trawler near a group of islands in the East China Sea, called the Senkaku by the Japanese and the Diaoyu by China. The Japanese said the trawler rammed a Japanese coast guard vessel. A few years ago such an incident would probably be sorted out quietly by low-level diplomats. However, this time the Chinese demanded the captain be returned to China. When Japan refused, China started to block shipments of rare earth minerals that are vital to Japan's electronic industries. The Japanese government quickly reversed its position and released the Chinese captain. While only one incident, many analysts cite this incident as being similar to China's increasingly assertive behavior in disputes

© H. Wiesenhofer/PhotoLink/Getty Images

over American military exercises in the Pacific and over border issues with India.

The ongoing Palestinian–Israeli conflict became front page news again during the spring of 2010 when Israeli commanders boarded an Irish-owned vessel carrying humanitarian supplies and a small group of pro-Palestinian activities. The vessel was trying to challenge the Israeli naval blockade of Gaza. The reaction of the United States to this and similar incidents was to condemn the Israel blockade of Gaza and to announce a one-year effort, spearheaded by President Obama and Secretary of State Hillary Clinton, to achieve a comprehensive Middle East peace agreement. While Hamas immediately rejected the new round of talks, Israeli and PLO representatives agreed to meet in Washington during the fall, even though neither side was particularly enthusiastic about the new initiative. Few analysts expect the new peace initiative to lead to a general peace accord. The recent refusal of the Israeli government to extend a moratorium on new buildings in the West Bank reduced the likelihood of a successful agreement even further. Aaron David Miller, in "The False Religion of Mideast Peace," outlines how the United States has been engaged in the Middle East peace process for decades because of a belief that lasting peace between Israel and the Palestinians and other Arab neighbors is possible. This belief now has the status as a religious doctrine with a "dogmatic creed that all incoming United States Presidents, including President Obama, have embraced." Miller's conclusion is that America currently lacks the opportunity or will to do "truly big things" on Arab-Israeli peacemaking.

The OSCE and the 2010 Crisis in Kyrgyzstan

Executive Summary

When Kazakhstan president Nursultan Nazarbayev met with U.S. president Barack Obama on several occasions during the former's April 11–14, 2010, visit to Washington, one of the issues the two leaders discussed was the volatile political situation in Kyrgyzstan. They were also joined on at least one occasion by Russian president Dmitry Medvedev, who was in Washington for the April 12–13 Nuclear Security Summit. The three governments were eager to share assessments about developments in Kyrgyzstan after the April 6–7 civil strife there killed about 80 people and wounded over 1,000. The ensuing chaos led Kazakhstan and other neighboring countries to close their borders with Kyrgyzstan and begin intensive consultations on an appropriate response.

Kazakhstan's role in dealing with the crisis was doubly important due to its considerable influence in Kyrgyzstan and its status as the 2010 chair-in-office of the Organization for Security and Co-operation in Europe (OSCE). The success of the OSCE in preventing the outbreak of a Kyrgyz civil war and promoting a peaceful resolution after days of civil unrest is attributable to the closeness of Kazakh-Kyrgyz relations as well as Kazakhstan's close ties with U.S. and Russian leaders. Although a desire to ensure stability in a neighboring country would have motivated a Kazakh response to the crisis in any case, the decision of the Kazakh government to address the crisis primarily through the OSCE was a consequence of Astana's status as OSCE chair. The chair gave Kazakhstan the mandate to act more prominently and more decisively during the Kyrgyz crisis. It managed to simultaneously promote its own regional security interests as well as bolster the international standing of the OSCE (and of Kazakhstan itself) by using the organization's diverse tools to help resolve the Kyrgyz crisis in a peaceful manner. The generally successful OSCE response to the crisis has in turn enhanced the prestige of both the organization and the Kazakh government.

Kazakhstan's Influence in Kyrgyzstan

Kazakhstan is Kyrgyzstan's most important neighbor. The two countries have established deep social, economic, and political ties. Their senior officials engage in frequent meetings, bilaterally and at multilateral gatherings, giving Kazakhstan many points of contact in Bishkek. Kyrgyz officials have demonstrated support for Nazarbayev's efforts to promote greater unity among Central Asian countries. In April 2007, the two governments signed an agreement to establish a bilateral International Supreme Council as a step toward a broader Central Asian Union.

Two-way trade between Kazakhstan and Kyrgyzstan amounts to almost half a billion dollars annually. Kazakhs also provide the main source of foreign capital in Kyrgyzstan, with over $300 million invested in various projects. The two governments established a common investment fund in 2007. Although Kazakhstan provides most of the capital for the fund, the larger part of the investment goes to projects in Kyrgyzstan in the form of joint Kazakh-Kyrgyz enterprises. Kazakh entrepreneurs have already created hundreds of joint ventures in Kyrgyzstan in the banking, construction, energy, and other sectors. According to one estimate, Kazakh investors hold one-third of the total equity of the banks in Kyrgyzstan. Bishkek imports about one-fifth of its wheat from Kazakhstan, and in recent years, Kazakhstan's booming economy has led more Kyrgyz labor migrants to seek work in Kazakhstan than in Russia. An estimated 200,000 Kyrgyz migrants work in Kazakhstan. Tourism, especially involving Kazakhs living near the Kyrgyz border, as well as cultural ties, also bind the two nations together.

Kazakh representatives have long urged their Kyrgyz counterparts to make greater progress in their domestic reform programs, especially in the economic sphere. During his April 2007 visit to Kyrgyzstan, Nazarbayev expressed interest in increasing Kazakhstan's support for the country's economic development. He told his hosts that, under the right conditions, Kazakhs were "ready to invest billions of dollars in Kyrgyzstan's economy." Nazarbayev offered to support Kyrgyzstan's hydropower sector by helping to finance its 1,900-megawatt Kambarata-1 and 240-megawatt Kambarata-2 power plants, despite the fact that Kazakhstan's own plants can generate electricity at cheaper prices than Kyrgyzstan. Investing in Kyrgyzstan's hydropower facilities—including the two Kambarata plans, whose combined projection costs could exceed $2 billion—would benefit Kazakhstan and other Central Asian countries, who share water and electricity. Recognizing that the investment could take some time to materialize, Nazarbayev pledged $100 million in emergency humanitarian aid, as well as wheat and fuel supplies, to help the country deal with an immediate food shortage due to a poor 2006–2007 harvest.

However, Nazarbayev bluntly warned during his April 2007 visit that political instability and widespread corruption were discouraging Kazakh businesses from investing in Kyrgyzstan, a view shared by the Asian Development Bank and other international financial experts. Nazarbayev urged all Kyrgyz political factions to negotiate a political compromise to their disputes, which remained acute even in 2007. Otherwise, he asserted that Kyrgyzstan could emulate Afghanistan and turn into an enclave of instability.

Kazakhstan and Kyrgyzstan have significant multilateral ties. Both are full members of the Commonwealth of Independent States (CIS), the Collective Security Treaty Organization (CSTO), the Shanghai Cooperation Organization (SCO), and the United Nations (UN). They also participate in NATO's Partnership for Peace and support the alliance's security mission in Afghanistan. Indeed, when Nazarbayev held a bilateral meeting with Obama on April 11, 2010, the Kazakh president announced Astana's agreement to permit U.S. planes conveying troops and equipment to Afghanistan to fly over Kazakhstan's territory en route to the U.S. military base at Manas Airport in Kyrgyzstan.

Although Kazak officials employed these diverse bilateral and multilateral tools during the recent crisis, they relied most heavily on the OSCE, which has developed some specific mechanisms to address urgent domestic political crises in Eurasia by resolving the immediate conflict. The decision to award Kazakhstan the OSCE chairmanship in 2010 acknowledged the country's growing importance in Eurasia. Kazakh officials viewed the decision as an endorsement of successful state building and economic development, their leading role in Central Asia, and their contribution as a bridge between the former Soviet republics and Europe's OSCE members. Other governments hoped that the OSCE chairmanship would bolster the organization's influence in the former Soviet bloc, as well as promote a greater commitment to all three OSCE baskets, including democracy and human rights.

Resolving the 2005 Kyrgyz Crisis

The OSCE played an important role in resolving the 2005 crisis in Kyrgyzstan. After a month of small-scale protests primarily in the southern part of Kyrgyzstan, on March 24, 2005, tens of thousands of demonstrators gathered in front of the main government building in the capital of Bishkek. The protestors were angry over the parliamentary elections held on February 27 and March 13, in which several opposition candidates were barred. Many international observers, including the OSCE, judged the ballot fundamentally flawed. After some skirmishes, a mob stormed the government headquarters, while other parts of Bishkek and other cities experienced widespread looting and violence. President Askar Akayev, who had ruled Kyrgyzstan since the breakup of the Soviet Union, fled the country, and Kyrgyzstan became the third former Soviet republic after Georgia in 2003 and Ukraine in 2004 to experience a "colored

revolution" in which a government fell due to mass demonstrations following the holding of fraudulent elections.

While the political confrontation over election results was similar to that of Georgia and Ukraine, the major driving forces for the 2005 protests in Kyrgyzstan were the low standard of living, widespread poverty, lack of economic opportunities, and government corruption. The protests were spontaneous, chaotic, and violent; they lacked political organization and coordination and even a clear political purpose. Therefore the rapid success of the "Tulip Revolution" in ousting President Akayev surprised everyone, including the opposition.

The OSCE's negative interpretation of the 2005 ballot helped contribute to the popular revolt. As the demonstrations grew in size, the OSCE center in Bishkek called on all sides to refrain from using violence in resolving their political differences. It urged all parties to observe the law, maintain constructive dialogue, and respect the basic principles of human rights and civil freedoms. The OSCE then assumed the important role of neutral mediator between President Akayev and the interim government established by the opposition. The OSCE chair-in-office, Foreign Minister Dimitrij Rupel of Slovenia, stressed that the OSCE did not want to take sides but would defend democratic processes. The OSCE focused on encouraging a political dialogue between Akayev and the new interim government aimed at finding a realistic and legal solution to their differences. When the two sides agreed to have the OSCE as the mediator, the personal representative of the OSCE chair-in-office flew to the country on March 24 to perform that role.

The OSCE played an important role in returing the country to the constitutional path of democratic elections. It sought to end the legal dispute between the two rival parliaments, both of which claimed legitimacy due to their different interpretations of the election results. The OSCE sent officials and legal experts to Bishkek to establish a procedure that would allow for holding early presidential elections. The OSCE recommended amendments to Kyrgyzstan's election legislation and the country's constitution. It also generated an action plan for implementing its strategy against corruption, which had been a major source of popular discontent that had helped precipitate the political instability. An August 2003 agreement provided for OSCE assistance to reform Kyrgyz law-enforcement bodies. Indeed, Kyrgyzstan was the only Central Asian country to receive such a special police assistance program. The goal was to enhance public safety, improve the work of law-enforcement agencies, their relations with the public, provide them with necessary equipment, and reform the internal security forces to meet international standards. Finally, the OSCE helped coordinate international efforts—including those of the United Nations, the European Union, international financial institutions, and national governments—to help stabilize the situation in Kyrgyzstan. The OSCE helped initiate regular meetings between representatives of embassies, international organizations, and nongovernmental organizations (NGOs) active in Kyrgyzstan.

The OSCE continued its reform efforts for several years after the crisis. It provided additional funding for the Kyrgyz police to help them ensure stability in the run-up to the July

2005 presidential elections. On June 1, 2005, the OSCE established a one-year police emergency support program. Police in Bishkek and their subunits acquired 38 vehicles, over 1,000 pieces of communication equipment, special equipment used by dog-handling teams, as well as Xerox machines and computers. Police officers received training from skilled experts to maintain public order. The project also established a police emergency call center. These measures aimed to increase the standards of service provided to citizens, the efficiency of operational measures to stop unlawful activities, and the supervision of officials and subunits responsible for organizing police in response to people's complaints. In July 2005, the OSCE, in collaboration with the UN Development Program, launched a conflict prevention project designed to monitor and alleviate political conflicts related to upcoming elections.

Three negative developments detracted from the subsequent OSCE efforts in Kyrgyzstan. First, Russian officials were suspicious of the March 2005 Tulip Revolution, seeing it as a foreign-inspired putsch organized by a small group of pro-Western politicians who used the OSCE to gain international legitimacy. They criticized the OSCE mission to the March 2005 parliamentary elections for employing double standards that denounced alleged government improprieties while ignoring infringements committed by the opposition. Second, as Martha Brill Olcott of the Carnegie Endowment for International Peace points out, each time nondemocratic elections lead to successful protests, it increases the stakes for the next country that tries to hold nondemocratic elections. Seeing what happened in Kyrgyzstan, following the previous "colored revolutions" in Georgia and Ukraine, made other former Soviet governments less inclined to hold their own free elections. Russian officials in particular saw a Western hand behind these three regime changes aimed at weakening Moscow's influence in the former Soviet Union. And third, Kyrgyzstan continued to experience political problems after 2005 despite the OSCE's efforts to place the country on a democratic path. The OSCE's Office for Democratic Institutions and Human Rights (ODIHR) criticized the December 16, 2007, parliamentary elections in Kyrgyzstan, in which President Kurmanbek Bakiyev's ruling Ak Zhol Party won each of the 90 contested legislative seats, for not meeting international standards.

The 2010 Kazakh-OSCE Crisis Response

The persistence of problems after 2005 set the stage for the April 2010 crisis in Kyrgyzstan, one of the most acute in recent Central Asian history. Widespread popular discontent grew due to the rising costs of food and electricity, government-tolerated nepotism and corruption, and the July 2009 presidential elections, which implausibly gave Bakiyev more than three-fourths of the vote. In late February and March, protests broke out in various cities against price increases in government services. The authorities sought to preempt the rising discontent by arresting opposition leaders. The move backfired and provoked widespread demonstrations in Bishkek and other areas

on April 6. The protesters, some of whom used violence, initially demanded the release of the arrested opposition leaders. After the beleaguered security forces responded with deadly force, the protesters expanded in numbers and demands. They overwhelmed the government's defenders and seized key government buildings, including the presidential residence. At least 83 people died and more than 1,500 were wounded in the resulting violence, in which looters joined the initial political protests.

President Bakiyev fled the capital and returned to his power base in Jalalabad, in southern Kyrgyzstan. Although the April 6–7 violence was not repeated, public safety and ethnic tensions continued to present problems. Of the country's 5.3 million people, three-fourths are ethnic Kyrgyz, but ethnic Russians, Turks, Uzbeks, and other minorities make up the remaining quarter. Additional deaths and injuries resulted when ethnic Kyrgyz forcefully tried to take back land from villages populated by ethnic Russians and Meskhetian Turks. Rural violence also broke out north of Bishkek. Five people were killed on April 19 when violence erupted between landowners and squatters in the village of Mayevka. Concerned members of the international community were especially eager to restore public safety and resolve the power struggle between Bakiyev and the new Kyrgyz provisional administration.

Following Bakiyev's departure from the country on April 15, the provisional government announced that it would hold a referendum on a new constitution, which would rebalance political power from the presidency to the parliament, followed by national elections within six months. Their planned domestic and foreign policies remain less clear, with different government leaders offering differing and sometimes conflicting statements. Tensions persist over such important issues as the degree of state control of the economy, how to reduce tensions between the northern and southern parts of the country, and what should be the main directions of the country's foreign policy. The country's economic situation remains dire as Kyrgyzstan lacks the oil, natural gas, and other natural resources of some of its well-endowed neighbors. The leadership of the transitional authority has remained in flux, with even key posts frequently changing hands. Nonetheless, many of the incumbents have had previous government experience under Akayev or Bakiyev.

The OSCE's response to the April 2010 crisis in Kyrgyzstan differs somewhat in how the organization addressed previous political crises in a member country. Often, the foreign minister of the country holding the OSCE chair would meet with competing political factions to promote agreement on how to resolve the crisis. A common solution was for the competing factions to agree that the OSCE would organize new national elections and help monitor them to ensure that the ballot was free and fair. ODIHR would send its well-respected electoral observers, while other OSCE bodies, assisted by its members and other international institutions such as the United Nations, would support these efforts. Various NGOs would also dispatch election observers and provide humanitarian assistance. The OSCE followed this process in both the 2005 and the 2010 crises in Kyrgyzstan.

Under Kazakhstan's chairmanship, the OSCE roughly followed this standard crisis management script during the April 2010 crisis, with some modifications. The immediate OSCE priority was to avert further civil strife and restore peaceful economic and political life in Kyrgyzstan. On April 7, the OSCE chair-in-office, Kanat Saudabayev, who is also Kazakhstan's state secretary and foreign minister, conducted a phone conversation with Kyrgyz foreign minister Kadyrbek Sarbayev over the unrest in Kyrgyzstan. Saudabayev conveyed the OSCE's readiness to facilitate dialogue between the incumbent government and the opposition. On the same day, the OSCE representative on freedom of the media, Dunja Mijatovic, called for restoring information flows to journalists who were covering the deteriorating situation in Kyrgyzstan following reports that the authorities were blocking media broadcasts.

On April 8, Saudabayev initiated the multinational conflict resolution process by telephoning a number of senior European and Eurasian officials, including the heads of several other international organizations and foreign ministries as well senior Kyrgyz officials. Saudabayev's most important act was to appoint a special envoy, Zhanybek Karibzhanov, to go to Kyrgyzstan and manage the crisis in the field. Karibzhanov was an excellent candidate for that position since he is deputy speaker of the Majilis (lower house of parliament) of Kazakhstan and chair of the Kazakh-Kyrgyz interparliamentary group. Using the knowledge and contacts he had previously developed through Kazakh-Kyrgyz exchanges, Karibzhanov rapidly identified and met with key members of the provisional government and other influential members of Kyrgyz society. After he arrived in Bishkek later on April 8, he immediately urged the parties to stop fighting and engage in dialogue. Karibzhanov took a nonjudgmental attitude. Using his status as special envoy of the OSCE chair-in-office, he convened meetings with leaders of the provisional government and representatives of political parties to facilitate dialogue and assess the need for further OSCE involvement.

That same day, UN secretary general Ban Ki-moon attended a special session of the OSCE Permanent Council in Vienna. The Permanent Council is the main decisionmaking body of the 56-country OSCE. The UN secretary general addressed the OSCE Permanent Council. He called for a return to constitutional order and emphasized the need to improve coordination between the United Nations and the OSCE on the ground. While reminding the council that chapter 8 of the UN Charter calls for members to work together to manage crises, he commended the OSCE's role in regional conflict prevention. Ban had fortuitously visited Kyrgyzstan a few days before the April 6 riots as part of a trip to all five Central Asian countries. He therefore had a better understanding and interest in the Kyrgyz crisis than would normally be expected of a UN secretary general.

The international team of special envoys and other international representatives also took shape at this time, with Kazakh diplomats coordinating the multinational response under OSCE leadership. While in Vienna, Ban announced that the UN special envoy, Jan Kubis, would collaborate with Karibzhanov in Kyrgyzstan to help restore constitutional order. Kubis was a valuable choice for this mission since, as OSCE secretary general in 2005, he helped resolve the previous major political crisis in Kyrgyzstan. Also on April 8, the EU special representative for Central Asia, Pierre Morel, joined Karibzhanov in Kyrgyzstan. Ambassador Herbert Salber, director of the OSCE Conflict Prevention Centre in Vienna, went to Bishkek to support these efforts. Meanwhile, the OSCE parliamentary president, Joao Soares, expressed concern over the situation in Kyrgyzstan and the ensuing fatalities. He offered the support of the Parliamentary Assembly in facilitating broad-based political dialogue. Soares appointed Kazakh senator Adil Akhmetov, who is also the OSCE personal representative on combating intolerance and discrimination against Muslims, as his special envoy to Kyrgyzstan.

Other foreign governments worked with OSCE representatives to ensure the safety of their nationals living in Kyrgyzstan during the riots and their immediate aftermath. Although few foreigners were injured during the April unrest, some Chinese businessmen suffered property losses when their shops were looted and burned along with most other business establishments in Bishkek. The Chinese-owned Guoying commercial center, a four-story building containing 4,800 square meters for business operations, was completely gutted. Kyrgyz security guards defending the Dangtang Chinese market killed a rioter and injured six others. Some of these Chinese commercial establishments were also attacked during the 2005 Tulip Revolution, when they lost over $5 million.

After arriving in Kyrgyzstan, Karibzhanov indicated that his first step would be to consult with all influential local and foreign actors. Karibzhanov made clear that unless the parties in conflict were prepared to talk with each other, the intervention of the OSCE or other groups would likely fail. He urged members of the interim government to engage in talks with President Bakiyev, using an international mediator rather than a Kyrgyz national. Although the OSCE declined to mediate the domestic crisis without the approval of both sides, the OSCE Center in Bishkek, following an appeal from the interim administration, began providing assistance to citizen patrols and other bodies seeking to maintain law and order.

After meetings in Bishkek with representatives of the provisional administration, parliment, and civil society, OSCE envoy Karibzhanov reported on April 12 that the discussions had identified spheres where the OSCE could make an effective contribution. Karibzhanov listed his immediate priorities as guaranteeing public safety, restoring commercial activities, and working with the provisional administration to strengthen the country's legal framework. He reaffirmed these priorities when he met with Roza Otunbayeva, head of the country's interim administration, on April 13. He told her that stability would require restoring the rule of law, public safety, and human rights and working closely with the international community. Summing up his efforts during the five days since his appointment and arrival in Kyrgyzstan, Karibzhanov asserted that he and his team had "established contacts with key political figures and facilitated dialogue between them, formed a comprehensive picture of the situation in the country, and assessed the need for potential enhanced OSCE assistance to Kyrgyzstan." These potential areas for greater OSCE efforts included: "support to public safety, targeted economic and environmental activities, legislative reform, electoral assistance, monitoring of human rights and fundamental freedoms, and support to public participation." Throughout his mediation efforts, Karibzhanov collaborated with his counterparts from the other main international organizations that had sent special envoys to Kyrgyzstan—Jan Kubis of the United Nations, Pierre Morel of the European Union, Adil Akhmetov of the OSCE Parliamentary Assembly, and Valeriy Semerikov of the Collective Security Treaty Organization—as well as the local embassies of important foreign countries.

After a tense week, Saudabayev announced on April 15 that Bakiyev had agreed to leave Kyrgyzstan following an agreement with the interim government. Saudabayev described Bakiyev's departure as an important step toward stability and the prevention of civil war in Kyrgyzstan. The OSCE chair-in-office credited this development to the joint efforts of Kazakh president Nursultan Nazarbayev, U.S. president Barack Obama, and Russian president Dmitry Medvedev, as well as active mediation by the OSCE, the United Nations, and the European Union. It became evident that Kazakh officials played the pivotal role in persuading Bakiyev to abandon his efforts to remain in office, potentially by force of arms, and instead go into exile. They arranged for him and his immediate family to fly on the evening of April 15 on a Kazakh Air Force plane from the southern Kyrgyz town of Jalalabad to the regional center of Taraz in Kazakhstan. They also helped secure Bakiyev's signed letter of resignation beforehand.

Although the precise guarantees offered to Bakiyev to induce his departure remain unknown, Kazakh officials might have guaranteed his personal safety, as well as that of his immediate family members, many of whom were also threatened with prosecution by members of the new Kyrgyz administration. Bakiyev later thanked Nazarbayev for his assistance in an interview shown on Kazakhstan's Habar channel. On April 16, a few days before Bakiyev's television interview, Nazarbayev offered some details about how the political crisis was resolved. He explained that he feared Bakiyev would rally armed supporters in the south who were prepared to wage a civil war to maintain him in power. The interim administration was also reluctant to compromise and wanted to punish Bakiyev and his allies for their alleged crimes in office. "It was extremely hard to make an agreement with the new government to get flight permission for our planes," Nazarbayev recalled, "and it was hard to convince President Bakiyev to leave the country." With the immediate crisis over, Nazarbayev urged the new government to concentrate on the country's political and economic reconstruction. Astana offered emergency fuel and lubrication materials necessary for planting crops. According to Kazakh officials, this aid was essential because, if Kyrgyz did not plant crops in the spring, there would be another humanitarian crisis in the fall.

Dampening Great Power Rivalry

Not only did Kazakh leaders enjoy good relations with the leading political factions in Kyrgyzstan, but they also had close ties with their counterparts in Russia and the United States,

the two largest bilateral aid donors to Kyrgyzstan. Both states had significant regional security interests at stake in the crisis. Kyrgyzstan is the only country in the world to host both a Russian and an American military base, and both facilities are located on the outskirts of Bishkek. The Russian base symbolizes Moscow's preeminent security role in the region, while the U.S. facility plays a vital role in sustaining American and NATO military operations in Afghanistan. Kyrgyzstan also borders China's sensitive western province of Xinjiang, which Chinese officials fear could be infiltrated by terrorists and narcotics traffickers. Chinese businesses also have been expanding their economic presence in Kyrgyzstan. These diverse interests could easily have led to intense conflict among the larger powers, but they did not. Both Russian and U.S. officials were content to empower the Kazakh government to resolve the crisis. The Chinese, EU, and other foreign governments, including the other Central Asian republics, also followed Kazakhstan's lead in Kyrgyzstan. On April 9, for instance, the German, French, and Turkish foreign ministers expressed their "full support" for Saudabayev's efforts in Kyrgyzstan and "confirmed their readiness to assist Astana in every possible way."

According to Bakiyev and other sources, many Russian policymakers had grown dissatisfied with the Kyrgyz president. Russia's leaders allegedly believed that Bakiyev had reneged on what Russian officials interpreted as an earlier deal to close the American base at Manas after having received considerable Russian aid. They also believe Bakiyev had double-crossed them on another agreement, reached last year, to establish a new military training center in southern Kyrgyzstan under CSTO auspices and was instead allowing the Pentagon to open its own training facility in Batken. Paradoxically, given the extent of official corruption in Russia, Moscow also alleged embezzlement by the Bakiyev family of millions of dollars of Russian financial aid, as well as fraud committed against Russian companies.

Before the April 2010 uprising, Russian officials had cultivated good ties with the Kyrgyz political opposition and were well positioned to exploit their influence within the country's internal security forces. Russia was the first country to recognize the new Kyrgyz government and the first to offer major financial assistance in the form of a $20-million grant and a $30-million concessional loan to help stabilize the economy. Medvedev offered additional economic assistance to Kyrgyzstan after the country established effective governmental institutions able to maintain order. Russian officials rejected Bakiyev's subsequent efforts to contest the legitimacy of his resignation. The Russian government gained further goodwill in Bishkek by arresting Bakiyev's former interior minister, Moldomusa Kongantiyev, in Moscow and sending him back to Kyrgyzstan for trial for his involvement in the April 7 crackdown.

As OSCE chair, however, President Nazarbayev was able to address Kyrgyzstan as an equal with President Medvedev, something that became apparent when the two men discussed the crisis on the phone on April 8. Russia chaired the CIS and the CSTO. Kazakhstan was a member of both organizations, but chose to rely primarily on the OSCE and its more extensive political mediation tools when addressing the crisis. In a speech at the Brookings Institution on April 13, Medvedev warned that Kyrgyzstan was "on the verge of civil war" and could become a "second Afghanistan." Medvedev seemed sufficiently alarmed by the situation that he apparently accepted the need for Kazakhstan and the OSCE to diffuse the immediate crisis, which would still offer Moscow opportunities to exploit the crisis for long-term strategic gains. For example, officials in the new Kyrgyz government have expressed interest in joining the customs union recently formed by Russia, Belarus, and Kazakhstan.

In addition, the Kyrgyz crisis also led President Islam Karimov of Uzbekistan to move closer to Russia. Signs of Uzbek concern became evident when the government closed its border with Kyrgyzstan following the outbreak of widespread riots. On April 20, Karimov made his first visit to Moscow in more than two years. After consulting with Medvedev and other Russian officials, he claimed that their viewpoints coincided completely. In what could be seen as a warning to Karimov and the leaders of other post-Soviet republics that resist Moscow's dominance, Medvedev refused to exclude "the possibility of similar scenarios in ex-Soviet states or other countries—everything is possible in this world, if people are not happy with the authorities, if the authorities do not make efforts to support their people."

During his April 11–14 visit to Washington, Nazarbayev was told by Medvedev, Obama, and leaders of other OSCE member states about their fears over the dangerous situation in Kyrgyzstan. Nazarbayev later related that Obama and Medvedev separately "asked me to work on it and to keep them informed," which he did. The three governments also coordinated their pressure on Bakiyev to resign and leave the country in order to end the immediate standoff.

When Robert Blake, U.S. assistant secretary for South and Central Asian affairs, visited Bishkek on April 15, he sought assurances that the provisional government was working with the OSCE to draft a new constitution that would result in national elections within the next six months. "The U.S. strongly supports the efforts of the OSCE and the Kazakhstan chair-in-office to find a resolution to the situation involving Mr. Bakiyev," he told a press conference, later adding that "we support the efforts by the interim government and the OSCE special envoy to find a peaceful solution to this impasse in a way that is in accordance with the Kyrgyz constitution." To achieve legitimacy, Blake advised the interim government to work closely with the OSCE to ensure that steps to restore democracy and human rights were in accordance with OSCE standards. He concluded the press conference by observing "that the U.S. has been in close touch with the government of Kazakhstan, both because it is a friend of the U.S., but also because it plays a very important role now as the OSCE chair-in-office, and I think Kazakhstan shares our interest in a return to democracy and in a peaceful outcome of the Bakiyev situation in accordance with the Kyrgyz constitution." That same day, State Department spokesman Philip Crowley said in Washington that, while the United States had not yet recognized the provisional government, it was encouraged by the fact that Bishkek was committed to OSCE principles regarding democracy and human rights. Crowley confirmed that Nazarbayev,

Obama, and Medvedev had discussed the Kyrgyz issue a few days earlier, saying this trilateral consultation "points to strong international cooperation to hopefully resolve a difficult situation peacefully." Crowley added that "this was an international effort led by the OSCE. Kazakhstan is currently the chair of the OSCE, and we're just happy that this has been successfully resolved peacefully." On April 16, Senator Benjamin L. Cardin, cochair of the U.S. Helsinki Commission, in a press release praised Kazakhstan's leadership of the OSCE, especially its government's contribution to securing Bakiyev's peaceful departure. "Kazakhstan's Chairmanship of the OSCE has been vital in resolving this crisis."

On April 20, Saudabayev met with interim government officials in Bishkek to address local and regional security concerns. He argued that because the immediate crisis had passed it was time to move toward reestablishing longer-term political and economic stability in the country. Saudabayev told journalists in Bishkek that "the interim government now has conditions for implementing the declared programme, ensuring the supremacy of the law and, afterwards, dealing with the main socio-economic problems." He added that "conditions, which would make it possible to shift to further democratization, carry out constitutional reforms, parliamentary elections and ensure the lawfulness of the new Kyrgyz authorities, will be created only after this." Prior to visiting Bishkek, Saudabayev consulted with UN secretary general Ban Ki-moon, EU high representative for foreign policy Catherine Ashton, Spanish foreign minister Miguel Moratinos (representing the EU presidency), Russian foreign minister Sergey Lavrov, and Chinese foreign minister Yang Jiechi. These discussions focused on how to integrate the new interim government rapidly into the international community.

Limited International Institutional Alternatives

As in earlier crises, one reason why foreign governments felt comfortable working with the OSCE was that, irrespective of its weaknesses, it was still a more appropriate tool for resolving an internal political crisis within a member country than the competing regional security institutions in Europe or Eurasia. Although some of these organizations possessed greater financial and military resources than the OSCE, they lacked the legitimacy the OSCE had acquired through its longstanding efforts to promote democracy and counter internal conflict in the broader European region. Moreover, Kazakhstan's decision to work primarily through the OSCE in addressing the Kyrgyz crisis further bolstered that organization's primary role. Other countries deferred to Astana's lead during the crisis given Kazakhstan's status as Kyrgyzstan's most influential neighbor, as well as its understanding of the complex nature of Kyrgyz politics. Although Kazakhstan was also a member of several other institutions that could have intervened more vigorously in Kyrgyzstan, the Kazakh government chose to address the crisis in their neighbor mainly under the OSCE's auspices.

The membership of Kyrgyzstan, Kazakhstan, and Russia in the CSTO, together with Armenia, Belarus, Russia, Tajikistan, and Uzbekistan, made that institution a possible player in the Kyrgyz crisis. However, the CSTO declined to intervene in what was seen as an internal political event within a member country rather than an act of foreign aggression requiring a collective response. CSTO secretary general Nikolai Bordyuzha said that the current situation is purely a domestic affair for Kyrgyzstan. The organization's new Collective Rapid Reaction Force, which included special internal security units, was designed to defend members against international terrorist groups, while the regular combat forces aimed to protect members from attacks by foreign militaries. Since these contingents remain under the national jurisdiction of the member states, the dispatch of any force would require an official request of the Kyrgyz government, a collective decision of the CSTO, and the consent of the national government of the unit concerned. Meanwhile, the CIS remained in a general state of decay. As chair of both the CSTO and the CIS, Russia might have sought to use either institution to exert greater influence on Kyrgyz developments. However, Russian leaders felt comfortable deferring to the OSCE to promote a peaceful resolution while pursuing their own bilateral ties with the new authorities in Bishkek.

The European Union's effort during the Kyrgyz crisis, led by EU special envoy Pierre Morel, was primarily devoted to gathering information and supporting OSCE-led mediation efforts. Morel spent April 9–14 in Kyrgyzstan and returned to Brussels to brief EU ambassadors about the situation on April 14. The EU's high representative for foreign policy, Catherine Ashton, deferred to the OSCE's lead, which does not appear to have included any additional actions besides calling Saudabayev and listening to Morel's reports. On April 20, after the acute crisis ended, Ashton told the European Parliament that the European Union would provide financial and political support to the new Kyrgyz government, which it had yet to recognize, only if the government demonstrated a commitment to democracy and human rights.

Shortly after the riots in Kyrgyzstan, the secretary general of the Shanghai Cooperation Organization (SCO), Muratbek Imanaliyev, issued a statement expressing concern over events in Kyrgyzstan. However, the SCO remained disengaged from the turmoil until after it had largely ended. It was not until April 19 that Imanaliev visited Kyrgyzstan to meet with officials of the new provisional government. The head of the interim administration, Roza Otunbayeva, pledged to fulfill all of the country's SCO obligations. Acting Kyrgyz defense minister Ismail Isakov tried to reassure Imanaliev that the interim administration had restored internal and border security, while Imanaliev promised to work with other SCO members to supply the new government with assistance.

The United Nations assumed a more important role than usual due to Ban's fortuitous visit to Kyrgyzstan a few days before the April 6 riots and his attendance at a session of the OSCE Permanent Council during the early crisis period. For a while, his special envoy, Jan Kubis, offered the only means by which Akaev and the political opposition could communicate. After Bakiyev left Kyrgyzstan, however, Kubis ended his role, leaving it up to the UN headquarters in New York and the UN

About CSIS and IND

The U.S.-Kazakhstan OSCE Task Force Policy Case Study is produced by the New European Democracies Project at the Center for Strategic and International Studies (CSIS) and the Institute for New Democracies (IND). CSIS is a private, tax-exempt institution focusing on international public policy issues. Its research is nonpartisan and nonproprietary. IND is a nonpartisan and nonprofit organization dedicated to promoting good governance, human rights, and the rule of law in countries undergoing political transformation. CSIS and IND do not take specific policy positions.

CSIS-IND Taskforce Policy Brief team: Margarita Assenova, IND Director; Natalie Zajicova, Program Officer (IND); Janusz Bugajski, CSIS NEDP Director; Ilona Teleki, Deputy Director and Fellow (CSIS); Besian Boçka, Program Coordinator and Research Assistant (CSIS)

Regional Center for Conflict Prevention in Central Asia to help restore normal political life to Kyrgyzstan.

Next Steps

The OSCE Permanent Council advises participating states on the situation in Kyrgyzstan and will continue consultations on plans to restore stability in the country. In the longer term, the OSCE will need to address what Kazakh and OSCE officials have acknowledged are the major political, economic, and social causes of the unrest in Kyrgyzstan. President Nazarbayev, for instance, has repeatedly pointed to the country's lagging economic development as a source of continuing discontent.

The OSCE has offered to support the interim government pending the holding of a referendum on a new constitution that would decrease presidential powers, as well as new national parliamentary elections. Both of these ballots are scheduled for later this year. In the interim, the OSCE is urging the interim authorities to address the country's most urgent social and economic problems. ODIHR and the OSCE representative on freedom of the media are seeking to restore respect for human rights and fundamental freedoms in Kyrgyzstan. These and other OSCE bodies are also providing assistance to ensure continued public safety, monitor human rights and fundamental freedoms, and promote legislative and other political reforms in preparation for national elections.

There are clear limits on what an intergovernmental body such as the OSCE can do in terms of averting domestic conflict within a member country. Its rules of consensus, as well as the norms about tolerating diversity among members' political systems as long as they broadly conform to democratic norms, make it difficult for the organization to change flawed policies and practices other than publicize them through OSCE reports and the speeches of OSCE officials. That said, the OSCE might review in greater detail what went wrong in Kyrgyzstan after 2005 and try to ensure that similar mistakes are not repeated in the aftermath of the more recent political turnaround. Certainly the OSCE mandate, if fulfilled, would more effectively address many of the common causes of domestic unrest, including fraudulent elections, economic problems, and state-sanctioned corruption. In addition, continuing unrest in southern Kyrgyzstan that some fear could precipitate a civil war and provoke territorial fracture and the involvement of neighboring countries, underscores the necessity for continuing and effective OSCE involvement.

Critical Thinking

1. Describe the core missions of the organization for Security and Co-operation in Europe (OSCE) and why it intervened to stop civil strife in Kyrgyzstan in 2010.

2. Access recent news sources to determine the current conditions related to civil strike in Kyrgyzstan and whether the OSCE is still involved in the conflict.

From *CSIS-IND Task Force,* May 14, 2010, pp. 1–11. Copyright © 2010 by Institute for New Democracies (IND), Center for Strategic & International Studies. Reprinted by permission.

Chinese Military Seeks to Extend Its Naval Power

Edward Wong

Yalong Bay, China—The Chinese military is seeking to project naval power well beyond the Chinese coast, from the oil ports of the Middle East to the shipping lanes of the Pacific, where the United States Navy has long reigned as the dominant force, military officials and analysts say.

China calls the new strategy "far sea defense," and the speed with which it is building long-range capabilities has surprised foreign military officials.

The strategy is a sharp break from the traditional, narrower doctrine of preparing for war over the self-governing island of Taiwan or defending the Chinese coast. Now, Chinese admirals say they want warships to escort commercial vessels that are crucial to the country's economy, from as far as the Persian Gulf to the Strait of Malacca, in Southeast Asia, and to help secure Chinese interests in the resource-rich South and East China Seas.

In late March, two Chinese warships docked in Abu Dhabi, the first time the modern Chinese Navy made a port visit in the Middle East.

The overall plan reflects China's growing sense of self-confidence and increasing willingness to assert its interests abroad. China's naval ambitions are being felt, too, in recent muscle flexing with the United States: in March, Chinese officials told senior American officials privately that China would brook no foreign interference in its territorial issues in the South China Sea, said a senior American official involved in China policy.

The naval expansion will not make China a serious rival to American naval hegemony in the near future, and there are few indications that China has aggressive intentions toward the United States or other countries.

But China, now the world's leading exporter and a giant buyer of oil and other natural resources, is also no longer content to trust the security of sea lanes to the Americans, and its definition of its own core interests has expanded along with its economic clout.

In late March, Adm. Robert F. Willard, the leader of the United States Pacific Command, said in Congressional testimony that recent Chinese military developments were "pretty dramatic." China has tested long-range ballistic missiles that could be used against aircraft carriers, he said. After years of denials, Chinese officials have confirmed that they intend to deploy an aircraft carrier group within a few years.

China is also developing a sophisticated submarine fleet that could try to prevent foreign naval vessels from entering its strategic waters if a conflict erupted in the region, said Admiral Willard and military analysts.

"Of particular concern is that elements of China's military modernization appear designed to challenge our freedom of action in the region," the admiral said.

Yalong Bay, on the southern coast of Hainan island in the South China Sea, is the site of five-star beach resorts just west of a new underground submarine base. The base allows submarines to reach deep water within 20 minutes and roam the South China Sea, which has some of the world's busiest shipping lanes and areas rich in oil and natural gas that are the focus of territorial disputes between China and other Asian nations.

That has caused concern not only among American commanders, but also among officials in Southeast Asian nations, which have been quietly acquiring more submarines, missiles and other weapons. "Regional officials have been surprised," said Huang Jing, a scholar of the Chinese military at the National University of Singapore. "We were in a blinded situation. We thought the Chinese military was 20 years behind us, but we suddenly realized China is catching up."

China is also pressing the United States to heed its claims in the region. In March, Chinese officials told two visiting senior Obama administration officials, Jeffrey A. Bader and James B. Steinberg, that China would not tolerate any interference in the South China Sea, now part of China's "core interest" of sovereignty, said an American official involved in China policy. It was the first time the Chinese labeled the South China Sea a core interest, on par with Taiwan and Tibet, the official said.

Another element of the Chinese Navy's new strategy is to extend its operational reach beyond the South China Sea and the Philippines to what is known as the "second island chain"—rocks and atolls out in the Pacific, the official said. That zone significantly overlaps the United States Navy's area of supremacy.

Japan is anxious, too. Its defense minister, Toshimi Kitazawa, said in mid-April that two Chinese submarines and eight destroyers were spotted on April 10 heading between two Japanese islands en route to the Pacific, the first time such a large Chinese flotilla had been seen so close to Japan. When two Japanese destroyers began following the Chinese ships, a Chinese helicopter flew within 300 feet of one of the destroyers, the Japanese Defense Ministry said.

Since December 2008, China has maintained three ships in the Gulf of Aden to contribute to international antipiracy patrols, the first deployment of the Chinese Navy beyond the Pacific. The mission allows China to improve its navy's long-range capabilities, analysts say.

A 2009 Pentagon report estimated Chinese naval forces at 260 vessels, including 75 "principal combatants"—major warships—and more than 60 submarines. The report noted the building of an aircraft carrier, and said China "continues to show interest" in acquiring carrier-borne jet fighters from Russia. The United States Navy has 286 battle-force ships and 3,700 naval aircraft, though ship for ship the American Navy is considered qualitatively superior to the Chinese Navy.

The Pentagon does not classify China as an enemy force. But partly in reaction to China's growth, the United States has recently transferred submarines from the Atlantic to the Pacific so that most of its nuclear-powered attack submarines are now in the Pacific, said Bernard D. Cole, a former American naval officer and a professor at the National War College in Washington.

The United States has also begun rotating three to four submarines on deployments out of Guam, reviving a practice that had ended with the cold war, Mr. Cole said.

American vessels now frequently survey the submarine base at Hainan island, and that activity leads to occasional friction with Chinese ships. A survey mission last year by an American naval ship, the Impeccable, resulted in what Pentagon officials said was harassment by Chinese fishing vessels; the Chinese government said it had the right to block surveillance in those waters because they are an "exclusive economic zone" of China.

The United States and China have clashing definitions of such zones, defined by a United Nations convention as waters within 200 nautical miles of a coast. The United States says international law allows a coastal country to retain only special commercial rights in the zones, while China contends the country can control virtually any activity within them.

Military leaders here maintain that the Chinese Navy is purely a self-defense force. But the definition of self-defense has expanded to encompass broad maritime and economic interests, two Chinese admirals contended in March.

"With our naval strategy changing now, we are going from coastal defense to far sea defense," Rear Adm. Zhang Huachen,

deputy commander of the East Sea Fleet, said in an interview with Xinhua, the state news agency.

"With the expansion of the country's economic interests, the navy wants to better protect the country's transportation routes and the safety of our major sea lanes," he added. "In order to achieve this, the Chinese Navy needs to develop along the lines of bigger vessels and with more comprehensive capabilities."

The navy gets more than one-third of the overall Chinese military budget, "reflecting the priority Beijing currently places on the navy as an instrument of national security," Mr. Cole said. China's official military budget for 2010 is $78 billion, but the Pentagon says China spends much more than that amount. Last year, the Pentagon estimated total Chinese military spending at $105 billion to $150 billion, still much less than what the United States spends on defense. For comparison, the Obama administration proposed $548.9 billion as the Pentagon's base operating budget for next year.

The Chinese Navy's most impressive growth has been in its submarine fleet, said Mr. Huang, the scholar in Singapore. It recently built at least two Jin-class submarines, the first regularly active ones in the fleet with ballistic missile capabilities, and two more are under construction. Two Shang-class nuclear-powered attack submarines recently entered service.

Countries in the region have responded with their own acquisitions, said Carlyle A. Thayer, a professor at the Australian Defense Force Academy. In December, Vietnam signed an arms deal with Russia that included six Kilo-class submarines, which would give Vietnam the most formidable submarine fleet in Southeast Asia. Last year, Malaysia took delivery of its first submarine, one of two ordered from France, and Singapore began operating one of two Archer-class submarines bought from Sweden.

Last fall, during a speech in Washington, Lee Kuan Yew, the former Singaporean leader, reflected widespread anxieties when he noted China's naval rise and urged the United States to maintain its regional presence. "U.S. core interest requires that it remains the superior power on the Pacific," he said. "To give up this position would diminish America's role throughout the world."

Thom Shanker contributed, reporting from Washington.

Critical Thinking

1. Where are Chinese naval operations today? Does their positioning pose a theat to the United States? Explain.

2. What is an "exclusive economic zone" and how does the definition used by the United States and China differ?

3. Explain why you agree or disagree with the prediction that the U.S. and Chinese military are likely to clash more often in the future. Provide two examples to support your position.

The False Religion of Mideast Peace

And Why I'm no Longer a Believer.

AARON DAVID MILLER

O n October 18, 1991, against long odds and in front of an incredulous press corps, U.S. Secretary of State James A. Baker III and Soviet Foreign Minister Boris Pankin announced that Arabs and Israelis were being invited to attend a peace conference in Madrid.

Standing in the back of the hall at the King David Hotel in Jerusalem that day, I marveled at what America had accomplished. In 18 months, roughly the time it took Henry Kissinger to negotiate three Arab-Israeli disengagement agreements and Jimmy Carter to broker an Egypt-Israel peace treaty, the United States had fought a short, successful war—the best kind—and pushed Iraq's Saddam Hussein out of Kuwait. And America was now well-positioned to bring Arabs and Israelis across the diplomatic finish line.

Or so I thought.

Baker, who lowballed everything, was characteristically cautious. "Boys," he told a few of us aides in his suite after the news conference, "if you want to get off the train, now might be a good time because it could all be downhill from here." But I wasn't listening. America had used its power to make war, and now, perhaps, it could use that power to make peace. I'd become a believer.

I'm not anymore.

Etymologists tell us that the word "religion" may come from the Latin root *religare,* meaning to adhere or bind. It's a wonderful derivation. In both its secular and religious manifestations, faith is alluring and seductive precisely because it's driven by propositions that bind or adhere the believer to a compelling set of ideas that satisfy rationally or spiritually, but always obligate.

And so it has been and remains with America's commitment to Arab-Israeli peacemaking over the past 40 years, and certainly since the October 1973 war gave birth to serious U.S. diplomacy and the phrase "peace process" (the honor of authorship likely goes to a brilliant

veteran State Department Middle East hand, Harold Saunders, who saw the term appropriated by Kissinger early in his shuttles). Since then, the U.S. approach has come to rest on an almost unbreakable triangle of assumptions—articles of faith, really. By the 1990s, these tenets made up a sort of peace-process religion, a reverential logic chain that compelled most U.S. presidents to involve themselves seriously in the Arab-Israeli issue. Barack Obama is the latest convert, and by all accounts he too became a zealous believer, vowing within days of his inauguration "to actively and aggressively seek a lasting peace between Israel and the Palestinians, as well as Israel and its Arab neighbors."

Like all religions, the peace process has developed a dogmatic creed, with immutable first principles. Over the last two decades, I wrote them hundreds of times to my bosses in the upper echelons of the State Department and the White House; they were a catechism we all could recite by heart. First, pursuit of a comprehensive peace was a core, if not the core, U.S. interest in the region, and achieving it offered the *only* sure way to protect U.S. interests; second, peace could be achieved, but *only* through a serious negotiating process based on trading land for peace; and third, *only* America could help the Arabs and Israelis bring that peace to fruition.

Like all religions, the peace process has developed a dogmatic creed.

As befitting a religious doctrine, there was little nuance. And while not everyone became a convert (Ronald Reagan and George W. Bush willfully pursued other Middle East priorities, though each would succumb at one point, if only with initiatives that reflected, to their critics, varying degrees of too little, too late), the exceptions have mostly proved the rule. The iron triangle that drove Richard Nixon, Gerald Ford, Jimmy Carter, George H.W. Bush, Bill Clinton, and now Barack Obama to accord the Arab-Israeli issue such high priority has turned out to be both durable and bipartisan. Embraced by the high priests of the national security temple, including State Department veterans like myself, intelligence analysts, and most U.S. foreign-policy mandarins outside government, these tenets endured and prospered even while the realities on which they were based had begun to change. If this wasn't the definition of real faith, one wonders what was.

That Obama, burdened by two wars elsewhere and the most severe economic crisis since the Great Depression, came out louder, harder, and faster on the Arab-Israeli issue than any of his predecessors was a remarkable testament to just how enduring that faith had become—a faith he very publicly proclaimed while personally presiding over the announcement of George Mitchell as his Middle East envoy in an orchestrated ceremony at the State Department two days after his swearing-in.

At first, it seemed that Obama, the poster president for America's engagement with the world, had found a cause uniquely suited to his view of diplomacy, one whose importance had been heightened by his predecessor's neglect of the issue and the Arab and Muslim attachment to it. Even before the Gaza war exploded three weeks prior to his inauguration, Obama had been bombarded by experts sagely urging a renewed focus on Middle East peace as a way to regain American prestige and credibility after the trauma of the Bush years. The new president soon hit the Arab media running as a kind of empathizer-in-chief, ratcheting up expectations even as Israelis increasingly found him tone-deaf to their needs.

Obama surrounded himself with key figures, such as chief of staff Rahm Emanuel and Secretary of State Hillary Clinton, who believed deeply in the peace religion. He named as his chief peacemaker Mitchell, a man with real stature and negotiating experience; and his national security advisor is James L. Jones, himself a former Middle East envoy who made the stunning pronouncement last year: "If there was one problem that I would recommend to the president" to solve, "this would be it."

All these veteran leaders were not only believers, but had extra reason to encourage a tougher line toward Israel; they had seen the Benjamin Netanyahu movie before and were determined not to let their chance at Middle East peace end the same way. In his first turn as prime minister in the 1990s, the brash hard-liner Netanyahu had driven Bill Clinton crazy. (I remember being briefed on their first meeting in 1996, after which the president growled: "Who's the fucking superpower here?") Confronted with Netanyahu again, Obama and his team needed no encouragement to talk tough on the growing Israeli settlements in the West Bank, an issue that experts inside and outside government were clamoring for Obama to raise as the first step in his renewed push for peace.

At the time, it looked to be a magical convergence of leader and moment: The Arab-Israeli issue seemed perfectly suited to Obama's transformational objectives and his transactional style. If Obama wanted to begin "remaking America," why not try to remake the troubled politics of peace, too? After all, this was the engagement president, who believed deeply in the power of negotiations.

Obama was not alone in his belief, of course. The peace-process creed has endured so long because to a large degree it has made sense and accorded with U.S. interests. The question is, does it still? Does the old thinking about peacemaking apply to new realities? Is the Arab-Israeli conflict still the core issue? And after two decades of inflated hopes followed by violence and terror, and now by directionless stagnation, can we still believe that negotiations will deliver?

Sadly, the answers to these questions seem to be all too obvious these days. And Obama's first 15 months as a disciple of the old creed tells you why. In 2009, the president pushed the Israelis, the Arabs, and the Palestinians to get negotiations going and was rebuffed by all three. He later told *Time* magazine ruefully that "we overestimated our ability to persuade." In March of this year, provoked by the Netanyahu government's incomprehensible announcement of new housing units in East Jerusalem smack in the middle of U.S. Vice President Joe Biden's visit to Israel, Obama pushed the Israelis again, harder this time, though it seems without much of a strategy to put the crisis to good use.

Obama is clearly determined not to take no for an answer. Fresh from his victory on health care, he's King of the World again and in no mood to let the King of Israel frustrate his plans. This willfulness is impressive, and it makes it even more imperative now that he's engaged in the faith to give that old-time religion a fresh look, based not just on what's possible but on what's probable. We don't have the right to abandon hope, but we do have the responsibility to let go of, or at least temper, our illusions.

I can't tell you how many times in the past 20 years, as an intelligence analyst, policy planner, and negotiator, I wrote memos to Very Important People arguing the centrality of the Arab-Israeli issue and why the United States needed to fix it. Long before I arrived at the State Department in 1978, my predecessors had made all the same arguments. An unresolved Arab-Israeli conflict would trigger ruinous war, increase Soviet influence, weaken Arab moderates, strengthen Arab radicals, jeopardize access to Middle East oil, and generally undermine U.S. influence from Rabat to Karachi.

From the 1940s through the 1980s, the power with which the Palestinian issue resonated in the Arab world did take a toll on American prestige and influence. Still, even back then the hand-wringing and dire predictions in my Cassandra-like memos were overstated. I once warned ominously—and incorrectly—that we'd have nonstop Palestinian terrorist attacks in the United States if we didn't move on the issue. During those same years, the United States managed to advance all of its core interests in the Middle East: It contained the Soviets; strengthened ties to Israel and such key Arab states as Egypt, Jordan, and Saudi Arabia; maintained access to Arab oil; and yes, even emerged in the years after the October 1973 war as the key broker in Arab-Israeli peacemaking.

Today, I couldn't write those same memos or anything like them with a clear conscience or a straight face. Although many experts' beliefs haven't changed, the region has, and dramatically, becoming nastier and more complex. U.S. priorities and interests, too, have changed. The notion that there's a single or simple fix to protecting those interests, let alone that Arab-Israeli peace would, like some magic potion, bullet, or elixir, make it all better, is just flat wrong. In a broken, angry region with so many problems—from stagnant, inequitable economies to extractive and authoritarian governments that abuse human rights and deny rule of law, to a popular culture mired in conspiracy and denial—it stretches the bounds of credulity to the breaking point to argue that settling the Arab-Israeli conflict is the most critical issue, or that its resolution would somehow guarantee Middle East stability.

The unresolved Arab-Israeli conflict is still a big problem for America and its friends: It stokes a white-hot anger toward the United States, has already demonstrated the danger of confrontation and war (see Lebanon, 2006; Gaza, 2008), and confronts Israel with a demographic nightmare. But three other issues, at least, have emerged to compete for center stage, and they might prove far more telling about the fate of U.S. influence, power, and security than the ongoing story of what I've come to call the much-too-promised land.

First, there are the wars in Iraq and Afghanistan, where tens of thousands of Americans are in harm's way and are likely to be for some time to come. Add to the mix the dangerous situation in Pakistan, and you see volatility, threat, and consequences that go well beyond Palestine. Second, though U.S. foreign policy can't be held hostage to the war on terror (or whatever it's now called), the 9/11 attacks were a fundamental turning point for an America that had always felt secure within its borders. And finally there's Iran, whose nuclear aspirations are clearly a more urgent U.S. priority than Palestine. Should sanctions and/or diplomacy fail, the default position—military action by Israel or even the United States—can't be ruled out, with galactic consequences for the region and the world. In any event, it's hard to imagine Netanyahu making any big decisions on the peace process until there's much more clarity on what he and most Israelis regard as the existential threat of an Iran with a bomb.

As Obama surely reckoned, moving fast on Arab-Israeli peacemaking would help the United States deal with these issues. But that linkage wasn't compelling when Bush used it to suggest that victory in Iraq would make the Arab-Israeli conflict easier to resolve; it's not compelling now as an exit strategy from Iraq either, as if engaging in Arab-Israeli diplomacy will make the potential mess we could leave behind in Iraq easier for the Arabs to swallow. Nor can the Arab-Israeli issue be used effectively to mobilize Arabs against Iran, because the United States could never do enough diplomatically (or soon enough) to have it make much of a difference. Finally, linking the United States' willingness to help the Israelis with Iran to their willingness to make concessions on Jerusalem and borders isn't much of a policy either. If anything, it risks the United States losing its leverage with Israel on the Iranian issue and raising the odds that Israel would act alone.

Surely the United States can do more than one thing at once, the foreign-policy equivalent of walking and chewing gum at the same time. But America must also do multiple things *well*. Obama can't have an inch-deep and mile-wide approach in which he commits to everything without a cruel and unforgiving assessment of what's really possible and what's not. Nor can the United States afford another high-profile failure based on what a brilliant and committed Clinton told us shortly before we went to Camp David: "Guys, trying and failing is a lot better than not trying at all." This is an appropriate slogan for a high school football team; it's not a substitute for a well-thought-out strategy for the world's greatest power. Obama already has made a commitment to the American people to end two wars, keep them safe from attack at home, and stop Iran from obtaining a nuclear weapon, not to mention tackling the challenges of a severe recession and growing deficit.

Governing is about choosing; it's about setting priorities, managing your politics, thinking strategically, picking your spots, and looking for genuine opportunities that can be exploited—not tilting at windmills. And these days, Arab-Israeli peacemaking is a pretty big windmill.

Even if you could make the case for the centrality of the Arab-Israeli conflict, could you make peace?

Americans are optimists. Our idealism, pragmatism, and belief in the primacy of the individual convince us that the world can be made a better place. Unlike many countries that grapple with existential questions of political identity and physical survival, Americans today don't live on the knife's edge or hold (whatever our Puritan or Calvinist beginnings) a dark deterministic view of human nature.

All this drives our conviction that talking is better than shooting. Rodney King-like, we believe that if people would only sit down and discuss their differences rationally and compromise, a way might be found to accommodate conflicting views. After all, America is the big tent under which so many religious, political, and ethnic groups have managed to coexist, remarkably amicably. Perhaps this spirit is best embodied by Obama's Mideast envoy George Mitchell, who once told me that any conflict created by human beings could be resolved by them. Mitchell is truly convinced that solutions can be found and that serious diplomacy is what you do until that time comes. But he ended his first foray into Arab-Israeli diplomacy with three emphatic no's: from Israel on a comprehensive settlement freeze, from Saudi Arabia on partial normalization, and from the Palestinians on returning to negotiations.

Much of our earlier experience in the tough world of Arab-Israeli peacemaking seemed to bear out Mitchell's initial conviction. In the time from the 1973 war to 1991, two Republican secretaries of state (Kissinger and Baker) and one Democratic president (Carter) succeeded in hammering out a series of Arab-Israeli agreements that established America's reputation as an effective, even honest, broker—seeming to validate the simple proposition that negotiations can work.

If there was anyone who represented the faith in that proposition, it was me. I recall giving a talk in Jerusalem in the fall of 1998, after Clinton had brokered the Wye River accords (never implemented), in which I argued that Arab-Israeli negotiations and the move toward peace were now irreversible. That remark, one of the great howlers of the decade, prompted a note from Efraim Halevy, then Israel's deputy Mossad chief, rightly questioning my logic, and though Halevy was too polite to say it in his note, my judgment as well. Still I believed.

And I continued to do so, all the way through the 1990s, the only decade in the last half of the 20th century in which there was no major Arab-Israeli war. Instead, this was the decade of the Madrid conference, the Oslo accords, the Israel-Jordan peace treaty, regional accords on economic issues, and a historic bid in the final year of the Clinton administration to negotiate peace agreements between Israel, Syria, and the Palestinians. But for a variety of reasons, not the least of which was the Arab,

Palestinian, Israeli (and American) unwillingness to recognize what price each side would have to pay to achieve those agreements, the decade ended badly, leaving the pursuit of peace bloody, battered, and broken. Perhaps the most serious casualty was the loss of hope that negotiations could actually get the Arabs and Israelis what they wanted.

And that has been the story line ever since: more process than peace.

Looking ahead, that process looks much, much tougher—and peace more and more elusive—for three reasons.

First, Arab-Israeli peacemaking is politically risky and life-threatening. Consider the murders of Egyptian President Anwar Sadat and Israeli Prime Minister Yitzhak Rabin. At Camp David, I heard Palestinian leader Yasir Arafat say at least three times, "You Americans will not walk behind my coffin." Leaders take risks only when prospects of pain and gain compel them to do so. Today's Middle East leaders—Israel's Netanyahu, Syria's Bashar al-Assad, and Palestine's Mahmoud Abbas—aren't suicidal. It was Netanyahu, after all, who once told me: "You live in Chevy Chase. Don't play with our future."

Second, big decisions require strong leaders—think Jordan's King Hussein or Israel's Menachem Begin—because the issues on the table cut to the core of their political and religious identity and physical survival. This requires leaders with the legitimacy, authority, and command of their politics to make a deal stick. But the current crop are more prisoners of their constituencies than masters of them: Netanyahu presides over a divided coalition and a country without consensus on what price Israel will pay for agreements with Palestinians and Syria; Abbas is part of a broken Palestinian national movement and shares control over Palestine's guns, authority, and legitimacy with Hamas. It's hard to see how either can marshal the will and authority to make big decisions.

Third, even with strong leaders, you still need a project that doesn't exceed the carrying capacity of either side. In the past, U.S. diplomacy succeeded because the post-1973-war disengagement agreements, a separate Egypt-Israel accord, and a three-day peace conference at Madrid aligned with each side's capabilities. Today, issues such as Jerusalem (as a capital of two states), borders (based on June 1967 lines), and refugees (rights, return, and compensation) present gigantic political and security challenges for Arabs and Israelis. One accord will be hard enough. The prospect of negotiating a comprehensive peace; concluding three agreements between Israel and the Palestinians, between Israel and Syria, and between Israel and Lebanon; dismantling settlements in the Golan Heights and West Bank; and withdrawing to borders based on June 1967 lines seems even more fantastical.

Bottom line: Negotiations can work, but both Arabs and Israelis (and American leaders) need to be willing and able to pay the price. And they are not.

Under these circumstances, the refrain from many quarters is that America must save the day. If the Arabs and Israelis are too weak or recalcitrant, then the United States must support and/or push them to make the deal.

Such forceful U.S. diplomacy succeeded in the past. Indeed, it's a stunning paradox that with the exception of the 1994 Israel-Jordan peace treaty, every other successful accord came not out of direct negotiations, but as a result of U.S. mediation. The Oslo accords, often touted as the miracle produced by direct talks between Israelis and Palestinians, proved to be a spectacular failure. All that's missing now, the argument goes, is the absence of American will.

I understand the logic of this view, and having spent more than 20 years in frustrating talks with the Arabs and Israelis, I can also see how it can be emotionally satisfying. But because I know a thing or two about failure and don't want to see the United States fail (yet again), I simply don't buy the argument. If I genuinely believed America could impose and deliver a solution through tough forceful diplomacy, I'd be more sympathetic—but I don't. And here's why:

Ownership: Larry Summers, Obama's chief economic advisor, said it best: In the history of the world, no one ever washed a rental car. We care only about what we own. Unless the Arabs and Israelis want political agreements and peace and can invest enough in them to give them a chance to succeed, we certainly can't. The broader Middle East is littered with the remains of great powers that wrongly believed they could impose their will on small tribes. Iraq, Afghanistan, Iran ... need I continue? Small tribes will always be meaner, tougher, and longer-winded than U.S. diplomats because it's their neighborhood and their survival; they will always have a greater stake in the outcome of their struggle than the great power thousands of miles away with many other things to do. You want to see failure? Take a whack at trying to force Israelis and Palestinians to accept an American solution on Jerusalem.

The negotiator's mystique: It's gone, at least for now. When Americans succeeded in Arab-Israeli diplomacy, it was because they were respected, admired, even feared. U.S. power and influence were taken seriously. Today, much of the magic is gone: We are overextended, diminished, bogged down. Again Summers: Can the world's biggest borrower continue to be the world's greatest power? Our friends worry about our reliability; our adversaries, including Hamas, Hezbollah, and Iran,

believe they can outwait and outmaneuver us. Nor does there appear much cost or consequence to saying no to the superpower. After Obama and Mitchell's fruitless first year, I worry that the mediator's mystique of a Kissinger or a Baker, or the willfulness and driving force of a Carter, won't return easily.

Domestic politics: The pro-Israel community in the United States has a powerful voice, primarily in influencing congressional sentiment and initiatives (assistance to Israel in particular), but it does not have a veto over U.S. foreign policy. Lobbies lobby; that's the American way, for better or worse. Presidents are supposed to lead. And when they do, with a real strategy that's in America's national interests, they trump domestic politics. Still, domestic politics constrain, particularly when a president is perceived to be weak or otherwise occupied. This president has been battered of late, and his party is likely to face significant losses in the 2010 midterm elections. Should there be a serious chance for a breakthrough in the peace process, he'll go for it. But is it smart to risk trying to manufacture one? The last thing Obama needs now is an ongoing fight with the Israelis and their supporters, or worse, a major foreign-policy failure.

U.S.-Israeli relations: America is Israel's best friend and must continue to be. Shared values are at the core of the relationship, and our intimacy with Israel gives us leverage and credibility in peacemaking when we use it correctly. But this special relationship with the Israelis, which can serve U.S. interests, has become an exclusive one that does not. We've lost the capacity to be independent of Israel, to be honest with it when it does things we don't like, to impose accountability, and to adopt positions in a negotiation that might depart from Israel's. It's tough to be a credible mediator with such handicaps.

Fighting with Israel is an occupational reality. It's part of the mediator's job description. Every U.S. president or secretary of state who succeeded (and some who didn't) had dust-ups, some serious, with Israel. (Remember how Bush 41 and Baker used housing loan guarantees? In 1991, the United States denied Israel billions in credit to borrow at reduced interest rates because of Prime Minister Yitzhak Shamir's determination to build settlements.) But the fight must produce something of value—like the Madrid conference—that not only makes the United States look good but significantly advances the negotiations. In short, we need a strategy that stands a chance of working. Otherwise, why would any U.S. president want to hammer a close ally with a strong domestic constituency?

And this was the problem with Obama's tough talk to Israel on settlements. Not only was the goal he laid out—a settlements freeze including natural growth—unattainable,

So Why Have We Failed?

More than 60 years after Israel's stunning victory in the 1948 war that birthed the Jewish state, an end to the world's most exasperating conflict seems more distant than ever. U.S. President Barack Obama is trying to drag both sides kicking and screaming to the negotiating table after nearly a decade of no progress. But is there still any reason for hope? We asked leading Americans, Israelis, and Palestinians who've tried and failed to make peace to answer three crucial questions: What have you learned, who's primarily to blame, and what's your out-of-the-box idea to solve the conflict? Here are excerpts from what they told us.

Zbigniew Brzezinski

National security advisor to U.S. President Jimmy Carter from 1977 to 1981

Who's to blame: The United States. On more than one occasion it pledged to become seriously engaged in promoting peace, but in fact its engagement has been more rhetorical than real, lacking in will to use the obvious dependence of both the Israelis and the Palestinians on American support.

Out-of-the-box idea: To announce to the world America's commitment to a framework for peace based on four key points, namely (1) no right of return for Palestinian refugees to Israel proper; (2) West Jerusalem as the seat for Israel's capital and East Jerusalem as the seat of the Palestinian capital with some internationally based sharing of the Old City; (3) the drawing of borders between the two states along the 1967 lines, adjusted on the basis of one-for-one swaps as the frontiers; and (4) an essentially demilitarized Palestinian state with U.S. or NATO forces on the west bank of the Jordan River.

Saeb Erekat

Head of the Palestine Liberation Organization's Steering and Monitoring Committee and the organization's chief negotiator

What I learned: At the beginning of the peace process I honestly thought I knew Israel better. I used to believe that Israel's fears and concerns were about security and recognition. But when Arab and Islamic countries offered recognition to Israel in exchange for Israeli withdrawal to the 1967 borders in the 2002 Arab Peace Initiative and Israel chose to continue its colonization, I started rethinking Israel's goals.

Who's to blame: If you ask me as a Palestinian, I would tell you the Israeli occupation. But it is also important to say that Israel has not been seriously challenged to stop its illegal policies against the peoples of the region. Therefore I also blame the third parties for turning a blind eye to Israeli actions and consolidating a culture of impunity, which allows Israel to continue creating facts on the ground. Without this blind support, Israel would have never been able to settle over half a million settlers within the occupied Palestinian territory.

Daniel Kurtzer

U.S. ambassador to Israel under President George W. Bush and ambassador to Egypt under President Bill Clinton; professor of Middle East studies at Princeton University

What I learned: Almost everything the United States tries to achieve in the Middle East is informed by what we do or fail to do in the peace process. When we are active diplomatically, Arab states are more willing to cooperate with us on other problems; when we are not active, our diplomatic options shrink. The Arab-Israeli conflict is not just another squabble among "tribes" over land; it has become a signature issue in international relations that encompasses dimensions of territory, security, historical rights, and religion. Achieving peace between Arabs and Israelis is a significant U.S. national interest.

Out-of-the-box idea: Nearly 43 years since the 1967 war, it is astounding that the United States has not articulated its view on what a final settlement should look like on borders and territory, settlements, Jerusalem, refugees, security, and the like. Today, we have worn-out guidance on some of these issues—mostly focused on what we oppose—but we lack a clear vision of what we support. In other words, it is time for us to act like a great power in resolving one of the world's festering and dangerous conflicts.

Gen. Anthony Zinni

Former head of U.S. Central Command and U.S. envoy to the Middle East peace process in 2001 and 2002

What I learned: By now, we should realize what doesn't work: summits, agreements in principle, special envoys, U.S.-proposed plans, and just about every other part of our approach has failed. So why do we keep repeating it?

but it wasn't part of a broader strategy whose dividends would have made the fight worthwhile. Going after the Israelis piecemeal on settlements to please the Arabs or to make ourselves feel better won't work unless we have a way of achieving a breakthrough. That a tough-talking Obama ended up backing down last year when Netanyahu said no to a comprehensive freeze tells you why.

And that remains the president's challenge after the Biden brouhaha over housing units in East Jerusalem. In the spring of 2010 we're nowhere near a breakthough, and yet we're in the middle of a major rift with the Israelis. Unless we achieve a big concession, we will be perceived to have backed down again. And even if the president manages to extract something on Jerusalem, the chances that Netanyahu will be able to make a far greater move on a core issue, such as borders, will be much reduced. Unless the president is trying to get rid of Netanyahu (and produce a new coalition), he'll have no choice but to find a way to cooperate with him.

So now Obama faces a conundrum. A brilliant, empathetic president, with a Nobel Peace Prize to boot, has embraced the iron triangle and made America the focal point of action and responsibility for the Arab-Israeli issue at a time when the country may be least able to do much about it.

Trying to compensate for the absence of urgency, will, and leadership among Arabs and Israelis by inserting your own has always been a tough assignment. The painful truth is that faith in America's capacity to fix the Arab-Israeli issue has always been overrated. It's certainly no coincidence that every breakthrough from the Egypt-Israel treaty to the Oslo accords to the Israel-Jordan peace agreement came initially as a consequence of secret meetings about which the United States was the last to know. Only then, once there was local ownership or some regional crisis that the United States could exploit, were we able to move things forward.

America's capacity to fix the Arab-Israeli issue has always been overrated.

Right now, America has neither the opportunity nor frankly the balls to do truly big things on Arab-Israeli peacemaking. Fortuna might still rescue the president. The mullahcracy in Tehran might implode. The Syrians and Israelis might reach out to one another secretly, or perhaps a violent confrontation will flare up to break the impasse.

But without a tectonic plate shifting somewhere, it's going to be tough to re-create the good old days when bold and heroic Arab and Israeli leaders strode the stage of history, together with Americans, willing and able to do serious peacemaking.

I remember attending Rabin's funeral in 1995 in Jerusalem and trying to convince myself that America must and could save the peace process that had been so badly undermined by his assassination. I'm not a declinist. I still believe in the power of American diplomacy when it's tough, smart, and fair. But the enthusiasm, fervor, and passion have given way to a much more sober view of what's possible. Failure can do that.

The believers need to re-examine their faith, especially at a moment when America is so stretched and overextended. The United States needs to do what it can, including working with Israelis and Palestinians on negotiating core final-status issues (particularly on borders, where the gaps are narrowest), helping Palestinians develop their institutions, getting the Israelis to assist by allowing Palestinians to breathe economically and expand their authority, and keeping Gaza calm, even as it tries to relieve the desperation and sense of siege through economic assistance. But America should also be aware of what it cannot do, as much as what it can.

Alfred, Lord Tennyson, who probably didn't know much about the Middle East, said it best: "There lives more faith in honest doubt, believe me, then in half the creeds." And maybe, if that leads to more realistic thinking when it comes to America's view of Arab-Israeli peacemaking, that's not such a bad thing.

Critical Thinking

1. What is the current U.S. position in terms of the Middle East peace process?

2. Explain why you believe the latest U.S. effort to foster negotiations between Israel and the Palestinians is or is not likely to succeed in the near term.

AARON DAVID MILLER served as an advisor on the Middle East to Republican and Democratic secretaries of state. He is currently a public policy scholar at the Woodrow Wilson International Center for Scholars and the author of *The Much Too Promised Land: America's Elusive Search for Arab-Israeli Peace.*

UNIT 5

North-South Interstate Conflicts and Rivalries

Unit Selections

18. **The Next Empire?,** Howard W. French
19. **Obama and Latin America: New Beginnings, Old Frictions,** Michael Shifter

Learning Objectives

- What Chinese national interests are maximized by increased investments in African countries?

- What African national interests are maximized by increased Chinese investments in African countries?

- Which countries in Latin America are seeking to diversify their alliances and relationships beyond North America? Why?

- Provide an example where the national interests of most Latin American states diverge from those of the United States.

Student Website

www.mhhe.com/cls

Internet References

The National Defense University Website
   www.ndu.edu
African Center for Strategic Studies (ACSS)
   www.africacenter.org
AllAfrica.com
   http://allafrica.com
Centre for Chinese Studies
   www.ccs.org.za
United States Africa Command (AFRICOM)
   www.africom.mil
United States Southern Command (USSOLUTHCOM)
   www.southcom.mil/appssc/index.php
The North American Institute
   www.northamericaninstitute.org
American Dialogue
   www.iadialog.org
Observatory of Cultural Policies in Africa (OCPA)
   http://ocpa.irmo.hr/resources/index-en.html

Mao made famous the phrase the "Third World," in referring to the large number of countries that were united by their economic status and historical experiences. Mao and many others urged the countries in the "Third World" to remain apart from the Western "First World" or the former communist "Second World" during the Cold War and unite instead, in a new coalition. Since the 1960s, there has been a growing recognition that most of the developing countries of the "Third World" are located south of the equator and thus, share a number of common problems related to climate, geography, and transportation that make economic development difficult. Many writers in countries that were former colonies also emphasize the continuing multifaceted dependency that many former colonies experience in their international relations with former colonial powers.

The "North-South" label has increasingly been adopted to designate both an informal and formal grouping of nation-states based on their economic level of development, shared history, and common continuing problems. Negotiations over many issues between Northern and Southern countries take place in the United Nations General Assembly, and in more specialized U.N. organizations such as the United Nations Conference on Trade and Agricultural Development or UNCTAD. UNCTAD has continued to operate as a forum for dialogue between the poor and wealthy states. However, by the 1980s, the unity of the South's Group of 77 (G77) had largely collapsed. Most analysts cite the rise of OPEC and the newly industrialized countries in Asia as important trends that helped shatter the facade of a united developing world. Throughout the 1990s and continuing into the early 21st century, many of the most important multinational economic negotiations have occurred between developing country members of the G-20 and members of the G-8, i.e., France, United States, United Kingdom, Russia, Germany, Japan, Italy, and Canada.

Most observers believe that such labels as the "North-South conflict" are too simplistic to capture the diverse range of issues among countries at different levels of development. However, the term continues to be used as a convenient shorthand label. The label is useful for referencing the fact that there are frequent conflicts between developed and developing countries over a host of nontraditional security issues (i.e., economic and environmental) that result in very different interests and experiences among large numbers of countries in the developed and developing world. Another simplifying device often used to understand complex political conflicts are analogies often framed as "lessons of history." As the American surge in Afghanistan failed to swiftly defeat the Taliban, many analysts started noting similarities between the closing days of Vietnam and Afghanistan. During 2010 one important difference emerged: The Karzai government of Afghanistan entered into informal negotiations with certain segments of the Taliban without waiting, to consult with and for advice from their American allies.

One of the most dramatic changes in North-South political relations in recent years has been the increased presence of China throughout much of the developing world as investors, workers, and role models of how centralized, "top-down" development plans are implemented. Although China has been

investing abroad for decades, she has only recently became the biggest investor and trade partner for several nation-states in the Southern hemisphere. Nowhere is this trend more apparent than in Africa. Howard W. French in, "The Next Empire?," details how "all across Africa, new tracks are being laid, highways built, ports deepened, commercial contracts signed—all on an unprecedented scale, and led by China, whose appetite for commodities seems insatiable." Many analysts are now speculating about the longer-term significance of China's increased involvement in the continent. Will China's increased capital, technology, and support for large new infrastructure projects be the needed impetus to transform neo-colonial economies into vibrant centers or growth, or does the higher profile adopted by the Chinese government and investors in recent years merely reflect the latest round of exploitation by outsiders?

Much like in Africa, the "North-South," and even the "Third World" labels still resonate with many leftist politicians and intellectuals is Latin America. For nearly two centuries, the United States viewed Latin America as being within its exclusive sphere of influence. Over the past three decades, most countries in the region shifted from military dictatorships to democracies to civilian-led governments that adopted neoliberal economic reforms. Political changes and economic growth occurred, but few economic benefits trickled down to most citizens. The result was a wave of leftist leaders elected in several Latin American countries who have promised to bring more tangible results to the people.

After two decades of privatization and trade liberalization across the hemisphere, leftist leaders were elected first in Venezuela with the election of Hugo Chavez and next in Brazil. Evo Morales was elected in Bolivia, all leaders promising to exert more state control over their nations' economies to promote wealth distribution. The return of leftist even extends to Nicaragua where a nemesis of the Reagan administration, Daniel Ortega, was elected in 2006. While some analysts warn that recent leftist-populist alliances threaten United States interests in the region, others are not so alarmed. Chávez and other leftist leaders were losing support even before the financial crisis of 2008. Regardless of how one interprets the varying support for more radical leaders in key Latin American countries, a basic reality facing the current generation of leaders is that they must find ways to produce tangible results to everyday problems for increased numbers of middle class and poor citizens. In "No Longer Washington's Backyard," Michael Shifer and Daniel Joyce describe the desire of Latin American leaders to diversify their alliances, citing the fact that Latin America's largest country, Brazil, held a mega-summit in December 2008 without the United States. For many Latin American states, China and other rising powers, such as India, offer attractive alternative models of development, markets, and sources of capital, technology, and possibly also alternative allies for the future.

The Next Empire?

All across Africa, new tracks are being laid, highways built, ports deepened, commercial contracts signed—all on an unprecedented scale, and led by China, whose appetite for commodities seems insatiable. Do China's grand designs promise the transformation, at last, of a star-crossed continent? Or merely its exploitation? The author travels deep into the heart of Africa, searching for answers.

HOWARD W. FRENCH

A porter helped me with my bags as I made my way, sweating, into the train station in Dar es Salaam. In addition to my normal complement of luggage, I had brought a carton full of provisions, including several gallons of water, for a trip of uncertain duration. With the carton perched on his head, the porter led me through the vast, densely packed concourse and into the waiting salon.

There, a clock sat high on the wall, its hands frozen since who knows when. Around the perimeter of the room, above the upholstered benches, the faded yellow walls bore what looked like a generation's worth of oily stains, laid down in layers in the shape of heads and shoulders by people leaning back, like me, bludgeoned by the thick afternoon heat and waiting for the call to board.

I was about to embark on one of the world's great train rides, a journey from this muggy Indian Ocean port city, the commercial capital of Tanzania, to the edge of the Zambian Copper Belt, deep in the heart of southern Africa. The official who'd sold me my ticket had seemed puzzled when I asked when the train would arrive at its final destination, and he refused to guess; in recent years, the 1,156-mile trip has been known to take anywhere from its originally scheduled two days to an entire week.

The railroad—known as the Tazara line—was built by China in the early 1970s, at a cost of nearly $500 million, an extraordinary expenditure in the thick of the Cultural Revolution, and a symbol of Beijing's determination to hold its own with Washington and Moscow in an era when Cold War competition over Africa raged fierce. At the time of its construction, it was the third-largest infrastructure project ever undertaken in Africa, after the Aswan Dam in Egypt and the Volta Dam in Ghana.

Today the Tazara is a talisman of faded hopes and failed economic schemes, an old and unreliable railway with too few working locomotives. Only briefly a thriving commercial artery, it has been diminished by its own decay and by the roads and air routes that have sprung up around it. Maintenance costs have saddled Tanzania and Zambia with debts reportedly as high as $700 million in total, and the line now has only about 300 of the 2,000 wagons it needs to function normally, according to Zambian news reports.

Yet the railway traces a path through a region where hopes have risen again, rekindled by a new sort of development also driven by China—and on an unprecedented scale. All across the continent, Chinese companies are signing deals that dwarf the old railroad project. The most heavily reported involve oil production; since the turn of the millennium, Chinese companies have muscled in on lucrative oil markets in places like Angola, Nigeria, Algeria, and Sudan. But oil is neither the largest nor the fastest-growing part of the story. Chinese firms are striking giant mining deals in places like Zambia and the Democratic Republic of the Congo, and building what is being touted as the world's largest iron mine in Gabon. They are prospecting for land on which to build huge agribusinesses. And to get these minerals and crops to market, they are building major new ports and thousands of miles of highway.

In most of Africa's capital cities and commercial centers, it's hard to miss China's new presence and influence. In Dar, one morning before my train trip, I made my way to the roof of my hotel for a bird's-eye view of the city below. A British construction foreman, there to oversee the hotel's expansion, pointed out the V-shaped port that the British navy had seized after a brief battle with the Germans early in the First World War. From there, the British-built portion of the city extended primly inland, along a handful of long avenues. For the most part, downtown Dar was built long ago, and its low-slung concrete buildings, long exposed to the moisture of the tropics, have taken on a musty shade of gray.

"Do you see all the tall buildings coming up over there?" the foreman asked, a hint of envy in his voice as his arm described an arc along the waterfront that shimmered in the distance. "That's the new Dar es Salaam, and most of it is Chinese-built."

I counted nearly a dozen large cranes looming over construction sites along the beachfront Msasani Peninsula, a sprawl of resorts and restaurants catering mostly to Western tourists. Near them, sheltered coyly behind high walls, lie upscale brothels worked by Chinese prostitutes. In the foreground, to the northwest, sits Kariakoo, a crowded slum where Chinese merchants flog refrigerators, air conditioners, mobile phones, and other cheap gadgets from narrow storefronts. To the south lies Tanzania's new, state-of-the-art, 60,000-seat national sports stadium, funded by China and opened in February 2009 by President Hu Jintao.

"Statistics are hard to come by, but China is probably the biggest single investor in Africa," said Martyn Davies, the director of the China Africa Network at the University of Pretoria. "They are the biggest builders of infrastructure. They are the biggest lenders to Africa, and China-Africa trade has just pushed past $100 billion annually."

Davies calls the Chinese boom "a phenomenal success story for Africa," and sees it continuing indefinitely. "Africa is the source of at least one-third of the world's commodities"—commodities China will need, as its manufacturing economy continues to grow—"and once you've understood that, you understand China's determination to build roads, ports, and railroads all over Africa."

Davies is not alone in his enthusiasm. "No country has made as big an impact on the political, economic and social fabric of Africa as China has since the turn of the millennium," writes Dambisa Moyo, a London-based economist, in her influential book, *Dead Aid: Why Aid Is Not Working and How There Is a Better Way for Africa*. Moyo, a 40-year-old Zambian who has worked as an investment banker for Goldman Sachs and as a consultant for the World Bank, believes that foreign aid is a curse that has crippled and corrupted Africa—and that China offers a way out of the mess the West has made.

"Between 1970 and 1998," she writes, "when aid flows to Africa were at their peak, poverty in Africa rose from 11 percent to a staggering 66 percent." Subsidized lending, she says, encourages African governments to make sloppy, wasteful decisions. It breeds corruption, by allowing politicians to siphon off poorly monitored funds. And it forestalls national development, which she says begins with the building of a taxation system and the attraction of foreign commercial capital. In Moyo's view, even the West's "obsession with democracy" has been harmful. In poor countries, she writes, "democratic regimes find it difficult to push through economically beneficial legislation amid rival parties and jockeying interests." Sustainable democracy, she feels, is possible only after a strong middle class has emerged.

In its recent approach to Africa, China could not be more different from the West. It has focused on trade and commercially justified investment, rather than aid grants and heavily subsidized loans. It has declined to tell African governments how they should run their countries, or to make its investments contingent on government reform. And it has moved quickly and decisively, especially in comparison to many Western aid establishments. Moyo's attitude toward the boom in Chinese business in Africa is amply revealed by the name of a chapter in her book: "The Chinese Are Our Friends." Perhaps what Africa needs, she notes, is a reliable commercial partner, not a high-minded scold. And perhaps Africa should take its lessons from a country that has recently pulled itself out of poverty, not countries that have been rich for generations.

"I would say this is a transformational moment for Africa," Moyo told me from London last spring. "I see the explosive development of infrastructure. I see people producing more food and having more jobs . . . And besides, I don't see how otherwise you are going to get a civil society, except by building up a middle class."

Even taking the recent global downturn into account, this has been a hopeful time for a historically downtrodden continent. Per capita income for sub-Saharan Africa nearly doubled between 1997 and 2008, driven up by a long boom in commodities, by a decrease in the prevalence of war, and by steady improvements in governance. And while the downturn has brought commodity prices low for the time being, there is a growing sense that the world's poorest continent has become a likely stage for globalization's next act. To many, China—cash-rich, resource-hungry, and unfickle in its ardor—now seems the most likely agent for this change.

But of course, Africa has had hopeful moments before, notably in the early 1960s, at the start of the independence era, when many governments opted for large, state-owned economic schemes that quickly foundered, and again in the 1970s, another era of booming commodity prices, when rampant corruption, heavy debt, and armed conflict doomed any hopes of economic takeoff.

China's burgeoning partnership with Africa raises several momentous questions: Is a hands-off approach to governmental affairs the right one? Can Chinese money and ambition succeed where Western engagement has manifestly failed? Or will China become the latest in a series of colonial and neocolonial powers in Africa, destined like the others to leave its own legacy of bitterness and disappointment? I was heading south on the Tazara—through the past and into the future, to the sites of some of China's most ambitious efforts on the continent—to try to get some early sense of how the whole grand project was proceeding.

The call to board the train came early, and I took my place in an orderly embarkation line in the departure hall, eventually walking down the central platform and past the luridly disheveled wreckage of a long-immobilized train. On the adjacent track, my train, the Kilimanjaro Express (which, curiously, goes nowhere near Mount Kilimanjaro), looked natty by comparison, its dark-olive paint unmarred. I clambered aboard and, after a brief confusion over seating assignments, settled with my three cabinmates into a tight little space with twin bunk beds along both walls and a table in the middle.

Isaac Mpotia, a 50-year-old Tanzanian electrical engineer who had studied in Germany, sat by the window, directly across from me. He was taking the train home to Iringa, in southern Tanzania, I later learned, after a long stint doing engine work for the Tazara in Dar. He was quiet and a little somber while the train sat in the station, but as it lurched away from the platform at 3:50 P.M., right on time, he smiled. "Today," he said, "we are operating on German time." With a look of mischief, he added: "From here out, we can break down at any time."

The slums on the southwestern edge of Dar, where women pounded their evening meals in mortars and half-naked children waved, quickly fell away, giving over to thickening bush. With nightfall's approach, we would be entering the Selous Game Reserve, one of the largest in Africa. (I had heard stories of collisions with elephants causing trains to derail.) All along the way, wreckage was strewn beside the tracks—railway cars hauled from where they'd derailed or broken down, and left to decay like great, dead beasts.

As we looked out at these rusting carcasses, my cabinmates began talking about the railroad, and what it said about their societies. "This is a good train," said Isaac, with a trace of bitterness, "but like any piece of equipment, it needs maintenance." Daniel Simwinga, a voluble, Bible-toting Zambian, responded, "Everyone knows you can't keep getting milk from a cow without feeding it grass." (Daniel was bringing a shipment of auto parts and other goods south. As a commercial trader, he rides the Tazara as often as twice a month, and is well versed in its shortcomings.)

"As soon as we have problems, we ask someone else to take care of them for us," Isaac continued. "We ask the Europeans. We ask the Americans. We ask the Chinese. We will run this train into the ground, and then we will tell the Chinese we need another one. This is not development." I thought of the wreckage by the tracks. In China, there is no such thing as metallic waste. Armies of migrant workers scour the countryside with hammers and chisels, collecting and selling every scrap to the insatiable smelters that feed the country's industries. Here, by contrast, was a land without industry.

The World Bank and the United Nations did surveys for a Tazara-like line in the early 1960s, and both concluded that such a railway would be neither economically feasible nor sustainable. But China built the line, between 1970 and 1975, at the behest of two African leaders: Julius Kambarage Nyerere, the first president of Tanzania, who wanted to open up the remote south of his country and bolster his pan-African credentials; and President Kenneth Kaunda of Zambia, whose landlocked country was seeking an alternative to the trade routes south through white-ruled Rhodesia.

Within a decade, the line was suffering from repeated breakdowns, landslides, and management failures. Planners had envisioned running 17 trains a day, but by 1978 there were only two. Tanzanians and Zambians tend to lay the railway's chronic operational problems at the doorstep of official corruption. Isaac and Daniel joked about this throughout the trip. For them, revenue-skimming explained every woe, from an unscheduled stop on our first night to replace a part, to an electrical short that plunged our stifling cabin into darkness after Daniel tried to turn on the cabin's antiquated fan.

As an example of top-down, state-driven development, the Tazara had also come up short. Planners had envisioned a new agricultural corridor nearly 10 miles wide on either side of the tracks, doubling regional food production. Yet much of the land—moist black soil and extraordinary verdure—was all but empty. The government had never invested in electrification, schools, or roads near the railway, nor had it provided access to credit so that farmers could buy fertilizer or good seed. During one 90-minute stretch in northeastern Zambia, beginning at Mkushi, I did not see a single farm or village.

The unrealized value of this fallow earth seemed to pain Daniel. And he was quite aware of the opportunity that it represented to foreigners, especially with crops in rising demand worldwide. "The Chinese have already begun coming," he said. "They covet our land. It seems there's no space for people there."

Chinese farmers have been trickling into Africa for years, buying small plots and working them using Chinese techniques. But China began to prioritize large-scale agricultural investment in Africa around the time of the lavish 2006 China-Africa summit in Beijing, a milestone in China's courtship of the continent. At the time, China promised to establish 10 agricultural demonstration centers promoting Chinese farming methods, and to send experts far and wide. Last June, the *Economic Observer,* an independent Chinese weekly newspaper, reported that China, "faced with increasing pressure on food security," was "planning to rent and buy land abroad to expand domestic food supply." Beijing had earmarked $5 billion for agricultural projects in Africa in 2008, with a focus on the production of rice and other cash crops.

Many Chinese agricultural initiatives are shrouded in mystery. In 2006, for instance, China offered a $2 billion soft loan to Mozambique for a project to dam the Zambezi River Valley, amid some of the continent's most fertile soils. The following year,

Chinese and Mozambican officials reportedly signed a memorandum of understanding allowing 3,000 Chinese settlers to begin farming in the area. But following a local uproar, Mozambique's government denied all reports of the plan, and little has been heard of it since.

Officials in Chongqing province—home to roughly 12 million farmers whose land either has already been lost in the flooding that accompanied the construction of the Three Gorges Dam, or is under pressure from urban growth in the province—have publicly encouraged mass emigration to Africa. In September 2007, Li Ruogu, the head of China's Export-Import Bank, told the *South China Morning Post,*

> Chongqing is well experienced in agricultural mass production, while in Africa there is plenty of land but food production is unsatisfactory . . . Chongqing's labour exports have just started, but they will take off once we convince the farmers to become landlords abroad.

Li pledged full financial support to those farmers at the time, but has since distanced himself from those remarks.

"China's interest in agricultural investment—in land—is a hot-button issue," wrote Deborah Bräutigam, a professor at American University and a leading expert on China's economic relations with Africa, in a recent paper. "For many, land is at the heart of a nation's identity, and it is especially easy to raise emotions about outsiders when land is involved."

The stop-and-go quality of major Chinese farming deals and the strong feelings that they've produced suggest that the honeymoon between the Chinese and Africans may not last long. During the course of my trip, land issues seemed to bring out the ugliest biases in the people I spoke to. "If you gave this land to Chinese people to work it, this place would be rich overnight," said one Chinese woman immigrant, a middle-aged trader in southern Congo: "They're too lazy, these Africans." Many Africans, for their part, were intensely wary of Chinese immigration; Daniel told me that this was a particularly raw issue among many of his friends. Conspiracy theories echoed frequently. In Dar, for instance, rumors had spread that the new national sports stadium was part of a secret deal to grant land to Chinese farmers in Tanzania.

Ultimately, the combustibility of Chinese farming initiatives may limit the plans' reach. Even so, Chinese investment in other industries has not slowed, and there's no reason to believe it will. The acquisition of the ores and oil underneath African soil is more easily hidden from public view than that of the land above.

To fully grasp China's economic approach in Africa, one must study European imperial history—as Beijing itself has been doing. "Recently, a very interesting Chinese delegation visited Brussels," I was told by Jonathan Holslag, head of research for the Brussels Institute of Contemporary China Studies. "And they asked to see all the old colonial maps of the Congo. These are the only maps that reflect reasonably accurate surveys of Congo's underground, and they want to use them for development plans in Katanga and elsewhere. If you look at Chinese policy documents, it is very obvious that they are focused on opening up the heart of the continent. There is clearly a long-term strategy for doing this, and it seeks to break up the north-south flow of minerals, to build east-west lines that will allow them to bypass South Africa."

To fully grasp China's economic approach in Africa, one must study European imperial history—as Beijing itself has been doing.

Jamie Monson, a historian of the Tazara line, writes lucidly about this strategy:

To construct a railroad was to command a region—the most famous manifestation of this being Cecil Rhodes's dream of linking "Cape to Cairo" through a continent-wide rail connection. To control a region in turn was to keep rivals out, or at least to restrict their trade participation through tariffs and other regulatory interventions.

The truest intellectual forerunner of China's strategy seems to be a plan once pursued by Germany. Before its defeat in World War I, Germany's leaders had dreamed of a continental empire, a *Mittelafrika* stitched together by railways stretching from Dar es Salaam to the Atlantic Ocean. A northern line from Dar to Moshi was completed in 1912. German surveys of a southern route, essentially the forerunner of the Tazara line, were carried out between 1904 and 1907, but the project was abandoned after a local rebellion against German rule.

Germany's railway schemes were driven by intense competition with Britain. Although China may claim to be a new kind of power, its plans, too, have always had a strategic component, including rivalry with the West, and lately a desire to circumvent the regional economic powerhouse, South Africa, and ultimately control the markets for key African minerals.

To succeed, Germany's *Mittelafrika* would have required cooperation from Belgium and Portugal in order for its trains to traverse the expanse of Congo and Angola on their way to the Indian Ocean. In five short years, China has solved this problem, rebuilding Angola's Benguela railroad and laying the groundwork for a vast new rail-and-road network to be built in Congo, Zambia, and other peripheral countries. China will not turn these railways over to African governments, as it did with the Tazara. Rather, it will retain majority control of its rail investments, operating the railways until its money is recouped by ticket and cargo revenues and by other fees.

The Zambian end of the Tazara line, Kapiri Mposhi, roughly marks the southeastern edge of southern Africa's vast copper belt, one of *Mittelafrika*'s choicest prizes. The Kilimanjaro Express pulled into town 72 hours after leaving Dar—we'd had two big delays along the way, but had been lucky to suffer no major breakdowns.

A scrum of porters and drivers beset the weary, baggage-laden travelers on the platform, competing noisily for the chance to haul the merchandise brought from Tanzanian ports. I met Daniel's wife and son as we disembarked, and we eventually said our goodbyes (Isaac had gotten off the train farther north).

The town itself is a dismal backwater. A desolate market sits behind the giant train station, a jumble of cinder-block storefronts, almost all abandoned and strewn with rubbish. The commerce, such as it is, takes place in a muddy square facing these deserted buildings. There, a handful of crude stalls have been made by lashing rough-hewn wood planks together with cord. Women sit wanly before little pyramids of tomatoes, onions, and oranges. The train, evidently, has not brought prosperity to this place.

Nonetheless, Kapiri Mposhi is a gateway to perhaps the most significant hubs of Chinese activity on the continent. About 120 miles to the south lies Lusaka, where Beijing's presence is long established and Chinese businesses abound. And about 45 miles to the north lies Congo, the stage for China's grandest experiment—and biggest bet—on the continent. I was heading to Lubumbashi, a Congolese mining city of 1.2 million people, where billions of dollars of Chinese investment are, for good or ill, just beginning to make themselves felt.

One of the largest and most populous countries in Africa, the Democratic Republic of the Congo is also perhaps the most star-crossed. It gained independence from Belgium in 1960 and promptly became the site of Africa's first coup d'état. It then suffered for 32 years under the dominion of the American-backed dictator Mobutu Sese Seko, the continent's most corrupt and influential despot. Over the past 10 years, it's been the scene of the world's deadliest conflict since World War II.

In spring 2008, Congo's beleaguered government unveiled a package of Chinese investments totaling $9.3 billion, a figure later reduced, for complex reasons involving International Monetary Fund pressure, to $6 billion—still roughly half of Congo's GDP. China will build massive new copper and cobalt mines; 1,800 miles of railways; 2,000 miles of roads; hundreds of clinics, hospitals, and schools; and two new universities. Speaking before the parliament, Pierre Lumbi, the country's infrastructure minister, compared the package to the Marshall Plan, and called it "the foundation on which the growth of our economy is going to be built."

In exchange, China will get almost 11 million tons of copper and 620,000 tons of cobalt, which it will extract over the next 25 years—a "resource for infrastructure" swap that China first pioneered, on a smaller scale, in Angola in 2004. Congo will choose from a menu of Chinese construction companies—pre-vetted and supplied with credit by China's Export-Import Bank—which typically begin (and end) their work quickly, dispatching hundreds or thousands of workers to do the job.

Much of the Chinese mining activity will center around Lubumbashi, founded by Belgium in 1910 and built up with forced labor in the 1930s. Lubumbashi has long lived by the whims of distant global markets, its booms unfailingly followed by busts. The Belgians, British, Americans, South Africans, and even the Congolese themselves, under Mobutu, have all enjoyed runs there.

During my visit, the city was drenched in seasonal rains, but it bathes year-round in a deep-set shabbiness. Still, traces of charm and bygone ambition survive. An imposing whitewashed courthouse faces a large traffic roundabout circling an antiquated steam locomotive once used to haul copper-laden cars. The once grand European-style post office still stands, though its concourse is given over to Chinese merchants selling cell phones from rickety glass cabinets.

Evidence of Chinese industry is not hard to find in Lubumbashi. In many neighborhoods, Chinese road crews are busy sealing muddy, potholed avenues with asphalt. They're also paving an old dirt route east to Kiniama, and building another road west, to copper-rich Kipushi.

Well before the new ore-for-development deal was signed, the city and its surroundings had become a sort of new Promised Land for Chinese fortune seekers. As copper prices rose fourfold between August 2003 and August 2008, thousands of migrants descended on the region, like forty-niners during the American gold rush. They were drawn by word of mouth about the mineral riches and the ease of doing business here. Congolese officials were reputedly easy to bribe. Visas could be cheaply bought, and so could mining permits, often in the name of poor Congolese front men.

Under a white-hot afternoon sun, I made my way to a vast, Chinese-dominated industrial zone at the city's northern edge, where copper-smelting operations sat behind high walls. There, I met Li Yan, a brisk, 30-ish man who manages a medium-size copper-mining company. Li's company, with its giant smelting oven, heavy rock-crushing equipment, and half-dozen oversize trucks, looks well funded and well run. But he shook his head in disgust as he spoke to me about the copper rush. "There's a belief among Chinese people that they can realize anything," he told me. "But the people who came here had no experience and no preparation. It was like children running around, really a mess."

Many Chinese fortune seekers had hired African work gangs to dig for copper, sometimes even in Lubumbashi's red-clay streets. "They were profiteers and speculators," said one local businessman. "Congo got nothing from them." Most of them dug "no more than 20 feet deep, which requires no investment at all." The government belatedly tried to reassert control, requiring all those who mined copper to smelt it as well, and to make more-substantial investments in equipment, in order to generate more jobs and tax revenue and to make the industry more sustainable. In response, small operators scrambled to build small, inefficient furnaces. In 2008, as prices tumbled from $9,000 a ton to a low of $3,500, the makeshift smelters closed down and the Chinese owners fled, leaving their Congolese workers unpaid and the landscape littered with industrial refuse.

Beijing's giant construction package, of course, is on an entirely different scale than the fly-by-night mine operations that have come and gone in Lubumbashi. But the conditions under which the deal was signed were in many ways similar to those under which many Chinese fortune seekers had obtained their permits. Negotiations, conducted in secret, were entrusted to one of President Joseph Kabila's close personal confidants, a man without a government portfolio. Since then, questions about whose interests are being served by the deal—those of everyday Congolese, or merely those of Kabila's cronies—have multiplied.

In the center of Lubumbashi, just off the roundabout with the old locomotive, I met with Kalej Nkand, director of the Congolese Central Bank for Katanga province. Inside, the bank faintly resembles a musty warehouse—cavernous, dimly lit, and mostly open. It was getting toward lunchtime, and a half-dozen employees sat at metal desks scattered about the office's large open floor. One woman pecked at an antiquated computer; the rest read old newspapers or dozed.

Kalej, a dapper young technocrat in a finely tailored olive suit, welcomed me into the deep chill of his office. In polished French, he told me that Congolese desperation had enabled the worst aspects of the early Chinese copper rush. "Most of these arrangements were negotiated at a time of great difficulty for the Congo because of the war," he said. "It was too easy for people to come, get their product, and take off." He described the big new Chinese package as "bait," with "terms that were a bit unconventional," but nonetheless appealing to a war-torn and bankrupt country.

For the rest of our conversation, Kalej studiously avoided criticizing the deal, often leaning forward and rocking slightly with his hands clasped before his face as he weighed his words. In Congo it was commonly said that President Kabila had bet his presidency on relations with China; for an official to say anything critical could be career-ending, or worse.

"We've got to remember the expectations of the populace," Kalej said. New roads built under the auspices of the deal will link "rural areas with urban centers. People will be able to get their goods to market. The price of produce and other goods will go down." *Such were the dreams for Tazara, too,* I thought, remembering the depressing little market in Kapiri Mposhi.

There was also the nettlesome question of where the new roads would actually go. Many of the package's details have not been released publicly. Word on the street has it that the first, 275-mile section in the long, arching route chosen for the gigantic highway project will lead from Lubumbashi to Pweto, a one-gas-station town of 20,000 people on Lake Mweru that has no industry and few natural resources. Pweto is the hometown of Augustin Katumba Mwanke, the man who negotiated the deal, and he has reportedly built a palatial residence there; with the highway in place, he'll be able to get to it from Lubumbashi in a few hours rather than the two days or more required now.

The company that will build the highway, China Railway, has been laying down another road leading out of Lubumbashi. It stretches eastward, and a crew of dozens of Chinese is working fast to scrape the existing dirt track smooth and complete the building of drainage culverts, before laying asphalt. This one, I discovered, leads to the regional police chief's estate, an immense domain complete with artificial lakes and luxurious guest houses, all enclosed behind a 10-foot-high electrified fence. As we passed, my driver warned nervously that the area was under electronic surveillance and stopping or slowing down would not be prudent.

A prominent Congolese lawyer who is part of a loose citizens' network that is investigating the Chinese package said the deal will leave Congo in the same position it was in after decades of exploitation by Belgium. "We could have said, 'You can have our copper, but we want some of it transformed here.' We've negotiated for billions of dollars without determining if those investments are productive, without thinking through the sequencing of things, without thinking about the creation of a metallurgy industry. We have cheap labor and abundant electricity," so refining would make economic sense. "But we negotiated without experts and without analysis."

I asked whether the huge building program—the roads and schools and hospitals—would produce dividends, and he shook his head grimly. "Six billion dollars in infrastructure is not development. Schools with desks are not going to educate our population. A road is not going to develop this country . . . Schools require a school system, and they need teachers. In this climate, roads last only 10 years without maintenance, and the Congo has no capacity in this regard."

Gilbert Malemba N'Sakila, a former law-school dean in Lubumbashi, expressed similar doubts: "The Chinese are not even making use of Congolese talent. They hire laborers, and that's it." Management and technical expertise are provided almost exclusively by Chinese workers. "When they pack up and go, the Congo will be left with nothing, not even an upgrade in our human resources. Our earth will be dug up, emptied, and left that way."

These views echo—and are informed by—those in Zambia, Congo's copper-rich neighbor to the south, which has a much longer record of business dealings with newly capitalist China. Zambians enthusiastically welcomed investment in 1998, when the China Non-Ferrous Metal Mining Company bought a mothballed copper mine at Chambishi, near the Congo border, for $20 million and promptly invested $100 million in its rehabilitation.

Things turned sour, though, when the new Chinese managers banned union activity and began paying Zambian employees less than the $67-a-month minimum wage. In 2005, more than 50 Zambians were killed in an accidental blast at an explosives factory that served the mine; witnesses said that Chinese staff members had fled the scene moments before the explosion, failing to warn the African employees. A year later, during protests over back pay and work conditions, a Chinese supervisor opened fire on Zambian workers with a shotgun, wounding several.

The turmoil at the Chambishi mine quickly bled into Zambian politics. Michael Sata, the leader of the Patriotic Front party, made China's business practices and growing presence in the country big issues in the presidential election of 2006; China threatened to cut off relations with Zambia if he won. Sata, whose party was young and relatively small at the time, won 28 percent of the vote. In the 2008 election, he won 38 percent, losing the election by just two points.

Few Zambians have been lifted into the middle class by Chinese mining activity, and today, Sata remains unrelenting in his criticisms of China. "Our [Chinese] friends are too numerous, and we know their resources cannot sustain them," Sata told me in his Lusaka office, taking phone calls from constituents and filling out a lottery card as he reeled off a catalog of reproaches. "Zambians . . . do not need labor being dumped here. The Chinese are scattering all over the world, but there is no such thing as Chinese investment, as such. What we're seeing is Chinese parastatals and government interests, and they are corrupting our leaders."

"The idea that big influxes of wealth will help Africa has never really panned out," Patrick Keenan, an Africa specialist at the University of Illinois, told me. "When the path to wealth goes through the presidential palace, there are enormous incentives to obtaining power and to holding on to it. This kind of wealth incites politicians to create economically wasteful projects, and it relieves them of the need to make politically difficult choices, like broadening the tax base."

Indeed, the same objections raised by the Zambian aid critic Dambisa Moyo—that foreign aid breeds corrupt, lazy, and ineffective government—can be applied toward any foreign investments that focus on mineral extraction, especially ones that deliver cash and services directly to governments with no conditions attached. All things considered, resource-based or infrastructure-driven development—even development as massive as the ongoing Chinese wave—appear unlikely to lead to a meaningful African renaissance.

China's rise, it is worth noting, did not begin with highways or factories or gleaming cities. It began with agriculture and rural development. "It is true that China has pushed infrastructure development, but that only began two decades after economic growth had taken off," says Justin Yifu Lin, who is the chief economist of the World Bank and the highest-ranking Chinese national in any international financial institution. "Providing economic incentive to farmers, incentives to workers, attracting foreign investment—those were the priorities at the beginning."

Many African farmers, Lin told me, "would strongly benefit from simple technology, like cheap diesel pumps to irrigate their fields." Chinese involvement in agriculture, he believes, could make a big difference. Through investment and demonstration, Chinese farmers could serve as an important catalyst in an African economic takeoff, much as they did a generation ago in China itself.

But agricultural transformation is the most unlikely part of the Chinese project. Farming, of course, takes place in plain view, and foreign encroachment on fertile land raises passions; African governments are likely to find it easier and more profitable to sell oil and mineral rights. Song Tingming, an official at a Chinese agricultural trade group, told the *Economic Observer* that he believes the best time for China to develop agriculture overseas has probably passed, because the purchase of farmland has become a hot-button issue, with Korea and some Persian Gulf states having already made or attempted big farmland investments in Africa.

And ironically, while Beijing is extremely well-positioned to help Africa improve its governance—a second area of great need throughout much of the continent—it seems deeply reluctant to do so. No developing country has understood the importance of a strong, results-oriented public administration better than China. But so far, in part because of China's history of subjugation by Westerners, as well as its defensive stance over its human-rights record, Beijing has remained attached to its rhetoric about noninterference.

Everywhere I traveled in Africa, people spoke in defense of conditionality—the attachment of good-governance strings to loans from the West. "Many people look at Western conditions as a good thing, because nowadays so many things can be discussed openly, unlike the past—like corruption, for example," said John Kulekana, a veteran Tanzanian journalist. "There are no more demigods here, and that is because of the growth of civil society, which has received lots of help from the West. Former ministers are called to account for their behavior. We are building accountability."

Well-governed states—where the people have a real say in choosing their leaders, where national priorities are openly discussed, and where legal institutions are strong—will undoubtedly benefit in lasting ways from Chinese commercial partnerships. But commercial partnerships alone seem unlikely to lead to good governance or enduring prosperity. A see-no-evil approach to governance would leave many countries with depleted resource bases and stunted political institutions, even as their population continues to grow rapidly.

Africans' attitudes toward China's recent initiatives on their continent are perhaps inevitably riddled with ambivalence. Many African intellectuals bridle at Western criticism of China's African full-court press. The West, they say, has long patronized their continent, and since the end of the Cold War, has subjected it to outright neglect. And all of that is true. But the question remains: How does their continent overcome a pattern of extractive foreign engagement—beginning with its first contact with Europe, when gold or slaves were acquired in exchange for cloth and trinkets—that is still discernible today?

This question, which one hears almost everywhere, was addressed most powerfully by the Congolese lawyer I met in

Lubumbashi. He received me in his office in his downtown home, where he bathes in water collected from an old parabolic satellite dish, and where he says the mail gets delivered once or twice a year, after he pays a bribe to the post office.

I asked him if the arrival of the Chinese was a new and great opportunity for the continent, as some have said. "The problem is not who is the latest buyer of our commodities," he replied. "The problem is to determine what is Africa's place in the future of the global economy, and up to now, we have seen very little that is new. China is taking the place of the West: they take our raw materials and they sell finished goods to the world . . . What Africans are getting in exchange, whether it is roads or schools or finished goods, doesn't really matter. We remain under the same old schema: our cobalt goes off to China in the form of dusty ore and returns here in the form of expensive batteries."

Critical Thinking

1. Describe the main types of investments China is making throughout Africa.
2. Explain why Chinese private and public firms have increased their investments in Africa so much in recent years.
3. Provide three reasons why many Africans welcome increased Chinese investments in their country and throughout the continent.
4. Explain why some Africans are critical or at least weary about the recent large increases in Chinese investments.

HOWARD W. FRENCH is the author of *A Continent for the Taking: The Tragedy and Hope of Africa.* He teaches at the Columbia University Graduate School of Journalism.

Obama and Latin America:
New Beginnings, Old Frictions

"Signs of frustration are unmistakable in Washington and in many Latin American capitals, despite Obama's immense personal appeal and the continued promise of a more productive partnership."

MICHAEL SHIFTER

Hugo Chávez's speech to the United Nations General Assembly on September 24, 2009, did not receive much attention. The speech was notably more restrained than his famous address on the same occasion three years earlier, in which the Venezuelan president had called George W. Bush the "devil" and referred to the "smell of sulfur." This time Chávez was forced to depart from his usual, incendiary script because of Barack Obama's favorable image and his preference for engagement—"We will extend a hand if you are willing to unclench your fist," the US president had declared in his inaugural address. Indeed, Chávez said the smell of sulfur had been replaced by "the smell of hope."

Nonetheless, Chávez—ever resourceful—hinted at what might become a common view regarding Obama's approach toward Latin America and the Caribbean. He referred to "two Obamas," one projecting a friendly, conciliatory image, and the other adhering to the course of Obama's predecessors, who typically treated the region as the "backyard" of the United States. Chávez raised doubts about whether old practices and concepts would in fact give way to more genuine and equitable cooperation. His speech referred directly to three issues that caused friction in hemispheric relations in 2009: Cuba policy, the US military presence in Colombia, and the Honduras crisis.

Three issues caused friction in hemispheric relations in 2009: Cuba policy, the US military presence in Colombia, and the Honduras crisis.

The past year has actually seen relatively little substantive change on a number of longstanding disputes. And toward the end of 2009, inter-American strains were further aggravated by the sensitive question of Iran's growing involvement in the region. The November visit of Iranian President Mahmoud Ahmadinejad to Venezuela, Bolivia, and, most significantly, Brazil coincided with deepening concerns in Washington and the international community about Iran's nuclear program.

The implications of the visit were serious enough that Secretary of State Hillary Clinton warned Latin American countries on December 11 that "if people want to flirt with Iran, they should take a look at what the consequences might well be for them." These words had a familiar ring, and predictably elicited a response from Chávez about "threats" leveled by the US government.

Also disconcerting, if not unexpected, for many Latin Americans was the absence of a sustained, high-level focus on the region during the first year of the Obama administration. Granted, the new president was inundated from the outset, and many other issues—from the economic crisis to health reform to changing conditions in Afghanistan—understandably took precedence. But Latin Americans were dismayed that a new assistant secretary for Western Hemisphere affairs was not in place until the end of November, and that Latin American policy degenerated into partisan bickering over issues like Honduras. Today, signs of frustration are unmistakable in Washington and in many Latin American capitals, despite Obama's immense personal appeal and the continued promise of a more productive partnership.

The Mood Swing

The fifth Summit of the Americas, involving every democratically elected head of state in the region, was fortuitously scheduled less than three months after Obama's historic inauguration. The summit in Trinidad and Tobago provided the new US president with an introduction to the region's leaders, political idiosyncrasies, and complex challenges. Obama had never been south of the border before, though he did stop in Mexico on his way to the summit. His prior meetings with Mexican President Felipe Calderón and Brazilian President Luiz Inácio

Lula da Silva were well orchestrated and entirely appropriate, given the importance of both countries.

Not surprisingly, the spotlight at the summit was on Obama, who aroused considerable curiosity. He performed in exemplary fashion, setting a refreshingly moderate tone, promising a "new beginning," and extending a hand even to hostile leaders such as Chávez. While this overture was somewhat controversial at home, Obama showed regional leaders that he would not view the Americas in ideological terms, as a region sharply divided between friends and adversaries. Rather, Obama called for "mutual respect," and although he was not the first US president to do so, his personal background and story lent the pledge greater credibility.

Further, Obama's decision to close the detention facility at Guantánamo Bay, Cuba—although implementation has been bogged down—was an enormously important and positive signal to the region. Obama also acknowledged failure regarding the two principal sources of irritation in US–Latin American relations: Cuba and counternarcotics policies. He promised to work cooperatively in devising alternative approaches to these and other questions on the hemispheric agenda.

At the very least, Obama's debut on the regional stage was highly successful in improving the mood in US–Latin American relations. Obama's likeability contrasted sharply with his predecessor's, significantly enhancing the favorable image of the United States. For example, according to the Pew Research Center, in Brazil last year confidence in Obama was at 76 percent, a dramatic jump from the 17 percent that Bush registered in 2008. A Latin American Barometer poll revealed an increase in the United States' favorability from 58 percent in 2008 to 74 percent in 2009—the highest rating ever reached by the United States since the survey began in 1995.

This shift mirrors a global upward trend and represents no meager accomplishment for the new administration. Improvement in America's image, though no substitute for substantive policy gains, is an essential step toward repairing the damage of preceding years and rebuilding trust in US foreign policy.

Along with projecting a friendlier face to the world, Obama's other major achievement in his first year was averting a widely feared economic collapse and all of its likely repercussions. In Latin America there was enormous apprehension about how the financial crisis would affect a region that had endured more than its share of such crises (even though this time the problem originated in the United States). To its great credit, Latin America largely avoided the effects of the economic turmoil; Brazil's quick rebound was particularly impressive.

By adopting effective economic measures, Obama in effect heeded Lula's suggestion that the best thing the United States could do for Latin America was to put its own economic house in order. Although severe problems in the region remain, including high unemployment, the worst-case scenarios were fortunately never realized. With the notable exception of Mexico, whose economy contracted by more than 7 percent in 2009, Latin America weathered the financial crisis substantially better than most experts predicted.

The Honduras Surprise

No one expected when Obama took office that Honduras would become an important test for the administration's new approaches toward democracy, relations with Latin American partners, and multilateral cooperation. Yet after Manuel Zelaya, the democratically elected president, was ousted by the Honduran military on June 28, a series of reactions—sometimes with comic opera qualities—ended up severely complicating US–Latin American relations.

The Obama administration's condemnation of the coup—Zelaya's prior unconstitutional power grab did not offset or justify such an egregious violation of the democratic order—was swift and firm. Obama said the coup was "illegal" and set a "terrible precedent." The president was keen to be on the "right side" of this issue, to work in concert with Latin American neighbors, and try to distinguish himself from Bush, whose administration had conveyed undisguised glee after a coup temporarily removed Chávez from power in April 2002. In what turned out to be an instance of remarkable political consensus, the United States and every other country in the hemisphere adopted a punitive stance toward the de facto regime in Honduras, pressing for Zelaya's return.

The regional consensus against the coup can be attributed to two factors in addition to the US reaction. The first is that Zelaya was a Chávez ally, which led the Venezuelan president and his supporters in the Bolivarian Alliance for the Peoples of our Americas (ALBA) to take a forceful stand. (Honduras had joined ALBA in 2008. Other ALBA members, besides Venezuela, include Cuba, Bolivia, Nicaragua, Ecuador, and a number of Caribbean nations.)

In addition, although some coups have occurred in Latin America in recent years (even military coups, such as Ecuador's in 2000), this one touched a nerve in the region. A widely shared calculation, which turned out to be entirely incorrect, was that a unified, principled position in the hemisphere would lead to a practical solution. Honduras's de facto government, it was believed, would be forced to succumb to sustained international pressure. As it happened, nearly everyone underestimated the government's resistance and ability to delay, as it ran out the clock until an election that had already been scheduled for November 2009.

As the crisis dragged on, the Obama administration tried to pursue a middle ground, which provoked criticism from both sides. Washington was reluctant to impose a solution and apply the full force of trade sanctions, though the Obama administration consistently insisted on Zelaya's return and employed some pressure on the de facto government (by withholding aid, for example). For such perceived ambivalence, Obama was criticized by some Latin American governments, such as Brazil's, which called on Washington to exercise its disproportionate leverage to ensure Zelaya's return. The calls for a more heavy-handed US approach seemed to irk Obama, who noted in August "the irony that the people that were complaining about the US interfering in Latin America are now complaining that we are not interfering enough."

At the same time, the Honduras controversy quickly became mired in US domestic politics. Some congressional Democrats echoed Brazil's sentiments. Republicans, however, were upset that Obama was pushing so vigorously for the return of Zelaya, an ally of the anti-US Chávez. They criticized what they perceived to be Zelaya's anti-democratic conduct and lauded the de facto government's resistance.

Republicans were particularly enraged when the Obama administration announced that it would not recognize the November 29 elections unless Zelaya presided over them. Jim DeMint, a Republican senator from South Carolina, was the most conspicuous critic of the administration's policy, expressing his disapproval by holding up the appointments of Arturo Valenzuela as assistant secretary of state and Thomas Shannon as ambassador to Brazil. The acrimony and partisan discord in Washington were reminiscent of the cold war battles that played out regarding Central America a generation ago.

In October, with the election in Honduras fast approaching, it became increasingly clear that efforts to resolve the issue pursued by the Organization of American States (OAS) and Costa Rican President Óscar Arias were unlikely to bear fruit. The de facto Honduran government showed no sign that it would allow Zelaya (who had been holed up in the Brazilian embassy since September) to return to the presidency. The Obama administration, eager to resolve both the Honduras crisis itself and the domestic political dispute regarding Honduras that jeopardized its Latin America policy, undertook a diplomatic mission that resulted in both Honduran parties signing an accord.

According to the agreement, Zelaya could return to power with the approval of the Honduran Congress, and the November election would proceed with everyone accepting the results. Although many initially applauded the accord as a breakthrough that would end the crisis, it soon became clear that the two sides interpreted the agreement differently, leaving the deadlock unresolved.

With the accord, the Obama administration decided that it would recognize the outcome of the election, leaving as a separate matter, and one in the hands of the Honduran Congress, the question of Zelaya's return to office. This distinction left Washington sharply at odds with other Latin American governments, which said they would recognize the election only if Zelaya were allowed to return.

Honduras's Congress in the end withheld its approval. But the US administration reckoned that if the elections proceeded reasonably well—with the result seen as legitimate by most Hondurans—then other governments would eventually come around to recognizing and dealing with the new government. (As a result of this policy stance, DeMint lifted his hold on the appointments of Valenzuela and Shannon.)

Porfirio Lobo of Honduras's National Party was elected the country's next president, and some governments have already joined the United States in recognizing the outcome. In this context, prospects for a solution to the Zelaya issue appear increasingly likely, preparing the ground for Honduras to resume full diplomatic and economic relations in the hemisphere.

For the Obama administration, the crisis is instructive in several respects. While the administration quickly and properly adopted a principled and punitive stand alongside its Latin American partners, it misread conditions on the ground

in Honduras, hindering a practical solution. Moreover, the administration's on-again, off-again involvement in the crisis hampered its ability to strike the delicate balance between supporting cooperative, hemispheric approaches and trying to shape a favorable outcome.

A tight economic relationship between Honduras and the United States made it even more crucial that the United States play such a diplomatic role. Yet the Obama administration, perhaps in a rush to resolve the crisis and partly as a result of domestic political problems, ended up carrying out a policy that left its Latin American friends unhappy, both because they were not adequately consulted and because they did not endorse the terms of the accord.

Colombia Confusion

A lack of consultation and of adequate diplomatic groundwork has also strained US–Latin American relations on another key issue: an agreement between Washington and Bogotá for US access to seven Colombian bases used for combating drugs and that country's insurgencies. The 10-year pact, news of which leaked in Colombia in August—it was signed at the end of October—has revived suspicions in South America about US military motives in the region. The announcement of the agreement, ineptly managed, struck Latin Americans as incongruous with the spirit of the Obama administration's stated regional approach.

The agreement moved forward and reached completion through inertia—it had been in the works during the Bush administration—and it was championed by the government of Colombian President Álvaro Uribe. In Colombia it was sold as a way to ensure the country's security in the face of potentially aggressive moves by Chávez. In Washington, the accord was driven by bureaucratic agencies, particularly the Defense Department's Southern Command, with scant strategic or political vision. A serious review of this military cooperation pact—and how it would be perceived in Latin America—was by all accounts not undertaken with the right focus and energy.

The deal was a political gift for Chávez, giving him new ammunition for his anti-US tirades. Chávez has long used the substantial security collaboration between the United States and Colombia as evidence of a military threat to his country and as justification for his own military spending, which has included the purchase of an estimated $5 billion to $7 billion worth of arms from Russia alone.

Venezuela's ambassador in Washington, Bernardo Álvarez, wrote in December that the agreement's "vague provisions and questionable motivations threaten regional stability and territorial sovereignty, alter the region's military balance, and threaten to push more of the violence and drug trafficking that is endemic to Colombia's conflict across its borders." Chávez has been unrelenting in his criticism, seizing on the pact to attack the Obama administration. In fact, it was predictable that the Venezuelan president, feeling increasingly encircled in the region and politically vulnerable at home, would lash out.

The Obama administration has responded by insisting that the agreement merely formalizes the existing security relationship with Colombia and does not signify an increased US military presence in the country (the current cap is 800 US military personnel and 600 private contractors) or any operation beyond Colombia's borders. It is doubtful, given Washington's other preoccupations and policy priorities in the region, that it has any interest whatsoever in carrying out the activities suggested by Chávez and others in Latin America.

Still, it is unclear that the new agreement was even necessary for achieving US policy goals. And even if the deal were deemed essential, it should have been accompanied by a high-level diplomatic effort and communications strategy aimed at assuaging persistent, understandable concerns among Latin American friends like Brazil about the role of the US military in the region.

Perhaps the most damaging aspect of the Colombia base agreement for US–Latin American relations has been the strong reaction registered by Brazil's government. The Brazilians, after all, just a year ago launched the Union of South American Nations, which is modeled after the European Union and seeks to deal with defense issues as part of a wide-ranging regional agenda.

Any agreement regarding the United States and its evolving security role in South America was bound to generate suspicion and controversy, so prior consultations with senior officials of the continent's leading power should have been a top priority. Although Brazilian criticism of the United States on this issue may have been overblown, Washington should have been able to anticipate such a reaction.

Cuba, Again

As Obama quickly discovered at the summit meeting in Trinidad and Tobago, no issue unifies Latin America in its posture toward the United States as much as the decades-long US embargo against Cuba. Obama's election to the presidency—including his victory in Florida, which has a sizeable Cuban-American community—was thought to signal a greater openness to ending the anachronistic embargo and engaging Cuba instead.

Obama fulfilled his campaign promises to lift Bush-era restrictions on travel and remittances by Cuban-Americans, and to authorize new US investments in telecommunications in Cuba. The administration renewed dialogue on migration and engaged in negotiations to establish regular postal service. The moves so far have been modest and incremental, but they clearly point to a more open-minded approach toward Cuba and a sharp departure from Bush administration policies.

Nonetheless, it is clear that lifting the embargo—as most Latin Americans have called for— remains politically unrealistic absent significant steps toward reform on Cuba's part, such as releasing political prisoners or holding free and fair elections. And there is no indication that Cuban President Raúl Castro intends to adopt such changes any time soon. The more politically feasible step of lifting a travel ban for all Americans has some congressional momentum, but some congressional resistance as well, and the Obama administration has been cautious.

Another key development affecting US–Latin American relations was lifting Cuba's suspension from the OAS, which

had lasted 47 years. This change came at the OAS General Assembly meeting in Honduras in early June, when a resolution that set a path for Cuba's return to the organization was unanimously approved (even though to date Cuba has shown no interest in coming back).

Although the resolution contained some political conditions and reflected a sound compromise, the process caused some irritation on both sides. Washington wanted tougher conditions, and some Latin American governments—especially the ALBA bloc—pressed for a resolution without conditions. The Obama administration preferred a more cautious, deliberate approach to an issue that in the United States remains highly charged.

The Real Agenda

The Obama administration's pragmatic and realist foreign policy orientation has logically meant an interest in deepening relationships with the two most significant Latin American countries: Brazil and Mexico. From the outset of his administration, Obama seems to have grasped the vital importance of Brazil in helping to advance US interests and priorities in the region. Brazil, increasingly active and influential in global forums such as the Group of 20, and with aspirations to gain a seat on the United Nations Security Council, is regarded as a central player on issues such as energy, climate change, nonproliferation, and the Doha round of trade negotiations.

During Obama's first year as president, the US-Brazil relationship regarding these and other global questions has been somewhat more productive than it has been regarding issues on the regional agenda, especially Honduras, the Colombian bases, and Cuba. Also, as mentioned, the Ahmadinejad visit to Brazil in late November provoked concern in Washington, particularly among some members of Congress. Differences on these issues highlight contrasting political realities and conflicting priorities in Washington and Brasília.

In Mexico, on the other hand, the realities of relentless crime and violence—aggravated by that country's profound economic crisis in 2009—have only deepened Mexico's ties with the United States. The bilateral agenda is impressively broad, encompassing issues such as trade, immigration, drugs, human rights, and the environment. To be sure, frustration remains on both sides. Washington wants the Calderón administration to push for long-awaited structural reforms. Many Mexicans resent unabated US demand for drugs, a continued flow of arms and drug money into their own country, lack of progress on immigration reform, and restrictions on Mexican trucks operating north of the border.

Nonetheless, the Obama administration is building on remarkable advances in the institutionalization of this essential relationship—in the executive, legislative, and judicial branches of government—an institutionalization that has evolved in recent years and has ensured reasonably effective management of problems when they emerge.

The Mexican case dramatically illustrates the pernicious consequences of organized crime throughout the Americas, much of it fueled by the drug trade. With the selection of former Seattle police chief R. Gil Kerlikowske as the head of the

US Office of National Drug Control Policy, or "drug czar," the Obama administration signaled a shift in strategy that would concentrate more resources and attention on reducing demand and consumption in the United States.

However, while widespread dissatisfaction with supply-side counternarcotics policies persists in Washington, there is still no alternative approach backed by political consensus to supplant this admittedly flawed strategy. A special commission on drug policy in the Americas, an initiative of the House Subcommittee on Western Hemisphere Affairs, will, pending Senate approval, be established to review Washington's current anti-drug approach and come up with recommendations for a more effective policy. Such a serious policy review is likely to be welcomed throughout Latin America, where a special regional commission headed by former presidents Fernando Henrique Cardoso (Brazil), Ernesto Zedillo (Mexico), and César Gaviria (Colombia) has highlighted the drug trade's detrimental effect on the rule of law and democratic governance.

On two other matters of great concern in Latin America—immigration and trade—the Obama administration has moved slowly, if at all. Both issues are politically contentious and risky to handle. Obama and the Democrat-controlled Congress have signaled, however, that they plan to undertake comprehensive immigration reform in 2010.

On two matters of great concern in Latin America—immigration and trade—the Obama administration has moved slowly, if at all.

The Hispanic congressional caucus in particular has applied enormous pressure on the administration to fix a broken and irrational immigration system, and to regularize the status of an estimated 12 million undocumented workers in the United States. Moving reform forward is apt to be difficult and will hinge on economic conditions and the unemployment picture. But at least there appears to be a will to pursue reform, and a strong political constituency is pushing hard for it.

On trade questions, in contrast, the Obama administration has been notably indifferent. Trade is much lower on the policy agenda than immigration, and is particularly sensitive with unions, an important Democratic Party constituency. To date, there is no indication the US Congress will soon approve a pending trade pact with Panama and particularly a more controversial deal with Colombia. The Free Trade Area of the Americas—the chief hemispheric goal that emerged from the first Summit of the Americas in 1994—is essentially moribund, with weak support in Washington and most Latin American capitals.

Tempering Expectations

Then-President Bill Clinton presided over that first summit, which was held in Miami, and which reflected considerable optimism for hemispheric cooperation. But Clinton also presided over the approval of a $1.3 billion counternarcotics assistance package in 2000, known as Plan Colombia. Whatever that program's merits, it was fundamentally bilateral and it heavily emphasized security assistance. Predictably, it was harshly denounced and wildly unpopular throughout Latin America. Clinton, though, somehow managed to escape criticism in the region for what was regarded as a misguided effort.

Obama may face a similar challenge in Latin America. While he is likely to remain an enormously popular and appealing figure, US policies will continue to attract criticism in the region, especially in the absence of a clear, strategic concept guiding future decisions. The costs of the Honduras crisis and the US-Colombia base agreement resulted from an abiding mix of intermittent policy attention, failure to consult widely, and inability to take fully into account Latin American concerns and sensibilities.

US policies will continue to attract criticism in the absence of a clear, strategic concept guiding future decisions.

This is not to say that more effective policy management and deeper understanding of the region would necessarily yield policy convergence. On the contrary, what is most instructive about the various episodes in US–Latin American relations during Obama's first year in office is the extent to which sharply contrasting political realities and constraints render cooperation on a range of issues much more difficult. The fundamental task is to minimize unnecessary irritations and to identify which of the political realities are most worthy of substantial investment of diplomatic and economic resources.

In this regard, the devastating earthquake in Haiti on January 12, 2010—described by former President Clinton as "one of the great humanitarian emergencies in the history of the Americas"—presented a particularly compelling need and opportunity for high levels of US commitment, combined with regional collaboration. Although Haiti, the Western Hemisphere's poorest country, has long been neglected and has not fit easily in any subregional group, it nonetheless illustrates the possibilities for effective multilateralism. The presence of 7,000 peacekeepers serving with a seven-year-old United Nations mission—including significant and varied Latin American representation, led by Brazil—had already marked a step forward in redressing Haiti's traditional isolation from collective hemispheric endeavors.

The Obama administration's notably swift and forceful response to the Haiti tragedy, and its interest in working in concert with Latin American neighbors, could help the United States recover some lost ground in inter-American relations this year, and could replenish a measure of goodwill with countries such as Brazil. Washington's response also serves as a reminder that, under some circumstances—and despite the recent emergence of exclusively Latin American groupings—the United States is uniquely suited and well-positioned to play a significant role in addressing critical regional challenges and advancing shared interests.

Nonetheless, it is important not to overstate the possible effects of the Haiti calamity for improving US–Latin American relations. Indeed, what was most striking about an ALBA meeting held in Havana in mid-December was that the pronouncements that came out of it about Obama were barely distinguishable from those aimed at Bush in preceding years. Chávez read a note from Fidel Castro, who had previously praised Obama, now saying "empire is on the offensive again. . . . under the friendly smile and African-American face of Barack Obama." Such language may not predict behavior, and it should not stop the Obama administration from looking for ways to engage ALBA members. But it does offer a dose of realism about what can be reasonably expected from a set of governments led by Chávez and his allies.

The continuing irritations in relations between the United States and Latin America make it all the more urgent that the Obama administration extensively consult with and even more deeply engage the most significant and largely friendly governments in the region, such as Brazil, Mexico, Chile, Colombia, and Peru—as well as some select nations like El Salvador and the Dominican Republic in too often overlooked Central America and the Caribbean.

Bolstering such ties and offering concrete reassurances of genuine partnership should be at the top of Washington's agenda in the Americas. The critical challenge is to pursue priorities of mutual interest and to avoid fueling polarization and getting sidetracked.

Critical Thinking

1. List two examples of how one or more Latin American states have tried to diversify their relationships beyond the United States in recent years.

2. Explain why many Latin American countries want to diversify their relationships and alliances beyond their northern neighbor.

3. Give an example of an important foreign policy dispute in recent years where many Latin American countries had very different positions due to differing interests from those of the United States.

MICHAEL SHIFTER, a *Current History* contributing editor, is vice president for policy at the Inter-American Dialogue and an adjunct professor at Georgetown University.

From *Current History,* February 2010, pp. 67–73. Copyright © 2010 by Current History, Inc. Reprinted by permission.

UNIT 6

Conflicts among Nation-States in the Global South, Sub-National Conflicts, and the Role of Non-State Actors in an Interdependent World

Unit Selections

Learning Objectives

- Provide some examples of how organized crime in Iraq complicated United States efforts to establish a stable Iraq.
- Why is organized crime likely to increase in Iraq in the future?
- Explain why some analysts call Guinea Bissau Africa's first narco-state.
- Explain why opportunistic conflicts in Africa may never end developing world.
- Explain why several Middle East investors targeted Ethiopia for new commercial agri-businesses.

Student Website
www.mhhe.com/cls

Internet References

George Mason's Center for Global Policy
http://globalpolicy.gmu.edu
George Mason's Terrorism, Transnational Crime, and Corruption Center (TraCCC)
http://policy-traccc.gmu.edu/abouttraccc/whoweare.html
U.S. Central Command (CENTCOM)
www.centcom.mil
AllAfrica.com
http://allafrica.com
Douglas Farah's Blog
www.douglasfarah.com/presentations.shtml

Civil wars are now the most common form of warfare in International Relations. Civil conflicts are extremely costly in terms of the number of lives lost, the damage to the local economy and environment, and the violence and disruption that spills over into neighboring countries. The durations of such conflicts vary widely depending on several factors. For example, when one or both parties are able to fund their cause with the proceeds from contraband such as opium, diamonds, or coca, the conflict tends to be a protracted affair. One dramatic example of this destructive trend is ongoing violence in the Congo, now called the Democratic Republic of the Congo. The second civil war in the Democratic Republic of the Congo (DRC) escalated to become Africa's first continental war. More lives were lost during the conflict than during World War II. Before, during and in the aftermath of this inter-state conflict, millions of refugees and civilians suffered at the hands of rival militias backed by governments and rebel groups. Virtually all of the actors in this conflict, including African Union/UN peacekeepers, have been accused of participating in illicit smuggling for self-enrichment reasons or to fund additional fighting.

Criminality is becoming an increasingly important aspect of other types of international conflicts as well. Phil Williams, in "Organized Crime in Iraq: Strategic Surprise and Lessons for Future Contingencies," details how the United States was surprised after the invasion of Iraq in 2003 by the "rise of organized crime and its emergence as a postconflict spoiler." This development was simply not anticipated and was a major destabilizing factor increasing the sense of lawlessness and public insecurity, undermining the efforts to regenerate the economy, and financing the violent opposition to the occupation forces. Attempts to counter crime remains fragmented and organized crime is likely to increase after the United States withdrawal and given the continued weakness of the Iraqi state.

Transnational criminal networks now span several continents. Illicit networks dedicated to moving and selling drugs, stolen merchandise, women, children, or able-bodied men looking for work are often global in scope. Some of these networks have the capacity to adapt quickly to shift transport hubs in response to governmental or regional crackdowns on crime to to other locations in the world. These actors often complicate ongoing domestic and international conflicts further. For example, as pressure increased on Latin America drug smugglers in the Caribbean and North America as part of the U.S.-led War on Drugs throughout the Western Hemisphere and due to an increase in demand for cocaine from Europe, some Latin American drug cartels shifted their smuggling routes from Colombia to Venezuela so they could more efficiently ship drugs by sea and air to West African states that have become new transit posts before cocaine is moved to Europe. These new criminal operations are disrupting and aggravating fragile efforts to restore peace in weak states, many of whom are still recovering from decades of civil conflict. In Guinea Bissau during 2009, the military killed the president in his urban home in the capital city of Bissau shortly after the Chief of the Military was killed in a bomb blast. No one was ever charged with the bomb blast, which contained materials never seen before in West Africa and a trigger

© www.marines.mil/unit/marforaf/PublishingImages/100211-M-1273D-004.JPG

purchased in Thailand. Many suspected Latin American drug cartel involvement in the killing of the Chief of the Military and several commentators now routinely refer to Guinea Bissau as the first de facto narco-state in Africa. Despite efforts by international and regional authorities to support security reform in Guinea Bissau, Latin American drug networks continue to use Guinea Bissau and other states in West Africa to smuggle illicit shipments of cocaine to Europe.

While millions of civilians are at risk of starvation due to civil and international conflicts, many of these conflicts are unlikely to end quickly. In "Africa's Forever Wars," Jeffrey Gettleman describes the harsh reality that some of Africa's most brutal wars may never end because they are not really wars in the traditional sense but rather "opportunistic, heavily armed banditry" by groups who assault civilians, rape women, and capture children to become child soldiers. According to Gettleman, the only way to stop these rebels is to kill the leaders who head these gangs rather than liberation movements. To support his thesis, Gettleman uses anecdotes from his interactions with several recent militias including Nkunda, former head of one of the militias in the eastern Congo, and Joseph Kony, leader of the Lord's Resistance Army.

Such prolonged conflicts, along with other man-made causes and weather fluctuations, create food shortages that aggravate the suffering of millions who are already malnourished or starving. Such shortages can develop very rapidly as was the case for world supplies of wheat in 2010. After losing much of the winter wheat crop, the government of Russia banned further wheat exports, which led to an immediate increase in wheat prices. One immediate result was the increase in the price of basic staples in poor countries, including Mozambique, where price increases for food staples resulted in widespread urban riots. As basic food supplies become scarce for prolonged periods due to weather and man-made disruptions, investors are looking further afield for new areas in the developing world to invest in commercial agri-businesses. The first losers are often subsistence farmers and urban dwellers whose governments cannot afford to purchase enough staples to sell at subsidized prices.

Organized Crime in Iraq: Strategic Surprise and Lessons for Future Contingencies

Dr. Phil Williams

After the invasion of Iraq in March 2003, the United States encountered a series of strategic surprises, including the hostility to the occupation, the fragility of Iraq's infrastructure, and the fractious nature of Iraqi politics. One of the least spectacular but most significant of these surprises was the rise of organized crime and its emergence as a postconflict spoiler. This development was simply not anticipated. Organized crime in Iraq in the months and years after March 2003 emerged as a major destabilizing influence, increasing the sense of lawlessness and public insecurity, undermining the efforts to regenerate the economy, and financing the violent opposition to the occupation forces. In 2003, the theft of copper from downed electric pylons made the restoration of power to the national grid much more difficult. In 2008, the capacity to generate funds through criminal activities enabled al Qaeda in Iraq (AQI) to continue resisting both the U.S. military and the Iraqi government. Moreover, with the planned U.S. withdrawal from Iraq, organized crime in the country will continue to flourish by maintaining well established crime-corruption networks. It might also expand by exploiting the continued weakness of the Iraqi state.

Although the ability of the U.S. Army and Marine Corps to adapt to conditions on the ground contributed enormously to a transformation in the security environment from 2005–2006 to 2007–2008, attempts to combat organized crime remained fragmented and sporadic. For the most part, organized crime remains peripheral to the core roles and missions for the U.S. military. The Department of Justice has several important programs in Iraq, as part of what is intended as a whole-of-government approach. Nevertheless, combating organized crime remains a low priority for the United States. Even though organized crime made the establishment of stability and security both more complicated and more costly, it is not clear that the lessons from this experience have been integrated into U.S. strategic thinking about Iraq, let alone strategic planning for similar contingencies elsewhere.

Against this background, this article delineates the key dimensions of organized crime in Iraq, identifies a number of factors that contributed to strategic surprise, and identifies several ways of reducing the prospects for similar surprises in future contingencies.

Dimensions of Organized Crime

In many respects, the intervention into Iraq was a rude awakening for the United States. It was not simply that Washington was ill prepared for the kind of resistance that developed, although that was clearly the case. The U.S. military, after several false starts, did a remarkable job of competitive adaptation to the environment and to its adversaries—a process that contributed enormously to the turnaround in 2007 and 2008. Yet the lessons from Iraq are not simply about the importance of counterinsurgency doctrine and strategy; they are about the need to go beyond a partial understanding of phenomena becoming stronger and more pervasive in a globalized world.

Organized crime in Iraq is neither an outlier nor an aberration; rather, it is a central feature of much of the global periphery. Indeed, insofar as there is integration of the periphery into the global economy, it has a lot of negatives. These became evident during the 1990s when the Cali drug trafficking organization, led by the Rodriguez Orejuela brothers and Santacruz Londono, became—at least for a few years—the developing world's most successful transnational corporation. Today, Afghanistan is hardly integrated into the licit global economy at all, yet it is a major supplier of one of the most lucrative products in the illicit global economy, where the problem is not a lack of integration but the embedding of local opium and heroin production in global trafficking and supply networks. In Iraq, the main moneymaker for organized crime, corrupt politicians, and officials (as well as insurgents, militias, and jihadis) was not drugs but oil. In spite of the important distinction between a product subject to prohibition and one under the monopoly control of a particular government, oil in Iraq was as important to organized crime and to the insurgency as opium is to warlords, criminal organizations, and the Taliban in Afghanistan. The theft, diversion, and smuggling of oil became a national pastime in Iraq, feeding into the coffers of insurgent and jihadi organizations, the militias, tribal groups, and criminal organizations alike. In fact, criminality related to the oil business had several different dimensions: the theft and smuggling of crude oil from the Al Basra oil terminal; the diversion, black market sale, or illicit reexport of imported petroleum products; and the theft and smuggling of refined products from the Baiji refinery.

Organized crime in Iraq is neither an outlier nor an aberration; rather, it is a central feature of much of the global periphery.

If oil was the focus of most criminal activity in Iraq, however, equally striking was the range of criminal activities perpetrated by traditional criminal enterprises interested only in profit and also political groups using crime to fund their cause. Extortion (and its less malevolent concomitant, protection) became pervasive. And the reconstruction efforts multiplied the opportunities. Large amounts of money for reconstruction were poured into Iraq with inadequate oversight and no comprehensive plan for its effective disbursement. Iraqis were awarded contracts with protection money almost invariably built in, some of which went to organized crime and some to the insurgency. Inadvertently, the United States was funding the very groups attacking its forces. As well as the natural focus on extortion and protection (particularly important where there was no effective Leviathan to provide security), criminals and combatants alike engaged in the illicit trafficking of antiquities, the theft and smuggling of cars, trafficking in human beings, drug smuggling (especially of synthetics), and the illicit weapons trade.

After oil crimes, however, the most important activity was kidnapping. The kidnapping of Iraqis became an enduring problem, reaching a peak in 2006 with an estimated 40 abductions a day, which provided major revenue for criminals, militias, and insurgents. The kidnapping of foreigners, in contrast, was relatively short-lived but often had dramatic impact as videos of the decapitation of hostages were posted on the Internet. Kidnapping sometimes involved tacit or explicit cooperation between kidnapping gangs concerned with profit and jihadi groups concerned with both fundraising and strategic impact. On occasion, the jihadis simply let it be known that they wanted a particular kind of hostage: at other times, kidnapping gangs took the initiative in the hope that they could sell their hostages directly to the jihadis or obtain a share of the proceeds after the jihadis obtained ransom payments. The willingness of governments—most notably those of France, Italy, and Germany—to make large ransom payments for the freedom of their citizens made kidnapping of foreigners particularly attractive. It also led to some strange situations, with the Italian government, for example, finding itself in a bidding war with AQI for the kidnapped journalist Giuliana Sgrena.

Yet if kidnapping was an important revenue source, it was also a strategic weapon used by the insurgents and jihadi groups in efforts to undermine coalition unity, coerce governments with military contingents or support workers into withdrawing, sow insecurity both in the general population and in the nongovernmental organization community, and undermine the effectiveness of the occupation forces and the Iraqi government. The ability to amplify kidnapping through executions posted on the Internet made it an even more powerful weapon that will almost certainly be used in other contingencies.

Another element of organized crime in Iraq was the linkage to corruption in government ministries. This simply reflects the dual nature of corruption as both a pervasive condition and an instrument of organized crime. Corruption in Iraq was also integrally related to violence. Indeed, violence played a key role in protecting crime-corruption networks, maintaining the political-criminal nexus, and limiting efforts to reform the system. Although it is difficult to separate violence used to intimidate members of anticorruption bodies and agencies from the more pervasive violence, a close examination reveals clearly that those fighting corruption—whether staff members of the Commission on Public Integrity or investigative journalists digging too deep—were particularly vulnerable to precisely targeted violence designed to inhibit their investigation, restrict or dilute their findings and proposals, and suppress anticorruption activities. A few Iraqi politicians and officials recognized this and referred specifically to the violent mafia in the oil ministry that prevented reform. It is likely that similar if less blatant efforts at intimidation were made in other ministries in order to maintain the lucrative revenue streams linked to corruption.

Officials at the U.S. Embassy in Baghdad performed an extremely perceptive assessment of corruption in the ministries (which was leaked and published on the Internet), but even this exposure did not sufficiently emphasize the role of violence and coercion in perpetuating corrupt activities and protecting the connections among organized crime, insurgents, and militias on the one side and between politicians and officials on the other. Unfortunately, while corruption-related violence was only a small part of the overall violence, it had a powerful and pervasive impact that made good governance more elusive and undermined faith in the new government. The post-Ba'athist Iraqi state was inevitably somewhat weak at the outset, and organized crime sought to perpetuate that weakness.

It is clear from all this that organized crime in Iraq was highly predatory. Yet it is also important to recognize what, in a very different context, Andre Standing shrewdly described as the "social contradictions of organized crime."[1] Writing specifically about the Cape Flats in South Africa, Standing shows how organized crime and criminal economy can play *positive* roles. In an analysis that has wide applicability, Standing argues that the criminal economy is "a core dimension of the community" rather than "a fringe activity perpetrated by outsiders who can be easily separated from a normal legal society containing good citizens."[2] This certainly applies to Iraq, where organized crime and illicit economic activity are pervasive. Moreover, in Standing's view, organized crime "delivers employment and goods to thousands of individuals" otherwise socially and economically excluded.[3] This notion of organized crime as a safety net is not far-fetched even in Iraq, although expressions of criminal "philanthropy" or criminal paternalism of the kind displayed elsewhere—most flamboyantly in Colombia by Pablo Escobar in his program "Medellin without slums"—seem lacking.

Recognizing that organized crime can act as a safety net is simply to recognize that it has benefits as well as costs. Organized crime is certainly not victimless—especially when violence or the threat of violence are integral to the crime, as it is with kidnapping and trafficking in persons—but it is a social and economic coping strategy, providing employment when unemployment is high and opportunities when opportunities in licit economies are severely constricted. Indeed, the economy in Iraq had been so devastated by successive wars, sanctions, and economic mismanagement that organized crime was one of the few sources of employment after March 2003. This is not to deny the pernicious nature and devastating consequences of organized crime; it is simply to suggest that complex phenomena often have paradoxical characteristics.

Recognizing that organized crime can act as a safety net is simply to recognize that it has benefits as well as costs.

The other critical component of organized crime in Iraq was the appropriation of criminal methods by political and military actors. Insurgents, jihadis, militias, and certain Sunni tribes were all involved in organized criminal activities. In many respects this was a familiar pattern. Groups as diverse as the Irish Republican Army, Liberation Tigers of Tamil Eelam, and Revolutionary Armed Forces of Colombia had long used criminal activities as a funding mechanism. For jihadi groups, especially AQI, criminal activities became a critical source of revenue. The willingness of European governments to make substantial payments for the release of their citizens made kidnapping of foreigners highly lucrative. Reports claim that France paid $15 million for the release of three hostages, Italy paid $11 million, and Germany paid $8 million to $10 million.[4] This revenue stream was surpassed only by the profits from the theft, diversion, smuggling, and black market sales of oil. Car theft was another source of funding for AQI and became particularly important in Mosul when AQI and its affiliates concentrated there after setbacks in Al Anbar and Baghdad. Extortion and various kinds of fraud were also core funding activities. Shiite militias, especially Jaish al-Mahdi (JAM), also became heavily involved in organized crime in Iraq, although how much was carried out under the direct control of the organization and how much by "rogue" factions is uncertain. Four criminal activities provided Mahdi army members with important revenue streams: extortion and protection, black market sales of petroleum, seizures of cars and houses under the guise of sectarian cleansing, and involvement in oil smuggling in Basra. The offensives in Basra and Sadr City in the first half of 2008 had some impact in reducing JAM criminal activities.

All this challenged the dominant paradigm of terrorist financing that emerged after September 11, 2001, and involved funneling funds through charities, the global financial system, and informal money transfer mechanisms to terrorists carrying out attacks. Following the money becomes difficult without a trail, or when funds are raised and spent locally or there is no distinction between fundraisers and those who commit acts of terrorism. Although the money brought into Iraq by foreign fighters was not negligible, the amounts seem to have been modest when compared with the funds raised through criminal activities. This was recognized by a 2006 intelligence report leaked to the *New York Times* that concluded insurgents and terrorists in Iraq were financially self-sufficient and not dependent on funds from outside the country, let alone from al Qaeda central.

Closely linked to this self-sufficiency, the informal, criminal, and conflict economies in Iraq overlapped and intersected in complex ways.[5] The insurgency, like organized crime, became an important source of employment. If the appropriation of organized crime methods helped insurgents and jihadis, however, it also provided opportunities for wedge-driving by the United States. In Anbar Province, in particular, tensions over the control of illicit activities between the Sunni tribes and AQI helped to create a major schism.[6] The U.S. military, as the "strongest tribe," became adjudicator and enforcer in criminal disputes dressed up as political differences, siding with one set of violent armed groups engaged in criminal activities against other groups judged more dangerous.[7] The tribes were losing the turf wars to AQI until the U.S. military came to the rescue. Moreover, the Anbar Awakening was in part an alternative employment program that encouraged the defection of major Sunni tribes from the insurgency. If the United States was able to lever what was effectively criminal competition, however, the tactical benefits were greatly outweighed by the strategic costs of failing to anticipate the rise of organized crime in Iraq and the far-reaching consequences it would have for reestablishing stability and governance after the toppling of Saddam Hussein. Although there were precedents, analogues, and commentaries that could have provided early warning, the obstacles to anticipating the rise of organized crime were systemic and powerful.

The U.S. military, as the "strongest tribe," became adjudicator and enforcer in criminal disputes dressed up as political differences.

Strategic Surprise

Ironically, Iraq is not the first case in which U.S. aspirations and expectations have been confounded by organized crime. The hope that Russia in the 1990s would undergo a smooth transition to liberal democracy and the free market was disappointed by widespread corruption, connivance, and violence associated with the rise of organized crime.[8] In part, this reflected a loss of social control by the state, a loss inherent amid transformation and upheaval. In retrospect, however, the rise of organized crime reflected the adoption of a new strategy by the political elite. Accepting the end of the Soviet Union, many members of the elite, working in collusion with criminals, positioned themselves to exploit the transition to capitalism. And with the absence of a regulatory framework for business, organized crime became protector, arbitrator of disputes, and debt collector of last resort. At times, organized crime appeared out of control, with contract killings being used to eliminate threats—whether in the form of reformist politicians, investigative journalists, or policemen resistant to the blandishments of corruption. Yet as Joseph Serio has argued, what was happening was in fact a fusion of crime, business, and politics.[9] The achievement of Vladimir Putin was primarily to reestablish the dominant role of the political elites in what has remained a symbiotic relationship with organized crime. At various points during the 1990s, it appeared that organized crime was taking over the state. In fact, the state was a willing partner. Under Putin, however, the state simply became a much more assertive partner, with the security services and law enforcement once again controlling, regulating, and facilitating (rather than neutralizing) organized crime.

The key point is that the role of organized crime in derailing the transition of Russia to a free market and liberal democracy was not anticipated. Fritz Ermarth has noted that although the State Department's Bureau of Intelligence and Research in 1992 produced an astute analysis of the likely impact of crime and corruption in Russia, "subsequently, neither American intelligence analysis nor American policymakers adequately appreciated the crime and corruption problem."[10] At the policymaking level there was a great deal of "customer sales resistance" driven in part by wishful thinking about the transition, which created skepticism about reports emphasizing the extent of Russian political corruption.[11] At the analytic level, it appears there was a desire to please policymakers by both emphasizing that the market would tame organized crime and downgrading the challenge that it posed by inappropriate analogies between Russian criminals and the "robber barons" in the United States.[12] As Ermarth noted, the robber barons operated in an environment constrained by laws.[13] They also built infrastructure rather than looting the state. The result was not a dramatic strategic surprise but a subtle and an insidious one. As a result, it was not one from which appropriate and valuable lessons were learned.

The evolution of organized crime in Russia was not the only experience that could have increased sensitivities to the potential role of organized crime in Iraq. The conflicts in the Balkans during the 1990s were inextricably linked to organized crime, which obtained an enormous boost from the imposition of international sanctions, acted as a major funding mechanism for ethnic factions, and helped to maintain the Slobodan Milosevic regime in Serbia. Competing factions and state structures appropriated criminal activities as a means of funding political agendas. The struggle over Kosovo, for example, was in part a clash between cigarette smugglers and heroin traffickers. Yet political animosities did not inhibit criminal cooperation when it was mutually convenient and beneficial. Serb and Albanian criminal networks, for example, were not averse to doing business with one another, in spite of political tensions. In a political economy dominated by illicit activities,

this was hardly surprising. The illicit economy and organized crime were not on the periphery of economic and political activities in the Balkans; they were *central* to those activities. Moreover, this was not some kind of regional aberration but the emergence of a pattern that is becoming increasingly common and that was certainly manifest in Iraq.

Although there is inevitably an element of what David Snowden termed "retrospective coherence" in this analysis of Iraq, it is worth emphasizing that several warning voices were raised about organized crime in the early months of the occupation.[14] One of these was Mark Edmond Clark of the Strategy Group, who noted in July 2003 that "the Balkans could possibly serve as a model for understanding what is now taking place in Iraq."[15] He also noted that "combating organized crime in Iraq will . . . demand further consideration as the humanitarian and reconstruction efforts get under way."[16] Perhaps even more important, in August 2003 a delegation from the United Nations Office of Drugs and Crime (UNODC) provided a comprehensive assessment, noting that organized crime was already contributing to instability and complicating reconstruction.[17] The UNODC report identified oil smuggling, trafficking in firearms, human trafficking, theft and trafficking of artifacts, kidnapping and extortion, car-jacking, and the large-scale theft of copper from pylons and power lines as key criminal activities, some of which had already reached "industrial scale" proportions.[18] The report also noted that "the conditions for the expansion of organized crime include the absence of the rule of law, the disintegration of state institutions and the promotion of various forms of smuggling under the previous regime."[19] Both Clark and the UNODC mission provided strategic warning about the rise of organized crime in post-Ba'athist Iraq. Their warnings, however, had little impact on high-level decision-making. Neither civilian leaders in the Coalition Provisional Authority nor members of the military leadership took the warnings as seriously as they should have—and the UN mission met a mixture of resistance and indifference.[20]

The UNODC report identified key criminal activities, some of which had already reached "industrial scale" proportions.

The indifference to the possible rise of organized crime and its profoundly debilitating consequences was reflected in two early decisions in Iraq, both of which had far-reaching consequences: the decision to stand by passively in the face of widespread looting, and the decision to disband the army. The decision to do nothing in the face of the looting seems to reflect both a lack of planning for the occupation and a belief that looting reflected a deep-seated anger at the regime and, therefore, was likely to have a highly cathartic effect. In fact, the looting both reflected and accentuated a condition of anomie: the degeneration of moral standards and permissible behavior. In an environment characterized by enormous uncertainty, a lack of clear rules and norms, and the absence of constraints imposed by a strong central government, allowing the looting gave the wrong signal. Not only did it embolden criminals and undermine faith in the occupation, but it also created a pervasive sense of personal insecurity. This proved difficult to dispel and ultimately fed into the emergent role of the militias as sectarian protectors. The looting also morphed into more focused and organized forms of crime. Perhaps most important, however, was the psychological impact of a lawless environment with high levels of impunity. The conclusion was that criminal activities had high payoffs and carried few risks.

The decision to dismantle the army, although more ideological than the decision to allow the looting, was another major boost to the rise of predatory forms of organized crime in Iraq. If more thought had been given to the consequences of creating a surplus of unemployed experts in violence in an environment characterized by weak governance mechanisms with low levels of legitimacy, multiple sectarian, tribal, and regional divisions, and very constricted employment opportunities, then the imprudent nature of the decision would have been obvious. Once again, experiences in the former Soviet Union and Balkans could have provided a vital insight: when experts in violence are removed from their traditional occupation in the armed forces or security services, they become what one Russian scholar termed "entrepreneurs of violence."[21] Although measures to limit the power of the Ba'athists were essential, the extent of de-Ba'athification was done with too little analysis of likely consequences. The result was the unleashing of groups that had always had a predatory approach to the society who also had managerial skills and expertise in violence and intimidation. Indeed, former regime elements from the military and the intelligence services became major players in the criminal world. Some of these people were able to use their detailed knowledge of the population to identify particularly lucrative targets for kidnapping for ransom. The families of many hostages discovered that the kidnappers had specific details of their finances, which both accentuated their sense of helplessness and limited their bargaining ability.

If the Coalition Provisional Authority failed to recognize how its own decisions and actions fed into the rise of organized crime in the country, some U.S. operational units appreciated the organized crime component of the challenges confronted. As early as July 2004, Marine commanders were acknowledging that it was difficult to:

> overemphasize the importance of organized crime in the insurgency. . . . The perpetrators are motivated by self-interest and greed. They not only plan and carry out violence but pay others to do the same. One commander compared the intransigence of Iraqi organized crime networks to that of the mafia in Sicily before World War II. It has the same stranglehold on whole local economies and populations, and is protected by family and tribal loyalties.[22]

Such an assessment, however, was not widely accepted, with the result that neither the extensive nature of criminal activities nor their pernicious consequences was anticipated and contained. As a result, the rise of organized crime in Iraq proved a strategic surprise for the United States. The reasons for this must now be examined.

Grooved Thinking and Labeling

Military planning appropriately focuses on overt military problems and challenges. One of the problems inhibiting both planning and analysis, however, is the simple labeling and categorizing of problems. Labels become important in defining problems and determining the locus of responsibility for responding to them.[23] In this connection, it bears emphasis that although military planning now includes an integral rule of law component, this was not initially the case in Iraq. Moreover, organized crime was seen as a law and order problem rather than a military challenge, even though it fed directly into the disorder, political violence, and pervasive insecurity. Consequently, criminal activities and criminal organizations were dealt with sporadically rather than systematically and at the tactical and operational levels rather than as a matter of strategy. This remained largely true even when the emphasis on counterinsurgency became more pronounced.

In Iraq, organized crime was seen as a law and order problem rather than a military challenge, even though it fed directly into the disorder, political violence, and pervasive insecurity.

Poor Use of Analogies and Precedents

It is often noted that historical analogies and history itself are used badly in both intelligence and national security decisionmaking. Part of the reason is the dominance of national experience, a failure to see broader patterns, and a reluctance to acknowledge the relevance of experience elsewhere. In this connection, the United States has an ethnocentric view of organized crime, which is traditionally seen as a law and order challenge rather than a fundamental threat to security. Indeed, the very concept of security in the United States has always referred primarily to national and sometimes to international security.

In Latin America, in contrast, security is seen much more in terms of public or citizen security. One reason for the difference is that traditional organized crime in the United States played by certain rules; policemen were regarded as touchable (in some places and on some occasions) by the bribe but untouchable by the bullet. In Latin America and other parts of the world, the inhibitions on attacking those who work for the state are much weaker. And while the United States was relatively successful—at least in the long term—in containing the Italian Mafia, in other countries organized crime was more pervasive and damaging.

Yet U.S. civilian and military leaders exhibited considerable reluctance to acknowledge not only that organized crime could exercise much more influence in some societies than it did in the United States but also that it might behave with less prudence and greater ruthlessness. Both the Balkans and many states of the former Soviet Union provided dramatic examples of how pervasive and corrosive organized crime could become in periods of state weakness, collapse, or even political transitions characterized by rapid social and economic dislocation. Although the United States during the 1990s developed considerable interest in political stability, state weakness, and the dangers of state failure, it rarely linked those issues to the role and rise of organized crime, even though the former Soviet Union and Balkans experienced bumpy transitions in which organized crime emerged as a major spoiler. Expectations about the free market economy and the aspirations for liberal democracy soon became mired in large-scale economic dislocation, unemployment, and the failure to develop the legal and regulatory structures for the governance of a capitalist economy.

As a result, organized crime became a proxy for the state, providing protection and enforcement unavailable through legal channels. In Iraq, the United States made the state fail—through a very successful decapitation strategy. The rapidity of state collapse and the dislocation created in a society rendered highly fragile by brutal dictatorship, successive wars, and the imposition of international sanctions provided multiple opportunities for the rise of organized crime. This was as inevitable as it was unexpected.

Dominance of Strategic Perspectives

The dominant assessment of Iraq prior to the U.S. invasion was of a rogue state with a regime intent on regional domination and likely involved in the development of weapons of mass destruction. Iraq was a strategic challenge, so little attention was given to its internal social and economic problems. Consequently, the debate over sanctions revolved around their effectiveness in inhibiting the behavior of Saddam Hussein. No consideration was given to the criminalization consequences of international sanctions.[24] Peter Andreas argues very persuasively, however, that "sanctions almost invariably have a criminalizing impact on the targeted country as well as its neighbors."[25] In his view, the criminalizing consequences of sanctions occur at several distinct but overlapping levels. First, while sanctions are in effect, the target state typically goes "into the business of organized crime to generate revenue, supplies, and strengthen its hold on power, fostering an alliance with clandestine transnational economic actors for mutual gain. This alliance may, in turn, persist beyond the sanctions period."[26] Iraq certainly exemplifies this, with its exploitation of the oil-for-food program for kickback schemes, as well as the oil protocols with its neighbors. Second, efforts to circumvent sanctions lead to the creation of regional smuggling linkages. In Iraq, such linkages survived the collapse of the Ba'athist regime and became an important factor in helping to fund opposition to U.S. presence. Third, sanctions and their circumvention result in the criminalization of the economy and society, enabling organized crime groups to move from the periphery to the core of economic life.

After the collapse of the regime, illicit activities in Iraq continued while, in effect, becoming more democratic and more diffuse. U.S. planners seem to have given this prospect scant attention, exhibiting little if any sensitivity to the acceptance of criminal behavior and criminal activities as the norm in Iraq. Although it is possible that intelligence assessments reflected a far deeper understanding, U.S. policymakers were oblivious to the degradation of norms and standards that had taken place in a country ruled by personal dictatorship and not law, a population wracked by a succession of internal and external wars, an economy in which sanctions had destroyed the middle class, and a society in which insecurity, desperation, opportunism, and greed had created a combustible combination only contained by repression.

> **U.S. policymakers were oblivious to the degradation of norms and standards that had taken place in a country ruled by personal dictatorship and not law.**

When the tyranny of fear was removed and the "fierce state" was destroyed, there was nothing to replace it as a source of order.[27] Mechanisms for managing disputes or resolving conflicts were absent, as were national institutions in which people could place their trust. The Ba'athist regime had done a good job of containing and even hiding these faultlines in society, and consequently it was hard for the United States, looking from the outside, to understand the deterioration. Nevertheless, the inability or unwillingness to recognize that "reestablishing societal acceptance of legal norms can be one of the most challenging tasks after the sanctions are lifted" was to have profound implications.[28] The failure to categorize Iraq as a high-risk country for organized crime meant that U.S. forces were ill prepared for the challenges they would face.

This is not to claim that domestic factors in Iraq were completely ignored. Insofar as there was an internal focus, however, it was on the Sunni-Shia divide and the likely impact of the U.S. intervention on reversing the balance of advantage in Iraq. The financial dimension of sectarian cleansing—through kidnappings, killings, and the associated theft of cars and houses—has received remarkably little attention, at least in the public debate.[29] Another surprise was the intensity of the political competition among Shia factions and parties. This competition came to the fore in Basra, where there was a violent struggle for the control of both licit and illicit trade in oil. Indeed, intra-Shia sectarianism and organized crime became bound up with one another, as elements in Moqtada al-Sadr's militia, Jaish al-Mahdi, became involved, at the very least, in providing protection for oil smugglers, and found itself competing with both the Fadhila party militia and the Badr Corps (which gradually became integrated into the army) for the "rents" on this trade.

Wishful Thinking: Regime Change without Pain

In many postmortems of intelligence and decisionmaking failures, it is clear that all too often those involved saw only what they expected to see. In some cases, that was compounded by a tendency to see what they wanted to see. In effect, preconceptions were reinforced by wishful thinking. Such a tendency seems to have been at work in Washington prior to the invasion of Iraq, particularly in decisions made at the political level.

Strong elements of wishful thinking encouraged a tendency to minimize the extent of the disruption and dislocation that would occur with the U.S. military intervention. Underlying this is an important cultural factor rooted in the ideals of American society, which creates an appealing but often unwarranted optimism about the capacity of the United States to bring about desired changes. This pattern of expectation was woven through a long series of U.S. military interventions and was crystallized in the resurgent Wilsonianism of a conservative Republican administration. An economic variant of Wilsonianism was evident in Thomas Barnett's *The Pentagon's New Map: War and Peace in the Twenty-first Century,* which encapsulated and extolled the virtues of global neoliberalism at a time when this had already been rejected in many parts of the world. For Barnett, the opportunity to integrate Iraq (and Afghanistan) into the core global economy was one of the major benefits of intervention. The underlying assumption is that the Western and especially the American conception of globalization, if not enthusiastically shared throughout the developing world, remains attractive.

The concomitant is that developing countries will accept liberal democratic norms and welcome U.S. power and presence that embodies these norms. The resulting expectation is that the West in general and the United States in particular will be able to expand the order, peace, and stability of the developed world to the zone of disorder in the periphery. Such thinking ignores three things: the rejection not only of liberal-democratic values but also modernity itself in large segments of the developing world; antipathy toward the United States, which is seen as seeking to impose its values and principles on unwilling populations even where this means supporting corrupt and autocratic governments in the meantime; and the capacity of others not to confront the United States directly but to act as spoilers in conflict and postconflict situations.

The diffusion and democratization of weapons systems, along with the ingenuity of substate and transnational networks in devising asymmetrical weapons, might not defeat great-power occupation but can make occupation very costly. Perhaps more fundamentally, it is not clear that the momentum is with the West. A close examination of events over the last two decades suggests not that order is flowing from the core to the periphery but that disorder is extending from the periphery to the core. One of the best encapsulations of the rise of organized crime and other violent nonstate actors as well as the development of alternative forms of governance is the term *the revenge of the periphery.*[30]

Ethnocentrism and Corruption

Hand-in-hand with the Wilsonian conception of the desirability of liberal democracies is the notion of well-regulated polities with clear distinctions between public and private activities, rules on conflicts of interest, institutional safeguards against abuse of position and authority for private gain, a high degree of transparency and accountability, and a deep and abiding sense of public service. In fact, Western democracies are the anomaly; "corruption" is not only endemic but is also deeply embedded in many traditional societies where it is linked to familial, tribal, and clan obligations that take precedence over

the rule of law. From this perspective, governing the state is not a burden that requires an unselfish tradition of public service but an opportunity to obtain and distribute resources. Access to the resources of the state is a prize to be won, and the spoils are distributed in ways that reflect traditional affiliations, obligations, and loyalties. This gives politics in many countries in the developing world a zero-sum quality that accentuates rather than bridges divisions within these societies.

> **"Corruption" is deeply embedded in many traditional societies where it is linked to familial, tribal, and clan obligations that take precedence over the rule of law.**

All this was reflected in high levels of official corruption in Iraq and the development of a symbiotic relationship between crime and politics. The relationships that had developed under Saddam between political elites, officials, and bureaucrats on the one side and criminal organizations on the other deepened as the new government was formed. The symbiosis was particularly pronounced in the Ministry of Oil where administrative corruption and political collusion greatly facilitated the theft, diversion, and smuggling of oil and petroleum products. The development of a "political-criminal nexus" mirrored that in many other parts of the world.[31] Yet the nexus undermined U.S. interests and complicated efforts to establish good governance. In other words, historical, cultural, and political factors in Iraq ensured the collective interest remained subordinate to individual and factional interests. These factors were reinforced and perpetuated by the links between organized crime and political and administrative elites. Moreover, the injection of large amounts of money for economic reconstruction without adequate control or oversight and no plan for effective disbursement exacerbated both crime and corruption. Reconstruction moneys tempted not only various factions in Iraq but also U.S. corporations and contractors—many of which performed abysmally in terms of task completion. Reconstruction was vital but its implementation, in spite of all the efforts of the Special Inspector General on Iraq Reconstruction, facilitated and encouraged the growth of corruption and organized crime.

The critical question, therefore, is how similar strategic surprises can be avoided in future conflict and postconflict contingencies.

Intelligence, Military Contingencies, and Organized Crime

In thinking about intelligence to combat organized crime, two main requirements stand out. First, intelligence assessments of organized crime must be incorporated into the decisionmaking process preceding the deployment of military forces. These assessments should anticipate the levels, forms, and scope of organized crime that might arise during the contingency itself and consider the impact on prospects for success. Second, during the deployment, intelligence about organized crime should enhance the effectiveness of the military forces in meeting their mission requirements.

In terms of intelligence and planning, one simple way to anticipate the possible rise of organized crime as a spoiler in military contingencies is to include an organized crime threat assessment prior to military deployment. A useful analogy is arms control impact statements, which were congressionally mandated requirements accompanying certain military budget requests between 1976 and 1993. An organized crime impact statement need not be formalized in the same way. Nevertheless, it should become a key component of military planning, a part of intelligence preparation of the battlefield at the strategic level and something that is given full consideration prior to deploying forces. Systematically thinking about how the military intervention—whether large-scale or more modest—is likely to change the opportunity space and incentive structures for organized crime in the target country and the surrounding region is critical. In this connection, it has become axiomatic that the deployment of peacekeepers expands the market for commercial sex and creates new incentives for trafficking in women to the deployment country.

While much will depend on the specific circumstances, it is likely that in most situations a team approach to the assessment that combines country specialists, political and economic analysts, and those with expertise on organized crime is appropriate. The assessment itself could be based on a checklist of key questions, broad enough to be asked in all cases but focused enough to elicit aspects of the problem unique to the particular target country and contingency under consideration. The assessment should consider organizations and markets, incentives and inhibitions, and ways in which a U.S. military deployment might have the inadvertent consequence of strengthening organized crime.

In most situations a team approach to the assessment that combines country specialists, political and economic analysts, and those with expertise on organized crime is appropriate.

If the assessment concludes that organized crime is likely to become a major problem, it must identify points of leverage that the United States can exploit to preempt or limit the problem. What follows is a preliminary checklist for such an assessment. It is not definitive and there is some overlap, but this is based on the notion that an organized crime threat assessment needs to be broad rather than narrow and that elements of overlap are preferable to gaps.

1. The Current State of Organized Crime in the Country:

- What is the current state of organized crime? Is it specialized or diverse? Is it widespread or restricted to a few sectors of the economy? Are there particular sectors where organized crime has or could develop a dominant position?

- How is crime organized? Is it through traditional hierarchies and pyramidal structures or through more horizontal networks? Are there many small groups and "mom and pop" operations, or are there a few large syndicates?

- What is the cultural basis for organized crime? Are trust and loyalty in the criminal world rooted in family, tribe, or clan relationships and affinities, or are they based simply on the threat of harsh reprisals for defection or disloyalty? Or is it a mix of affinity and fear?

- What traditions (for example, traditions of cross-border smuggling, patrimonial relationships, or lack of allegiance to the state structure) in the society encourage or feed into criminal activity? Conversely, what traditions might act as constraints on various forms of criminality?

- What level of legitimacy does the state have? Does the state provide adequate levels of protection and service to its citizens? If it does not, what alternative sources of protection, service, and even governance are available?

- Are political factions and violent groups that oppose the government using criminal activities for funding? If so, what kinds of activities are they engaged in, and what kinds of revenue streams are they obtaining?

- What kind of connections and cooperation exists, if any, between violent political actors and traditional criminal enterprises? If there is cooperation, is it based merely on mutual expediency or certain kinds of affinity among the different types of groups?

- Does the regime in power systematically engage in criminal activities? If so, what kinds of collaborative networks are involved? Are these networks likely to be self-sustaining and self-perpetuating in the absence of the regime and the accompanying linkages?

- What is the level of economic development of the state? What is its degree of control over key resources? What resources exist in the state, and how are their management and the distribution of profits organized? If control of key resources is a state monopoly, in what ways is this monopoly being challenged (for example, siphoning resources and moving them to illicit markets whether in the state or outside, or violent conflict for control of licit and/or illicit markets)? If control is contested, who are the challengers to the state?

- If there are major political divisions in the state, to what extent are rival factions exploiting criminal activities to fund political competition?

- What kind of state/regime is the target of possible intervention? Is it strong or weak, authoritarian or democratic? Are there capacity gaps and functional holes that could be exploited and/or filled by organized crime? What kinds of rents do the political elites obtain? Are these rents concentrated or distributed? Is there a political-criminal nexus in the country? If so, how is power distributed in relationships between the political elites and the criminal organizations?

123

- What is the level of civil society in the country? Are civil society institutions fully or poorly developed? Do elements of civil society in any way act as counterweights to organized crime and/or government corruption?
- Has the state been subjected to international sanctions? If so, how did it respond? Were attempts made to circumvent sanctions, and if so, how successful were they? Did sanctions and sanctions-busting result in the development of national and regional criminal networks? If so, are these networks likely to survive the removal of sanctions and develop other illicit business opportunities?

2. The Future Potential of Organized Crime:

- What are the propensity and capacity for criminal organizations to act as spoilers in the event of either regime change or postconflict peace-building?
- To what extent are there violent groups opposing the military presence and acting as spoilers to the reestablishment of good governance? Will these violent groups be able to appropriate organized crime methods, thereby becoming more powerful and effective spoilers?
- In the event of political and economic upheaval, what kinds of black markets are likely to emerge? Are these likely to be informal coping mechanisms, or will they provide opportunities for criminal enrichment? If new criminal markets do emerge, what kinds of incentives and opportunities exist for new entrants into these markets? What kinds of products are likely to be most important? What is the likely balance among wholly illicit prohibited products and services, regulated products or services, and licit products susceptible to theft, diversion, and smuggling? What kinds of criminal activities are likely to be most lucrative?
- How much does the successful pursuit of illicit opportunities require the perpetuation of a weak state as opposed to allowing the reemergence of a strong legitimate state?
- Is the state, the peacekeeping contingent, or intervening force able to provide security, or will key portions of the citizenry look for alternative forms of protection? Is the state, the peacekeepers, or an intervening force able to provide services, or will key portions of the citizenry look for alternative service providers? If there is a demand for services and protection, which groups are best positioned to meet that demand? How powerful and attractive are these alternative forms of governance? What is the balance between predation and protection in their activities?

3. Potential Points of Leverage:

- Is there invariably a zero-sum relationship between alternative forms of governance and the state, or can these rival power and authority centers be coopted by the state? If cooption is not feasible, in what ways might

alternative governance structures be simply encouraged to become less predatory?
- Are some forms of organized crime activities and certain kinds of criminal organization more pernicious than others? If such a distinction can be made, what opportunities might there be to exploit it?
- What is the relationship among the informal, illegal, and conflict economies? Are there sufficiently attractive incentives and opportunities in the legal economy to entice people away from the informal and illicit economies? Are there sufficiently attractive incentives and opportunities in the informal economy to encourage people to move away from the illicit and conflict/insurgent economies? How can these incentives and opportunities be strengthened?
- If legitimacy is low, what can be done in the short/medium and long terms to enhance it? Similarly, if the rule of law is weak, what can be done in the short/medium and long terms to enhance it?
- If reconstruction is a key part of either peacekeeping or military intervention, how can it best be managed so violent and criminal groups are not able to exploit the resources injected into the economy? In what ways can aid and reconstruction efforts be protected so they do not become targets for extortion, fraud, or exploitation?
- To what extent do intervention or peacekeeping disrupt or threaten traditional stakeholders and/or the dominance of certain political actors? Are there ways that a more inclusive and integrating strategy can be developed?
- What measures could preempt or inhibit alliances between criminal enterprises solely focused on profit and violent groups with political agendas, to whom criminal activities are simply a financial means to achieve political goals?
- Are there regional asymmetries, such as markedly different prices for commodities produced in the target country and/or its neighbors, that can encourage smuggling? If so, can these asymmetries be reduced?
- What kinds of actions by peacekeeping or intervention forces encourage the creation of alliances among criminal groups, among violent political groups, or between criminal and violent political groups? Do differential law enforcement and targeting priorities offer opportunities to break alliances between various groups or factions?
- What kind of precautions can be taken to avoid the emergence of kidnapping as a strategic weapon against the occupation or peacekeeping forces rather than simply as criminal activity?

As acknowledged above, this is not an exhaustive list. It does, however, provide essential questions that need to be framed prior to any military or peacekeeping contingency, even where it is not readily obvious that organized crime plays a major role or has the capacity to become a spoiler. Once the intervention or peacekeeping deployment is under way, however, a new set of collection and analytic requirements comes to the fore. One possible approach to meeting these operational demands is through systematic efforts to fuse national security and law enforcement intelligence.

An effective fusion of law enforcement intelligence on the one side and military and strategic intelligence on the other is difficult. Moreover, the Iraq experience is not particularly promising, as there was little if any integration of law enforcement and military intelligence. Even though military intelligence developed enormous insight into Iraqi culture, tribal traditions and relationships, and social and political networks, this process does not seem to have been extended in any systematic way to organized crime in Iraq. This is not surprising. One of the most important obstacles was the military's lack of interest in the law enforcement mission, especially complex investigations that are themselves a source of intelligence and understanding as well as crucial to prosecution and conviction. To overcome this, strategic and military intelligence has to acknowledge that the organized crime is not a peripheral issue but something that can contribute significantly to the funding of those who are hostile to U.S. forces and willing to use violence to eject them. The growing acknowledgment of the salience of the rule of law mission in the Department of Defense is an important sign of progress and suggests that the military's clear dichotomy between intelligence and military operations on the one side and reconstruction and rule of law operations on the other is breaking down. It is not that soldiers are expected to become policemen; it is simply that there has to be a more explicit recognition that some law enforcement intelligence skills are highly relevant to the military environment of the 21st century.[32]

Even though military intelligence developed enormous insight into Iraqi culture, this process does not seem to have been extended to organized crime.

Even with such an acknowledgment, however, difficulties remain. The rule of law mission is broad and does not focus adequately on organized crime. Military intelligence collectors and analysts are not trained for the specific requirements of criminal intelligence. They are even less suited for criminal investigations, which remain crucial in learning the nature and extent of criminal networks involved in the larger organized crime challenge. On the other side of the equation, civilian law enforcement agencies are reluctant to embed their own analysts and agents with military units for lengthy periods. Moreover, much law enforcement remains deeply rooted in the tactical and the operational, with emphasis on specific cases and indictment and conviction rather than knowledge acquisition and what might be termed the strategic dismantling of criminal organizations.

These difficulties are both systemic and serious. Even with highly adaptive organizations in the theater of operations,

they cannot be overcome once military forces are deployed. Traditional divides and bureaucratic silos must be overcome before deployment. It is argued here that this could be done with a set of initiatives explicitly designed to integrate law enforcement intelligence with strategic and military intelligence.

First, and most important, is the creation of a multiagency intelligence task force specifically designed to focus on organized crime in conflict and postconflict situations. This should include representatives from the Central Intelligence Agency, Defense Intelligence Agency, Department of the Treasury, Federal Bureau of Investigation, and Drug Enforcement Administration, with individuals designated as support personnel in other agencies who could be called on for additional assistance with both data and analysis. The task force could be organized as a network, but it would be preferable to have the members working together in the same location as this is essential to the creation of trust, the cross-fertilization of both methods and substantive insights, and the development of a distinctive sense of mission.

Second, there has to be a mutual learning process that will not be easy and therefore requires careful selection of personnel who are synthetic and eclectic in their approach, open to new methods, and dedicated to the mission irrespective of institutional affiliation. The key for law enforcement intelligence analysts is to think beyond the specific case and to combine the results of specific investigations (in which the priority is primarily knowledge acquisition and only secondarily arrest and indictment) with an overall strategic perspective. More traditional intelligence analysts should recognize that law enforcement has a great deal to offer to the intelligence process, particularly in complex environments. David Snowden has argued that the only way to understand a complex environment is by probing both the environment and adversaries and eliciting reactions that lead to enhanced understanding and awareness as well as knowledge acquisition.[33] Law enforcement is extremely good at probing behavior. For example, by temporarily detaining a critical figure in a criminal network while continuing to carry out surveillance on the network, it is possible to obtain insights into how criminal networks operate under stress. Such insights can facilitate the destruction of these networks.

A third essential pillar is a long-term program of increased personnel exchange between law enforcement and intelligence agencies with the notion that this would provide both a candidate pool for the task force and an analytic surge capability for specific contingencies. The integration of law enforcement intelligence into the training for strategic and military intelligence, and strategic and military analytic methods into law enforcement training, would augment this.

The final component would be the broadening of the intelligence mission in conflict and post-conflict situations to go beyond those who are using violence against U.S. forces and to develop strategic and targeting intelligence about both criminal enterprises and the criminal fundraising activities of political and military actors. In a sense, the shift of focus in Iraq from improvised explosive devices to the networks behind them was the kind of process being described, but it would need to be even broader and more explicit to be effective.

None of this is a panacea. Nevertheless, an organized crime threat assessment prior to military deployment and the creation of a multiagency intelligence task force focused on organized crime in conflict and postconflict situations would at least offer some prospect of avoiding the kind of strategic surprise that occurred in Iraq.

Notes

1. André Standing, *The Social Contradictions of Organized Crime on the Cape Flats,* Institute for Security Studies (ISS) Paper 74 (Pretoria, South Africa: ISS, June 2003), available at <www.iss.co.za/Pubs/Papers/74/Paper74.html>.

2. Ibid., 1.

3. Ibid.

4. Daniel McGrory, "How $45m Secretly Bought Freedom of Foreign Hostages," *The Times* (London), May 22, 2006, 8.

5. Jonathan Goodhand uses the terms *coping, shadow,* and *combat economies.* See "Frontiers and Wars: The Opium Economy in Afghanistan," *Journal of Agrarian Economy* 5, no. 2 (April 2005), 191–216. See also David S. Ramirez, "Gaining Control of Iraq's Shadow Economy" (Thesis, Naval Postgraduate School, September 2007), 20, 61–69; and Robert E. Looney, "The Business of Insurgency: The Expansion of Iraq's Shadow Economy," *The National Interest* (Fall 2005).

6. Austin Long, "The Anbar Awakening," *Survival* 50, no. 2 (April 2008), 67–94.

7. For the allusion, see Bing West, *The Strongest Tribe* (New York: Random House, 2008).

8. See Fritz W. Ermarth, "Seeing Russia Plain: The Russian Crisis and American Intelligence," *The National Interest* (Spring 1999), 5–14.

9. See Joseph D. Serio, *Investigating the Russian Mafia* (Durham, NC: Carolina Academic Press, 2008), especially 233–235.

10. Ermarth.

11. Ibid.

12. Ibid.

13. Ibid.

14. David Snowden, "Complex Acts of Knowing: Paradox and Descriptive Self-Awareness," *Journal of Knowledge Management* 6, no. 2 (May 2002).

15. Mark Edmond Clark, "Understanding Balkan Organized Crime: A Key to Success in Iraq?" interview by Sean Costigan, Columbia International Affairs Online, July 2003, available at <www.ciaonet.org/special_section/iraq/papers/clm10/clm10.html>.

16. Ibid.

17. United Nations Office of Drugs and Crime (UNODC), *Addressing Organized Crime and Drug Trafficking in Iraq: Report of the UNODC Fact Finding Mission 5–18 August* 2003 (Vienna: UNODC, August 25, 2003).

18. Ibid., 7.

19. Ibid., iii.

20. This point was made to the author in a conversation with one of the UNODC officials who authored the Iraq report.

21. Vadim Volkov, *Entrepreneurs of Violence: The Use of Force in the Making of Russian Capitalism* (Ithaca, NY: Cornell University Press, 2002).

22. Pamela Hess, "Analysis: Zen and the Art of Counterinsurgency," *The Washington Times,* July 29, 2004.

23. The author is grateful to James Cockayne of the International Peace Institute for this observation about the importance of labels.

24. Peter Andreas, "Criminalizing Consequences of Sanctions: Embargo Busting and Its Legacy," *International Studies Quarterly* 49, no. 2 (June 2005), 335–360.

25. Ibid., 335.

26. Ibid.

27. The notion of the "fierce" state is discussed in Nazih N. Ayubi, *Overstating the Arab State: Politics and Society in the Middle East* (New York: I.B. Tauris, 1996), especially chapter 12. For an excellent analysis of Iraq under Saddam Hussein that fits the notion of the fierce state, see Kanan Makiya, *Republic of Fear* (Berkeley: University of California Press, 1998).

28. Andreas, 337.

29. A notable exception to this was *Iraqslogger,* a journalistic blog that has provided highly perceptive reporting and valuable insights on developments in Iraq.

30. This phrase was used by Lilian Bobea at a Friedrich Ebert Stiftung Meeting on Organized Crime in Latin America, Mexico City, June 2008.

31. See Roy Godson, ed., *Menace to Society: Political-Criminal Collaboration Around the World* (New Brunswick, NJ: Transaction, 2003).

32. The author is grateful for many of the insights in this and the following paragraph to Marc Hess and Dr. Lawrence Cline.

33. Snowden.

Critical Thinking

1. Explain how organized crime might be a major factor destabilizing Iraq in the future.

2. What other factors may also play a role in destabilizing Iraq?

DR. PHIL WILLIAMS is Wesley W. Posvar Professor and Director of the Matthew B. Ridgway Center for International Security Studies at the University of Pittsburgh.

From *PRISM*, vol. 1, no. 2, March 2010, pp. 47–68. Copyright © 2010 by National Defense University Press. Reprinted by permission of NDU Press.

Africa's Forever Wars

JEFFREY GETTLEMAN

There is a very simple reason why some of Africa's bloodiest, most brutal wars never seem to end: They are not really wars. Not in the traditional sense, at least. The combatants don't have much of an ideology; they don't have clear goals. They couldn't care less about taking over capitals or major cities—in fact, they prefer the deep bush, where it is far easier to commit crimes. Today's rebels seem especially uninterested in winning converts, content instead to steal other people's children, stick Kalashnikovs or axes in their hands, and make them do the killing. Look closely at some of the continent's most intractable conflicts, from the rebel-laden creeks of the Niger Delta to the inferno in the Democratic Republic of the Congo, and this is what you will find.

What we are seeing is the decline of the classic African liberation movement and the proliferation of something else—something wilder, messier, more violent, and harder to wrap our heads around. If you'd like to call this war, fine. But what is spreading across Africa like a viral pandemic is actually just opportunistic, heavily armed banditry. My job as the *New York Times'* East Africa bureau chief is to cover news and feature stories in 12 countries. But most of my time is spent immersed in these un-wars.

I've witnessed up close—often way too close—how combat has morphed from soldier vs. soldier (now a rarity in Africa) to soldier vs. civilian. Most of today's African fighters are not rebels with a cause; they're predators. That's why we see stunning atrocities like eastern Congo's rape epidemic, where armed groups in recent years have sexually assaulted hundreds of thousands of women, often so sadistically that the victims are left incontinent for life. What is the military or political objective of ramming an assault rifle inside a woman and pulling the trigger? Terror has become an end, not just a means.

This is the story across much of Africa, where nearly half of the continent's 53 countries are home to an active conflict or a recently ended one. Quiet places such as Tanzania are the lonely exceptions; even user-friendly, tourist-filled Kenya blew up in 2008. Add together the casualties in just the dozen countries that I cover, and you have a death toll of tens of thousands of civilians each year. More than 5 million have died in Congo alone since 1998, the International Rescue Committee has estimated.

Of course, many of the last generation's independence struggles were bloody, too. South Sudan's decades-long rebellion is thought to have cost more than 2 million lives. But this is not about numbers. This is about methods and objectives, and the leaders driving them. Uganda's top guerrilla of the 1980s, Yoweri Museveni, used to fire up his rebels by telling them they were on the ground floor of a national people's army. Museveni became president in 1986, and he's still in office (another problem, another story). But his words seem downright noble compared with the best-known rebel leader from his country today, Joseph Kony, who just gives orders to burn.

Even if you could coax these men out of their jungle lairs and get them to the negotiating table, there is very little to offer them. They don't want ministries or tracts of land to govern. Their armies are often traumatized children, with experience and skills (if you can call them that) totally unsuited for civilian life. All they want is cash, guns, and a license to rampage. And they've already got all three. How do you negotiate with that?

The short answer is you don't. The only way to stop today's rebels for real is to capture or kill their leaders. Many are uniquely devious characters whose organizations would likely disappear as soon as they do. That's what happened in Angola when the diamond-smuggling rebel leader Jonas Savimbi was shot, bringing a sudden end to one of the Cold War's most intense conflicts. In Liberia, the moment that warlord-turned-president Charles Taylor was arrested in 2006 was the same moment that the curtain dropped on the gruesome circus of 10-year-old killers wearing Halloween masks. Countless dollars, hours, and lives have been wasted on fruitless rounds of talks that will never culminate in such clear-cut results. The same could be said of indictments of rebel leaders for crimes against humanity by the International Criminal Court. With the prospect of prosecution looming, those fighting are sure never to give up.

How did we get here? Maybe it's pure nostalgia, but it seems that yesteryear's African rebels had a bit more class. They were fighting against colonialism, tyranny, or apartheid. The winning insurgencies often came with a charming, intelligent leader wielding persuasive rhetoric. These were men like John Garang, who led the rebellion in southern Sudan with his Sudan People's Liberation Army. He pulled off what few guerrilla leaders anywhere have done: winning his people their own country. Thanks in part to his tenacity, South

Sudan will hold a referendum next year to secede from the North. Garang died in a 2005 helicopter crash, but people still talk about him like a god. Unfortunately, the region without him looks pretty godforsaken. I traveled to southern Sudan in November to report on how ethnic militias, formed in the new power vacuum, have taken to mowing down civilians by the thousands.

Even Robert Mugabe, Zimbabwe's dictator, was once a guerrilla with a plan. After transforming minority white-run Rhodesia into majority black-run Zimbabwe, he turned his country into one of the fastest-growing and most diversified economies south of the Sahara—for the first decade and a half of his rule. His status as a true war hero, and the aid he lent other African liberation movements in the 1980s, account for many African leaders' reluctance to criticize him today, even as he has led Zimbabwe down a path straight to hell.

These men are living relics of a past that has been essentially obliterated. Put the well-educated Garang and the old Mugabe in a room with today's visionless rebel leaders, and they would have just about nothing in common. What changed in one generation was in part the world itself. The Cold War's end bred state collapse and chaos. Where meddling great powers once found dominoes that needed to be kept from falling, they suddenly saw no national interest at all. (The exceptions, of course, were natural resources, which could be bought just as easily—and often at a nice discount—from various armed groups.) Suddenly, all you needed to be powerful was a gun, and as it turned out, there were plenty to go around. AK-47s and cheap ammunition bled out of the collapsed Eastern Bloc and into the farthest corners of Africa. It was the perfect opportunity for the charismatic and morally challenged.

In Congo, there have been dozens of such men since 1996, when rebels rose up against the leopard skin-capped dictator Mobutu Sese Seko, probably the most corrupt man in the history of this most corrupt continent. After Mobutu's state collapsed, no one really rebuilt it. In the anarchy that flourished, rebel leaders carved out fiefdoms ludicrously rich in gold, diamonds, copper, tin, and other minerals. Among them were Laurent Nkunda, Bosco Ntaganda, Thomas Lubanga, a toxic hodgepodge of Mai Mai commanders, Rwandan genocidaires, and the madman leaders of a flamboyantly cruel group called the Rastas.

I met Nkunda in his mountain hideout in late 2008 after slogging hours up a muddy road lined with baby-faced soldiers. The chopstick-thin general waxed eloquent about the oppression of the minority Tutsi people he claimed to represent, but he bristled when I asked him about the warlord-like taxes he was imposing and all the women his soldiers have raped. The questions didn't seem to trouble him too much, though, and he cheered up soon. His farmhouse had plenty of space for guests, so why didn't I spend the night?

Nkunda is not totally wrong about Congo's mess. Ethnic tensions are a real piece of the conflict, together with disputes over land, refugees, and meddling neighbor countries. But what I've come to understand is how quickly legitimate grievances in these failed or failing African states deteriorate into rapacious, profit-oriented bloodshed. Congo today is home to a resource

rebellion in which vague anti-government feelings become an excuse to steal public property. Congo's embarrassment of riches belongs to the 70 million Congolese, but in the past 10 to 15 years, that treasure has been hijacked by a couple dozen rebel commanders who use it to buy even more guns and wreak more havoc.

Probably the most disturbing example of an African un-war comes from the Lord's Resistance Army (LRA), begun as a rebel movement in northern Uganda during the lawless 1980s. Like the gangs in the oil-polluted Niger Delta, the LRA at first had some legitimate grievances—namely, the poverty and marginalization of the country's ethnic Acholi areas. The movement's leader, Joseph Kony, was a young, wig-wearing, gibberish-speaking, so-called prophet who espoused the Ten Commandments. Soon, he broke every one. He used his supposed magic powers (and drugs) to whip his followers into a frenzy and unleashed them on the very Acholi people he was supposed to be protecting.

The LRA literally carved their way across the region, leaving a trail of hacked-off limbs and sawed-off ears. They don't talk about the Ten Commandments anymore, and some of those left in their wake can barely talk at all. I'll never forget visiting northern Uganda a few years ago and meeting a whole group of

Africa Heats Up

Scientists have long warned that warming global temperatures and the resource scarcities that result will bring more violent conflicts. The U.S. government even directed its intelligence community to study the potential national security implications of climate change. But the evidence showing that rising temperatures cause armed conflict has been sketchy at best—until now.

In a recent study published in *Proceedings of the National Academy of Sciences,* a team of economists compared variations in temperature with the incidence of conflict in sub-Saharan Africa between 1981 and 2002 and found startling results: Just a 1 degree Celsius increase in temperature resulted in a 49 percent increase in the incidence of civil war. The situation looks even bleaker in coming decades. Given projected increases in global temperatures, the authors see a 54 percent increase in civil conflict across the region. If these conflicts are as deadly as the wars during the study period, Africa could suffer an additional 393,000 battle deaths by 2030.

The main reason for the projected violence is global warming's impact on agriculture, but there could be other factors as well. For instance, violent crime tends to increase when temperatures are high, while economic productivity decreases. In an especially depressing aside, the authors note that even under the "optimistic scenario" for economic growth and political reform in the coming decades, "neither is able to overcome the large effects of temperature increase on civil war incidence."

—Joshua E. Keating

women whose lips were sheared off by Kony's maniacs. Their mouths were always open, and you could always see their teeth. When Uganda finally got its act together in the late 1990s and cracked down, Kony and his men simply marched on. Today, their scourge has spread to one of the world's most lawless regions: the borderland where Sudan, Congo, and the Central African Republic meet.

Child soldiers are an inextricable part of these movements. The LRA, for example, never seized territory; it seized children. Its ranks are filled with brainwashed boys and girls who ransack villages and pound newborn babies to death in wooden mortars. In Congo, as many as one-third of all combatants are under 18. Since the new predatory style of African warfare is motivated and financed by crime, popular support is irrelevant to these rebels. The downside to not caring about winning hearts and minds, though, is that you don't win many recruits. So abducting and manipulating children becomes the only way to sustain the organized banditry. And children have turned out to be ideal weapons: easily brainwashed, intensely loyal, fearless, and, most importantly, in endless supply.

In this new age of forever wars, even Somalia looks different. That country certainly evokes the image of Africa's most chaotic state—exceptional even in its neighborhood for unending conflict. But what if Somalia is less of an outlier than a terrifying forecast of what war in Africa is moving toward? On the surface, Somalia seems wracked by a religiously themed civil conflict between the internationally backed but feckless transitional government and the Islamist militia al-Shabab. Yet the fighting is being nourished by the same old Somali problem that has dogged this desperately poor country since 1991: warlordism. Many of the men who command or fund militias in Somalia today are the same ones who tore the place apart over the past 20 years in a scramble for the few resources left—the port, airport, telephone poles, and grazing pastures.

Somalis are getting sick of the Shabab and its draconian rules—no music, no gold teeth, even no bras. But what has kept locals in Somalia from rising up against foreign terrorists is Somalia's deeply ingrained culture of war profiteering. The world has let Somalia fester too long without a permanent government. Now, many powerful Somalis have a vested interest in the status quo chaos. One olive oil exporter in Mogadishu told me that he and some trader friends bought a crate of missiles to shoot at government soldiers because "taxes are annoying."

Most frightening is how many sick states like Congo are now showing Somalia-like symptoms. Whenever a potential leader emerges to reimpose order in Mogadishu, criminal networks rise up to finance his opponent, no matter who that may be. The longer these areas are stateless, the harder it is to go back to the necessary evil of government.

All this might seem a gross simplification, and indeed, not all of Africa's conflicts fit this new paradigm. The old steady—the military coup—is still a common form of political upheaval, as Guinea found out in 2008 and Madagascar not too long thereafter. I have also come across a few non-hoodlum rebels who seem legitimately motivated, like some of the Darfurian commanders in Sudan. But though their political grievances are well defined, the organizations they "lead" are not. Old-style African rebels spent years in the bush honing their leadership skills, polishing their ideology, and learning to deliver services before they ever met a Western diplomat or sat for a television interview. Now rebels are hoisted out of obscurity after they have little more than a website and a "press office" (read: a satellite telephone). When I went to a Darfur peace conference in Sirte, Libya, in 2007, I quickly realized that the main draw for many of these rebel "leaders" was not the negotiating sessions, but the all-you-can-eat buffet.

For the rest, there are the un-wars, these ceaseless conflicts I spend my days cataloging as they grind on, mincing lives and spitting out bodies. Recently, I was in southern Sudan working on a piece about the Ugandan Army's hunt for Kony, and I met a young woman named Flo. She had been a slave in the LRA for 15 years and had recently escaped. She had scarred shins and stony eyes, and often there were long pauses after my questions, when Flo would stare at the horizon. "I am just thinking of the road home," she said. It was never clear to her why the LRA was fighting. To her, it seemed like they had been aimlessly tramping through the jungle, marching in circles.

This is what many conflicts in Africa have become—circles of violence in the bush, with no end in sight.

Critical Thinking

1. What are the main reasons why the war in Sierra Leone took so long to end or why violent conflict in the eastern part of the Democratic Republic of the Congo continues today?

2. Identify one of "Africa's Forever Wars" that is still simmering and explain how it differs from a conventional civil war or domestic conflict.

JEFFREY GETTLEMAN is East Africa bureau chief for the New York Times.

UNIT 7

Asymmetric Conflicts: Trends in Terrorism and Counterterrorism

Unit Selections

Learning Objectives

- Describe some ways that Al Qaeda has become a more adaptive and flexible organization and be able to provide a few examples.

- Explain what al-Shabab is and why it launched simultaneous attacks in Uganda during the World Cup.

- What are the three integrated pillars of a successful counterinsurgency campaign?

- Describe one program the United States military is using to try to reduce the number of young men attracted to jihadist terrorism in Asia.

Student Website
www.mhhe.com/cls

Internet References

Columbia International Affairs Online
www.ciaonet.org/cbr/cbr00/video/cbr-v/cbr-v.html
Stratfor Global Intelligence
www.stratfor.com/about_stratfor
Combating Terrorism Center at West Point
www./ctc.usma.edu
The Search for International Terrorist Entities
www.siteinstitute.org/index.html
Terrorism Research Center
www.terrorism.com
United States Government Counterinsurgency Initiative
www.usgcoin.org
AFPAK
www.nato.int/ISAF

The terrorist attacks against the World Trade Center and the Pentagon on September 11, 2001, and the anthrax letter attacks the following month highlighted the vulnerabilities of economically developed societies to attacks by disaffected radicals who can now pursue their political goals by killing large numbers of civilians. The United States' decision to pursue the al-Qaeda terrorists using the military as the lead agency in the Global War on Terrorism (GWOT) resulted in a comprehensive offensive that mobilized large amounts of the resources and time of the United States and allied governments. Although Osama bin Laden and Ayman al-Zawahiri remain at large, much of the leadership and organizational structure of al-Qaeda has been destroyed or disrupted.

For many observers, al-Qaeda's decision to take the fight directly to America was a strategic mistake, since it prompted an unprecedented and largely effective response from a previously distracted giant, the United States. During the early years of the war many analysts believed that the United States had succeeded in its struggle against terrorism. However, many analysts and United States voters concluded that the United States was also wrong to attack Iraq rather than finish the hunt for Osama bin Laden and eliminate the residual Taliban threat in Afghanistan. During 2008, some well-known western terrorist analysts pronounced al-Qaeda's military and strategic campaign against the United States and "near enemies" as having failed even though legacy residual groups would continue to operate worldwide.

The resurgence of the Taliban attacks and success at controlling large parts of Afghanistan and growing evidence that al-Qaeda leaders were living comfortably in houses, not caves, in several urban areas within the Tribal Trust areas of Pakistan led many of the same analysts to reassess the security situation in Afghanistan and Pakistan in recent years. Despite a renewed offensive by Pakistani and American forces in some of the border territories starting in 2009, al-Qaeda Central continues to work to destabilize the Pakistani government, divert United States attention from the fight in Afghanistan, and undermine Islamabad's alliance with the United States. The increased frequency of high profile suicide attacks widely attributed to al-Qaeda in several civilian locations in different urban areas of Pakistan is only one of several signs of a shift in al-Qaeda's strategy. Many Pakistanis blame the United States for the increased violence within their borders. Tensions between the United States and Pakistani government over unilateral U.S. manned and drone attacks in Pakistan reached a crisis point during the fall of 2010 when Pakistan closed one of the main transportation routes into Afghanistan. Meanwhile, bin Laden, acting in his self-proclaimed role of global statesman for the radical Islamic world, issued two audio proclamations urging more affluent governments in the Muslim world to do more to help the millions struggling to recover from historic flood damage in Pakistan.

While al-Qaeda Central may not yet be on the ropes, the leadership is now tightly constrained and must operate from secret locations. More threats now come from several decentralized and often self-financed small groups of radical jihadists who operate in Europe, Africa, and other locations around

the world. Many of these groups had their own agenda before pledging their allegiance to bin Laden. This diffusion of al-Qaeda inspired, and in a some cases al-Qaeda Central trained, terrorist attacks is why some analysts now predict that the battle against jihadist extremism may take 50 or more years to win even if bin Laden and his lieutenants are captured or killed. This more pessimistic view is based on the fact that al-Qaeda has proven to be a highly adaptive movement in the face of a successful Global War on Terrorism (GWOT), renamed "complex overseas operations" by U.S. Obama Administration officials. Scott Stewart notes in "Profiling: Sketching the Face of Jihadism," that al-Qaeda has no lack of operatives, including increased numbers of volunteers from the West. A recently foiled Mumbai-style plot to attack locations in Germany, the United Kingdom, and France simultaneously, including the iconic Eiffel Tower, illustrates the tactical flexibility of a movement that continues to attempt high profile attacks against both "near and far enemies" worldwide.

Al-Qaeda allies throughout Africa are among the most active in carrying out high-profile attacks in West, East, and the Horn of Africa. Since the withdrawal of Ethiopian troops from Somalia, the former youth movement al-Shabab has pledged its allegiance to al-Qaeda while continuing to consolidate its presence in the country and launching attacks into neighboring states. Al-Qaeda failed to disrupt the World Cup games in South Africa, but al-Shabab demonstrated its expanded operational reach with two simultaneous suicide bombings in the Ugandan capital of Kampala during July 2010. Tim Pippard, in "Al-Shabab's Agenda in the Wake of the Kampala Suicide Attacks," describes how the organization carried out twin bombings of a rugby club and Ethiopian restaurant that left 76 civilians, who were watching the World Cup final on televisions, injured or dead. These attacks suggest that al-Shabab and al-Qaeda in the Maghreb (AQIM) in West Africa will continue to evolve into greater regional threats to African and Western interests in the future.

Although the United States and other Western countries are helping foreign governments contain a growing threat from terrorists, the harsh reality remains that successful counter-terrorism program often take a long time. Dr. David J. Kilcullen emphasizes in "Three Pillars of Counterinsurgency" that the last time the United States attempted to implement an interagency counterinsurgency doctrine was in 1962, and it didn't work very well. Kilcullen warns that the conflict environment today is even more complicated and that the U.S. government must mobilize all its agencies along with host nations, multiple foreign allies, and coalition partners, non-government organizations, media, community groups, and business in order to win the war. In his article, Kilcullen proposes an interagency counterinsurgency framework based on three integrated pillars—economic, political, and security activities.

Western governments are also supporting a number of new programs that are designed to reduce the appeal among Muslim youths to joining jihadist terrorist organizations. Miemie Winn Byrd, in "Combating Terrorism with SocioEconomics: Leveraging the Private Sector," describes one such designed to counter the attraction to religious extremism for young Muslim males that was started by the United States Pacific Command (USPACOM) in the Philippines in 2002 that was used later in Iraq. The approach relies to a great extent on using DOD Reserves and Guard members and links with the private sector to open doors to the business community to develop non-traditional networks and partnerships.

Profiling: Sketching the Face of Jihadism

SCOTT STEWART

O n Jan. 4, 2010, the U.S. Transportation Security Administration (TSA) adopted new rules that would increase the screening of citizens from 14 countries who want to fly to the United States as well as travellers of all nationalities who are flying to the United States from one of the 14 countries. These countries are: Afghanistan, Algeria, Cuba, Iran, Iraq, Lebanon, Libya, Nigeria, Pakistan, Saudi Arabia, Somalia, Sudan, Syria and Yemen.

Four of the countries—Cuba, Iran, Sudan and Syria—are on the U.S. government's list of state sponsors of terrorism. The other 10 have been labeled "countries of interest" by the TSA and appear to have been added in response to jihadist attacks in recent years. Nigeria was almost certainly added to the list only as a result of the Christmas Day bombing attempt aboard a Detroit-bound U.S. airliner by Umar Farouk Abdulmutallab, a 23-year-old Nigerian man.

As reflected by the large number of chain e-mails that swirl around after every attack or attempted attack against the United States, the type of profiling program the TSA has instituted will be very popular in certain quarters. Conventional wisdom holds that such programs will be effective in protecting the flying public from terrorist attacks because profiling is easy to do. However, when one steps back and carefully examines the historical face of the jihadist threat, it becomes readily apparent that it is very difficult to create a one-size-fits-all profile of a jihadist operative. When focusing on a resourceful and adaptive adversary, the use of such profiles sets a security system up for failure by causing security personnel and the general public to focus on a threat that is defined too narrowly.

Sketching the face of jihadism is simply not as easy as it might seem.

The Historical Face of Terror

One popular chain e-mail that seemingly circulates after every attack or attempted attack notes that the attack was not conducted by Richard Simmons or the Tooth Fairy but by "Muslim male extremists between the ages of 17 and 40." And when we set aside the Chechen "Black Widows," the occasional female suicide bomber and people like Timothy McVeigh and Eric Rudolph, many terrorist attacks are indeed planned and orchestrated by male Muslim extremists between the ages of 17 and 40. The problem comes when you try to define what a male Muslim extremist between the ages of 17 and 40 looks like.

When we look back at the early jihadist attacks against the United States, we see that many perpetrators matched the stereotypical Muslim profile. In the killing of Rabbi Meir Kahane, the 1993 World Trade Center Bombing and the thwarted 1993 New York Landmarks Plot, we saw a large contingent of Egyptians, including Omar Abdul-Rahman (aka "the Blind Sheikh"), ElSayyid Nosair, Ibrahim Elgabrowny, Mahmud Abouhalima and several others. In fact, Egyptians played a significant role in the development of the jihadist ideology and have long constituted a very substantial portion of the international jihadist movement—and even of the core al Qaeda cadre. Because of this, it is quite surprising that Egypt does not appear on the TSA's profile list.

Indeed, in addition to the Egyptians, in the early jihadist plots against the United States we also saw operatives who were Palestinian, Pakistani, Sudanese and Iraqi. However—and this is significant—in the New York Landmarks Plot we also saw a Puerto Rican convert to Islam named Victor Alvarez and an African-American Muslim named Clement Rodney Hampton-el. Alvarez and Hampton-el clearly did not fit the typical profile.

The Kuwait-born Pakistani citizen who was the bombmaker in the 1993 World Trade Center bombing is a man named Abdul Basit (widely known by his alias, Ramzi Yousef). After leaving the United States, Basit resettled in Manila and attempted to orchestrate an attack against U.S. airliners in Asia called Operation Bojinka. After an apartment fire in Manila caused Basit to flee the city, he moved to Islamabad, where he attempted to recruit new jihadist operatives to carry out the Bojinka plot. One of the men he recruited was a South African Muslim named Istaique Parker. After a few dry-run operations, Parker got cold feet, decided he did not want to embrace martyrdom and helped the U.S. Diplomatic Security Service special agents assigned to the U.S. Embassy orchestrate Basit's arrest. A South African named Parker does not fit the typical terrorist profile.

The following individuals, among many others, were involved in jihadist activity but did not fit what most people would consider the typical jihadist profile:

- Richard Reid, the British citizen known as the "shoe bomber."
- Jose Padilla, the American citizen known as the "dirty bomber."
- Adam Gadahn, an al Qaeda spokesman who was born Adam Pearlman in California.
- John Walker Lindh, the so-called "American Taliban."
- Jack Roche, the Australian known as "Jihad Jack."
- The Duka brothers, ethnic Albanians involved in the Fort Dix plot.
- Daniel Boyd and his sons, American citizens plotting grassroots attacks inside the United States.
- Germaine Maurice Lindsay, the Jamaican-born suicide bomber involved in the July 7, 2005, London attacks.

- Nick Reilly, the British citizen who attempted to bomb a restaurant in Exeter in May 2008.
- David Headley, the U.S. citizen who helped plan the Mumbai attacks.

As reflected by the list above, jihadists come from many ethnicities and nationalities, and they can range from Americans named Daniel, Victor and John to a Macedonian nicknamed "Elvis," a Tanzanian called "Foopie" (who smuggled explosives by bicycle) and an Indonesian named Zulkarnaen. There simply is not one ethnic or national profile that can be used to describe them all.

An Adaptive Opponent

One of the big reasons we've witnessed men with names like Richard and Jose used in jihadist plots is because jihadist planners are adaptive and innovative. They will adjust the operatives they select for a mission in order to circumvent new security measures. In the wake of the 9/11 attacks, when security forces began to focus additional scrutiny on people with Muslim names, they dispatched Richard Reid on his shoe-bomb mission. And it worked—Reid was able to get his device by security and onto the plane. If he hadn't fumbled the execution of the attack, it would have destroyed the aircraft. Moreover, when Khalid Sheikh Mohammed wanted to get an operative into the United States to conduct attacks following 9/11, he selected U.S. citizen Jose Padilla. Padilla successfully entered the country, and it was only Mohammed's arrest and interrogation that alerted authorities to Padilla's mission.

But their operational flexibility in fact predates the 9/11 attack. For example, some of the operatives initially selected for the 9/11 mission were Yemenis and could not obtain visas to the United States. Since Saudis were able to obtain visas much easier, al Qaeda simply shifted gears and decided to use Saudis instead of Yemenis.

Pakistan-based militant groups Lashkar-e-Taiba and Harkat-ul-Jihad e-Islami likewise sought to fool the Danish and Indian security services when they dispatched an American citizen named David Headley from Chicago to conduct pre-operational surveillance in Mumbai and Denmark. Headley, who was named Daood Gilani at his birth, legally changed his name to David Coleman Headley, anglicising his first name and taking his mother's maiden name. The name change and his American accent were apparently enough to throw intelligence agencies off his trail—in spite of his very aggressive surveillance activity.

Most recently, al Qaeda in the Arabian Peninsula (AQAP) showed its cunning when it dispatched a Nigerian, Abdulmutallab, in the Christmas Day attack. Although STRATFOR was among the first to see the threat AQAP's innovative devices posed to aviation security, there is no way we could have forecast that the group would conduct an attack originating out of Nigeria using a Nigerian citizen. A Saudi or Yemeni, certainly; a Somali or American citizen, maybe—but a Nigerian? AQAP's use of such an operative was a total paradigm shift. (Perhaps this paradigm shift explains in part why U.S. officials chose not to act more aggressively on intelligence they had obtained on Abdulmutallab that could have prevented the attack.) The only reason Nigeria is on the list of 14 countries now is because of the Christmas Day incident, and there is no reason that jihadists couldn't use a Muslim from Togo, Ghana, or Trinidad and Tobago instead of a Nigerian in their next attack.

Jihadist planners have now heard about the list of 14 countries and, demonstrating their adaptability, will undoubtedly try to use operatives who are not from one of those countries and choose flights that originate from other places as well. They may even follow the lead of Chechen militants and the Islamic State of Iraq by employing female suicide bombers. They will also likely instruct operatives to "lose" their passports so that they can obtain new documents that contain no traces of travel to one of the 14 countries on the list. Jihadists have frequently used this tactic to hide operatives' travel to training camps in places like Afghanistan and Pakistan.

Moreover, jihadist groups have no lack of operatives from countries that are not on that list. Jihadists from all over the world have travelled to jihadist training camps, and in addition to the large number of Egyptian, Moroccan and Tunisian jihadists (countries not on the list), there are also Filipinos, Indonesians, Malaysians and, of course, Americans and Europeans. Frankly, there have been far more jihadist plots that have originated in the United Kingdom than there have been plots involving Nigerians, and yet Nigeria is on the list and the United Kingdom is not. Because of this, a British citizen (or an American, for that matter) who has been fighting with al Shabaab in Somalia could board a flight in Nairobi or Cairo and receive less scrutiny than an innocent Nigerian flying from the same airport.

In an environment where the potential threat is hard to identify, it is doubly important to profile individuals based on their behaviour rather than their ethnicity or nationality—what we refer to as focusing on the "how" rather than the "who." Instead of relying on pat profiles, security personnel should be encouraged to exercise their intelligence, intuition and common sense. A U.S. citizen named Robert who shows up at the U.S. Embassy in Nairobi or Amman claiming to have lost his passport may be far more dangerous than some random Pakistani or Yemeni citizen, even though the American does not fit the profile requiring extra security checks.

The difficulty of creating a reliable and accurate physical profile of a jihadist, and the adaptability and ingenuity of the jihadist planners, means that any attempt at profiling is doomed to fail. In fact, profiling can prove counter-productive to good security by blinding people to real threats. They will dismiss potential malefactors who do not fit the specific profile they have been provided.

Critical Thinking

1. Groups affiliated with al-Qaeda today in places such as Somalia or the United Kingdom are very different from the al-Qaeda led by Osama bin Laden over a decade ago. Pick one jihadist terrorist group that has pledged allegiance to al-Qaeda Central and describe this group's objectives, tactics, and methods of financing terrorist operations.

2. Use the same group discussed in prior question to provide examples of how the group differs from bin Laden's al-Qaeda prior to 9/11.

Al-Shabab's Agenda in the Wake of the Kampala Suicide Attacks

TIM PIPPARD

The Somali Islamist group al-Shabab demonstrated its expanding operational reach when it executed simultaneous suicide bombings in the Ugandan capital, Kampala, on July 11, 2010.[1] The attacks—targeting a rugby club and an Ethiopian restaurant in a neighborhood popular with expatriates as people watched the World Cup final—left 76 civilians dead, including one U.S. citizen.[2] While an investigation by Ugandan authorities into the attacks is ongoing (with some support from the U.S. Federal Bureau of Investigation), U.S. Department of State officials acknowledge that initial evidence confirms the al-Shabab connection to the blasts.[3]

Al-Shabab previously announced its internationalist ambitions on February 1, 2010 when it formally aligned with al-Qa'ida, stressing in a media release that the "jihad of the Horn of Africa must be combined with the international jihad led by the al-Qa'ida network."[4] Yet for the most part, this move had minimal immediate impact on al-Shabab's operational activities. Aside from a handful of minor incursions into northern and northeastern Kenya, the group has retained a focus on Somalia and foreign military and political targets in the capital city Mogadishu, as well as parts of central and southern Somalia.[5]

Therefore, the Kampala attacks—al-Shabab's first successful major foreign operation—constitute an important development, raising questions about the extent to which al-Shabab is evolving from an Islamic-nationalist group claiming to operate on behalf of Somalis, to one now seemingly incorporated more fully into a broader pan-Islamic campaign. This article will examine the group's capacity to pursue and sustain a campaign outside of Somalia's borders.

Al-Shabab's Foreign Focus

Al-Shabab emerged as an independent entity in early 2007 following the collapse of the Islamic Courts Union (ICU), which controlled much of central and southern Somalia during the latter half of 2006 until an Ethiopian invasion in late December ousted the Islamists from power.[6] Its central aims since that time have been to overthrow Somalia's

Transitional Federal Government (TFG), implement Shari'a, and eject all foreign security forces from the country.

The heavy presence of foreign military personnel in Somalia is one of the key drivers of al-Shabab's campaign, ensuring that the group has always incorporated a foreign-focused element. The African Union Mission in Somalia (AMISOM) is currently the only force capable of challenging al-Shabab's ascendency in Mogadishu, having replaced Ethiopian troops in early 2007 to bolster the TFG.[7] Critically, of the 6,000 AMISOM military personnel currently deployed in Somalia, all but four military staff officers have been provided by Uganda and Burundi—a level of involvement guaranteeing that both countries remain priority targets for Somali Islamists.[8] Al-Shabab has also characterized AMISOM as a mere continuation of the Ethiopian invasion, and thus Ethiopia too remains a key al-Shabab adversary.

In this respect, the Kampala attacks mark the continuation and intensification of al-Shabab's rhetorical and operational campaign directed at Ugandan and Burundian targets that has become increasingly pronounced and coherent in recent months. On July 9, 2010, just two days prior to the Kampala blasts, al-Shabab issued a statement encouraging Islamist militants in Chechnya, Pakistan, Afghanistan and elsewhere to attack the diplomatic missions of Uganda and Burundi in response to their continued support for the TFG.[9] Specific threats targeting the Ugandan and Burundian capital cities also featured in an al-Shabab statement dated October 22, 2009, in which senior al-Shabab commander Shaykh Ali Mohamed Hussein stressed: "We shall make their people cry. We will attack Bujumbura and Kampala . . . We will move our fighting to those two cities and we will destroy them."[10]

The Kampala attacks mark the continuation and intensification of al-Shabab's rhetorical and operational campaign directed at Ugandan and Burundian targets that has become increasingly pronounced and coherent in recent months.

Ugandan and Burundian troops have also come under sustained attack in al-Shabab-controlled areas of Mogadishu in IED attacks, raids, ambushes, targeted assassinations, and stand-off weapon operations. In one such exchange on June 3, 2010, mortar fire between al-Shabab militants and TFG troops (backed by AMISOM peacekeepers) in the Kaaraan, Yaqshid and Abdiazziz districts of the capital left 23 people dead and 66 others wounded; two of those killed were Ugandan troops.[11]

Radicalization and Centralization

Al-Shabab's operational capacity to project its campaign beyond Somalia's borders ultimately relates to a range of shifts in the group's internal dynamics during the past two years, culminating in the emergence of a highly centralized and radicalized organization that is far more capable of pursuing its extreme Islamist ideology.

Most notably, al-Shabab's loose network structure has been supplanted by a more centralized organizational hierarchy coalesced around several key Somali extremists.[12] These include the group's leader Ahmed Abdi Aw-Mahmoud (known as "Godane"), Ibrahim Haji Jama "al-Afghani," and Shaykh Fuad Mohamed "Shongole." These individuals are thought to be supported by several foreign al-Qa'ida operatives implicated in the 1998 U.S. Embassy bombings in Nairobi and Dar es Salaam, as well as the attacks on Israeli tourists in Mombasa in November 2002,[13] principal among them being Fazul Abdullah Muhammad (al-Qa'ida's leading figure in Somalia).[14] Many of these foreign fighters have settled in al-Shabab camps in southern Somalia and are involved in training Somali militants.[15] Their primacy in the upper echelons of al-Shabab's leadership hierarchy also facilitates and ensures the high degree of operational planning and preparedness required to successfully launch large-scale operations.

In addition, al-Shabab has increasingly incorporated tactics synonymous with sophisticated al-Qa'ida operations—a progression common to local groups seeking to solidify ties with al-Qa'ida.[16] Several al-Shabab attacks have involved multiple, simultaneous mass casualty suicide explosions. On September 17, 2009, two al-Shabab suicide bombers infiltrated AMISOM's headquarters in the capital city, killing 17 soldiers (including Burundian Major General Juvenal Niyonguruza, AMISOM's deputy commander) and injuring another 40.[17] On December 3, 2009, a suicide bomber blew himself up at a graduation ceremony being held at Mogadishu's Shamo Hotel, killing 24 people, including four TFG officials.[18]

Al-Shabab has also crafted a vigorous communications strategy designed to promote and garner domestic and international support for its extreme ideology, as well as discourage further external meddling in Somalia. Al-Shabab's media wing—the al-Kataib Foundation for Media Productions—frequently issues high quality video and audio statements containing threats of future attacks, or glorifying past operations (particularly martyrdom operations). A 10-minute video released by al-Shabab in early June 2010 titled "The African Crusaders" is one of the slickest productions to date, containing footage and images of heavy clashes with AMISOM troops in northern Mogadishu on May 27.[19] Speaking in English, the narrator questions the involvement of Ugandan and Burundian troops in Somalia, accusing them of "fighting America's war in a foreign land."[20]

Diaspora Support

Al-Shabab is also actively seeking material and physical support from Somali communities in Western Europe and the United States, further enhancing its international characteristics. For instance, in February 2008 three Somali immigrants were arrested in Sweden and three in Norway on suspicion of financing terrorism (five individuals were subsequently released without charge; one Norwegian national was charged in October 2009 with collecting money for Somali terrorist groups).[21]

Many of the individuals recruited into al-Shabab's ranks or suspected of providing material support to the group are U.S. nationals, some of whom have become highly radicalized. On November 23, 2009, as part of an ongoing U.S. investigation into Somali Islamist insurgent support networks, 14 individuals were charged with recruiting and financing some 20 Somali men in the Minneapolis area of Minnesota, who subsequently traveled to Somalia and trained at al-Shabab camps.[22] According to official court documents, a Somali-American who traveled to Somalia, Shirwa Ahmed, was one of five suicide bombers involved in simultaneous suicide attacks in northern Somalia in October 2008.[23] The central concern among U.S. counterterrorism officials is that more members of the Somali-American diaspora might embrace terrorism, and that al-Qa'ida will continue to exploit and develop its base in southern Somalia from which to target U.S. and Western interests.[24]

Another U.S. national recruited to al-Shabab, Omar Hammami (also known as Abu Mansur al-Amriki), has emerged as a high-profile media representative, appearing in numerous al-Shabab propaganda videos and providing a foreign face to the group.[25]

Conclusion

Each of these attributes—an increasingly radical agenda, a centralized leadership structure, refined propaganda machinery, and a foreign support network—suggests that al-Shabab will continue to evolve into a greater regional threat. Indeed, on July 15, 2010, al-Shabab threatened further attacks against Uganda and Burundi in an audio statement aired on Mogadishu radio stations, in which al-Shabab insisted that "what has happened in Kampala was only the beginning. We will keep revenging what your soldiers remorselessly did to our people."[26]

Each of these attributes suggests that al-Shabab will continue to evolve into a greater regional threat.

Concurrently, however, al-Shabab's evolution into a more overtly internationalist organization has undercut some of its appeal and support base within Somalia.[27] Al-Shabab's hard line interpretation of Islam (in which it is attempting to impose religious uniformity on Somali society at the expense of traditional clan structures and beliefs) has failed to resonate with many Somali citizens.[28] In addition, while al-Shabab's increasingly brutal operational tactics—specifically suicide bombings targeting civilians—have enabled it to retain territory in central and southern Somalia, such tactics have also caused public outrage and alienated supporters, even in traditional al-Shabab strongholds.[29]

Al-Shabab is also coming under increasing pressure from other Somali factions, particularly Hisbul Islamiyya (another of Somalia's Islamist organizations that emerged from the collapse of the ICU). Tensions between the two groups intensified in October 2009 when Hisbul Islamiyya and al-Shabab militants fought each other for control of the strategically important town of Kismayo.[30] Consequently, al-Shabab's efforts are now largely focused on re-establishing its political and military credentials, and vying for influence alongside other factions in Somalia's Islamist movement.

As such, while al-Shabab's successful execution of sporadic, large-scale attacks abroad seems quite feasible in the future, a protracted foreign campaign—in which al-Shabab develops and retains external networks responsible for launching attacks against Ugandan and Burundian targets—appears beyond the group's present capabilities.

Notes

1. Alisha Ryu, "Al-Shabab Leader Threatens More Attacks in Uganda," Voice of America, July 15, 2010.

2. "Somali Militants Claim Kampala World Cup Blasts," BBC, July 12, 2010; "Worldwide Alert Issued to Identify Kampala Suicide Bombers," Voice of America, July 18, 2010.

3. Al-Shabab also officially claimed responsibility for the blasts. Separately, Ugandan police announced on July 13 that they had found an explosives-laden vest (rigged to detonate by cell phone) at a nightclub in Kampala, possibly preventing another explosion. For details, see Josh Kron, "Uganda Says it Thwarted Another Bombing," *New York Times,* July 13, 2010; Philip J. Crowley, daily press briefing, U.S. State Department, July 12, 2010.

4. Sarah Childress, "Somalia's Al-Shabaab to Ally With Al-Qaeda," *Wall Street Journal,* February 2, 2010.

5. Fred Mukinda, "Al-Shabab Attacks Kenya Territory," *Daily Nation,* March 31, 2010; "Shabab Militants Attack Village in Kenya's North Eastern Province," Jane's Terrorism and Insurgency Centre, May 29, 2010.

6. "Somalia: The Tough Part is Ahead," International Crisis Group, January 26, 2007; Ravi Somaiya, "Who is Al-Shabab?" *Newsweek,* July 12, 2010.

7. Will Hartley, "Terrorism Trends—Jane's Intelligence Centre Seminar," IHS Jane's, June 22, 2010.

8. Although AMISOM's force size has failed to reach its mandated 8,000, Uganda's deployment of a fourth battalion in mid-March 2010 took the force size to 6,120 troops. Of this total, Ghana, Cameroon, Senegal and Zambia have contributed four military staff officers to AMISOM headquarters in Mogadishu. Nigeria, Sierra Leone and Zambia have also contributed to the 40-strong AMISOM civilian police deployment in Somalia. See "Report of the Secretary-General on Somalia," United Nations Security Council, May 11, 2010.

9. "Somalia's Shabab Calls on Global Islamist Militants to Attack Ugandan and Burundian Targets," Jane's Terrorism and insurgency Centre, July 9, 2010.

10. "Shabab Threatens to Attack Burundian and Ugandan Capitals," Jane's Terrorism and Insurgency Centre, October 23, 2009; "Shabab Threatens Uganda and Burundi," al-Jazira, October 23, 2009.

11. "Mortar Exchange Leaves 23 Dead in Somalia's Mogadishu," Jane's Terrorism and Insurgency Centre, June 3, 2010.

12. "Somalia's Divided Islamists," International Crisis Group, May 18, 2010.

13. Johnnie Carson, "Developing a Coordinated and Sustainable U.S. Strategy Toward Somalia," testimony before the U.S. Senate Select Committee on Foreign Relations, May 20, 2009.

14. Fazul Abdullah Muhammad became al-Qa'ida's lead operative in Somalia after the death of Salah Ali Salah Nabhan in a U.S. raid on September 14, 2009. See "Shabab's Mixed Messages," *Jane's Terrorism and Security Monitor,* January 27, 2010; "Somalia's Divided Islamists."

15. "Al Qaeda in Yemen and Somalia: A Ticking Time Bomb," report to the Committee on Foreign Relations, U.S. Senate, January 21, 2010.

16. For instance, in Algeria the Salafist Group for Preaching and Combat's (GSPC) alignment with al-Qa'ida in late 2006 led to a resurgence in violence characterized by large-scale suicide attacks in April, September and December 2007. See "JTIC Country Briefing—Algeria," Jane's Terrorism and Insurgency Centre, June 1, 2009.

17. "Shabab Attacks AMISOM," *Jane's Terrorism and Security Monitor,* July 12, 2010.

18. "Somalia's Divided Islamists."

19. "The African Crusaders," al-Kataib Foundation for Media Productions, June 2010.

20. "Shabab Attacks AMISOM."

21. "Somalis Arrested in Sweden," *Ice News,* March 11, 2008; Christian Nils Larson and Michael Jonsson, "Tax Evasion—Dealing with the Shabab's Funding," *Jane's Intelligence Review,* February 9, 2010.

22. "Terror Charges Unsealed in Minneapolis Against Eight Men, Justice Department Announces," U.S. Department of Justice, November 23, 2009.

23. Ibid.

24. Bronwyn Bruton, "In the Quicksands of Somalia," *Foreign Affairs* 88:6 (2009); "Al Qaeda in Yemen and Somalia: A Ticking Time Bomb."

25. Andrea Elliott, "The Jihadist Next Door," *New York Times,* January 31, 2010.

26. Mohamed Olad Hassan, "Al-Shabab Leader Threatens More Uganda Attacks," Associated Press, July 15, 2010.

27. "Somalia's Divided Islamists."

28. The International Crisis Group (ICG) has documented numerous instances of public disaffection at al-Shabab's attempts to impose its extreme vision of Islam on Somali society. ICG researchers also note that public disillusion with al-Shabab is being further fueled by its poor governance record in southern Somalia. See "Somalia's Divided Islamists."

29. Ibid.; Mark Landler, "After Attacks in Uganda, Worry Grows Over Group," *New York Times,* July 12, 2010.

30. Stig Jarle Hansen, "Faction Fluctuation—The Shifting Allegiances within Hizbul Islam," *Jane's Intelligence Review,* March 11, 2010. Tensions between Hisbul Islamiyya and al-Shabab commanders have continued, with clashes between the two groups occurring into mid-2010.

Critical Thinking

1. Define al-Shabab and describe its current activities in Somalia and neighboring countries.

2. What objectives did al-Shabab achieve by launching simultaneous attacks in Uganda during the 2010 World Cup in South Africa?

3. Provide three reasons why al-Shabab chose to strike Uganda rather than South Africa during the 2010 World Cup.

TIM PIPPARD is Senior Consultant in the Security and Military Intelligence Practice of IHS Jane's, and is currently Research Director of an IHS Jane's study entitled "Relationships and Rivalries: Assessing Al-Qa'ida's Affiliate Network." He is Assistant Editor of Perspectives on Terrorism (the journal of the Terrorism Research Initiative), and former managing editor of Jane's Terrorism and Insurgency Center (JTIC).

Three Pillars of Counterinsurgency

Dr. David J. Kilcullen[*]

Introduction

We meet today in the shadow of continuing counterinsurgencies that have cost thousands of lives and a fortune in financial, moral and political capital. And we meet under the threat of similar insurgencies to come. Any smart future enemy will likely sidestep our unprecedented superiority in traditional, force-on-force, state-on-state warfare. And so insurgency, including terrorism, will be our enemies' weapon of choice until we prove we can master it.[1] Like Bill Murray in *Groundhog Day,* we are going to live this day over, and over, and over again—until we get it right.

So we seek a common doctrine to integrate national power against the threat. This has happened before, it turns out.

The United States produced an inter-agency counterinsurgency doctrine in 1962. Called the *Overseas Internal Defense Policy* (OIDP),[2] it was "prepared by an Interdepartmental Committee consisting of representatives of State (Chair), DOD, JCS, USIA, CIA and AID."[3] It was approved under *National Security Action Memorandum 182* of 24 August 1962, signed by McGeorge Bundy[4] and overseen by a Special Group (Counter-Insurgency), comprising "the Chairman of the Joint Chiefs of Staff, the Deputy Secretary of Defense, the Director of Central Intelligence, the heads of AID and USIA, a staff member of the National Security Council, and . . . the Attorney General of the United States".[5] OIDP lays out a framework for whole-of-government counterinsurgency, assigns responsibilities and resources, and explains what each agency brings to the fight.

Why the history lesson? Because last time we tried this, it did not work very well. OIDP was classified, and while it informed senior leaders it filtered only fitfully down to the field. It was applied in only the minor campaigns of the day. And it lasted only until 1966. As Vietnam escalated, OIDP (used during the advisory phase of the war) was dropped and the campaign was handed off to the conventional military and the State Department's "A" Team of Europeanists and Cold Warriors.[6] And so, as many have observed, our problem is not that we lack doctrine but that we continually forget, relearn, discard our corporate knowledge, and treat as exceptional one of the most common forms of warfare.[7]

Today, things are even more complicated than in 1962. To be effective, we must marshal not only all agencies of the USG (and there are more than 17 agencies in the foreign policy arena alone[8]), but also all agencies of a host nation, multiple foreign allies and coalition partners, international institutions, non-government organizations of many national and political flavors, international and local media, religious and community groups, charities and businesses. Some have counterinsurgency doctrine that is more or less compatible with ours. Some have different doctrines, or none. Some reject the very notion of counterinsurgency—but all must collaborate if the conflict is to be resolved.

This means we need a way to generate purposeful collaboration between a host of actors we do not control. No doctrinal handbook will ever be flexible enough for such a fluid environment (though, something tells me, we will develop one anyway). Rather, we need an easily grasped mental model that helps individuals and agencies cooperate, creates platforms for collaboration, and forms a basis for improvisation. In conventional war we might call this an "operational design", or "commander's intent". I will call it a "model".

There are two parts to this model. The first is a description of the "conflict ecosystem" that forms the environment for 21st century counterinsurgency operations. The second is a tentative framework for whole-of-government counterinsurgency in that environment.

The Conflict Environment

An insurgency is a struggle for control over a contested political space, between a state (or group of states or occupying powers), and one or more popularly based, non-state challengers.[9] Insurgencies are popular uprisings that grow from, and are conducted through pre-existing social networks (village, tribe, family, neighborhood, political or religious party) and exist in a complex social, informational and physical environment.[10]

Think of this environment as a sort of "conflict ecosystem".

It includes many independent but interlinked actors, each seeking to maximize their own survivability and advantage in a

---

* Chief Strategist, Office of the Coordinator for Counterterrorism, U.S. Department of State. Correspondence address: 2201 C St. NW Washington D.C. 20520 e-mail kilcullendj@state.gov This presentation represents the author's personal opinions only.

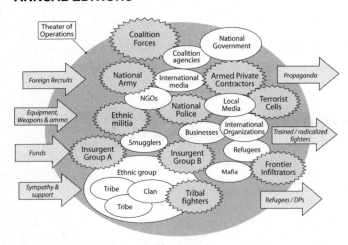

Figure 1 The Conflict Ecosystem.

chaotic, combative environment. Pursuing the ecological metaphor, these actors are constantly evolving and adapting, some seeking a secure niche while others seek to become "top predator" or scavenge on the environment. Some actors existed in the environment before the conflict. They include government, ethnic, tribal, clan or community groups, social classes, urban and rural populations, and economic and political institutions. In normal times, these actors behave in a collaborative or competitive way: but now, due to the internal power struggle, they are combative and destructive. The relatively healthy competition and creative tension that sustains normal society has spun out of control, and the conflict threatens to destroy the society.

This new state of the environment also produces new actors. These include local armed organizations, and foreign armed groups drawn into the conflict from outside. Often, that includes intervening counterinsurgent forces such as ourselves. Foreign terrorists are also increasingly "swarming" from one conflict to another in pursuit of their global agenda. In addition, the conflict produces refugees, displaced persons and sometimes mass migration. It creates economic dislocation, leading to unemployment and crime, and creating armed groups such as bandits, narcotics traffickers, smugglers, couriers and black marketeers.

This might be illustrated graphically as in Figure 1.

It is critically important to realize that we, the intervening counterinsurgent, are not outside this ecosystem, looking in at a Petrie dish of unsavory microbes. Rather, we are inside the system. The theater of operations is not a supine, inert medium on which we practise our operational art. Rather it is a dynamic, living system that changes in response to our actions and requires continuous balancing between competing requirements.

Where the counterinsurgent differs from other actors is largely a matter of intent. Like other players, we seek to maximize our survivability and influence, and extend the space which we control. But unlike some other players (the insurgents, for example) our intent is to reduce the system's destructive, combative elements and return it to its "normal" state of competitive interaction. This has sometimes been expressed as "bringing democracy" but, of course, democratic processes without the foundation of a robust civil society may simply create instability

and perpetuate conflict. Thus, whatever our political objective, our functional objective is to impose a measure of control on the overall environment. But in such a complex, multi-actor environment, "control" does not mean imposing order through unquestioned dominance, so much as achieving collaboration towards a set of shared objectives.

If this sounds soft, non-lethal and non-confrontational, it is not: this is a life-and-death competition in which the loser is marginalized, starved of support and ultimately destroyed. The actors mount a lethal struggle to control the population. There is no known way of doing counterinsurgency without inflicting casualties on the enemy: there is always a lot of killing, one way or another. But killing the enemy is not the sole objective—and in a counterinsurgency environment, operating amongst the people, force is always attended by collateral damage, alienated populations, feuds and other unintended consequences. Politically, the more force you have to use, the worse the campaign is going. Marginalizing and out-competing a range of challengers, to achieve control over the overall socio-political space in which the conflict occurs, is the true aim.

Remembering that this is simply a theoretical model, and thus a brutal oversimplification of an infinitely complex reality, how might we seek to operate in this environment?

A Framework for Inter-Agency Counterinsurgency

Obviously enough, you cannot command what you do not control. Therefore, "unity of command" (between agencies or among government and non-government actors) means little in this environment. Instead, we need to create "unity of effort" at best, and collaboration or deconfliction at least. This depends less on a shared command and control hierarchy, and more on a shared diagnosis of the problem, platforms for collaboration, information sharing and deconfliction. Each player must understand the others' strengths, weaknesses, capabilities and objectives, and inter-agency teams must be structured for versatility (the ability to perform a wide variety of tasks) and agility (the ability to transition rapidly and smoothly between tasks).

A possible framework for inter-agency counterinsurgency operations, as a means to creating such a shared diagnosis, is the "three pillars" model depicted at Figure 2.

This is a framework, not a template. It helps people see where their efforts fit into a campaign, rather than telling them what to do in a given situation. It provides a basis for measuring progress and is an aid to collaboration rather than an operational plan. And clearly, it applies not only to counterinsurgency but also to peace operations, Stabilization and Reconstruction, and complex humanitarian emergencies. The model is structured as a base (Information), three pillars (Security, Political and Economic) and a roof (Control). This approach builds on "classical" counterinsurgency theory, but also incorporates best practices that have emerged through experience in peacekeeping, development, fragile states and complex emergencies in the past several decades.

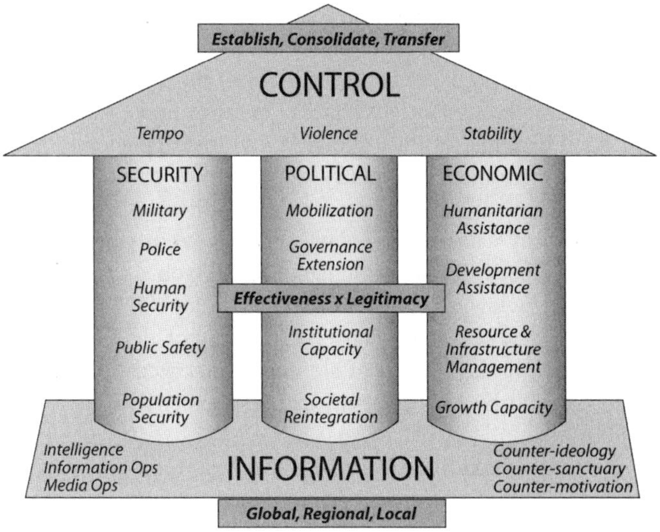

Figure 2 Inter-agency counterinsurgency framework.

Within this "three pillars" model, information is the basis for all other activities. This is because perception is crucial in developing control and influence over population groups. Substantive security, political and economic measures are critical but to be effective they must rest upon, and integrate with a broader information strategy. Every action in counterinsurgency sends a message; the purpose of the information campaign is to consolidate and unify this message. It includes intelligence collection, analysis and distribution, information operations,[11] media operations (including public diplomacy) and measures to counter insurgent motivation, sanctuary and ideology. It also includes efforts to understand the environment through census data, public opinion polling, collection of cultural and "human terrain" information in denied areas. And it involves understanding the effects of our operations on the population, adversaries and the environment. Clearly, not all actors will collaborate in these efforts; but until an information base is developed, the other pillars of counterinsurgency cannot be effective. Importantly, the information campaign has to be conducted at a global, regional and local level—because modern insurgents draw upon global networks of sympathy, support, funding and recruitment.

Resting on this base are three pillars of equal importance. Indeed, as Figure 2 illustrates, unless they are developed in parallel, the campaign becomes unbalanced: too much economic assistance with inadequate security, for example, simply creates an array of soft targets for the insurgents. Similarly, too much security assistance without political consensus or governance simply creates more capable armed groups. In developing each pillar, we measure progress by gauging effectiveness (capability and capacity) and legitimacy (the degree to which the population accepts that government actions are in its interest). This approach is familiar to anyone who has participated in a USAID conflict assessment, or worked on fragile states or complex humanitarian emergencies. It has a solid basis in empirical field experience in the aid and development community.[12]

Article 24. Three Pillars of Counterinsurgency

The security pillar comprises military security (securing the population from attack or intimidation by guerrillas, bandits, terrorists or other armed groups) and police security (community policing, police intelligence or "Special Branch" activities, and paramilitary police field forces). It also incorporates human security, building a framework of human rights, civil institutions and individual protections, public safety (fire, ambulance, sanitation, civil defense) and population security. This "pillar" most engages military commanders' attention, but of course military means are applied across the model, not just in the security domain, while civilian activity is critically important in the security pillar also. Clearly, also, security is *not* the basis for economic and political progress (as some commanders and political leaders argue). Nor does security depend on political and economic progress (as others assert). Rather, all three pillars must develop in parallel and stay in balance, while being firmly based in an effective information campaign.

The political pillar focuses on mobilizing support. As for the other pillars, legitimacy and effectiveness are the principal dimensions in which it is developed. It comprises efforts to mobilize stakeholders in support of the government, marginalize insurgents and other groups, extend governance and further the rule of law. A key element is the building of institutional capacity in all agencies of government and non-government civil institutions, and social re-integration efforts such as the disarming, demobilization and reintegration (DDR)[13] of combatants. Like the security pillar for military forces, the political pillar is the principal arena for diplomatic and civil governance assistance efforts—although, again, civil agencies play a significant role in the security and economic pillars also.

The economic pillar includes a near-term component of immediate humanitarian relief, as well as longer-term programs for development assistance across a range of agricultural, industrial and commercial activities. Assistance in effective resource and infrastructure management, including construction of key infrastructure systems, is critically important. And tailoring efforts to the society's capacity to absorb spending, as well as efforts to increase absorptive capacity, underpin other development activities.

These three pillars support the overarching objective of control, which—as we have seen—is the counterinsurgent's fundamental aim. The aim is not (as some have argued) simply to create stability. Stability may actually not be our objective, as the President emphasized in his recent speech to the United Nations General Assembly, when he observed that "on 9/11, we realized that years of pursuing stability to promote peace left us with neither. Instead, the lack of freedom made the Middle East an incubator for terrorism. The pre-9/11 status quo was dangerous and unacceptable."[14] Moreover, even if we do seek stability, we seek it as a means to an end, a step on the way to regaining control over an out-of-control environment, rather than as an end in itself.

In achieving control, we typically seek to manage the tempo of activity, the level of violence, and the degree of stability in the environment. The intent is not to reduce violence to zero or to kill every insurgent, but rather to return the overall system to normality—noting that "normality" in one society may look different from normality in another. In each case, we seek not only to establish control, but also to consolidate that control and then transfer it to permanent, effective and legitimate institutions.

Operationalizing the "Three Pillars"

If this model represents a possible framework for inter-agency counterinsurgency, how might we apply it in practice? Arguably, the basis for doing so exists already, in National Security Presidential Directive 44 (NSPD 44) which authorizes the creation of civilian capabilities for stabilization and reconstruction. True enough, the words "insurgency", "insurgent" or "counterinsurgency" do not appear in NSPD 44, but it clearly envisages the need to deploy integrated whole-of-government capabilities in hostile environments.

Personnel policies to develop human capital also require effort, but might be less of a burden than we currently envisage. Rather than sweeping policy changes, we simply need relatively minor modifications such as the ability to identify and record civilian officials with appropriate skills for conflict environments, track them throughout their careers, provide financial and legal cover for deployments, give them the necessary individual and team training to operate in hostile areas, and create career structures (perhaps in the form of "additional skills identifiers") that recognize time in conflict zones as equivalent, for career purposes, to time in standard postings.

Organizations, again, perhaps need less modification than we might imagine. We already have a near-perfect instrument for inter-agency counterinsurgency in the form of the Country Team, a 1950s innovation that has proven highly effective in adapting to complex environments. It remains the only standing inter-agency organization in the USG that can deliver integrated whole-of-government effects. It is thus an extremely valuable tool that we should be working to improve even further. Other organizational approaches, such as the Provincial Reconstruction Team (PRT), provide a basis for adaptation. PRTs were invented in 2003 in Afghanistan and have often been treated as a panacea for civilian counterinsurgency. They are not. But careful analysis of why PRTs succeed in some areas and do less well in others can help tailor approaches for specific situations. In this context, the efforts of private firms like Aegis Defence Services, whose Reconstruction Operations Centres and Regional Liaison Teams are flexible inter-agency organizations that have worked extremely well in Iraq, are worth emulating. Similarly, while NSPD 44 envisions a civilian reserve corps deploying field personnel and middle-management into conflict environments, we could also use it to establish a smaller expert cadre of advisors who could assist Ambassadors, Country Teams or force commanders.

Systems capabilities (electronic and otherwise) require significant work. These might include skills registers, personnel databases, and field capabilities such as communications, transportation and protection equipment. We could also benefit from electronic platforms to enable sharing of information between agencies, including non-government organizations. ReliefWeb is a good example of this, allowing multiple agencies to post and share information, identify opportunities to collaborate, and deconflict efforts. Security protocols allow information to be shared only with authorized participants, while public information can be widely disseminated. ReliefWeb's Afghanistan page (http://www.reliefweb.int/rw/dbc.nsf/doc104?OpenForm &rc=3&cc=afg) covers many components of the "three pillars" model, in the context of a complex emergency. Building on this would be less difficult, and less expensive, than one might think.

Training and education (for civil, military, and non-government personnel) would also create shared understanding, and spread best practices throughout a "counterinsurgency community"—again helping us achieve collaboration across a wide variety of players whom we cannot control. Besides specific educational outcomes, these programs develop personal relationships and erode institutional paranoia. Specific training needs include the development of civilian teams capable of "early entry" into environments not yet secured by military or police forces, with the movement, communications and self-protection skills and equipment to operate in these areas. Other needs are a capability for "denied area ethnography" to collect human terrain and population data for effective planning, and education for military leaders in the significant body of expertise that aid, humanitarian assistance and development communities have built up over time.

Finally, doctrine—a common USG handbook, common funding and legal authorities, and common operating standards—might be useful. And so we come full circle, to the OIDP of 1962. But it should now be clear that, without a common mental model for the environment and the pillars of a counterinsurgency effort, and without the personnel, organizations, systems, training and education elements of capability in place, merely producing a doctrinal handbook is likely to be as little use in 2006 as it was in 1962.

Conclusion

These thoughts are tentative; they need a large amount of work. The "three pillars" model is clearly incorrect—all models are, in that they are systematic oversimplifications of reality. But this, or something like it, might be a basis for further development.

And time is of the essence: regardless of the outcome of current campaigns, our enemies will keep applying these methods until we show we can defeat them. Thus, this is one of the most important efforts that our generation of national security professionals is likely to attempt. Our friends and colleagues' lives, the security of our nation and its allies, and our long-term prospect of victory in the War on Terrorism may, in part, depend on it.

Notes

1. United States Department of Defense, *Quadrennial Defense Review Report 2006,* U.S. Government Printing Office, Washington D.C. 2006, Chapter 1 for a detailed exposition of this argument.

2. See State Department, Office of the Historian, *Foreign Relations of the United States, 1961–63,* Volume VIII, Document 106, U.S. Government Printing Office, Washington D.C., 1990, pp. 382–383

3. *Ibid.* p. 3

4. *Ibid,* Document 105.

5. Charles Maechling, "Camelot, Robert Kennedy, and Counter-Insurgency: A Memoir", in *The Virginia Quarterly Review,* at http://www.vqronline.org/printmedia.php/prmMediaID/7976 accessed Sep 06.

6. *Ibid.*

7. See Robert R. Tomes, "Relearning Counterinsurgency Warfare" in *Parameters,* Spring 2004, pp.16–28. See also John A. Nagl, *Learning to East Soup with a Knife: Counterinsurgency Lessons from Malaya and Vietnam,* 2nd Edition, University of Chicago Press, Chicago, 2005; Robert M. Cassidy, "Back to the Street Without Joy: Counterinsurgency Lessons from Vietnam and Other Small Wars" in *Parameters,* Summer 2004 pp. 73–83; and N. Aylwin-Foster, "Changing the Army for Counterinsurgency Operations" in *Military Review,* November–December 2005, pp. 2–15.

8. Including, but not limited to, the Department of State, Agency for International Development, Department of Homeland Security, Department of Justice, Federal Bureau of Investigation, Department of Treasury, Central Intelligence Agency, Department of Commerce (International Trade Administration), Department of Defense, Department of Energy (National Nuclear Security Administration), Department of Labor (Bureau of International Labor Affairs), International Trade Commission, National Security Agency, National Security Council, United States Trade Representative, etc.

9. This definition follows that put forward by Gordon H. McCormick, who suggests that "an insurgency is a struggle for power (over a political space) between a state (or occupying power) and one or more organized, popularly based internal challengers". (McCormick, "Things Fall Apart: The 'Endgame Dynamics' of Internal Wars," RAND, draft paper, forthcoming, p. 2). But, to take into account the trans-national nature of several contemporary insurgencies, I have replaced McCormick's notion of a single state entity facing an internal challenger with the broader concept of a state *or group of states* confronting one or more (internal or external) *non-state* challengers.

10. I am indebted to Dr. Gordon McCormick of the Naval Postgraduate School, Monterrey, and to Colonel Derek Harvey for insights into the "small world, scale-free" aspects of insurgent social networks and the enduring influence of the pre-war Iraqi oligarchy on the current Iraqi insurgency.

11. Including psychological operations, electronic warfare, computer network operations, military deception and operations security. See U.S. Department of Defense, *Joint Publication 3–13 Information Operations*, 13 February 2006.

12. For a description of this approach, see United States Agency for International Development, *Fragile States Strategy*, January 2005, PD-ACA-999, USAID, Washington D.C. 2005, p. 3 ff.

13. See United Nations, Department of Peacekeeping Operations, *Disarmament, Demobilization and Reintegration of ex-Combatants: Principles and Guidelines*, United Nations, New York, 1999, available online at http://www.un.org/Depts/dpko/lessons/DD&R.pdf

14. See The White House, "President Bush Addresses United Nations General Assembly" at http://www.whitehouse.gov/infocus/mideast/ accessed September 2006.

Critical Thinking

1. After listing the three pillars of a successful counterinsurgency campaign, explain which ones in your opinion are being successfully implemented in Afghanistan today?

From *U.S. Government Counterinsurgency Conference,* September 2006. (U.S. Department of State)

Combating Terrorism with Socioeconomics: Leveraging the Private Sector

MIEMIE WINN BYRD

It is widely recognized that leaders of terrorist organizations come from the ranks of the educated and are mostly driven by extremist ideologies. The foot soldiers of terrorism, however, are often recruited from the deprived masses at the bottom of the socioeconomic and political pyramid. The leaders exploit impoverished and hopeless environments and circumstances to attract the large numbers of people needed to advance their agendas.[1]

Recently, the U.S. Army War College hosted a conference on the underlying conditions of terrorism and the military role in addressing these conditions. The participants agreed that the U.S. military has been successful in its efforts to attack and disrupt key terrorist organizations since 9/11; however, these organizations are able to replenish their ranks faster than we can reduce them because "poverty and inequality still prevail in many parts of the Muslim world with high illiteracy rates, lack of human development, and poor infrastructure."[2] Moreover, the "center of gravity for war and terror are the populations that can provide sanctuaries, safe havens, and/or recruitment for terrorists."[3] These conditions are pervasive throughout the Asia-Pacific region.

According to Asian Development Bank statistics, for example:[4]

- The Asia-Pacific region is home to two-thirds of the world's poor.
- Nearly 1.9 billion people in the region live on less than US$2 a day.
- At least 30 percent of the population in countries such as Cambodia, Laos, the Philippines, and Vietnam still live in extreme poverty.
- A conservative estimate of Asian unemployment is 500 million, and 245 million new workers are expected to enter the labor markets over the next decade.

Millions of Muslim boys in Asia are coming of age and creating a "youth bulge." When governments are not able to deliver a vision of hope, mutual respect, and opportunity these young men end up desperate, frustrated, and humiliated. These are ripe conditions for religious extremism, which can provide a perversely attractive escape from the grinding hopelessness and despair.[5]

According to Lieutenant General Wallace Gregson, former commander U.S. Marine Forces Pacific, the decisive terrain of the war on terror is the vast majority of people not directly involved, but whose support, either willing or coerced, is necessary to insurgent operations around the world.[6] This populace is equivalent to American swing voters, whose ballots have contributed significantly to the outcome of many U.S. Presidential elections. As President Ronald Reagan said during the midst of the Cold War, we have to turn these potential enemies into friends.

Thus, it is crucial for U.S. Pacific Command (USPACOM) to develop a concept of operations to alleviate these conditions. Since the launch of Operation *Enduring Freedom–Philippines* in 2002, the island of Basilan, where a reign of terror had ruled since the early 1990s, has achieved a secure environment. However, as we have seen in Iraq, this success will be short-lived if the local, state, and central governments are unable to provide a sustained secured atmosphere and meet the expectation of the populace. Lieutenant General Peter Chiarelli, USA, commander of Multinational Corps in Iraq, stated, "If we don't follow up with a build phase, then I don't think Baghdad can be secure." The same article pointed out:

> The imperative to provide economic benefits to ordinary Iraqis is not born out of some vague humanitarian impulse, U.S. military officials [in Iraq] emphasize, but one that directly affects the security of the country and the viability of the government.[7]

Although Basilan has made great strides in achieving better economic conditions in recent years, poverty and lack of opportunity are still pervasive. Therefore, our long-term counterterrorism efforts by, through, and with the government of the Philippines must focus on creating sustainable socioeconomic conditions on Basilan island.

Applying Principles of War

To put this concept in terms of a principle of war, this is equivalent to conducting an exploitative offensive operation following a successful attack. Exploitation takes advantage of tactical opportunities gained by the initiative. It pressures the enemy and compounds his disorganization.[8]

Creating sustainable socioeconomic conditions should be viewed as an exploitative offensive operation. We conduct this type of operation by shaping, changing, and maintaining the popular support for the armed forces of the Philippines and its government on Basilan. How do we maintain long-term popular support for our cause—that is, how do we deny popular support for the terrorist organizations? We do so by encouraging socioeconomic development that creates jobs, opportunities, and alternatives to violent extremism.

Network of Stakeholders

The U.S. military alone does not have the skills or resources to create sustainable socioeconomic development. This type of operation requires an extensive network of stakeholders: the host-nation government (including the military), local populace, international organizations, nongovernmental organizations, private sector, academia, and the U.S. Government (including the military). To attract all the necessary stakeholders, we need to activate the interagency process because the core competency needed for this phase lies in other Federal agencies, such as the Department of Commerce, the Department of State's Bureau of Economic and Business Affairs and Coordinator for Reconstruction and Stabilization, and the U.S. Agency for International Development (USAID). However, the Department of Defense (DOD) should and could be a proactive member of this interagency team.

Building this nontraditional network of stakeholders with varying interests and organizational cultures will be an arduous task. Therefore, all interagency players, including the military, must think and act outside the box. The Quadrennial Defense Review Execution Roadmap published in May 2006 directed DOD to develop a long-term, focused approach to build and increase the capacity for the international partners to deny sanctuary to terrorists and to separate terrorists from populations by utilizing all instruments of national power. To do so, DOD was authorized to partner and cooperate with:

- other departments and agencies of the U.S. Government
- state and local governments
- allies, coalition members, host nations, and other nations
- multinational corporations
- nongovernmental organizations
- the private sector.

Leveraging the Private Sector

DOD does not have to look far to reach into the private sector. The U.S. military employs thousands of Reserve and Guard citizen-Soldiers, Sailors, Airmen, and Marines who work in the private sector. Many of them hold significant decisionmaking positions with multinational corporations and regional and small firms. Many have valuable skills in such fields as public relations, marketing, business development, supply-chain management, finance, economics, agribusiness, and investment banking. We need to tap into not only this wealth of skills from these citizen-soldiers, but also their relationship with the business community. They can open many doors to the business community as we develop the nontraditional network and partnerships.

Citizen-soldiers can open doors to the business community as we develop the nontraditional network and partnerships.

The story of Lieutenant Colonel Allen McCormick, USAR, demonstrates the power of our Reserve and Guard members as invaluable assets already embedded inside the U.S. military. McCormick, or Army Reserve officer with Special Operations Command, Pacific (SOCPAC), is a brand manager who leads marketing campaign developments for Procter & Gamble in Cincinnati. He holds a Masters of Business Administration from Webster University.

While participating in an exercise at Camp H.M. Smith, Hawaii, in September 2006, McCormick heard about the USPACOM initiative to partner with the private sector. He quickly put us in touch with the appropriate point of contact at Procter & Gamble, and we are communicating with the company to explore how it can collaborate with USPACOM in Indonesia. Procter & Gamble has been working on water purification products to be marketed in developing countries such as Indonesia and the Philippines. They also collaborated with USAID and the Centers for Disease Control during the relief efforts after the tsunami of late 2004. Lieutenant Colonel McCormick is teaching SOCPAC to apply commercial marketing methods to trigger, diffuse, and measure the penetration of messages in "word-of-mouth" cultures to counter extremist messages.

Also, there is a remarkable phenomenon of new thinking gaining ground within the business community. The concept of eradicating poverty through profits involves ways that businesses can gain advantage in today's highly competitive global environment by servicing the needs of those who are at the bottom of the socioeconomic pyramid. By doing so, they trigger sustainable economic growth in those areas. Peace through commerce enhances the powerful role that commerce plays in promoting peace. According to *The Wall Street Journal,* many U.S. business schools are adopting the new mission of promotion in this way.[9] The Association to Advance Collegiate Schools of Business (AACSB), which accredits business schools around the world, has assembled a program called Peace through Commerce, with the aim of raising awareness about what business schools can do to promote peace. Michael Porter, a professor at Harvard Business School and a leading authority on competitive corporate strategy, stated:

it is becoming more and more apparent . . . that treating broader social issues and corporate strategy as separate and distinct has long been unwise [and] never more so than today. . . . [W]e are learning that the most effective way to address many of the world's most pressing problems is to mobilize the corporate sector. . . . In modern competition, economic and social policy can and must be integrated. . . . Not only can corporate and social needs be integrated, but the success of the developing world in improving prosperity is of fundamental strategic importance to almost every company.[10]

We must tap into and harness this new thinking. A recent strategy paper published by the Department of State's Bureau of Economic and Business Affairs stated that it is trying to explore ways that the private sector can help eradicate the underlying conditions that terrorists exploit.[11] The bureau convened a meeting in September 2006 to discuss this initiative, and USPACOM was asked to participate as a member of the interagency community. This meeting demonstrates that the U.S. Government is beginning to accept the idea of engaging the private sector and recognizing the untapped resources and capabilities that the business community possesses.

Military partnership with the private sector is not a new concept. Close cooperation at both the political and technological level gave the United States an advantage during World War II in aviation, communication, and radar developments.[12] Civilian-military collaboration was a critical ingredient for innovations necessary for America to gain an advantage over the enemy. Specific circumstances for including the private sector may be different today, but the concept is the same. The private sector has the capabilities, skills, resources, and innovations to solve the underlying socioeconomic conditions that foster terrorism.

Beyond Economics

While this article focuses primarily on the sustainable economic development and partnering with the private sector, it is not suggesting that this approach is a universal solution. The purpose is to bring attention to the importance of the economic element in shaping and changing the environment as we prosecute the war on terror. Other strategic elements—diplomatic, informational, and military—cannot be dismissed. An economic development can begin to occur only when basic security and physical needs are met. Efforts toward improved infrastructure (such as transportation systems, power, water, and telecommunications), developed human/social capital (health care and education), and good governance (to include sound macroeconomic policies) are the prerequisites for a continuous and sustained economic development. Enduring development strategies require equity, populace participation, and ecological preservation.[13] Therefore, the capabilities and interests of other stakeholders, in addition to the military and the private sector, are still needed to develop and maintain the foundation for sustainable economic development.

Economic development can begin to occur only when basic security and physical needs are met.

To initiate this process of engagement with the various stakeholders, a series of meetings may be warranted. These gatherings should facilitate an environment for these diverse organizations to explore and understand each other's organizational goals, capabilities, and requirements. By holding them, we hope to overcome organization-level cultural biases, build trust, and develop working relationships to generate synergy among the participating organizations. The military role within the network would be to facilitate the gatherings, point out the areas that are most vulnerable to terrorist recruitment, and provide assessments of the security situation in specific locations, such as the island of Basilan. A unified vision and situational awareness among the participants would be the expected outcome from these gatherings.

In addition to sponsoring the meetings, we need to attend private sector roundtables, such as AACSB annual meetings, Business Executives for National Security board meetings, conferences sponsored by the Institute for Defense and Business, FLOW (a grass-roots global network of entrepreneurs practicing conscientious capitalism for sustainable peace) networking events, and the Global Microcredit Summit. We need to let the private sector know that the U.S. Government and international community need their business expertise in creating products, services, and jobs for those who are at the bottom of the socioeconomic pyramid. By doing so, they can create hope and opportunities for the populace as well as additional markets for their products and services. The byproduct is creating environments inhospitable to violence and terrorism.

Beyond the Basilan Model

The success of Operation *Enduring Freedom–Philippines* has been attributed to the Basilan model, which built host-nation capacity, met basic physical needs of the local populace, enhanced Filipino government legitimacy and control, and disrupted insurgent safe havens. The emphasis on civil-military operations resulted in improved infrastructure, increased availability of water, and secured mobility for commerce. Therefore, this model was extremely effective in winning back public support and improving security in Basilan by reducing terrorist strongholds. It also laid the cornerstone for the beginning of social and economic progress in Basilan, but more work is needed for sustainable socioeconomic development.

Since 2002, the U.S. military, USAID, local and international nongovernmental organizations, and the government of the Philippines have been working together. We need to expand this network to include additional stakeholders, such as private businesses, multinational corporations, local and international investment firms, local and international financial institutions, and academe to build the capacity of the local populace and of the host-nation government.

For example, the Asian Development Bank initiated a process to cultivate a strategy for the Philippines to achieve long-term sustainable economic growth. In March 2005, the bank hosted the Philippines Development Forum, which was a meeting of the Philippines Consultative Group and other stakeholders. The forum addressed development issues and other factors, such as instability, weak infrastructure, an inefficient financial sector, corruption, large bureaucracy, and extensive national debt. The group recognized that the private sector accounted for 86 percent of gross domestic product and is responsible for the majority of job creation. Accordingly, it is the key to sustainable economic development.

We should leverage the Asian Development Bank's ongoing efforts and synchronize our plans, programs, and activities with them and facilitate the further expansion of the stakeholders' network. We should also leverage its expertise, interests, goals, and resources toward creating sustainable social and economic progress in Basilan. That island and the Philippines in general could be the next success story in the same line as Ireland, which was one of the poorest countries in Europe 15 years ago. Evidence shows that the unprecedented economic growth there had significant impact on reducing violence in Northern Ireland, which was considered the most violent region of northern Europe for the previous 40 years. In 20 years (1986 to 2006), unemployment declined from 17.6 percent to 4.5 percent.[14] Ireland's steady economic growth was led by private sector businesses.

It is crucial that we expose a critical mass of international business sector players to Basilan. As always with new startup investments and companies, the risk is extremely high, so the failure rate could be high also. Therefore, attracting a critical mass of private sector players, maintaining the network, and preserving their interests are the keys to netting a handful of successful new ventures and a steady stream of new investments.

A Horizontal World

A big challenge for the U.S. military would be to overcome its need for control. It is embedded in our organizational DNA to want to run things because military organizations are traditionally hierarchical and have a topdown structure. We must recognize that the military will be unable to exercise any control over the actions of its nonmilitary partners. We have to inspire them into collaborating with us. Hierarchical relationships are dissolving and more horizontal and collaborative ones are emerging within businesses, governments, and many organizations across the spectrum.[15] Therefore, success depends on how well we are able to influence and persuade them to help us. This can only be accomplished if we truly take the time and effort to understand their requirements, interests, and concerns. This is where we could leverage our Reserve and Guard members of the Armed Forces.

Notes

1. Jesus Felipe and Rana Hasan, *The Challenge of Job Creation in Asia,* ERD Policy Brief Series No. 44 (Manila, The Philippines: Asian World Development Bank, April 2006), available at www.adb.org/Documents/EDRc/Policy_Briefs/PB044.pdf.

2. Statement by Datuk Seri Abdullah Ahmad Badawi, Prime Minister of Malaysia.

3. Kent H. Butts, Terry Klapakis, and Art Bradshaw *The Military's Role in Addressing the Underlying Conditions of Terrorisre,* Issue Paper (Carlisle Barracks, PA: U.S. ArmyWar College, June 2006), 2, available at www.carlisle.army.mil/usacsl/Publications/IP05-06.pdf.

4. Felipe and Hasan.

5. Stuart Hart, *Capitalism at the Crossroads: The Unlimited Business Opportunities in Solving the World's Most Difficult Problems* (Philadelphia: Wharton School Publishing, 2005), 215.

6. Wallace C. Gregson, "Ideological Support: Attacking the Critical Linkage ," in *The Struggle Against Extremist Ideology: Addressing the Conditions That Foster Terrorism* (Carlisle Barracks, PA: U.S. Army War College, 2005), 22.

7. Linda Robinson, "The Battle for Baghdad," *U.S. News and World Report,* September 5, 2006, 56.

8. Field Manual 3–0, *Operations* (Washington, DC: Department of the Army, June 2001), 7–22.

9. Rhea Wessel, "Business School's New Mission: Promoting Peace," *The Wall Street Journal,* June 2, 2006.

10. World Resource Institute, *Tomorrow's Markets: Global Trends and Their Implications for Business* (Baltimore : World Resource Institute, 2002).

11. Department of State's Bureau of Economic and Business Affairs, *Using Economic Power to Combat Terrorism* (Washington, DC: Department of State, September 2006).

12. Allan R. Millett, "Pattern of Military Innovation," in *Military Innovation in the Interwar Period,* ed. Williamson R. Murray and Allan R. Millett (Cambridge: Cambridge University Press, 1998), 365.

13. Robin Broad, John Cavanagh, and Walden Bello, "Development: The Market Is Not Enough," in *International Political Economy : Perspectives on Global Power and Wealth,* ed. Jeffry A. Frieden and David A. Lake, 3d ed. (New York: St. Martin's, 1995), 397.

14. Michael Strong, "Understanding the Power of Economic Freedom to Create Peace," available at <www.flowproject.org/Downloads/Economic-Freedom-and-Peace.pdf>.

15. Thomas L. Friedman, *The World Is Flat: A Brief History of the Twenty-first Century* (New York: Farrar, Straus and Giroux, 2005), 45.

Critical Thinking

1. Explain why the U.S. military is involved in programs in Asia that are designed to reduce the number of young men joining jihadist extremist terrorist groups.

2. After becoming familiar with one program the U.S. military is backing in Asia to deter young men from joining jihadist terrorist groups, explain why you do or do not feel this type of program promotes U.S. national interests.

MAJOR MIEMIE WINN BYRD, USAR, is Deputy Economic Advisor for U.S. Pacific Command.

From *Joint Force Quarterly,* issue 46, 3rd quarter 2007, pp. 127–130. Copyright © 2007 by National Defense University Press. Reprinted by permission.

UNIT 8

Contemporary Foreign Policy Debates

Unit Selections

Learning Objectives

- What are some future possible policy outcomes in Afghanistan that might allow the United States to declare victory while reducing the number of U.S. and NATO forces in Afghanistan?

- Explain why security by in rural villages may be the key to a successful military campaign in Afghanistan.

Student Website
www.mhhe.com/cls

Internet References

AFPAK Channel
   http://afpak.foreignpolicy.com
Pajhwok Afghan News
   www.pajhwak.com/l
ArabNet
   www.arab.net

Although Barak Obama campaigned on a pledge to bring most United States troops home from Iraq, his position in Afghanistan was less clear during the campaign. After winning the election, United States President Obama approved additional troop increases to Afghanistan and declared that the United States strategy was to defeat the Taliban. After Obama's newly appointed head general in Afghanistan, Army General Stanley McChrystal, warned the President and Congress that the security situation was deteriorating so fast that he needed 40,000 more troops to prevent the Taliban from taking control of the country, Obama received a request by his military commanders for more resources for training Afghan military and police and to hire a thousand more civilian experts to help with development projects designed to win the hearts and minds of rural Afghans. In December 2009, he authorized an additional 30,000 troops to be deployed to Afghanistan. At the same time the United States president set a deadline of 2011 for reassessing how well the Afghani surge strategy was working. In 2010, the president asked Congress for about $33 billion to pay for the surge of 30,000 troops while proposing a three-year freeze on federal spending. While the president and Congress agreed to consider this expenditure separate from the proposed $700 billion budget and exempt the Pentagon from the proposed spending freeze, a deepening recession and a budget stalemate between Democrats and Republicans before the midterm elections further complicated the options available to the Obama Administration. Congress approved a $60 billion war effort funding bill in the fall as partisan lines were being drawn for a future budgetary struggle over the rest of the requested FY2011 budget.

In 2010, Obama fired General McChrystal for highly critical remarks the general and his advisers made to *Rolling Stone* magazine reporters and replaced McChrystal with General Petraeus, the chief architect of the successful surge strategy in Iraq. The jury is still out on whether the new strategy will work. The immediate effect of the troop buildup has been an escalation of fighting and a dramatic increase in the number of causalities and wounded U.S. soldiers. Critics note that there are important differences between Iraq and Afghanistan. One major difference is that the Taliban insurgency operates in every province and controls many districts, including areas surrounding the capital. The Taliban has also formed a parallel government that includes websites with 24-hour propaganda that rivals many Western organizations. A second importance different between the two conflicts is the absence of large numbers of rival seasoned militias and former government military personnel who might be persuaded to fight with the Americans in Afgahnistan. Even the most optimistic analyst estimates that it will take several years before the Afghanistan military and police are an effective fighting force who can counter the Taliban without United States military forces.

For several years before the military surge in 2010, it was evident to those with experience on the ground that the U.S. engagement in Afghanistan was floundering due to a large extent because neither the Karsi government or allied forces were able to protect rural villages and immunize them against

© Library of Congress, Prints & Photographs Division [LC-DIG-ppmsca-02037]

insurgency. According to Johnson and Mason, the U.S. needed to reconfigure its operations, creating small development and security teams at new compounds in every district in the south and east of the country. Writing in 2008, these authors claimed that "this approach would not necessarily require adding troops," although that would help—200 district based teams of 100 people would require 20,000 personnel. It remains to be seen if the substantially larger U.S. military presence now on the ground can succeed on preventing the Taliban from retaking areas in the absence of a significant United States military presence. Preliminary indications are not encouraging.

Complicating the military mission is the fact that the political environment in Afghanistan grew much more complicated in recent years at the same time that popular support for the war declined in the United States A UN-led review commission in 2009 declared the first round of voting for a new Afghanistan president to have been so corrupt that a second round of presidential elections was required. President Karzai, who received less than 50 percent of the vote during the first round, despite the massive cheating, only agreed to a run-off election after extensive outside pressure. The run-up to the second election was the deadliest for U.S. and allied forces since 2001. Parliamentary elections during 2010 were also characterized by widespread corruption. There was a brief flurry of activity on the part senior officials in Kabul to try to pressure the Karzai government to replace corrupt officials, including ones very close to the president in 2010. However, U.S. senior officials had to back off increasingly critical rhetoric of the Kabul government or risk a complete rupture in relations with the Karzai government.

Allied forces also experienced heightened casualties and increased pressures at home to scale back their forces in Afghanistan during 2010. As NATO allies reduced the size of their military commitment, the Afghani conflict increasingly became a predominantly American military intervention. However, the American military repeatedly found that offensive actions had very real costs both in terms of casualties and negative reactions from allied governments, especially their allies in Afganistan and Pakistan. Although United States and Pakistani forces initially cooperated in a new offensive in some of the Pakistani territorial provinces, a sharp increase in CIA air strikes on the Pakistani side of the border had raised tensions so much by the fall of 2010 that the Pakistan government closed the main supply route into Afghanistan. Meanwhile, in Kabul,

President Karzai began stating in public that he doubted the United States could defeat the Taliban forces militarily.

Against this background, political discussions inside and outside of government circles began to reassess the U.S. objectives, strategies, and options. In "Defining Success in Afghanistan: What Can the United States Accept?," Stephen Biddle, Fotini Christia, and J. Alexander their note that "many Americans are now skeptical that even a stable and acceptable outcome in Afghanistan is possible. While none are perfect, there is a range of acceptable and achievable outcomes for Afghanistan." The authors outline some future possible outcomes whereby the United States could frame a workable definition of success in Afghanistan. To date, senior officials such as United States Secretary of State Clinton and the new U.S. commander of international troops, Gen. David Petraeus, continue to defend the war effort and repeatedly call for strategic patience while the United States increases Afghani ownership of the process.

President Karzai's effort to organize a peace conference or jirga in the capital that included an invitation to Taliban representatives was disrupted in the first days by a failed suicide bombing attack and in subsequent days by a successful spectacular rocket attack. Much like its predecessors, the Obama Administration has taken an increasingly hard line against leaks of information crucial to the war effort to the press. The Obama Administration is proving to be even more aggressive than the Bush Administration in seeking to punish unauthorized leaks. To date, President Obama has already outdone every previous president in pursuing leak prosecutions.

Another new factor that is likely to complicate efforts to reach a negotiated settlement became public during the summer of 2010. In a public report, the United States government noted that nearly $1 trillion dollars in untapped mineral deposits had been found in Afghanistan. These heretofore unknown deposits include huge veins of iron, copper, cobalt, gold, and critical industrial metals like lithium that are so big they will undoubtedly influence any future peace negotiations and may eventually transform the current Afghan economy based largely on poppy cultivation for illegal opium exports into one of the most important mining centers in the world.

Defining Success in Afghanistan: What Can the United States Accept?

Stephen Biddle, Fotini Christia, and J. Alexander Thier

The original plan for a post-Taliban Afghanistan called for rapid, transformational nation building. But such a vision no longer appears feasible, if it ever was. Many Americans are now skeptical that even a stable and acceptable outcome in Afghanistan is possible. They believe that Afghanistan has never been administered effectively and is simply ungovernable. Much of today's public opposition to the war centers on the widespread fear that whatever the military outcome, there is no Afghan political end state that is both acceptable and achievable at a reasonable cost.

The Obama administration appears to share the public's skepticism about the viability of a strong, centralized, Western-style government in Kabul. But it does not think such an ambitious outcome is necessary. As U.S. Secretary of Defense Robert Gates observed in 2009, Afghanistan does not need to become "a Central Asian Valhalla." Yet a Central Asian Somalia would presumably not suffice. Success in Afghanistan will thus mean arriving at an intermediate end state, somewhere between ideal and intolerable. The Obama administration must identify and describe what this end state might look like. Without clear limits on acceptable outcomes, the U.S. and NATO military campaign will be rudderless, as will any negotiation strategy for a settlement with the Taliban.

In fact, there is a range of acceptable and achievable outcomes for Afghanistan. None is perfect, and all would require sacrifice. But it is a mistake to assume that Afghanistan is somehow ungovernable or that any sacrifice would be wasted in the pursuit of an unachievable goal. Afghanistan's own history offers ample evidence of the kind of stable, decentralized governance that could meet today's demands without abandoning the country's current constitution. By learning from this history and from recent experience in Afghanistan and elsewhere, the United States can frame a workable definition of success in Afghanistan.

Consent of the Governed

From the end of the Second Anglo-Afghan War in 1880 to the coup of Mohammad Daud Khan in 1973, Afghanistan underwent a relatively stable and gradual period of state building. Although the country was an absolute monarchy until 1964, Afghanistan's emirs, on the whole, needed the acquiescence of the population in order to govern. The central government lacked the strength and resources to exercise local control or provide public goods in many parts of the country. Instead, it ruled according to a series of bargains between the state and individual communities, exchanging relative autonomy for fealty and a modicum of order. Over time, as Kabul improved its capacity to offer services and to punish transgressors, this balance shifted, and local autonomy gradually eroded. But whenever this process went too quickly—most notably in the 1920s under Amanullah Khan and in the 1970s under the Soviet-backed People's Democratic Party—conflict in the periphery erupted and local power brokers challenged the central authority. The Soviet invasion in 1979 led to a fundamental breakdown of centralized authority and legitimacy, which resulted in the diffusion of political, economic, and military power across a number of ethnic and geographic groups. The era of dynastic control of the state by Pashtun elites is thus now over.

Although war, migration, and the emergence of regional strongmen have destabilized the Afghan countryside, local communities remain a fundamental source of Afghan identity and a critical base of governance and accountability. This is especially clear in the case of the local *jirga* or *shura* (community council). Traditionally, the community council was a place to solve problems and negotiate over common goods and burdens, with its more prominent members serving as liaisons to the central government. These bodies may differ in their power and representation, but they are still found today in virtually every community. This traditional and local base of legitimacy offers a potential foundation for stable governance in the future.

Washington, of course, would prefer to see Afghanistan—much as it would like to see any country—ruled in accordance with the will of the governed, its people prosperous, and the rights of its minorities and women respected. But the United States' two main security interests in Afghanistan that justify waging a war are much narrower: one, that terrorists who wish to strike the United States and its allies not use Afghanistan as their base, and two, that insurgent groups not use Afghanistan's territory to destabilize its neighbors, especially Pakistan.

There are many possible end states for Afghanistan, but only a few are compatible with these national security interests.

Afghanistan could become a centralized democracy, a decentralized democracy, a regulated mix of democratic and non-democratic territories, a partitioned collection of ministates, an anarchy, or a centralized dictatorship. The first and the last are unlikely; partition and anarchy are unacceptable. But decentralized democracy and internal mixed sovereignty are both feasible and acceptable.

The Failure of Centralization

Since 2001, Hamid Karzai's government, with international support, has pursued the model of centralized democracy. As first envisaged in the 2001 Bonn agreement and then codified in the 2004 Afghan constitution, this approach places virtually all executive, legislative, and judicial authority in the national government. It has created one of the most centralized states in the world, at least on paper. The president appoints every significant official in the executive branch, from provincial governors down to midlevel functionaries serving at the subprovincial level. All security forces are national forces. Although there are provisions to elect provincial, district, municipal, and village councils, only provincial council elections have been held thus far. Kabul holds all policy, budgetary, and revenue-generating authority. In March 2010, Karzai approved a new governance policy that devolves some local administrative and fiscal authority to appointed officials and provides modest auditing and budgetary powers to elected subnational bodies. Still, the Afghan state retains a remarkably centralized blueprint.

Political figures close to Karzai pushed for such a highly centralized government against the wishes of many non-Pashtun minorities—and despite Afghanistan's prior experience with failed, albeit non-democratic, centralization efforts. From 1919 to 1929, for example, Amanullah Khan aspired to be Afghanistan's Kemal AtatÜrk, but his strategy ultimately led to serious rural upheaval, which ended his rule. The radical attempts at centralization under the Soviet-backed regimes that followed the 1978 coup helped spark the mujahideen resistance and led to years of civil war.

After the Taliban were removed from power, in 2001, strong Pashtun support, combined with fears of a return to the civil war of the 1990s, created a majority in favor of a centralizing constitution. But Afghan central governments have never enjoyed the legitimacy required by such an organizing principle. The last 30 years of upheaval and radical devolution of political, economic, and military authority have only made this problem worse. Put simply, the current model of Afghan governance is too radical a departure in a place where the central state has such limited legitimacy and capacity. To create a lasting peace that includes the country's main ethnic and sectarian groups—as well as elements of the insurgency—Afghanistan will require a more inclusive, flexible, and decentralized political arrangement.

Stable Devolution

Power sharing would be easier under a decentralized democracy, in which many responsibilities now held by Kabul would be delegated to the periphery. Some of these powers would surely include the authority to draft and enact budgets, to use traditional alternatives to centralized justice systems for some offenses, to elect or approve important officials who are now appointed by Kabul, and perhaps to collect local revenue and enforce local regulation.

Increasing local autonomy would make it easier to win over Afghans who distrust distant Kabul and would take advantage of a preexisting base of legitimacy and identity at the local level. The responsibility for foreign policy and internal security, however, would remain with the central government, which would prevent even the more autonomous territories from hosting international terrorist groups or supporting insurrection against the state.

A decentralized democracy along these lines should be an acceptable option for the United States. Its reliance on democracy and transparency is consistent with American values. Individual territories with the freedom to reflect local preferences may adopt social policies that many in the United States would see as regressive. But the opposite could also occur, with some places implementing more moderate laws than those favored by a conservative center. By promoting local acceptance of the central government, this option would remove much of the casus belli for the insurgency. And it would preserve a central state with the power and incentive to deny the use of Afghan soil for destabilizing Pakistan or planning attacks against the United States.

A decentralized democracy would comport with much of the post-Cold War experience with state building elsewhere. A range of postconflict states in Africa (Ethiopia and Sierra Leone), Europe, (Bosnia and Macedonia), the Middle East (Iraq and Lebanon), and Asia (East Timor and, tentatively, Nepal) have used some combination of consociationalism, federalism, and other forms of decentralized democratic power sharing. Although it is too early to make definitive claims of success, to date not one of these states has collapsed, relapsed into civil war, or hosted terrorists. And some, such as Bosnia and Ethiopia, have remained tolerably stable for over a decade. This is, of course, no guarantee that decentralized democracy would work in Afghanistan. But its track record elsewhere and its better fit with the country's natural distribution of power suggests that it offers a reasonable chance of balancing interests and adjudicating disputes in Afghanistan, too.

A decentralized democracy in Afghanistan would face three critical challenges. The first, of course, is the Taliban, who oppose democracy on principle and are likely to resist this approach as aggressively as they now resist centralized democracy. The second challenge is the limited administrative capacity of the Afghan state. Decentralization would distribute power among a larger number of officials; for a state such as Afghanistan, which has a limited pool of competent bureaucrats, this could exceed the country's current human capital and require a major expansion of training efforts. Third, the country's malign power brokers would likely resist such an option. A transparent electoral democracy would threaten their status, authority, and ability to profit from corruption and abuse.

Yet decentralized democracy could actually offer some important counterbalances in each of these areas. Hard fighting will be required to marginalize the Taliban under any democratic system, decentralized or not. The odds of success are much higher, however, when the population supports the government. Counterinsurgency can be described as a form of violent competition in governance; it is much easier to win when the form of government offered is closer to the natural preference of the governed. And if the Taliban come to see their military prospects as limited, a decentralized system might entice some of their members to reconcile with the government in the hope of securing a meaningful local role in areas where their support is strongest.

It will not be easy to combat high-level corruption or to improve administrative capacity. But a transparent system in which locals make most decisions would allow Afghanistan's traditional community leaders to police the use of power and public funds. A faraway national ministry in Kabul is beyond the oversight of a village or district *shura*. In contrast, local councils can see how officials are spending money and can take issue with uses they find objectionable. Decentralization may also improve the Afghan government's basic competence by allowing local officials to focus on smaller, more local issues. For example, the most widely hailed development program in Afghanistan in the last eight years has been the National Solidarity Program, under which the central government provides grants to democratically elected community councils for local development projects. The NSP was designed at the national level but is administered locally. To date, it has been fiscally efficient and effective, reaching more than 20,000 villages.

Although decentralized democracy offers no easy guarantee of success, it has much better odds of success than a centralized model. But it would not come cheaply: the United States would have to wage a sustained counterinsurgency campaign, provide major administrative assistance to the Afghan government, and conduct vigorous anticorruption measures.

A Mixed Bag

Mixed sovereignty is an even more decentralized model. Much like decentralized democracy, this approach would take many powers that are now held in Kabul and delegate them to the provincial or district level. But mixed sovereignty would go one step further, granting local authorities the additional power to rule without transparency or elections if they so chose—as long as they did not cross three "redlines" imposed by the center.

The first redline would forbid local authorities from allowing their territories to be used in ways that violated the foreign policy of the state—namely, by hosting terrorist or insurgent camps. The second would bar local administrations from infringing on the rights of neighboring provinces or districts by, for example, seizing assets or diverting water resources. The third would prevent officials from engaging in large-scale theft, narcotics trafficking, or the exploitation of state-owned natural resources.

Beyond these limited restrictions, local authorities could run their localities as they saw fit, with the freedom to ignore the will of the governed or engage in moderate-scale corruption. The central government in Kabul would retain total control over foreign policy and the ability to make war and enforce narcotics, customs, and mining laws and limited authority over

interprovincial commerce. Under such an arrangement, sovereignty is mixed to a much greater degree than in the other possible systems, with many, but not all, of the ordinary powers of sovereign government delegated to the provincial or district level.

The mixed-sovereignty model would signal a more serious break with the direction of Afghan state building as it was conceived in 2001 than would decentralized democracy. But it would also be a partial acknowledgment of the de facto arrangements that have taken shape since 2001. Many of the governors and other local officials appointed by Karzai have ruled not by virtue of a legal mandate from Kabul but rather through their own local security and economic power bases, which operate outside the law but with the tacit acceptance of Kabul. In provinces such as Balkh (under Governor Atta Mohammad Noor) and Nangarhar (under Governor Gul Agha Sherzai), this has led to relative peace and a drastic reduction of poppy cultivation. Such warlords have settled into a stable equilibrium in which they profit from the theft of customs duties and state property but maintain order and keep their predation within limits so as to avert a mutually costly crackdown by Kabul.

In other areas, however, strongmen have caused instability. In Helmand, for example, several years of corrupt rule by Sher Mohammad Akhundzada alienated significant groups in the province and sent poppy cultivation soaring, fueling the insurgency. Even in Afghanistan's relatively stable north, the rule of warlords has led to ethnic violence and criminal excess. To ensure stability, mixed sovereignty cannot amount to partition under local strongmen who rule with impunity in private fiefdoms. Redline restrictions that forbid the sort of excesses that fuel insurgency are thus essential.

Mixed sovereignty has some important advantages: it is less dependent on the rapid development of state institutions and offers a closer fit with the realities of Afghanistan. Restricting the central government's involvement in local issues to a limited—but aggressively enforced—set of redlines could encourage the country's power brokers to moderate their excesses, which now drive many toward the Taliban. At the same time, a mixed-sovereignty system would depend less on transparency and efficiency, thus requiring less international mentoring, oversight, and assistance. Local autonomy would create incentives for Taliban members to participate in reconciliation negotiations, since a more purely democratic option would subject them to electoral sanction.

However, mixed sovereignty also carries risks and disadvantages that make it less consistent with U.S. interests than either centralized or decentralized democracy. First, governors would be free to adopt regressive social policies and abuse human rights. This would represent a retreat from nearly nine years of U.S. promises of democracy, the rule of law, and basic rights for women and minorities, with costs to innocent Afghans and the prestige of the United States.

Corruption would also be prevalent—indeed, for prospective governors, the opportunity for graft would be an essential part of the system's appeal. The Afghan government would have to contain the scale and scope of this corruption, lest official acceptance of abuse renewed support for the insurgency. To prevent this, Kabul would have to rein in the worst of today's excesses—if mixed sovereignty is merely a gloss for the status quo, it will fail. At the same time, the Afghan state would have to crack down on the narcotics trade, which if left unchecked could dwarf the revenues provided by foreign aid and make such aid a less convincing incentive for compliance with the center. The central government would have to strike a bargain with the country's power brokers, requiring them to refrain from large-scale abuses in exchange for tolerance of moderate local corruption and a share of foreign assistance. Even this kind of bargain, however, would probably be resisted by the country's strongmen, who have grown used to operating without restraint. Thus, mixed sovereignty would not free Kabul from the need to confront local power centers, and even this limited confrontation could be costly and difficult.

Under this style of governance, there would be a potential threat of instability as powerful governors periodically tested the waters to see what they could get away with. The central government would presumably need to carry out periodic enforcement actions, including violent ones.

Mixed sovereignty is thus not ideal, but it could be viable and meet U.S. security requirements if Washington and Kabul were willing to fulfill their roles as limited but important enforcers. The model offers the central government two means of imposing the essential redlines. The first is the threat of punitive military action ordered by Kabul. This would require security forces that have the capability to inflict serious costs on violators. (They need not have a monopoly on violence, but a meaningful national military of some sort is necessary.) The other enforcement mechanism is Kabul's control over foreign aid and its ability to direct aid to some provinces but not others.

Washington would not be powerless, either—it would retain its influence through the disbursement of foreign aid and its deep engagement with the Afghan National Security Forces. In order to maintain Afghanistan's internal balance of power, the United States and its NATO allies would need to pay constant attention. Otherwise, the country could slip into unrestrained warlordism and civil war. A workable mixed-sovereignty model is not a recipe for Western disengagement: it would require not only continued aid flows but also sustained political and military engagement. Regional diplomacy would be particularly important. To keep Afghanistan from becoming a magnet for foreign interference and a source of regional instability, the United States would have to ensure that the country was embedded in a regional security framework. Such a framework would facilitate aid flows and discourage intervention by Afghanistan's neighbors.

As with decentralized democracy, internal mixed sovereignty has produced tolerable outcomes in the developing world. Afghanistan itself was governed under a similar model for much of the twentieth century: Muhammad Nadir Shah and his son Muhammad Zahir Shah ruled for five decades as nominally absolute monarchs, but with limited state bureaucracy and a certain degree of autonomy for the periphery. The rule of law was generally administered locally, and some Pashtun tribes in the south and the east were exempted from military service. Nevertheless, a national army and a national police force remained ready to enforce a few key royal prerogatives. The government earned revenue not from internal taxation but from foreign trade, foreign aid (starting in the late 1950s), and the sale of natural gas to the Soviet Union (beginning in the late 1960s). Over time, as the government's capacity and resources increased, it was able to extend its writ, trying criminals in state courts, regulating the price of staple goods, and bringing community land under its authority.

There are also external parallels. After the end of the Nigerian Civil War in 1970, Nigeria had a weak federal government and a strong regional system, in which individual governors were free to organize local administration as they wished. Even today, the country retains some traits of internal mixed sovereignty. States in the Muslim north have sharia law, whereas others use secular judicial systems. The central government intervenes selectively to suppress unrest, such as in the Delta region. Although there are signs that Nigeria may now be deteriorating, for most of the last 40 years it has functioned tolerably.

The Unacceptable Others

Many other outcomes for Afghanistan are possible—but would fail to meet core U.S. security requirements. The country could, for example, split up in a form of either de facto or de jure partition. The most likely such split would divide the Pashtun south from the largely Tajik, Uzbek, and Hazara north and west. Such a result could come about if a reconciliation deal with the Taliban granted the group too much leeway in the country's south, its historical power base. Any outcome that leaves the Taliban relatively free to operate in the south could create safe havens for cross-border terrorism and insurgency, similar to the use of Iraqi Kurdistan by the Kurdistan Workers' Party, or PKK, or the use of Congolese border havens by Hutu guerillas. Partition would also set the stage for regional proxy battles and internal competition for control of Kabul and key border areas.

If the Karzai government collapses, Afghanistan could break down into the kind of anarchy and atomized civil warfare of the 1990s. Such a state would resemble the one that was taken over by the Taliban in the 1990s, or present-day Somalia, where lawlessness has created an opening for al Shabab, a violent, al Qaeda-supported Islamist movement—with obvious consequences for U.S. interests.

Lastly, Afghanistan could become a centralized dictatorship, although this is hard to imagine. A single strongman is unlikely to be able to consolidate power in post-Taliban Afghanistan, where political, military, and economic might is dispersed among numerous power brokers. In this environment, any prospective dictator—whether pro- or anti-Western—would find it very difficult to prevent the country from descending into civil war. A coup d'etat or other antidemocratic power grab (amending the constitution, for example, to allow for a president for life) is entirely possible but unlikely to yield stability in its wake.

Salvaging the Good

Afghanistan has been a failing experiment in centralized democracy, heading toward de facto partition, with Taliban control in some areas and unstable, ill-regulated strongman governance in many others. This trend can be reversed. But clinging to the original, centralized model will not help. Centralized governance matches neither the real internal distribution of power in Afghanistan nor local notions of legitimacy. There can be no effective military solution if the intended political goal is so badly misaligned with the country's underlying social and political framework.

To its credit, the Obama administration appears to have recognized that centralized democracy is a bridge too far for Afghanistan. Current policy is moving toward decentralization—the question is how far this should go and whether Afghan and U.S. officials can manage the transition successfully.

This shift toward decentralization can work, although it is no panacea. A system of either decentralized democracy or internal mixed sovereignty would have its drawbacks, and each would involve sacrifice and risk. In Afghanistan—as in most places—the more optimal a system of governance, the longer and harder the fight to get it. The question of whether to strive for the preferable outcome of decentralized democracy or to accept the less appealing alternative of internal mixed sovereignty will largely be determined by the efforts and sacrifices the United States and its partners are willing to undertake. Yet for all their drawbacks, either approach would meet core U.S. national security requirements if properly implemented. And either model is more achievable than today's goal of centralized democracy.

Moreover, a decentralized democracy would not require the Afghan government to abandon or amend the existing constitution. The 2004 constitution is flexible enough to allow many powers to be devolved through legislation, as demonstrated somewhat by the new sub-national governance policy, which provides limited administrative and budgetary authority to local officials. A mixed-sovereignty model would clash with the spirit and letter of the 2004 constitution, but such a system would likely evolve on a de facto basis, averting the need for a new constitution in the near term.

Afghanistan is not ungovernable. There are feasible options for acceptable end states that would meet core U.S. security interests and place the country on a path toward tolerable stability. The United States will have to step back from its ambitious but unrealistic project to create a strong, centralized Afghan state. If it does, then a range of power-sharing models could balance the needs of Afghanistan's internal factions and constituencies in ways that today's design cannot, while ensuring that Afghanistan does not again become a base for terrorists. In war, as in so many other things, the perfect can be the enemy of the good. The perfect is probably not achievable in Afghanistan—but the acceptable can still be salvaged.

Critical Thinking

1. Describe one possible outcome in Afghanistan that you would define as a success from the U.S. perspective. Be sure to justify your answer with specific, recent examples from the Afghanistan conflict.

2. Describe one possibe outcome in Afghanistan that you would define as a failure from the U.S. perspective. Be sure to justify your answer with specific, recent examples from the Afghanistan conflict.

STEPHEN BIDDLE is Roger Hertog Senior Fellow for Defense Policy at the Council on Foreign Relations. **FOTINI CHRISTIA** is Assistant Professor of Political Science at the Massachusetts Institute of Technology. **J. ALEXANDER THIER** is Director for Afghanistan and Pakistan at the U.S. Institute of Peace. For a selection of articles on Afghanistan from the Foreign Affairs archives, see the collection at www.foreignaffairs.com/collections/afghanistan.

From *Foreign Affairs*, vol. 89, no. 4, July/August 2010, pp. 48–60. Copyright © 2010 by Council on Foreign Relations, Inc. Reprinted by permission of Foreign Affairs. www.ForeignAffairs.com

All Counterinsurgency Is Local

Prosecuting the war in Afghanistan from provincial capitals has been disastrous; we need to turn our military strategy inside out.

THOMAS H. JOHNSON AND M. CHRIS MASON

June was the deadliest month for the U.S. military in Afghanistan since the invasion in October 2001. July became the second straight month in which casualties exceeded those in Iraq, where four times as many U.S. troops are on the ground. More Americans have been killed in Afghanistan since the invasion began than in the first nine years of the Vietnam War, from 1956 to 1964.

As in Vietnam, the U.S. has never lost a tactical engagement in Afghanistan, and this tactical success is still often conflated with strategic progress. Yet the Taliban insurgency grows more intense and gains more popular traction each year. More and more, the American effort in Afghanistan resembles the Vietnam War—with its emphasis on body counts and air strikes, its cross-border sanctuaries, and its daily tactical victories that never affected the slow and eventually decisive erosion of rural support for the counterinsurgency.

As the Russian ambassador to Afghanistan, Zamir Kabulov, noted in a blunt interview with the BBC in May, the current military engagement is also beginning to look like the Soviets' decade-long Afghan adventure, which ended ignominiously in 1989. That intervention, like the current one, was based on a strategy of administering and securing Afghanistan from urban centers such as Kabul and the provincial capitals. The Soviets held all the provincial capitals, just as we do, and sought to exert influence from there. The mujahideen stoked insurgency in the rural areas of the Pashtun south and east, just as the Taliban do now.

The backbone of the international effort since 2003—extending the reach of the central government—is precisely the wrong strategy.

The U.S. engagement in Afghanistan is foundering because of the endemic failure to engage and protect rural villages, and to immunize them against insurgency. Many analysts have called for more troops inside the country, and for more effort to eliminate Taliban sanctuaries outside it, in neighboring Pakistan. Both developments would be welcome. Yet neither would solve the central problem of our involvement: the paradigm that has formed the backbone of the international effort since 2003—extending the reach of the central government—is in fact precisely the wrong strategy.

National government has never much mattered in Afghanistan. Only once in its troubled history has the country had something like the system of strong central government that's mandated by the current constitution. That was under the "Iron Emir," Abdur Rehman, in the late 19th century, and Rehman famously maintained control by building towers of skulls from the heads of all who opposed him, a tactic unavailable to the current president, Hamid Karzai.

Politically and strategically, the most important level of governance in Afghanistan is neither national nor regional nor provincial. Afghan identity is rooted in the *woleswali:* the districts within each province that are typically home to a single clan or tribe. Historically, unrest has always bubbled up from this stratum—whether against Alexander, the Victorian British, or the Soviet Union. Yet the *woleswali* are last, not first, in U.S. military and political strategy.

Large numbers of U.S. and NATO troops are now heavily concentrated in Kabul, Kandahar, and other major cities. Thousands of U.S. personnel are stationed at Bagram Air Force Base, for instance, which is complete with Burger King, Dairy Queen, and a shopping center, but is hundreds of miles from the heart of the insurgency. Meanwhile, the military's contact with villagers in remote areas where the Taliban operate is rare, typically brief, and almost always limited to daylight hours.

The Taliban are well aware that the center of gravity in Afghanistan is the rural Pashtun district and village, and that Afghan army and coalition forces are seldom seen there. With one hand, the Taliban threaten tribal elders who do not welcome them. With the other, they offer assistance. (As one U.S. officer recently noted, they're "taking a page from the Hezbollah organizations in Lebanon, with their own public works to assist the tribes in villages that are deep in the inaccessible regions of the country. This helps support their cause with the population, making it hard to turn the population in support of the Afghan government and the coalition.")

The rural Pashtun south has its own systems of tribal governance and law, and its people don't want Western styles of either. But nor are they predisposed to support the Taliban, which espouses an alien and intolerant form of Islam, and goes against the grain of traditional respect for elders and decision by consensus. Re-empowering the village councils of elders and restoring their community leadership is the only way to re-create the traditional check against the powerful political network of rural mullahs, who have been radicalized by the Taliban. But the elders won't commit to opposing the Taliban if they and their families are vulnerable to Taliban torture and murder, and they can hardly be blamed for that.

To reverse its fortunes in Afghanistan, the U.S. needs to fundamentally reconfigure its operations, creating small development and security teams posted at new compounds in every district in the south and east of the country. This approach would not necessarily require adding troops, although that would help—200 district-based teams of 100 people each would require 20,000 personnel, one-third of the 60,000 foreign troops currently in the country.

Each new compound would become home to roughly 60 to 70 NATO security personnel, 30 to 40 support staff to manage logistics and supervise local development efforts, and an additional 30 to 40 Afghan National Army soldiers. The troops would provide a steady security presence, strengthen the position of tribal elders, and bolster the district police. Today, Afghan police often run away from the superior firepower of attacking Taliban forces. It's hard to fault them—more than 900 police were killed in such attacks last year alone. But with better daily training and help only minutes away, local police would be far more likely to put up a good fight, and win. Indirectly, the daily presence of embedded police trainers would also prevent much of the police corruption that fuels resentment against the government. And regular contact at the district and village levels would greatly improve the collection and analysis of intelligence.

Perhaps most important, district-based teams would serve as the primary organization for Afghan rural development. Currently, "Provincial Reconstruction Teams," based in each provincial capital, are responsible for the U.S. military's local development efforts. These teams have had no strategic impact on the insurgency, because they are too thin on the ground—the ratio of impoverished Afghan Pashtuns to provincial reconstruction teams is roughly a million to one. Few teams are able to visit every district in their province even once a month; it's no wonder that rural development has been marred by poor design and ineffective execution.

Local teams with on-site development personnel—"District Development Teams," if you will—could change all that, and also serve to support nonmilitary development projects. State Department and USAID personnel, along with medics, veterinarians, engineers, agricultural experts, hydrologists, and so on, could live on the local compounds and work in their districts daily, building trust and confidence.

Deploying relatively small units in numerous forward positions would undoubtedly put more troops in harm's way. But the Taliban have not demonstrated the ability to overrun international elements of this size, and the teams could be mutually reinforcing. (Air support would be critical.) Ultimately, we have to accept a certain amount of risk; you can't beat a rural insurgency without a rural security presence.

As long as the compounds are discreetly sited, house Afghan soldiers to provide the most visible security presence, and fly the Afghan flag, they need not exacerbate fears of foreign occupation. Instead, they would reinforce the country's most important, most neglected political units; strengthen the tribal elders; win local support; and reverse the slow slide into strategic failure.

Critical Thinking

1. Describe the key features of the counter-insurgency program advocated by Thomas Johnson and Chris Mason and explain why you believe this strategy can or cannot still work in Afghanistan. Be specific.

2. Identify which aspects of the counter-insurgency program advocated by Johnson and Mason are being implemented in Afghanistan today and which ones are not.

THOMAS H. JOHNSON directs the Program for Culture and Conflict Studies at the Naval Postgraduate School at Monterey, California. **M. CHRIS MASON** is a senior fellow at the Center for Advanced Defense Studies, in Washington, D.C. He recently served in the U.S. Foreign Service on the Pakistan-Afghanistan border.

UNIT 9

International Organizations, International Law, and Global Governance

Unit Selections

Learning Objectives

- List the Millennium Development Goals and target dates for implementation.

- Explain why you do/do not think these are realistic goals that can be achieved.

- Describe the proposal to form an All Africa Standby Force.

- What are the main reasons why the All Africa Standby Force was not achieved by 2010?

- Describe the "responsibility to protect norm" (R2P) and some of the reasons for it being proposed.

- Explain why the author has concluded that the R2P norm needs a "rethink."

Student Website
www.mhhe.com/cls

Internet References

African Center for Strategic Studies
http://africacenter.org

African Union
www.africa-union.org

AllAfrica.com
http://allafrica.com

End Poverty 2015 Millennium Campaign
www.endpoverty2015.org/2010_mdg_review_summit

The Digital Library in International Conflict Management
www.usip.org/library/diglib.html

Genocide Watch Home Page
www.genocidewatch.org

International Court of Justice (ICJ)
www.icj-cij.org

International Criminal Court
www.icc-cpi.int/home.html&l=*en*

IRIN
www.irinnews.org

United Nations
www./untreaty.un.org

United Nations Home Page
www.un.org

United Nations Peacekeeping Home Page
www.un.org/Depts/dpko/dpko

Amnesty International
www.amnesty.org

Global Policy Forum
www.globalpolicy.org

Human Rights Web
www.hrweb.org

InterAction
www.interaction.org

International organizations consist of members who are sovereign nation-states and other inter-government organizations, such as the European Union (EU) and the World Trade Organization (WTO). The most visible international organization throughout much of the post–World War II era was the United Nations (UN). Membership grew from the original 50 in 1945 to 185 in 1995. There are 192 members today. The United Nations, across a variety of fronts, achieved noteworthy results, such as the eradication of disease, immunization, provision of food, shelter to refugees and victims of natural disasters, and help to dozens of countries that have moved from colonial status to self-rule.

In recent years the link between human and traditional security concerns has become more obvious. At the 2000 UN Millennium Summit, world leaders from developed and developing countries committed themselves to a set of eight time-bound targets that, when achieved, will end extreme poverty worldwide. The Millennium Development Goals (MDGs) are to eradicate extreme poverty and hunger, achieve universal primary education, promote gender equality and empower women, reduce child mortality, improve maternal health, combat HIV/AIDS, malaria and other diseases, and achieve environmental sustainability and greater global partnerships.

The financial and economic world crises of the past few years forced a slowdown in progress toward reaching the MDGs in many developing countries during the past few years. In response, UN Secretary General Ban Ki-moon hosted a high-level Plenary Meeting on the Millennium Development Goals, better known as the "MDG Summit" in September 2010 to reassess progress toward achieving the MNG goals by the target date of 2015. Despite continuing economic problems in many countries, the MDG Summit noted that remarkable progress had been made in fighting poverty, increasing school enrollment, and improving health in many countries. The meeting adopted a new global action plan to achieve the eight anti-poverty goals by 2015 and announced major new commitments for women and children's health and other initiatives against poverty, hunger, and disease. Citing examples of success and lessons learned over the last 10 years, the final summit document spelled out steps that all stakeholders can take to accelerate progress on each of the eight goals. While skeptics doubt the targets will be reached by 2015, there is a remarkably international consensus now about what needs to be done to improve global well-being in the short-to-medium term.

In contrast to the progress being made on reaching agreement about what needs to be done to improve human security within the UN, several UN-sponsored peacekeeping missions suffered serious setbacks in recent years. The African Union peacekeeping mission in Somalia (AMISOM) has been unable to maintain peace beyond a few blocks in downtown Mogadishu, Somalia, despite additional troops sent under the auspices of the UN and additional troop deployments from several African countries to the AU force in recent years. During 2010, AMISOM forces were also unable to stop the consolidation of al-Shabab control in much of central and southern Somalia, nearly lost their toehold command post within Mogadishu, and failed in their mission of protecting civilians in several repeated attacks.

Similarly, for several years now there have been charges and growing confirmatory evidence that the United National Organization Mission in the Democratic Republic of Congo (MONUC) has failed to prevent several different militias and rouge government troops from raiding, raping, and killing innocent civilians in large sections of the eastern province. Even more shocking are charges that some MONUC forces were involved in illicit trafficking of goods and people while failing to stop combatant forces, who continued to use rape as a weapon against numerous villages in large parts of eastern DRC. During the fall of 2010, reports started filtering out about another round of mass rapes of civilians by members of illegal armed groups. While the UN

© Royalty-Free/CORBIS

Assistant Secretary-General in the UN Department of Peacekeeping operations was immediately dispatched from UN headquarters to DRC for a fact-finding mission, there are no indications that the world community is going mobilize for new efforts to support civilians in this war-torn crisis zone of central Africa. Instead, publication of such horrific abuses of human rights, much like reports of continuing abuses in Sudan's Darfur region despite the presence of a combined UN/African Union peacekeeping force known as UIAMID since 2008, seemed to be largely ignored by most observers in the West.

Unfortunately, the successes of international peacekeeping forces receive much less attention in the press. Instead, press sorties often fail to make clear to readers that UN peacekeeping forces typically operate under detailed mandates that permit them to observe and keep rival forces apart while not getting involved once fighting breaks out. Peace-making mandates that allow international peacekeepers to become active participants have rarely been approved by the Security Council after the experiences in the early years of the organization when the UN became militarily involved in the Korean War in the late 1950s and the civil war in the early days of the independence in the Congo in the 1960s. Taking an active role militarily in these conflicts nearly destroyed the United Nations. Since then, much more limited peacekeeping mandates are the main ones that have received political support by member nations of the UN, especially the permanent members of the Security Council. These limitations are a frequent source of frustration and criticism of UN peacekeeping activities. However, little can be done until such time that the member states of the United Nations reach a consensus on the need to amend the UN Charter or pass resolutions giving UN peacekeepers more authority. In the meantime there is a real possibility that without the financial backing of major international powers such as the United States, European countries, China, and Japan, the United Nations will be unable to fulfill an ever-growing list of requests in such diverse areas as military deployment, weapons proliferation, economic, social issues, and the environment.

Instead of supporting major changes in the role of the UN in maintaining peace and security, all of the major powers today are attempting to shift as much of the responsibility for maintaining international security onto regional alliances and organizations as is possible. In "The African Standby Force, Genocide, and International Relations Theory," Stephen Burgess details how important states in the world agreed to but failed to deliver security by implementing long-standing treaties such as the 1948 Genocide Convention, which obliges all nation-states to prevent and punish. The world community of nation-states have more often than not failed to stop genocide in modern conflicts (i.e., Rwanda,

Darfur, Bosnia) due to a lack of political will, and often also due to a lack of military capacities of African militaries whose government are willing to become involved in regional peacekeeping missions.

Africa is one region where nearly all countries agree that it would be best for African countries and regional organizations, such as the Economic Community of West African States (ECOWAS)'s military group (ECOMOG), to take the lead role in international peacekeeping missions. Burgess's Study is useful for detailing why the commitment to form an African standby Force (ASF) by 2010 was not implemented. Key factors include the lack of political will to intervene in other African states, the lack of military capacity, and the lack of coordination among key organizations within the African Union or among outside powers to implement the concept of "African solutions for African problems." Many of these same factors are also evident in other regions of the world. This harsh reality suggests that recent efforts to build up regional capabilities to deal with inter-state and intra-state conflicts may not be able to succeed in most cases without the support of the United Nations and the financial backing of the wealthiest nation-states.

The Obama Administration's emphasis on using multilateral diplomacy and institutions to solve international issues suggest that U.S. support for the battered international organization may be increasing compared to past U.S. policies toward the UN. This shift may lead to meaningful change in the capacity of regional bodies to maintain the peace if United States rhetoric is backed up by renewed amounts of resources and followed up by additional funds and support by other major powers. One early indication that the UN may receive more U.S. support was the fact that one of the first acts of the Obama Administration was to order the United States to pay back U.S. dues that had been withheld from the organization in previous years. This shift in U.S. policy is a tacit recognition that the United Nations, despite all of its problems, remains an important actor in global areas to combat disease, poverty, and global crime. However, most observers acknowledge that the organization is in a crisis period and requires some major overhauls if it is to function effectively throughout the century.

Among the recommendations made by UN Secretary General Ban Ki-moon to make the organization run more efficiently after his appointment was to chop deadwood and cut red tape within the organization and to accept that certain organs, such as the Human Rights Council, the Security Council, or the General Assembly may not be "fixable." Other analysts note that so many efforts to reach new international agreements within the United Nations and elsewhere have failed repeatedly that it is time to focus on a strategy of achieving a coalition of the smallest possible number of countries needed to have an impact on a particular international problem. Such a more minimalist approach may be a more effective way to break the gridlock that so often develops in international and regional international organizations.

The inability of the United Nations Security Council's permanent members to reach a consensus on many resolutions has delayed implementing proposals that might have stopped the killing of innocent civilians in places such as Darfur, Sudan, or in the Democratic Republic of the Congo. One idea that has received a great deal of discussion in recent years is the international norm called the "Responsibility to Protect" or R2P. The R2P principle embodies the notion that the international community has a responsibility to protect citizens even if the national government in question objects to outside intervention. Since this new norm is in direct conflict with the long-standing norms of national sovereignty and non-intervention into the affairs of independent nation-states without the permission of the national government, it is extremely controversial. However, creating a new international norm is one way to break the current deadlock in the Security Council over whether the UN should be given authority to intervene militarily in conflicts that have or threaten to kill thousands of innocent civilians. The idea was floated years ago by Canada's former Foreign Minister, Lloyd Axworthy, as a new doctrine that could give the UN authority and an obligation to shield people all over the world from genocide and ethnic cleansing.

The new doctrine has been picking up support among American neo-conservatives and evangelical Christians alike and is reflected in the wording of a recent UN Security Council statement that recognizes the right of the United Nations to intervene in a sovereign country if the national government fails to protect its own people. However, the new doctrine also appears to lay the groundwork for future UN military interventions in civil conflicts, even if the host nation-state objects to outside intervention. Alan Kuperman in "Rethinking the Responsibility to Protect," argues that the Responsibility to Protect doctrine not only often fails to achieve its goal of protecting at-risk civilians, but may also unintentionally put others in danger. Even though the doctrine is quite new, it already requires a major rethinking if it is to promote its intended purpose of maximizing protection for innocent civilians. The lack of a global consensus about what role the United Nations should play in protecting citizens of sovereign nation-states reflects an even more basic disagreement among world elites about what security should entail and who should be responsible for guaranteeing global security.

Another approach for dealing with perpetrators of collective violence and crimes against humanity has been to establish special international tribunals. These special courts, established in Rwanda and Yugoslavia, have spent a vast amount of human and monetary resources and resulted in few convictions. Most of these courts have been established to deal with specific instances of crimes against humanities under the auspices of the International Criminal Court. The trial of the former Liberian President and warlord, Charles Taylor, was moved to The Hague in The Netherlands as there was concern that holding the trial in West Africa might contribute to additional instability and prove difficult to accomplish from a logistic and resource perspective. To date, none of the criminal tribunals, set up in Rwanda, the former Yugoslavia, or Liberia that were suppose to bring justice to oppressed peoples have succeeded in directly advancing human rights or implementing the wishes of victims. All of these trials have been lengthy affairs costing billions of dollars. Many important countries, including the United States, continue to refuse to recognize the jurisdiction of the ICC due to sovereignty concerns and unwillingness to agree to allow United States military personnel to be liable for charges that would be tried under the ICC's jurisdiction.

During the spring of 2010 more than 100 nations, contingents of human-rights groups and lawyers from around the globe met in Kampala, Uganda, to try to tackle some of the most difficult issues in international law. One of the thorniest was a proposal to give the International Criminal Court in the Hague the power to prosecute the crime of aggression. While many smaller countries and Germany favor such a change as it is seen as a form of legal protection, others, including Britain and France were opposed. The United States, Russia, and China could not vote because they have not joined the court and were in Kampala only as observers. Since these three countries, along with France and Britain hold United Nations Security Council veto power, none of these powerful nation-states support such measures that could weaken the Council's influence.

Before the meeting, many supporters and critics alike have argued that the court, which opened its doors in 2002 and has started only two trials, should focus on becoming more efficient and on the complex tasks before it, rather than risk getting bogged down so soon in the intensely political issue of aggression. One or more of these reasons are why some have concluded that is would be better to abandon these special courts. In contrast, others argue that such fledgling institutions as the ICC and new norms, such the Responsibility to Protect or R2P, should be supported because it will take decades to establish new effective international institutions and norms. Some international legal experts now advocate rewriting or possibly even scrapping the Geneva Convention, written to prevent the same type of atrocities that occurred during World War II, from occurring again. This argument is based on the assumption that many of the old rules no longer apply to many actors in the international system today.

Millennium Development Goals: At a Glance

MDG 1—Eradicate Extreme Poverty & Hunger

Halve, between 1990 and 2015, the proportion of people whose income is less than $1 a day.

Achieve full and productive employment and decent work for all, including women and young people.

Halve, between 1990 and 2015, the proportion of people who suffer from hunger.

Facts and Figures

The world is on track to meet the MDG target of halving the proportion of people living on less than $1 a day between 1990 and 2015.

The proportion of people living in extreme poverty in developing regions dropped from 46% to 27%—on track to meet the target globally.

The absolute number of people living under the international poverty line of $1.25 a day—the international poverty line as adjusted by the World Bank in 2008—declined from 1.8 billion to 1.4 billion between 1990 and 2005.

The economic crisis is expected to push an estimated 64 million more people into extreme poverty in 2010.

The proportion of people suffering from hunger is declining only slowly. The estimated number of people suffering chronic hunger in 2010 is 925 million, down from 1.023 billion in 2009, but still more than the number of undernourished people in 1990 (about 815 million).

About one in four children under the age of five is underweight in the developing world, down from almost one in three in 1990.

Country Progress

Through a national input subsidy programme, **Malawi** achieved a 53% food surplus in 2007, from a 43% national food deficit in 2005.

Vietnam's investment in agriculture research and extension helped cut the prevalence of hunger by more than half, from 28% in 1991 to 13% in 2004–06. The prevalence of underweight children also more than halved from 45% in 1994 to 20% in 2006.

Nicaragua reduced its hunger rate by more than half, from 52% in 1991 to 21% in 2004–06.

In Northeast **Brazil**, stunting, an indicator of child malnutrition, decreased from 22.2% to 5.9% between 1996 and 2006–07.

Between 1991 and 2004, the number of people who suffer from undernourishment in **Ghana** fell by 34%, to 9% of the population.

In **Argentina**, the *Jefes y Jefas de Hogar* programme employed 2 million workers within a few months after its initiation in 2002, contributing to the country's rapid poverty reduction, from 9.9% in 2002 to 4.5% in 2005.

MDG 2—Achieve Universal Primary Education

Ensure that, by 2015, children everywhere, boys and girls alike, will be able to complete a full course of primary schooling.

Facts and Figures

Despite great strides in many countries, the target is unlikely to be met.

In the developing regions, net enrolment in primary education reached 89% in 2008, up from 83% in 2000.

In sub-Saharan Africa, enrolment increased by 18% between 1999 and 2008, and by 11% and 8% in Southern Asia and Northern Africa, respectively.

About 69 million school-age children are not in school, down from 106 million children in 1999. Almost half (31 million) are in sub-Saharan, and more than a quarter (18 million) are in Southern Asia.

Country Progress

In **Ethiopia**, the net enrolment rate for primary school was 79% in 2008, an increase of 95% since 2000.

In **Tanzania**, the primary school enrolment ratio had doubled to 99.6% by 2008, compared to 1999 rates, thanks to the abolition of school fees.

In **Bolivia**, bilingual education has been introduced for three of the most widely used indigenous languages, covering 11% of all primary schools in 2002 and helping expand access to education among indigenous children in remote areas.

Mongolia has been providing innovative mobile schools ("tent schools") to cater to children in the countryside who may otherwise not have regular access to educational services. One hundred mobile schools have been spread out over 21 provinces.

MDG 3—Promote Gender Equality and Empower Women

Eliminate gender disparity in primary and secondary education, preferably by 2005, and in all levels of education no later than 2015.

Facts and Figures

Gender gaps in access to education have narrowed, but disparities remain high in university-level education and in some developing regions.

In developing regions, there were 96 girls for every 100 boys enrolled in primary school in 2008, and 95 girls for every 100 boys in secondary school.

Women's share of national parliamentary seats increased to 19% in 2010, a gain of 73% since 1995, but far short of gender parity.

Globally, the share of women in paid non-agricultural wage employment is slowly increasing and reached 41% in 2008.

In 2010, just nine of 151 elected heads of state and 11 of 192 heads of government were women. Globally, women hold only 16% of ministerial posts.

Country Progress

Mexico's programme *Generosidad* awards 'Gender Equity Seals' to companies who achieve specific standards related to gender equity. By 2006, 117 companies held the Seal.

In 2008, Rwanda elected a majority of women (56%) to its lower chamber of parliament, the highest level of female representation of any country.

Starting from a very low gender parity index in primary education (0.35) in 1980s, Bangladesh closed the gender gap in primary and secondary education within a decade.

Tanzania's Land Act and Village Land Act of 1999 secured women's right to acquire title and registration of land, addressed issues of customary land rights, and upheld the principles of non-discrimination based on sex for land rights.

In Ethiopia's Amhara Province, promotion of functional literacy, life skills, reproductive health education and opportunities for savings for girls has significantly reduced marriage of girls aged 10 to 14.

In Guyana, help for teenage mothers to improve their competencies through education and life skills training has significantly empowered them to make decisions for better lives for themselves and their children.

MDG 4—Reduce Child Mortality

Reduce by two thirds, between 1990 and 2015, the under-five mortality rate

Facts and Figures

Child deaths are falling, but not quickly enough.

Almost nine million children still die each year before they reach their fifth birthday.

The highest rates of child mortality continue to be found in sub-Saharan Africa, where, in 2008, one in seven children died before their fifth birthday.

Of the 67 countries defined as having high child mortality rates, only 10 are currently on track to meet the MDG target.

In the developing regions as a whole, the under-five mortality rate decreased from 100 deaths per thousand live births in 1990 to 72 in 2008. This corresponds to a 28% decline, well short of the target of a two-thirds reduction.

Since 1990, child mortality rates have been more than halved in Northern Africa, East Asia, South-Eastern Asia, and Latin America and the Caribbean.

Sub-Saharan Africa's child mortality rate declined by 22% between 1990 and 2008. However, sub-Saharan Africa still accounted for half of the 8.8 million deaths of the world's children under the ago of five in 2008.

Country Progress

The under-five child mortality rate has fallen by 40% or more since 1990 in Ethiopia, Malawi, Mozambique and Niger. In Malawi, for example, the under-five child mortality rate fell 56% between 1990 and 2008.

The under-five child mortality rate was reduced by 50% or more since 1990 in Bangladesh, Bhutan, Bolivia, Eritrea, Laos and Nepal.

Since 1990, China's under-five child mortality rate has declined from 46 deaths for every 1000 live births to 18 per 1000 in 2008, a reduction of 61%.

From 1990 to 2008, child mortality declined by 25% in Equatorial Guinea and by 14% in Zambia.

Cambodia increased exclusive breastfeeding from 13% to 60% from 2000 to 2005, strengthening children and reducing their vulnerability to illnesses.

MDG 5—Improve Maternal Health

Reduce by three quarters the maternal mortality ratio.

Achieve universal access to reproductive health.

Facts and Figures

Maternal mortality remains unacceptably high, even though most maternal deaths could be avoided.

More than 350,000 women die annually from complications during pregnancy or childbirth, almost all of them—99%—in developing countries.

The number of women dying due to complications during pregnancy and childbirth has decreased by 34%, from an estimated 546,000 in 1990 to 358,000 in 2008.

Progress is notable, but the annual rate of decline is less than half of what is needed to achieve MDG target of reducing the maternal mortality ratio by 75% between 1990 and 2015.

In sub-Saharan Africa, a woman's maternal mortality risk is 1 in 30, compared to 1 in 5,600 in developed regions.

Every year, more than 1 million children are left motherless. Children who have lost their mothers are up to 10 times more likely to die prematurely than those who have not.

Country Progress

In **Malawi** and **Rwanda,** removal of user fees for family planning services has contributed to significant increases in use of family planning services.

In **Rwanda,** contraceptive prevalence among married women aged 15–49 jumped from 9% in 2005 to 26% in 2008.

The contraceptive prevalence rate among married women aged 15–49 in **Malawi** has more than doubled since 1992 to 33% in 2004.

In **Rwanda,** the skilled birth attendance rate increased from 39% to 52% from 2005 to 2008.

MDG 6—Combat HIV/AIDS, Malaria and Other Diseases

Have halted by 2015 and begun to reverse the spread of HIV/AIDS.

Achieve, by 2010, universal access to treatment for HIV/AIDS for all those who need it.

Have halted by 2015 and begun to reverse the incidence of malaria and other major diseases.

Facts and Figures

The global response to AIDS has demonstrated tangible progress toward the achievement of MDG 6. The number of new HIV infections fell steadily from a peak of 3.5 million in 1996 to 2.7 million in 2008. Deaths from AIDS-related illnesses also dropped from 2.2 million in 2004 to two million in 2008.

Still, every day over 7,400 people are infected with HIV and 5,500 die from AIDS-related illnesses.

HIV remains the leading cause of death among reproductive-age women worldwide.

An estimated 33.4 million people were living with HIV in 2008, two thirds of them in sub-Saharan Africa.

Access to HIV treatment in low-and middle-income countries increased ten-fold over a span of just five years.

Malaria kills a child in the world every 45 seconds. Close to 90% of malaria deaths occur in Africa, where it accounts for a fifth of childhood mortality.

There were an estimated 243 million cases of malaria in 2008, causing 863,000 deaths, 89% of them in Africa.

Major increases in funding have recently helped control malaria. Global production of mosquito nets rose from 30 million to 150 million annually between 2004 and 2009.

31% of African households owned an anti-malaria insecticide-treated net in 2008, a 14 percentage point increase since 2006.

The number of new cases of tuberculosis fell from 143 to 139 per 100,000 people between 2004 and 2008.

1.8 million people died from tuberculosis in 2008, about 500,000 of whom were HIV-positive.

Country Progress

In **Uganda,** the adult HIV prevalence rate dropped from 8% in 2001 to 5.4% in 2007.

Cambodia has managed to halt and reverse the spread of HIV, with the prevalence falling from 1.8% in 2001 to 0.8% in 2007.

The number of new HIV infections among children has declined five-fold in **Botswana,** from 4,600 in 1999 to 890 in 2007.

In **Peru,** improved TB case detection and cure rates through DOTS (Directly Observed Treatment Short Course) saved an estimated 91,000 lives between 1991 and 2000. TB incidence declined at a rate of 5% per year over 2006–8.

Between 1991 and 2000, improved TB control in **China** reduced prevalence by over a third.

In **India,** the tuberculosis mortality rate dropped by 43% between 1990 and 2008.

By 2008, 71% of targeted households in **Togo** had a bed net and nearly one million children had benefited from treatment for parasites.

MDG 7—Environmental Sustainability

Integrate the principles of sustainable development into country policies and programmes and reverse the loss of environmental resources.

Reduce biodiversity loss, achieving, by 2010, a significant reduction in the rate of loss.

Halve, by 2015, the proportion of the population without sustainable access to safe drinking water and basic sanitation.

By 2020, to have achieved a significant improvement in the lives of at least 100 million slum dwellers.

Facts and Figures

The world is on track to achieve the safe water target. Some 1.7 billion people have gained access to safe drinking water since 1990. Yet 884 million people worldwide still do not have access to safe drinking water.

In 2008, an estimated 2.6 billion people—more than 37% of the world's population—did not have access to toilets, latrines or other forms of improved sanitation.

The proportion of people living without access to improved sanitation decreased by only 8 percentage points between 1990 and 2006.

1.2 billion people in the world practice open defecation, posing enormous health hazards to entire communities—87% of these people are in rural areas.

The number of slum dwellers in the developing world continues to grow. Globally, 828 million people are living in slums today, compared to 657 million in 1990 and 767 million in 2000.

Since 2000, more than 200 million slum dwellers have gained access to improved water, sanitation or durable and less crowded housing.

The world has missed the 2010 target for biodiversity conservation. Based on current trends, the loss of species will continue throughout this century.

Country Progress

Between 1999 and 2005, **Costa Rica** prevented the loss of 720 sq km of forests in biodiversity priority areas and avoided the emission of 11 million tons of carbon.

In 2006, 80% of the rural population in **Ghana** had access to an improved drinking water source, an increase of 43% on 1990 levels.

In **Mali,** the percentage of the population with at least one point of access to improved sanitation rose from 35% in 1990 to 45% in 2006.

Guatemala has increased its investment in water and sanitation resources, which contributed to an increase in access to improved drinking water from 79% in 1990 to 96% in 2006 and to improved sanitation from 70% in 1990 to 84% in 2006.

In **Burkina Faso,** a water tower and pipe system were installed for 1,300 villagers in 2006, resulting in 20 litres of affordable clean water a day available to each household.

South Africa successfully achieved the MDG target of halving the proportion of people lacking access to safe water, as lack of access to improved drinking water was reduced from 19% in 1990 to 7% in 2006.

In **Senegal,** the proportion of people living in cities with access to improved water reached 93% in 2006.

Since 2002, **Brazil** has been implementing the One Million Rural Cisterns Programme to bring clean water to about 36 million people in North-Eastern Brazil.

MDG 8—Global Partnership

Develop further an open, rule-based, predictable, nondiscriminatory trading and financial system.

Address the special needs of least developed countries, landlocked countries and small island developing states.

Deal comprehensively with developing countries' debt

In cooperation with pharmaceutical companies, provide access to affordable essential drugs in developing countries.

In cooperation with the private sector, make available benefits of new technologies, especially ICTs.

Facts and Figures

Official development assistance (ODA) stands at 0.31% of the combined national income of developed countries, still far short of the 0.7% UN target.

ODA reached $120 billion in 2009—an all-time high—and is projected to be around $126 billion in 2010—well short of the $146 billion for 2010 pledged by donor countries at the Gleneagles Group of Eight Summit and the UN World Summit in 2005.

The proportion of imports from developing countries admitted free of duty into developed countries reached close to 80% in 2008, a jump from 54% a decade earlier.

Debt burdens have eased for developing countries and remain well below historical levels.

Access to information and communications technology (ICT) is expanding. Globally, an estimated 4.6 billion people had access to mobile phone by the end of 2009.

In 2008, 23% of the world's population was using the Internet, although the percentage remains much higher in developed regions than in the developing world. Only 1 in 6 people in the developing world has access to the Internet.

Country Progress

Only five donor countries reached or exceeded the UN target of aid corresponding to 0.7% of gross national income in 2009: **Denmark, Luxem-bourg, the Netherlands, Norway** and **Sweden.**

In terms of aid volume, the largest donors in 2009 were the **United States, France, Germany, the United Kingdom** and **Japan.**

China, India, Iran and **Uzbekistan** succeeded in lowering private sector prices for generic medicines to less than twice the international reference price.

The share of **world trade** belonging to economies that are developing and in transition has increased to over 40%, from 35% in 2000, despite the inability to successfully resolve the Doha development round of trade talks.

Sources: *Millennium Development Goals Report 2010,* United Nations; *Keeping the Promise* (Secretary-General's report, March 2010); *Accelerating Progress on the MDGs,* UNDP 2010; reports by UN agencies, funds and programmes.

Note: Country progress examples are for illustrative purposes for the media—not an official record.

Statistics and examples are drawn from the *UN Millennium Development Goals Report 2010* and other sources from across the UN System, including UNDP, UNICEF, UNFPA and WHO.

The African Standby Force, Genocide, and International Relations Theory

STEPHEN BURGESS

I n international politics, the tendency of the leaders of states and organizations to make promises to supply international security and other public goods and then not deliver is common. In domestic politics, "political entrepreneurs" are usually punished, particularly in democracies, if they do not at least partially fulfill promises to deliver public goods, including national security. The anarchical nature of international politics means that there is little or no incentive that prevents leaders from making promises to supply international security and other public goods that they know may not be delivered.[1] Furthermore, using international organizations to make agreements to supply public goods allows member state leaders to "scapegoat" the organization when the goods are not supplied; thereby leaders escape responsibility for failure.

In seeking explanations for why leaders over-promise or make unattainable promises to supply international security and other public goods, motivations vary, including a desire for prestige and earnest efforts to solve difficult international problems. Some leaders make promises without realizing that there may be a lack of political will and capability to respond. Weaker states and organizations wish to demonstrate strength and independence from stronger states. Stronger states cooperate by "burden shifting" to less capable states in exchange for aid thereby compounding the problem. In regard to leaders of organizations, such as the United Nations (UN) or African Union (AU), they over-promise because of a desire to prove the usefulness of their organizations or because of pressures from member states to respond to demands for security.[2]

Burden-shifting by powerful states, which have the capability to provide security, to weaker states and organizations adds to the shortfall in international security caused by over-promising. The tendency is explained by the difficulty and costliness of supplying security combined with the low salience/lack of interest of more powerful states. As an alternative, major powers persuade and pressure smaller and weaker states to assume burdens that they lack the capability and will to manage. In sum, the gap between over-promising and burden-shifting

causes is a large collective action problem which explains failure in international security, including the failure to intervene to stop genocide.

One of the thorniest international security issues is stopping genocide. Most states have ratified the 1948 Genocide Convention, which obliges them to "prevent and punish genocide."[3] However, states have not acted to prevent or stop genocide, especially in Rwanda (1994), Darfur (2003-4), and Bosnia (1992-5). A principal limiting factor has been a lack of political will on the part of leaders of states, both strong and weak, to send forces to intervene in the internal affairs of sovereign states in order to stop genocide. A secondary factor has been a lack of military capacity by states in the region affected that might have an interest in preventing genocide and keeping it from spilling over their borders.

The case of over-promising international security that is analyzed in this paper is that of the African leaders who approved the formation of the African Standby Force (ASF) and signed off on the promise that the ASF would be prepared by 2010 to intervene to stop genocide. In 2003, the AU Peace and Security Commission and the African Chiefs of Defense Staff (ACDS) devised the ASF with six "typical conflict scenarios" which were used to develop the ASF proposals. By 2010, the ASF would be able to meet the challenges of six scenarios laid out by the ACDS. The most challenging would be: Scenario 6 - deployment of a robust military presence in 14 days to stop genocide:

> 1.6 A number of typical conflict scenarios, outlined below were used to develop the proposals in this document:
>
> f. **Scenario 6.** AU intervention—e.g. genocide situations where international community does not act promptly.

The document specifies the capabilities that would be required by the ASF to respond to "genocide situations":

> 2.8 The speed with which forces will be required to deploy has particular implications for standby force structures and arrangements. Linked to this is the type

of conflict into which they will deploy. Given the fluid and uncertain nature of conflict, particularly in Africa, coherence on deployment will be critical. This demands that units and HQ staff will have trained together prior to deployment. Significant implications of varying readiness levels are:

At 14 days readiness collective training involving field exercises with all units is essential prior to activation. At this level of readiness there is also a clear requirement for a standing fully staffed brigade HQ and HQ support. There is also a requirement for an established and fully stocked logistics system capable of sustaining the entire brigade. Apart from large military alliances such as NATO, individual Member States may be best placed to provide this capability.

The document stipulates the need for rapid reaction capability to respond in two weeks' time:

2.9　　Bearing this in mind, the Meeting recommends the following long-term deployment targets for the ASF (all timings are from an AU mandate resolution):

c.　Due to the nature of situations demanding intervention operations, Scenario 6, it will be important the AU can deploy a robust military force *in 14 days*.[4]

The July 2004 AU heads of state summit in Addis Ababa, Ethiopia approved the ASF proposal, including the response to Scenario 6, and work began on building the standby force.

The methodology of the paper is to examine genocide, the failure to act and the lack of political will and capability to stop genocide. Plausible explanations for over-promising are examined and logical explanations, based upon evidence and theory, are selected. Given the problem of over-promising, the paper first determines that the political will does not exist to fulfill the promise to respond to genocide and explains why—examining the history of African leaders' responses to massive humanitarian abuses inside African countries and demonstrating that there has been little will to intervene in the sovereign affairs of African states. Second, the paper demonstrates that African states and the ASF do not and will not have the military capability to respond to Scenario 6 by examining African military capabilities and especially those of the ASF sub-regional brigades in relation to the task of intervening to stop genocide. Third, the paper explains why African leaders and officials would make such a promise by examining the "African solutions for African problems" concept and African nationalist ideology that lie behind several grand schemes and promises, including the ASF. Fourth, the paper examines "burden shifting" by the United States, Britain and France and why they would accept the AU's unattainable promise to stop genocide.

Given the lack of accountability in international politics, an additional question is how far are leaders, states and organizations willing to push their promises? Is there anything that constrains them from making wildly unrealistic promises? It would seem that there is a certain point at which incredulity arises about the promises of weaker states and organizations and where stronger powers must step in to provide the international security and other public goods or turn to the United Nations to do so, which is what happened after the AU failed to stop genocide in Darfur and was supplemented by the UN.[5]

Genocide and What It Takes to Stop It

As defined by the Genocide Convention, "genocide means any of the following acts committed with intent to destroy, in whole or in part, a national, ethnical, racial or religious group, as such:

　a.　Killing members of the group;

　b　Causing serious bodily or mental harm to members of the group;

　c　Deliberately inflicting on the group conditions of life calculated to bring about its physical destruction in whole or in part;

　d　Imposing measures intended to prevent births within the group;

　e　Forcibly transferring children of the group to another group."[6]

The most important phrase of the Convention is ". . .with *intent to destroy,* in whole or in part. . ." The difficulty of proving "intent to destroy" has led to disagreements about whether or not the mass killings and displacement of people in Bosnia, Kosovo and Darfur constituted genocide or the more euphemistic, "ethnic cleansing." Subsequently, former President Slobodan Milosevic of Serbia and President Omar el-Bashir of Sudan were indicted by international courts on charges of genocide.

Only in the case of Kosovo in 1999, was NATO, led by the United States, able to stop ethnic cleansing, only after 850,000 people had been expelled from their homes by Serbian forces. A key factor was the political will of President Bill Clinton, Secretary of State Madeline Albright and other NATO leaders to prevent the ethnic cleansing that had dragged on in Bosnia from 1992 to 1995 from repeating itself. Also, the United States and other NATO countries had the forces which were capable of coercing Serbia to stop the ethnic cleansing process and allow Kosovar Albanians to return to their homes. The Bosnia case demonstrates that weak political will and under-mobilized capability can lead to failure, while the Kosovo case shows that a combination of strong political will and high capability can prevent genocide.

The Lack of Political Will to Stop Genocide in Africa

There is a large body of evidence to prove that there is a lack of political will on the part of leaders of African states and organizations to stop genocide. Since the formation of the Organization of African Unity (OAU) in 1963, African leaders have agreed on the importance of sovereignty and non-interference in the internal affairs of member states.[7] When genocide happened in Burundi in 1972 and 1993 and Rwanda in 1994, African states and organizations did nothing to intervene. When Tanzania intervened in Uganda in 1979 to overthrow the murderous Idi Amin regime, widespread protests were raised by OAU member states.

With the founding of the AU in 2002, it was hoped that the new organization, with South African leadership, could be more assertive in providing greater Africa-wide security and perhaps even stopping genocide. However, the AU did not respond in 2003 and 2004 to stop genocide in Darfur due again to a lack of political will; South African leadership did not make a difference. The Sudanese military dictatorship was determined to continue its scorched earth campaign and resisted all efforts to place an effective international force in Darfur. Only after hundreds of thousands were killed and millions displaced from their homes and after considerable international pressure did the Sudanese government agree to the sending of an AU peacekeeping force. This force proved inadequate as the Sudanese military and militias continued to destroy villages and murder and displace people.

The lack of political will to stop genocide has been recently manifested in African leaders' refusal to accept the 2009 indictment of President Omar El-Bashir of Sudan by the International Criminal Court for ordering massive crimes against humanity, including genocide, in Darfur. A 2009 African Union heads of state summit called on the UN Security Council to delay the ICC indictment from coming into effect.[8] Evidently, some African leaders feared that they too eventually might be targeted by the ICC.

Political resistance to genocide prevention has also been evidenced by the controversy over the "responsibility to protect" principle, in which governments have the responsibility to protect civilians or call on international assistance if unable to do so. Many African states have resisted signing up to the principle in the UN due to fears of external intervention in their own internal affairs. Efforts to separate the responsibility to protect principle from humanitarian intervention that would be needed to stop genocide have met with limited success.[9]

Evidence does exist of African intervention at the invitation of sovereign rulers, which has incidentally stopped massive human rights abuses. In the case of Liberia in 1990, Nigeria and other West African (ECOWAS) states entered the country under the pretense of keeping the peace for an agreement between the regime of President Samuel Doe, which extended an invitation to intervene to save his regime and stop mass killings, and rebels led by Charles Taylor. When the peace agreement collapsed, Nigeria insisted on continuing with the intervention as a peace enforcement mission, which coincided with the interests that Nigeria's military dictator, General Ibrahim Babangida, had developed in Liberia.

The Lack of Military Capability to Stop Genocide

On paper and in practice, the ASF and African militaries lack the enforcement and counter-insurgency capabilities needed to intervene, stop genocide and defeat spoilers. At present, the ASF mainly consists of a dozen or so infantry battalions.[10] The ASF possesses little of the armor, airborne and air power capabilities that an intervention to stop genocide requires.[11] Furthermore, a multinational force will be unable to achieve the unity of effort to deploy and stop genocide.

More specifically, full implementation of the ASF subregional commands entails the development of a number of other capabilities; these include airlift as well as sealift and ground transportation to dispatch the rapid deployment units and main ASF brigades and their equipment to conflict zones and re-supply them. On a positive note, the development of early warning mechanisms may mean that the Rapid Development Capabilities (RDC) will not have to be in a high state of readiness for prolonged periods and might be able to react within 14 days. Considerable logistics and maintenance capabilities are needed to sustain the brigades on a multinational basis. Interoperability, including interoperable communications, is required for the brigades to achieve unity of effort in the field. Intelligence capabilities are needed to allow the brigades operate effectively in their areas of responsibility.

Full implementation means full cost bearing by each of the sub-regional commands and their member states. Effective command and control by sub-regional organizations and force commanders over the brigades requires combined training exercises plus sound communications with sub-regional headquarters and the AU Peace and Security Commission. The sub-regional brigades are charged with developing the ability to deploy field level headquarters that take orders from the AU mission planning cell in Addis Ababa. All of these capabilities are presently lacking to one degree or another. At present, it is highly unlikely that the ASF and the sub-regional brigades will achieve full implementation by December 2010 and even more unlikely that the ASF will be able to "intervene in genocidal situations where the international community does not act promptly."

Even over the long run, it is not likely that the ASF subregional commands will be a force for rapid response in "genocidal situations." Africa's poverty and lack of state capacity are major impediments that will prevent the ASF sub-regional commands from being fully implemented. Most of the ASF sub-regional commands are less than halfway to full implementation by the due date of December 2010. Some brigades will be more effective than others. ECOWAS and ECOBRIG appear to better organized, led and planned, but they have not proven their effectiveness. SADC and SADCBRIG with South African leadership will probably be more effective, if the level of commitment continues to increase. EASBRIG suffers from the detachment of Ethiopia from the countries of the East African Community. The Central African countries of ECCAS have relied on France for leadership, organization and logistics, especially in peacekeeping operations in the Central African Republic (CAR). The North African brigade is organizing under Egyptian, Libyan and Algerian leadership, but unity of effort may prove difficult. The hardest part, effective ASF operationalization, remains. There are chronically unstable states, such as Somalia, Sudan, CAR, Chad and the Democratic Republic of the Congo (DRC), that will continue to pose military challenges from insurgents, warlords and militias that the ASF will not be able to confront and defeat.

In practice, the operational cases of African peacekeepers in conflict zones—Darfur (AMIS) and Somalia (AMISOM)—are not encouraging. AMIS was undersubscribed with only a few thousand peacekeepers without helicopters or other mobility, which meant that the mission was largely ineffectual for four years.[12] In 2008, the UN established a hybrid mission which expanded the peacekeeping force from 5,000 troops to 19,500 troops and 6,500 police and which proved more effective. AMSIOM has been even worse, with only 1,500 troops deploying and with Nigeria, Ghana and Malawi refusing to fulfill pledges to deploying battalions. As a result, AMISOM peacekeepers have been confined to Mogadishu and have become targets for Al Shabaab militia fighters. Other relevant examples include Côte d'Ivoire in 2002, where ECOWAS forces were inadequate to stabilize the situation in the wake of civil war and where French forces had to enforce a cease-fire. Nigeria and ECOWAS intervened in Liberia in August 2003 in the wake of a cease-fire but needed the threat of force from a US Marine Expeditionary Unit to ensure stability. In October 2003, ECOWAS quickly handed over authority to a UN mission UNMIL) which possessed the capacity to build up the peacekeeping force and sustain it over more than six years.

The fundamental problem for the ASF is a lack of resources and sustainability. Future economic growth may provide some African states with greater resources for possible use in building the ASF and sub-regional brigades. However, this will still leave the ASF and its brigades short on the type of resources to fully develop, achieve self-sufficiency and be successful in scenario six. More specifically, airlift, logistics and maintenance are difficult for poor countries lacking trained personnel to develop. Most small militaries will not be able to afford maintaining standby units and keeping them in a state of readiness for extended periods. There is the possibility that donor fatigue will arise and that ASF structures and functions will atrophy.[13]

Comparing the AU and ASF in resource-poor Africa with the resource-rich European Union and NATO demonstrates that resources are not sufficient to develop and sustain multinational forces and the commitment that can lead to effective interventions in conflict zones, such as Afghanistan in this decade and in Bosnia during the ethnic cleansing from 1992-5. Political will and force projection capabilities are the missing ingredients that can only be provided by the United States, Britain and France.[14]

Why African Leaders Promised to Stop Genocide

The motivation to promise to stop genocide came in the wake of criticism of the OAU and African leaders who did nothing as the Rwandan genocide unfolded over 100 days. Nelson Mandela, who came to power in South Africa on May 10, 1994 during the midst of the genocide, strove to find a way to stop mass killings in Burundi. In 2000, Mandela assumed control of negotiations to end civil war in Burundi and develop a power-sharing arrangement. In the later 1990s, Mandela's successor as South African president, Thabo Mbeki, promoted an "African Renaissance" to end violence, elitism, corruption and poverty in Africa and create the basis for progress. Mbeki's leadership, South African diplomacy, and cooperation by a number of prominent African leaders led to the New Partnership for African Development (NEPAD) and the African Peer Review Mechanism (APRM) in which African states would submit to review of their security and governance situations. The African renaissance, NEPAD and APRM were manifestations of African nationalism plus liberal internationalist repackaging by South Africa to attract more aid from the West. The slogan, "African solutions to African problems," became prominent among African leaders at this time.[15]

The African Renaissance campaign by Mbeki, South Africa and other African leaders culminated in the 2002 founding of the African Union. The AU was given greater powers to intervene in conflict situations and to monitor the human rights situations in member states. Thus, sovereignty was no longer as powerful as it had been under the OAU. After the founding of the AU and the Peace and Security Council and Peace and Security Commission, South African leadership was also significant in influencing the African Chiefs of Defense Staff to adopt the ASF concept including Scenario 6, AU intervention in genocide situations. In July 2004, African leaders signed off on the ASF without paying much attention to Scenario 6. It was more important to launch the ASF with the prospect of attracting Western aid. In conclusion, over-promising to stop genocide was more an act of carelessness than deliberateness.

Burden Shifting

In explaining why the United States and other major powers as well as the UN would allow the AU's promise to go unchallenged, powerful states seek to "burden shift" when an intervention is not in their interest. The ASF fit into their burden shifting interests. Ever since the collapse of the UN peacekeeping mission (UNOSOM II) in Somalia in 1993 and the failure to respond to genocide in Rwanda in 1994, the United States and other powers sought to burden shift to African states, while providing financial and technical assistance. The United States launched the Africa Crisis Response Initiative, 1997-2001, to train African peacekeepers and followed it with the Africa Contingency Training and Assistance program, from 2002 onward. In 2004, the United States joined with European states in the Global Peace Operations Initiative to cooperate in training 75,000 African peacekeepers. The vast majority of training by the United States and other countries was suitable for peacekeepers to serve once a cease-fire had been secured. Very little was suitable for intervention in genocide situations, like the Rwandan genocide, which had motivated the United States and other countries to initiate the training in the first place.

The gap between great power burden shifting and over-promising by weak states and organizations is such that international security is often not provided. The most glaring example of this has been the lack of response to genocide in Rwanda and Darfur. Great powers can avoid blame for inaction by taking the issue to the UN Security Council. Thus, the UN was made the scapegoat for failure to act in the 1994 Rwandan genocide, and the AU for the 2004 Darfur genocide. Also, China was faulted for vetoing resolutions in the Security Council that may have stopped the killing and displacement.

The ASF concept and the commitment to stop genocide let the United States, France, and Britain off the hook in dealing with genocide. Only those three powers have the operational capability and can generate the political will to stop genocide. If genocide is ever to be stopped, the GPOI and ASF programs need to be altered to call on those three powers to lead in the stopping of genocide with support from willing African coalition partners.

Conclusion

This paper has demonstrated that African leaders have over-promised to stop genocide, given their lack of political will and weak military capability. As leaders of weak states, they over-promise because of a combination of African nationalist ideology and a desire for aid from major powers, captured in the nationalist slogan—"African solutions for African problems"[16]—which is also popular with the United States and other powers seeking to burden shift. Thus, a curious combination of nationalism and dependence trump a highly needed international public good—the political will and military capability to stop genocide. Throughout the world, weak states and organizations exhibit similarly contradictory behavior.

The lack of political will and capability to stop genocide explicitly highlights problems with the ASF concept. One must question if this is the way that African militaries should be organized and led in peace and stability operations. Given the scarcity of resources and dependence on donors and the likelihood of more internal conflict in weak African states, the ASF and the sub-regional commands are not sustainable and will not be for a very considerable period of time to come. Donor fatigue will eventually pose problems for the ASF. The ASF represents a diversion of scarce resources and time that Africa and its militaries could invest in alternative methods for enhancing African security. The ASF may make African militaries more cosmopolitan and more communicative with each other, but it will not make them dramatically more capable operationally. The lack of logistics, airlift and training prevents operational progress. Also, it is easier to maintain national units rather than a multinational force with elaborate and difficult command and control and planning mechanisms.

Resources being spent on ASF sub-regional brigades and the AU Peace and Security Commission could be used to better effect on developing the capability of the armed forces of individual states to serve in UN peacekeeping missions. A greater number of highly effective national battalions and brigades could be developed that could be deployed, supported and commanded by the UN. Most UN operations have a proven record of sustainment and resolution of many African conflicts followed by peacebuilding. The UN has the resources based on financial contributions of developed member states and combine developed country military resources and developing country troops. A related option would be to train the battalions of the most effective African militaries, such as Rwanda's, which would ensure the deployment of more capable African brigades.[17]

In regard to Scenario 6, stopping genocide, a problem for the UN and the Permanent Five is the lack of political will to stop genocide and the reluctance of China and Russia to authorize intervention in the internal affairs of member states. However, political will is also lacking in Africa, as has been demonstrated by the cases of Rwanda and Darfur and failing to intervene in Zimbabwe. Furthermore, the ASF goal of stopping genocide provides the United States, Britain and France (with the most capable militaries) the excuse not to act (as was the case with Darfur).

Ultimately, priority should be placed on effectiveness with dependence on the UN and the West rather than suboptimal security with self-reliance through the ASF. The ASF should remain a long-term goal—perhaps by 2020 or 2030. African peacekeepers would continue to be deployed with the authorization of the AU or sub-regional organizations before being taken over by the UN. The UN would continue to assume control over the operations and provide the financing, logistics, and other resources.

The ASF goals to be fully operational by 2010 and to stop genocide reflect the African tendency to set unattainable goals. This can be seen in the 2015 target for achieving the Millennium Development Goals for Africa, which will not be met. It can also be seen in unrealistic goals for the New Partnership for African Development (NEPAD), especially the African Peer Review Mechanism (APRM), which promises that African states will make major changes to their governance in response to peer review and the desire to increase foreign investment. Challenging timetables may prod African militaries to develop, but they also lead to unrealistic expectations, which can result in suboptimal performance, such as in Darfur (as well as the AU mission in Somalia). The alternative is realistic strategic concepts and directing scarce resources where they will be the most effective.

The ASF will not be fully implemented for the foreseeable future, because African states are too poor and lack capacity. In spite of this reality, African leaders, organizations and advisers have set up a scheme that promises to stop genocide and fully deploy but will not be able to do so by December 2010 or December 2020. Nevertheless, African leaders are attempting to demonstrate that African states and organizations are making an organized effort to posture for action and will ask the major powers to fill shortfalls in financial and military resources. This game of posturing should require that African leaders and organizations openly admit that Africa will not be fully capable to stop genocide, while they call on the major powers to fill the gaps and intervene. The international community, led by human rights NGOs, needs to continue to pressure the major powers and African states and organizations to establish a compact to stop genocide and other major man-made humanitarian disasters. A stepping stone to such a compact would be a commitment by African states to the "responsibility to protect" human rights norm.[18] With such a commitment, the ASF and developed country forces would find it easier to overcome sovereignty claims and intervene to stop genocide. Finally, the international community should pressure the African Union and African states to give an honest accounting of ASF progress and the lack thereof and what steps need to be taken to fill the gaps.

In regard to stopping genocide, commitment and political will by the United States and other powers in cooperation with a coalition of the willing in Africa appears to be the way to stop genocide. A way must be found to construct a coalition of the willing in which NGOs such as ENOUGH can play a constructive role. The question is in Africa, where political will is questionable and military capability is suspect, what formula will it take to prevent genocide? The United States and other developed countries need to must muster the political will and provide rapid reaction and air power capabilities and logistics to stop genocide.

In Liberia in 2003, high capability (the US MEU) and high willingness (ECOMIL in Liberia) were able to prevail in a volatile cease-fire situation. The Nigerian desire to end rule of Charles Taylor and pressure on the United States to act led to the end of a dangerous stalemate in 2003. Thus, salience is important; if deployment is within the sub-region, high salience will motivate the brigades to respond more effectively than if deployed outside of the sub-region. If regional military cooperation develops and flourishes, as perhaps in the case of ECOWAS and ECOBRIG, sub-regional capability to deal with some of the more challenging scenarios, requiring enforcement, will be enhanced.

There are questions for further international relations research. Given the lack of accountability in international politics, one question is how far are leaders, states and organizations willing to push their promises? Is there anything that constrains them from making unrealistic promises? It would seem that there is a certain point at which incredulity arises about the promises of weaker states and organizations and where stronger powers must step in to provide the international security and other public goods or turn to the United Nations to do so. Why would African leaders promise to stop genocide when they know that they cannot deliver? Why has no one objected?

Notes

1. Charles P. Kindleberger, "International Public Goods without International Government," *The American Economic Review,* Vol. 76, No. 1, March 1986, 1–13. Charles Lipson, "International Cooperation in Economic and Security Affairs," *World Politics,* Vol. 37, No. 1, October 1984, 1–23.

2. Percy S. Mistry, "Africa's Record of Regional Co-operation and Integration," *African Affairs,* 91 (397) 2000: 533–552. Keith Gottschalk and Siegmar Schmidt, "The African Union and the New Partnership for Africa's Development: Strong Institutions for Weak States?" *Internationale Politik und Gesellschaft,* 4, 2004, 138–159. Paul-Henri Bischoff, "Pan-African Multilateralism: Transformative or Disconnected?" *Politikon: South African Journal of Political Studies,* Volume 35, Number 2, August 2008, pp. 177–195. James D. Fearon and David D. Laitin, "Neotrusteeship and the Problem of Weak States," *International Security,* Vol. 28, No. 4 (Spring 2004), pp. 17–18.

3. "Convention on the Prevention and Punishment of the Crime of Genocide," United Nations, New York, December 9, 1948, Article I. Entry into Force, January 12, 1951. www.preventgenocide.org/law/convention/text.htm. There are more than 130 contracting parties including the United States. Article I states, "The Contracting Parties confirm that genocide, whether committed in time of peace or in time of war, is a crime under international law which they undertake to prevent and to punish."

4. "Policy Framework for the Establishment of the African Standby Force and the Military Staff Committee," Part I, Document Adopted by the Third Meeting of the African Chiefs of Defence Staff, 15-16 May 2003, pages 3, 6 and 7, www.africa-union.org/root/au/AUC/Departments/PSC/Asf/Documents.htm, accessed February 3, 2010.

5. The advocacy group, ENOUGH, www.enoughproject.org/, was founded with the express purpose of pressuring the US government and other entities to muster the political will and develop the diplomatic instruments to prevent genocide and protect civilians and publish perpetrators.

6. Genocide Convention, Article II.

7. Robert H. Jackson, *Quasi-States: Sovereignty, International Relations and the Third World,* Cambridge University Press, 1990, 13–31. Christopher Clapham, *Africa and the International System: The Politics of State Survival,* Cambridge University Press, 2002, 3–27.

8. "Decision on the Meeting of African States Parties to the Rome Statute of the International Criminal Court (ICC)," Doc. Assembly AU/13(XIII), Adopted by the Thirteenth Ordinary Session of the Assembly Of Heads of State and Government in Sirte, Great Socialist People's Libyan Arab Jamahiriya, July 3, 2009.

9. Alex J. Bellamy, "Realizing the Responsibility to Protect," *International Studies Perspectives,* Vol. 10, No. 2, May 2009, 111–128. Alex J. Bellamy, *The Responsibility to Protect: The Global Effort to Stop Mass Atrocities,* Cambridge, UK: Polity Press, 2009.

10. Jeffrey E. Marshall, "Building an Effective African Standby Force to Promote African Stability, Conflict Resolution and Prosperity," Crisis States Discussion Papers, London School of Economics, Development Studies Institute, Discussion Paper 16, 2009, 1–31.

11. Alan Kuperman, *The Limits of Humanitarian Intervention,* Baltimore, Johns Hopkins University Press, 2002, 52–77.

12. Interview with a European Union official, Addis Ababa, Ethiopia, May 29, 2007. The AU mission in Darfur, which the European Union heavily assisted, led EU officials to become disenchanted with the AU and led some to question the value of contributing to the AU Peace Facility.

13. Interview with EU official, May 2007. It is unfortunate that another Rwandan or Darfur genocide may be required to regenerate donor interest.

14. Dickens, "Can East Timor Be a Blueprint for Burden Sharing?" 29–40. An additional ingredient in stopping genocide is the adoption of the "responsibility to protect" norm. See also Bellamy, *Responsibility to Protect.*

15. Chris Fomunyoh, "African Solutions for African Problems: A Slogan Whose Time Has Passed," *AllAfrica.com,* February 9, 2005, http://allafrica.com/stories/200502090005.html

16. Chris Fomunyoh, "African Solutions for African Problems: A Slogan Whose Time Has Passed," *AllAfrica.com,* February 9, 2005, http://allafrica.com/stories/200502090005.html,

17. However, more trained Rwandan battalions could skew the balance of power in East and Central Africa and could harm civil-military relations inside Rwanda.

18. Bellamy, *Responsibility to Protect,* Bellamy. "Realizing the Responsibility to Protect,"

Critical Thinking

1. In your own words describe what the purpose of the All Africa Standby Force and how far from the core objective is the project.

2. Visit the African Union's All Africa Standby Force web page and briefly summarize what types of activities have been undertaken recently by the African Union to bring this entity to fruition.

STEPHEN BURGESS, US Air War College International Studies Association Annual General meeting 17–20 February 2010

Paper presented by Stephen F. Burgess, PhD, US Air War College, at the International Studies Association 2010 Annual General meeting.

Rethinking the Responsibility to Protect

ALAN J. KUPERMAN

One of the most recent innovations of institutional liberalism in international politics is the so-called Responsibility to Protect. Defined in 2001 by an international commission established by Canada, this emerging norm challenges the Westphalian tradition by arguing that sovereignty is neither absolute nor an entitlement of statehood, but rather a privilege that states may earn only by protecting their people. Moreover, if a state refuses to protect its people, or intentionally harms some of them, the international community has not merely the right, but the responsibility, to violate that state's traditional sovereignty to protect the at-risk population—if necessary, through military intervention.

As with many aspects of institutional liberalism, however, this noble principle has faltered in practice. Most obviously, as Darfur illustrates, the international community lacks the political will for the collective action necessary to protect vulnerable citizens. But even if the international community could muster the requisite political will, humanitarian intervention would remain bedeviled by two substantial obstacles—the logistical requirements of effective intervention and the perverse unintended consequences that result from moral hazard. Based on recent experience, the Responsibility to Protect not only often fails to achieve its goal of protecting at-risk civilians, but it may also unintentionally put others in danger. Even though the doctrine is quite new, it already requires a major rethinking if it is to promote its intended purpose of maximizing protection for innocent civilians.

The Emerging Norm

The norm of humanitarian intervention has emerged since the end of the Cold War, which broke the logjam in the UN Security Council and freed major powers to focus on more altruistic objectives.[1] The first case was in northern Iraq in April 1991, when a failed Kurdish rebellion sparked retaliation by Saddam Hussein's army, imperiling hundreds of thousands. The United States spearheaded a military intervention that protected civilians in several ways: by deterring ground attacks, facilitating the delivery of humanitarian aid, and preventing aerial attacks with a no-fly zone. Over the next four years, the international community launched similar high-profile humanitarian military interventions, of varying effectiveness, in southern Iraq, Bosnia, Somalia, and Zaire.

US President Bill Clinton enunciated the emerging norm in 1999, during NATO's aerial intervention in Kosovo, telling CNN, "If the world community has the power to stop it, we ought to stop genocide and ethnic cleansing."[2] Two years later, the Canadian-appointed commission formalized that declaration as the "Responsibility to Protect."[3] In December 2004, a UN panel concurred: "We endorse the emerging norm that there is a collective international responsibility to protect . . . in the event of genocide and other large-scale killing, ethnic cleansing or serious violations of international humanitarian law."[4] The following year, at the World Summit, the UN General Assembly codified this principle as the "responsibility to use appropriate diplomatic, humanitarian, and other peaceful means . . . to help protect populations from genocide, war crimes, ethnic cleansing, and crimes against humanity." However, because members of the Group of 77 harbored concerns about threats to their own sovereignty, the General Assembly refused to endorse military intervention unless authorized "through the Security Council . . . on a case-by-case basis . . . should peaceful means be inadequate."[5]

Inadequate Political Will

Although the international community has intervened in many conflicts since 1991, and even declared a responsibility to do so, it has typically lacked the political will to halt the violence until many civilians have already been victimized. Even in the midst of intervention, political will often disintegrates when intervention forces are confronted with casualties. In Bosnia, for example, the UN deployed peacekeepers in 1992, but did not authorize or equip them to end the violence until 1995, by which time some 100,000 Bosnians had died.[6] In Somalia, the UN and the US did not deploy a significant military intervention until late 1992, after tens of thousands of civilians already had died from conflict-related famine. These forces then were withdrawn prematurely after 18 US soldiers were killed in October 1993.[7] In Rwanda, when the genocide started in 1994, the UN quickly voted to withdraw most of its peacekeepers because ten of them had been killed on the first day.[8] In Sierra Leone, British peacekeepers intervened successfully in 2000 to end a civil war, but only after less robust regional and UN interventions had failed to prevent gruesome atrocities and tens of thousands of killings over the previous nine years.[9] Likewise, in

Liberia, US Marines and regional peacekeepers led a successful intervention to end civil war in 2003, but only after previous regional interventions had failed to avert tens of thousands of killings during the previous 13 years of civil war.[10]

Although the international community has intervened in many conflicts since 1991, and even declared a responsiblity to do so, it has typically lacked the political will to halt the violence until many civilians have already been victimized.

The Darfur region of northwest Sudan has witnessed the same pattern since 2003. Violence raged most intensely from mid-2003 to mid-2004, as state-supported Janjaweed Arab militias perpetrated a scorched-earth counter-insurgency against villages suspected of supporting African rebels, displacing approximately 2 million people within Sudan and as refugees to neighboring Chad, while killing thousands more. During this bloodiest phase, the international community failed to muster the political will for any military intervention, instead providing only humanitarian aid to the small portion of the affected population it could reach.[11] Not until August 2004 did the African Union deploy 132 military observers and approximately 300 peacekeepers, but without the mandate or equipment to protect civilians. Over the next year, the AU force increased to nearly 7,000 peacekeepers and police, but still lacked materiel and logistical support, such as helicopters and fuel, for effective reconnaissance and rapid reaction. In many areas, the peacekeepers could neither escort humanitarian aid convoys nor protect camps for internally displaced persons, let alone protect villages.[12] In 2007, the United Nations authorized a larger, joint UN-AU force (UNAMID) of 26,000 personnel, including nearly 20,000 troops. But as of late 2008, the deployment had yet to reach half that size and still awaited the requested helicopters.[13] Western states have repeatedly proved reluctant to deploy forces to Darfur, partly in fear of sparking a violent Islamist opposition against the occupying troops, as already confronts such troops in Iraq and Afghanistan.

Logistical Obstacles

Even if the international community could muster the political will for rapid and robust intervention in such conflicts, it would be impossible to protect at-risk populations in many cases where the perpetrators can act more quickly than the interveners. In Bosnia, for example, although the conflict dragged on for more than three years, the majority of ethnic cleansing was carried out in the spring of 1992. By the time Western media arrived on the scene later that summer, ethnic Serb forces had already occupied two-thirds of the republic and displaced more than one million residents. In Rwanda, at least half of the eventual half-million Tutsi victims were killed in the first three weeks of genocide in April 1994. When Croatia's army broke

a three-year cease-fire in August 1995, it ethnically cleansed virtually all of the more than 100,000 Serbs from the Krajina region in less than a week. In March 1999, when Serbian forces in Kosovo switched from a policy of counter-insurgency to ethnic cleansing, in response to NATO's decision to launch air strikes, they expelled nearly half of the province's ethnic Albanians in the first two weeks. Later that year, in East Timor, following a vote for independence, Indonesian-backed militias damaged the majority of the province's infrastructure and displaced most of its residents in little more than a week.

By contrast, even with sufficient political will, it is physically impossible to deploy properly equipped intervention forces so quickly over long distances. For example, when Iraq's army invaded Kuwait in August 1990, the United States unquestionably possessed the political will to deploy forces to Saudi Arabia as soon as possible in order to protect oil fields. Nevertheless, the first unit of only 2,300 US troops required 9 days to reach the area, and another week to prepare itself for venturing beyond its makeshift base. Even though the United States has by far the best force-projection capability in the world, and Saudi Arabia offered strong airfield infrastructure and a warm welcome, this small force still required more than two weeks to deploy. The reasons for such delay are numerous, but stem mainly from three factors: modern militaries cannot operate without their equipment, their equipment is extremely heavy, and there are limits to the rate at which such equipment can be airlifted to remote countries. Indeed, delays would be much longer for other potential interveners, larger forces, interventions that face armed resistance, or deployments to states with inferior infrastructure (as is typical in humanitarian crises).[14]

In Rwanda, even if the United States had acted as soon as the genocide came to light, at least six weeks would have been required to deploy a task force of 15,000 personnel and their equipment. A larger US force—matching those deployed previously to Haiti, Panama, and the Dominican Republic—would have taken longer. A multi-lateral intervention would have required even more time because other potential troop contributors lack the US capacity for rapid deployment. Unfortunately, by the time the international community realistically could have deployed an intervention force to Rwanda, the vast majority of the targeted population would have already been dead.[15]

The fact that much civil violence is carried out more rapidly than intervention forces could arrive to stop it is no excuse for failing to intervene; indeed, some lives could still be saved, even by belated intervention. However, the life-saving potential of humanitarian military intervention is smaller than commonly realized. This is important as the following section considers the unexpected costs of intervention.

Moral Hazard

The most counter-intuitive aspect of the Responsibility to Protect is that it sometimes contributes to the tragedies that it intends to prevent. The root of the problem is that genocide and ethnic cleansing often represent state retaliation against a sub-state group for rebellion, or armed secession, by some of its members. The emerging norm, by raising hopes of diplomatic and military intervention to protect these groups, unintentionally fosters rebellion by lowering its expected cost and raising its likelihood of success. Intervention does sometimes help rebels attain their political goals, but it is usually too late or inadequate to avert retaliation against civilians. Thus, the emerging norm resembles an imperfect insurance policy against genocidal violence. It creates a moral hazard that encourages the excessively risky behavior of rebellion by members of groups that are vulnerable to genocidal retaliation, but it cannot fully protect these groups against the backlash. The emerging norm thereby causes some genocidal violence that otherwise would not occur.[16]

In the early 1990s, for example, Bosnia's Muslim leaders sought to secede from Yugoslavia so that they could establish their own state in which Muslims would enjoy a near ethnic majority. But because they faced opposition from ethnic Serbs in Bosnia and the rest of Yugoslavia, who possessed considerably greater military power, the Muslims initially eschewed secession as suicidal. By 1992, however, the international community had pledged to recognize Bosnia's independence if it seceded. This pledge, combined with the Muslim leaders' knowledge of previous humanitarian interventions in Iraq and Croatia, led them to believe that they had a guarantee of protection if they armed themselves and seceded from Yugoslavia—which they proceeded to do with the support of Bosnia's ethnic Croat minority.[17] The Serbs retaliated in April 1992, but the international community did not intervene with decisive force until 1995, by which time tens of thousands of fighters and civilians were already dead.

A similar scenario played out a few years later in the Serbian province of Kosovo. The local ethnic Albanian majority sought independence but, in the face of Serb military superiority, they prudently hewed to peaceful resistance throughout the early 1990s. Even after an influx of light weapons from neighboring Albania in 1997, most of Kosovo's ethnic Albanians, including the rebel Kosovo Liberation Army, believed that, by themselves, they were no match for heavily armored Serb forces. Nonetheless, the rebels expected that if they could provoke the Serbs into retaliating against Albanian civilians, the international community would intervene on their behalf, thereby facilitating independence.[18]

The plan played out almost perfectly. In late 1997, the rebels started shooting large numbers of Serb police and civilians, which provoked the Serb forces to retaliate in 1998 with a counter-insurgency that killed approximately 1000 ethnic Albanian rebels and civilians. In 1999, NATO intervened on behalf of the Albanians with air strikes that, after 11 weeks, compelled Serb forces to withdraw and accept a NATO occupation. In 2007, this intervention culminated when the United States and most European states recognized Kosovo's independence.

But NATO's intervention had initially backfired, as noted, by compelling the Serbs in March 1999 to commence ethnic cleansing, which displaced about 850,000 Albanians and killed approximately 10,000. Then, when Serb forces withdrew in June 1999, the Albanians took revenge by ethnically cleansing some 100,000 Serb civilians, killing several hundred. Notably, the rate of violent death in Kosovo was roughly thirty times higher during the NATO bombing campaign than it had been during the year of conflict prior to intervention.

Much of this death and displacement in the Balkans was a direct consequence of the emerging norm of the Responsibility to Protect. Research in Bosnia and Kosovo, including interviews with top Muslim and Albanian militant leaders, reveals that they launched their armed challenges—provoking violent state retaliation—based entirely on the prospect of sympathetic foreign assistance.[19] The unavoidable conclusion is that the emerging norm of humanitarian intervention sometimes causes the tragedies that it aims to prevent.

Darfur is the most recent case in which the Responsibility to Protect has backfired. From 1983 to 2005, Sudan endured a brutal civil war between the northern-based regime and southern rebels, in which southern civilians bore the brunt of the violence. Starting in 2001, consistent with the emerging norm, the United States expanded an international campaign to protect the southern civilians by pressuring Sudan's government to share power and wealth with the rebels. By 2003, the intervention succeeded in compelling Sudan to agree to a tentative peace with the south. However, this had the unintended consequence of spurring rebellion in Darfur by militants who hoped to emulate the southern strategy of attracting humanitarian intervention to gain a share of power and wealth. Despite the state's brutal response to rebellion in Darfur, the international community, at first, responded only with condemnation and sanctions.

This initially feeble implementation of the emerging norm merely emboldened the rebels to continue fighting, with the hope of soliciting greater intervention. The tragic consequence was to exacerbate and prolong the suffering of civilians. In 2006, Sudan's government signed a US-brokered peace agreement, but two of the three main rebel factions refused to join because they demanded additional concessions and greater foreign intervention "like in Bosnia."[20] This recalcitrance triggered a further fractioning of the rebellion, a breakdown in the peace process, and anarchic violence. In light of the fact that the rebels have never had any chance of battlefield victory on their own, one can reasonably conclude that their repeated refusal to make peace is driven by the hope of larger international intervention under the Responsibility to Protect.[21] Once again, the emerging norm, which was intended to reduce genocidal violence, has produced the opposite effect.

Enabling Rapid Reaction

The shortcomings of the Responsibility to Protect do not necessitate its abandonment; but the emerging norm does require a serious rethinking, in terms of conception and implementation, in order to achieve its intended goal. Even if the political will for intervention could be mustered more frequently and rapidly, the above analysis indicates that reform is needed in at least two other broad areas: the structure of forces for military intervention, and the strategy for all intervention—whether diplomatic, economic, or military.

States that want to play a leading role in humanitarian military intervention should adjust their force structure to reflect the empirical reality that violence against civilians can be perpetrated very quickly. One option is to modify some power-projection forces so they can deploy faster. Lighter forces, with fewer heavy weapons and less armor, would require fewer cargo flights, enabling them to arrive sooner to start saving lives. But shedding protective armor and weaponry can also increase casualties, as the coalition forces in Iraq initially learned the hard way.[22] Such a trade-off cannot be made lightly.

An alternative strategy is to pre-position forces, or at least their heavy equipment, at forward bases closer to where they are most likely to be needed for humanitarian intervention, such as in Africa. Interventions could be launched from these bases using small cargo aircraft, which are more plentiful and better able to land at rudimentary African air fields than wide-body inter-continental airlifters. The cargo aircraft could make several round-trips per day to a conflict zone from forward bases, rather than one trip every few days from distant US or European bases, sharply reducing deployment time from weeks to days. One obstacle, however, is that many African states oppose foreign military bases as tantamount to neo-colonialism, as recently demonstrated by the Pentagon's difficulty in establishing a proposed continental headquarters for its new Africa Command (AFRICOM).[23] An even bigger obstacle is that the world's major powers, so far, have proved unwilling to make significant military investments in missions other than those defined by traditional national interests.

In recognition of the West's lack of will to deploy ground troops to Africa, the United States, in the mid-1990s, launched the first in a series of programs to train indigenous African forces for peace operations. This initiative had a reasonable premise—African states would be more willing than others to risk the lives of their troops to stop conflict on the continent; nonetheless, it has faced several obstacles. First, due to inadequate resources and some concern about unintended consequences, the programs have provided little, if any, weaponry or combat training. This means that the participating African forces are prepared only for the permissive environment of peacekeeping after a conflict ends, such as in Liberia in 2003.[24] Second, these initiatives, so far, have failed to pre-position heavy weapons, armored personnel carriers, or helicopters at African bases. As a result, such equipment would have to be transported and joined up with intervention forces on an ad hoc basis in the event of a crisis, wasting precious time. Third, most training has been conducted only within national units, so that the few trained forces remain unprepared for the multi-national coalition operations that would be necessary for any large-scale intervention. The African Union has recently established the framework for an African Standby Force of five regional, multi-national brigades. But even after receiving some foreign assistance, the project is so woefully under-funded that it remains skeletal, adding little to the few high-quality national military units that already existed on the continent.[25] In light of these shortfalls, an all-African force has little hope, any time soon, of quelling violence or providing security in a situation such as Darfur.

A final alternative is to create a UN rapid response capability, as proposed in 2000 by an international commission headed by Algerian diplomat Lakhdar Brahimi. This panel called for expanding UN standby arrangements "to include several coherent, multi-national, brigade-size forces and the necessary enabling forces, created by Member States working in partnership, in order to better meet the need for the robust peacekeeping forces."[26] One problem with this concept is that it makes no provision for airlift operations. Only the US military has a sizeable, long-haul cargo air fleet, which means that rapid reaction to most parts of the world is wishful thinking unless the United States participates.[27] Another problem is that even if UN member states were willing to pledge troops in advance for humanitarian intervention, it is uncertain whether they would actually deploy them when called upon. Relying on a UN force that might not materialize when needed could actually delay the collective response to humanitarian emergencies by encouraging individual states, initially, to "free ride" on the expected institutional response.

Reducing Moral Hazard

Potential interveners should also modify their implementation of the Responsibility to Protect in order to mitigate the problem of moral hazard. As currently implemented, the emerging norm has the unintended consequence of encouraging rebellion by members of vulnerable sub-state groups, prompting states to retaliate with genocidal violence before intervention can stop it. A theoretical solution would be for the international community to launch timely military interventions in response to every instance of state violence. But this is unfeasible for two reasons. First, even if the political will for intervention could be mustered, the pervasiveness of such violence would soon exhaust global resources. The decade of the 1990s witnessed major civil violence in at least 16 states (some on several occasions): Albania, Algeria, Angola, Azerbaijan, Bosnia, Cambodia, Congo Republic, Croatia, Ethiopia, Liberia, Kosovo, Sierra Leone, Somalia, Sudan, Tajikistan, and Zaire (later renamed the Democratic Republic of Congo). Moreover, by the logic of moral hazard, each instance of humanitarian intervention raises expectations of future intervention, thereby encouraging rebellions that may provoke additional state violence, further overwhelming the international capacity for intervention.

As currently implemented, the emerging norm has the unintended consequence of encouraging rebellion by members of vulnerable substate groups, prompting states to retaliate with genocidal violence before intervention can stop it.

Instead, the international community should modify its implementation of the Responsibility to Protect in five ways, so as to mitigate moral hazard and reduce the incidence of genocidal violence. This proposal builds on lessons from the economics literature on moral hazard and several case studies of humanitarian intervention.[28] The first reform is the most important: the international community should refuse to intervene in any way—diplomatic, economic, or military—to help sub-state rebels unless state retaliation is grossly disproportionate. This would discourage militants within vulnerable sub-state groups from launching provocative rebellions that recklessly endanger civilians, in hopes of garnering foreign intervention. At the same time, by retaining the intervention option for extreme cases, this reform would also discourage states from responding disproportionately to rebellion by intentionally harming civilians. All sides in civil conflicts would effectively be incentivized toward less violent action.

Second, when the international community intervenes in an internal conflict to deliver purely humanitarian aid (food, water, sanitation, shelter, and medical care), it should do so in ways that minimize the benefits to rebels. Typically, rebels benefit from such deliveries by intercepting aid convoys or transforming refugee and Internally Displaced Persons (IDP) camps into training and recruitment centers. To prevent this, the interveners should militarily escort the aid convoys and provide well-trained troops or police to secure the perimeter of camps in order to prevent the entry of weapons.

Third, the international community should expend substantial resources to persuade states to address the legitimate grievances of non-violent domestic groups. In combination with the first point, this would undo the perverse incentive that arises from the emerging norm's current implementation, which effectively ignores non-violent groups because they do not provoke state retaliation, but rewards militants by intervening in ways that help them, thereby promoting violence. Rather than punishing states when they defend themselves against armed challenges, the international community should incentivize states to address non-violent demands in hopes of averting such rebellions.

Fourth, the international community should not apply coercive leverage to compel a state to hand over territory or authority to a domestic opposition, unless it first deploys a robust peacekeeping force to defend against the potential violent backlash. Failure to do so can have disastrous consequences, as exemplified in Bosnia, Rwanda, Kosovo, and East Timor.[29] In each case, international coercion backfired when the state resisted and retaliated against domestic civilians, who were perceived as allies of the enemy.

Finally, interveners should avoid falsely claiming humanitarian motives for interventions that are driven primarily by other objectives, such as securing resources, fighting terrorism, or preventing nuclear proliferation. The reason is that every ostensible "humanitarian" intervention increases the expectations of sub-state groups elsewhere that they too will benefit from intervention if they rebel and provoke a humanitarian emergency. Thus, a false justification for intervention in one case can inadvertently promote civil war in others. When states intervene for self-interest, they obviously have incentive to claim falsely, or exaggerate, their altruistic motivation. But before doing so, they should weigh seriously the potential unintended consequences.

> **. . . every ostensible "humanitarian" intervention increases the expectations of sub-state groups elsewhere that they too will benefit from the intervention if they rebel and provoke a humanitarian emergency.**

Although these five proposed reforms could foster the goals of the Responsibility to Protect, their implementation could be hindered by several factors. First, there is no international institution strong enough to dictate when states may intervene. Second, despite the logic of the reforms, some states may still prefer to aid provocative rebels or ignore non-violent movements for reasons of national interest. Third, norms can be difficult to change quickly because they both reflect and perpetuate past habits and bureaucratic procedures.

On the other hand, the Responsibility to Protect might prove relatively easy to modify because it is so recent (it is, after all, still an "emerging" norm) and because only a handful of states have the potential for major intervention. The United States, in light of its preeminent military power and economic leverage, can and should take the lead. By modifying its implementation of the Responsibility to Protect, the new administration of President Barack Obama could set an example that would help maximize protection for innocent civilians around the globe.

Notes

1. Martha Finnemore, *The Purpose Of Intervention: Changing Beliefs About The Use Of Force* (Cornell University Press, 2004). Gary J. Bass, *Freedom's Battle: The Origins of Humanitarian Intervention* (New York: Knopf, 2008). Humanitarian intervention has occurred historically, though rarely, prior to the emergence of the modern norm.

2. President Bill Clinton, interview by Wolf Blitzer, *Late Edition*, CNN. Transcript located at www.cnn.com/ALLPOLITICS/ stories/1999/06/20/clinton.transcript/ Accessed 9 July 2004.

3. International Commission on Intervention and State Sovereignty, *The Responsibility to Protect* (2001), www.iciss .gc.ca/Report-English.asp. Accessed 22 April 2002.

4. United Nations, High Level Panel on Threats, Challenges and Change, *A More Secure World: Our Shared Responsibility* (2004), www.un.org/secureworld/. Accessed 3 December 2004.

5. United Nations, *World Summit Outcome,* A/RES/60/1 (2005).

6. Alan J. Kuperman, "Humanitarian Intervention," in *Human Rights: Politics and Practice,* Michael Goodhart, ed. (Oxford University Press, 2009).

7. John L. Hirsch and Robert B. Oakley, *Somalia and Operation Restore Hope: Reflections on Peacemaking and Peacekeeping* (USIP Press, 1995).

8. L. R. Melvern, *A People Betrayed: The Role of the West in Rwanda's Genocide* (New York: Zed Books, 2000). Alan J. Kuperman, *The Limits of Humanitarian Intervention: Genocide in Rwanda* (Washington, DC: Brookings Institution Press, 2001).

9. Leslie Hough, "A Study of Peacekeeping, Peace-Enforcement and Private Military Companies in Sierra Leone," *African Security Review* 16, no 4 (2007): 8–21.

10. Alan J. Kuperman, "A Small Intervention: Lessons from Liberia 2003," in *Stability from the Sea: Challenges for the US Navy,* Jim Wirtz and Jeff Larsen, eds. (Abingdon: Routledge, 2009), pp. 153–169.

11. United Nations Office for the Corrdination of Humanitarian Affairs, "Authorities forcibly close IDP camps in southern Darfur," *Integrated Regional Information Networks,* January 16, 2004. In January 2004, the UN estimated that humanitarian aid could reach only 15 percent of 900,000 war-affected persons in Darfur.

12. Alex De Waal, ed., *War in Darfur and the Search for Peace* (Harvard University Press, 2007). Julie Flint and Alex De Waal, *Darfur: A Short History of a Long War* (Zed Books, 2006). Gérard Prunier, *Darfur: The Ambiguous Genocide* (Cornell University Press, 2005). Emily Wax, "Peace Force In Darfur Faces Major Challenges: African Troops Stymied By Shortages, Mission," *Washington Post,* November 21, 2005. For a breakdown of the AU personnel in early 2007, see "Strength of AMIS," www.amis-sudan.org/AMIS%20Strength.html. Accessed 2 November 2008.

13. United Nations-African Union Mission in Darfur, "Darfur—UNAMID - Facts and Figures," www.un.org/depts/dpko/missions/unamid/facts.html. Accessed 23 December 2008. "Darfur peacekeepers offer no protection," *Integrated Regional Information Networks,* UN Office for the Coordination of Humanitarian Affairs, October 20, 2008.

14. Kuperman, *The Limits of Humanitarian Intervention.*

15. Kuperman, *The Limits of Humanitarian Intervention.*

16. Timothy W. Crawford and Alan J. Kuperman, eds., *Gambling on Humanitarian Intervention: Moral Hazard, Rebellion and Civil War* (New York: Routledge, 2006).

17. Alan J. Kuperman, "The Moral Hazard of Humanitarian Intervention: Lessons from the Balkans," *International Studies Quarterly* 52,1 (March 2008), pp. 49-80.

18. Kuperman, "The Moral Hazard of Humanitarian Intervention: Lessons from the Balkans."

19. Kuperman, "The Moral Hazard of Humanitarian Intervention: Lessons from the Balkans."

20. Alex de Waal, "Darfur's Deadline: The Final Days of the Abuja Peace Process," in Alex de Waal, ed., *War in Darfur and the Search for Peace* (Harvard University Press, 2007), p. 276. The quote is from Abdel Wahid Mohamed al-Nur, founder of Darfur's rebel Sudan Liberation Army and leader of its faction that rejected the peace agreement.

21. Alan J. Kuperman, "Strategic Victimhood in Sudan," *New York Times,* op-ed, May 31, 2006, p. 19. Alan J. Kuperman, "Next Steps in Sudan," *Washington Post,* op-ed, September 28, 2004. Roberto Belloni, "The Tragedy of Darfur and the Limits of the 'Responsibility to Protect,'" *Ethnopolitics* 5, no 4 (2006): pp 327–346.

22. R. Jeffrey Smith, "Study Faults Army Vehicle," *Washington Post,* March 31, 2005.

23. Peter Fabricius, "SADC shuns spectre of US Africom plans," *Sunday Independent* (South Africa), July 15, 2007. Gideon Nkala, "We are damned if we do, damned if we don't," *The Reporter* (Botswana), June 27, 2008.

24. Ian Rudge, "Operation Focus Relief: A Program Evaluation," LBJ School of Public Affairs, University of Texas at Austin, unpublished manuscript, December 14, 2005.

25. Benedikt Franke, "Enabling a Continent to Help Itself: U.S. Military Capacity Building and Africa's Emerging Security Architecture," *Strategic Insights* 6, no 1 (2007).

26. United Nations, "Report of the Panel on United Nations Peace Operations," 21 August 2000, www.un.org/peace/reports/peace_operations/. Accessed 24 October 2008.

27. Michael E. O'Hanlon, *Expanding Global Military Capacity for Humanitarian Intervention* (Brookings Institution Press, 2003).

28. Alan J. Kuperman, "Mitigating the Moral Hazard of Humanitarian Intervention: Lessons from Economics," *Global Governance* 14, no 2 (April-June 2008), pp. 219–240.

29. Alan J. Kuperman, "Ripeness Revisited: The Perils of Muscular Mediation," in *Terrence Lyons and Gilbert Khadiagala,* eds., *Conflict Management and Africa: Negotiation, Mediation, and Politics* (Abingdon: Routledge, 2008), pp. 9–21. Alan J. Kuperman, "Once Again, Peacekeepers Arrive Too Late," *Wall Street Journal,* op-ed, September 21, 1999.

Critical Thinking

1. In your own words, explain what the "Responsibility to Protect" (R2P) norm is and provide three reasons why it came into existence in recent years.

2. Identify one ongoing international conflict where large number of civilians are at risk and explain why you think the R2P norm might be applied in the future to protect civilians. Be specific.

ALAN J. KUPERMAN is an Associate Professor at the Lyndon Baines Johnson School of Public Affairs at the University of Texas at Austin and a Senior Fellow at the Robert S. Strauss Center for International Security and Law.

From *Whitehead Journal of Diplomacy and International Relations,* vol. X, no. 1, Winter/Spring 2009, pp. 33–43. Copyright © 2009 by Whitehead Journal of Diplomacy and International Relations. Reprinted by permission via Copyright Clearance Center.

UNIT 10

The International Economic System

Unit Selections

Learning Objectives

- What are some of the ways the Chinese are seeking to rebalance their economy after the worldwide slowdown and declines in the values of their foreign exchange reserves?

- What are some future perils for the United States in maintaining the current trade relationship with China?

- How likely do you think it will be that the BRIC countries function in the future as a bloc?

Student Website

www.mhhe.com/cls

Internet References

The Earth Institute at Columbia University
www.earth.columbia.edu

Graphs Comparing Countries
www.humandevelopment.bu.edu/use_exsisting_index/start_comp_graph.cfm

Centre for Chinese Studies
www.ccs.org.za

Goldman Sachs/BRICs
www2.goldmansachs.com/ideas/brics/index.html

International Monetary Fund
www.imf.org

Transparency International
www.transparency.org

World Bank
www.worldbank.org

World Mapper Project
www.sasi.group.shef.ac.uk/worldmapper

World Trade Organization
www.wto.org

There were signs of economic problems in several of the West's strongest economies in recent decades. However, until 2008 a downturn in Asia or Europe was short lived and out of sync with periods of economic slowdowns in the United States. These cycles helped to prevent a widespread global downturn. This compensatory mechanism failed during 2008 as the United States, Europe, and much of Asia, including key sectors in China and key emerging markets, started to experience the worse economic downturn since the Great Depression of the 1930s at the same time. As parallels in international economic conditions today and during the Great Depression of the 1930s increase, many analysts started to warn that governments in the developed world were making many of the same policy mistakes, including implementing rapid and deep spending cuts, increasing taxes, and imposing trade protectionist policies and tariffs before a widespread economic recovery had occurred. Throughout much of 2010, debates continued about whether the developed countries were slowly coming out of recession or were transitioning instead through a new "L" or even a "double-dip" type of world recession.

Many citizens in the developing world also saw a deterioration in their standards of living that was even more serious than in the developed world because many of the poorest of the least developed countries that lacked strategic natural resources had failed to grow during the boom years of the 1980s and 1990s. Thus, while many citizens living in the developing world had seen their economic standard of living decline in the decades prior to the 2008, a small number of elites had grown richer during the same time period. Increased economic inequality and the loss of jobs among many newly middle-class workers in developing countries was one of the most important trends experienced by developing and middle-income countries as the international slowdown took hold. Some countries, which rely primarily on natural resource exports, have recovered and are registering positive growth rates largely due to the rapid recovery experienced in the aftermath of the recent international downturn. Thus, while a few have managed to prosper since 2008, the majority in both the developed and developing world suffered real and painful economic losses in recent years.

The global slowdown appeared first as a series of interrelated economic crises in the financial, mortgage, and credit markets in the United States. Each of these crises soon was evident to some degree in many countries in Europe, Asia, and worldwide. The $700 billion United States rescue package, which quickly grew to US$820 billion, passed during the closing days of the Bush Administration, and a series of additional stimulus measures passed by Barak Obama and the Democratic Party-controlled Congress after the 2008 election, may have averted catastrophic economic meltdown but failed to prevent a worsening economic slowdown in the United States or worldwide. The rate of decline slowed markedly in the United States toward the end of 2009, but it is still unclear whether a series of interrelated economic global crises and continued sluggish growth and high rates of unemployment in the United States will hamper what seemed at first to be an anemic and slow recovery.

The most dramatic economic crisis stories during 2010 came from Europe, where even the most affluent countries started cutting back public expenditures, including long-entrenched social welfare programs despite widespread public opposition. As a whole, the European Community (EC) also experienced another round of financial shocks after it became known that key EC governments in southern Europe, e.g., Greece and Portugal, and among newer Economic Community members in Central Europe, such as Poland and Estonia, were on the verge of bankruptcy. These dire balance sheets forced the EC to devise a bailout plan that cost nearly a trillion United States dollars. Just as these budgetary crises in several countries were addressed, a new financial crisis developed in the private sector as it became public that some of the largest banks and financial organizations in the EC were on the

© S. Pearce/PhotoLink/Getty Images

verge of collapse due to huge losses and unsecured non-performing loans. This latest round of economic crises that started with a debt crisis in Greece continued to ripple out from Europe to Asia and the United States throughout 2010. More than 10 countries among the wealthiest 20 have had to postpone public bond offerings during the past few years, and nearly every country in the world is now looking for ways to cut public expenditures.

Since 2008 presidents and prime ministers from major countries around the world have met in attempts to avoid a deepening worldwide recession and to restore confidence in the world markets. However, it proved difficult to agree on specific proposals. Key European allies of the United States pushed for broad new roles for international organizations, empowering them to monitor everything from the global derivatives trade to the way major banks are regulated across borders. But United States officials have been reluctant to go that far, fearing that such proposals could potentially co-opt the independence of the United States financial system or compromise free markets. While signaling a willingness to listen to new proposals, the Obama Administration has yet to agree to any of the new proposals designed to sharpen existing international regulatory tools or to create new international organizations. Instead, the focus in the United States has been on passing new legislation that attempts to regulate the domestic market in an effort to avoid another series of economic crises.

In contrast to the American view, representatives of China tend to support the call made by European leaders for new international coordination. However, China, like the United States, is reluctant to cede national control or support the formation of new international organizations. As one senior Chinese official involved in the discussions noted, "It is important to have an agency which can coordinate the global market and policies of different countries . . . but China doesn't like the idea of having a global SEC since no organization should affect the sovereignty of countries."

The multiple international economic crises also served to underscore just how interdependent the economies of the world have become, especially those of the major powers such as the United States and

China. China had already become a major investor in the United States before the economic slowdown and had piled up so much excess saving in the United States that it willingly participated in the widespread trend of lending money at low rates, underwriting American consumption and fueling the financial and mortgage bubbles in the United States. The Chinese also invested heavily throughout the world, especially in other developed countries, and have recently become the major investor and importer in many of the mineral-rich countries in the developing world. Thus, the Chinese suffered along with the West as their economies started to melt down. The first place in China to suffer was the export sector specializing in consumer goods. More than half of all toy factories in China were forced to close immediately and millions of workers in manufacturing sectors lost their jobs. However, after the initial downturn, China was able to recover lost revenue from imports by effectively moving to meet growing demands at home for all types of consumer and commercial goods and services. The share size of its domestic market is turning out to be a key factor in helping China to recover from the recent economic downturn.

China's economic foreign policies have started to change in some subtle but important ways since the economic slowdown. In term of foreign investments, the country no longer invests nearly all of its more than $2 trillion in safe foreign currency bonds and other holdings such as United States Treasury bonds. Instead, as part of a broader diversification strategy, China's sovereign wealth fund quietly invested more than $9 billion worth of shares over the past year in some of the biggest United States corporations, including Morgan Stanley, Bank of America, Citigroup, Apple, Coca-Cola, Motorola, and Visa. The continuing increased foreign exchange reserves being amassed by China and the slow implementation of prior promises to allow the national currency to more freely float, and no doubt re-appreciate, is increasingly triggering a growing backlash in a number of western countries, including the United States. Toward the end of 2010 a bill was introduced into the United States Congress that called for tariffs and, ultimately for trade sanctions against China if the country continues to delay implementation of currency reforms that would undoubtedly reduce at least some of China's current comparative advantage in world trade.

Another important strategic shift in China's foreign investment strategy that was evident by 2010 was a greater willingness to enter into major new political and defense cooperative agreements with some of the country's most important suppliers of vital national resources. Thus, in 2010 China conclude military and political agreements with increasingly important suppliers of oil, such as Angola and Equatorial Guinea, and with important trade partners such as Nigeria, South Africa, and Brazil.

These shifts in China's foreign economic policies are dramatic when viewed against the backdrop of post–World War II when the United States was the sole world economic and political nation-state that had the resources and political clout necessary to shape the postwar economic era. This is not the case today, even though most central bankers and elected leaders around the world still look to the United States to help resolve international economic and political crises. However, in a world system that is transitioning to multipolar, where the constellation of key actors varies with the issue areas, no single country has a comprehensive strategy to protect one or all countries from the global economic slowdown. Instead, the depth and breath of the economic problems that started in 2008 has underscored the reality that effective financial regulation and reforms will require the coordination and cooperation of a broader and more unwieldy group, including emerging economies, many of them loaded with foreign exchange reserves, foreign debts, and influence over global financial markets. World leaders and publics are just now beginning to learn that economic interdependence has a dark and uncertain downside.

With foreign reserves totaling $2,270 billion even after recent loses are subtracted, there is a vigorous debate occurring inside China about when and how to convert foreign currency reserves from United States dollars and for more demand that the dollar be replaced as the global reserve currency. A more feasible idea that is gaining popularity in China that can be implemented relatively quickly is for China to start investing more of the reserves into the BRIC nations, i.e., Brazil, Russia, India, China, as well as other developing countries. This strategy involves more than the current rate of Chinese investments in foreign oil and other natural resources. The goal would be to help stimulate new development and trade between China and the developing world that would approximate a "Marshall plan" in the amounts of money lent to developing countries in Africa, Asia, and Latin America. If successful, such an approach would create new international demand for Chinese goods and a fundamental shift in the interests of many nation-states worldwide as most projects assume future economic growth and prosperity will require countries in the developing world to become important future "engines of economic growth."

New discussions and concerns involving the "BRIC" countries reflect a gradual and still subtle shift from countries located in the North to those in the South. Many predictions now forecast that the emerging and developing economies, including China, will match those in the North by 2020. In "Can the BRICs Become a Bloc?," Timothy M. Shaw discusses how these emerging economies offer an attractive host environment for many multinational corporations while also supporting such new and important sources of capital as Sovereign Wealth Funds. While the importance of the BRICs (Brazil, Russia, India, and China) has increased in recent years, questions remain as to how cohesive is this new "global middle?" These countries have distinctive histories, geographies, economies, and political structures. The BRICs complicated, multiple, and varying interests often cause tensions within the group. Nevertheless, the BRIC contribute to new multilateralism as an embryonic bloc, "especially given the decline of United States unilateralism." Whether this amounts to a "Beijing Consensus" remains contentious.

Future scenarios such as the one projecting the BRICs evolving into a de facto alliance assumes that key countries in the developing world will not only learn the correct lessons from the current economic downturn but will also be able to overcome decades-old problems tied to poor governance, endemic corruption, growing economic inequality, shoddy and too often fraudulent business and scientific practices, and high rates of poverty. Many of the less-developed countries will also have difficultly recovering from and growing in light of world slowdown unless their political regimes achieve and sustain macroeconomic stability and promoting. Whether such trends are possible throughout the developing world remains an unanswered but important question.

In the short-run, the most serious type of threat to international economic recovery may a new round of protectionist measures being imposed through national protectionist trade and investment measures in response to domestic pressures to do more to protect the welfare of nation-states' citizens. A wave of protectionist measures worldwide could quickly erode progress made throughout the post–World War II era to liberalize the movement of goods, people, and money across borders. While the impulse behind such measures is understandable in light of the continuing hard economic times, if such provisions spread worldwide, they could trigger another world dip that could led to an even more serious worldwide recession.

China to the Rescue
Growing out of the Financial Crisis

China has the wherewithal to lead the global economy out of its doldrums.

JOERGEN OERSTROEM MOELLER

While there is an emerging consensus on what ails the world economy there is no agreement on the treatment. Instead of a global economic policy a variety of national ones are being cooked up to satisfy national tastes that often contradict each other. The time has come—it is actually overdue—to recognize that stimulating global demand, bringing it into line with global supply, is the only cure.

> **The time has come—it is actually overdue—to recognize that stimulating global demand, bringing it into line with global supply, is the only cure.**

The diagnosis reveals that global demand is too low, resulting in excess production capacity, exercising downward pressure on investment, wages, and property prices. The prescription calls for a rebalancing of demand and supply. Excess supply over investment in the 'fat' years, combined with an inventory build up, aggravate the policy dilemma. Experience tells us that cutting excess supply is an agonizing process that easily undermines confidence in a recovery, harming long-term growth prospects.

Individual countries may try to remedy excess production capacity by exporting more goods, but this shifts the calamity from one country to another doing no good for the global economy. If policy makers are allowed to walk down this path, protectionism will throw a spanner in the works of recovery as countries race to retaliate against each other.

But first we have to do away with the illusion that global growth will return to five percent. Growth will likely land one, maybe two, percentage points lower and stay there for a while, as the world waits to see how a rebalanced and restructured global economy will fare.

Taken together the United States, Europe, and Japan account for more than half and may be even two-thirds of the global economy depending upon the calculating method. Europe is trying hard to reform its economy, but results are still disappointing. Japan is facing a low-trend growth, if growth at all, due to demographics and the inability to restructure.

And we are unlikely to see private consumption drive U.S. economic growth as it has done for many years. The paradigm has changed. The halving of the oil price from summer 2008 to summer 2009 should have led to higher private consumption, but it didn't. A number of factors—the stock market, bankruptcies, and bailing out of GM to mention a few—depressed the willingness to spend and it is not clear to which extent better data will renew consumer confidence.

> **We are unlikely to see private consumption drive U.S. economic growth as it has done for many years.**

Personal saving as a percentage of disposable income has rocketed from zero in April 2008 to nearly seven percent in May 2009; the highest figure in more than six years. Demographics too are turning against the United States. Economics tells us that private consumption for an individual peaks around 45–50 years of age and the baby boomers have passed that mark. There is no basis, then, to expect private consumption in the United States to rise or even correspond to the level around and prior to 2007. And without private consumption a recovery is unthinkable.

This leads to the conclusion that increasing demand can only be found outside the traditional heavyweights. The newcomers are China, India, and Southeast Asia plus a number of other countries around the globe. But as only China—and partly India—is playing in the big league, examining that country should prove instructive.

And it looks pretty good.

But the first step is to repudiate the thesis that China's domestic demand is still weak, signaled by the persistent balance of payments surplus. If domestic demand were rising as share of GDP, imports would pull the balance of payments towards a smaller surplus, runs the argument. But it is falling. The World Bank predicts China's surplus will fall to 8.3 percent of GDP in 2010 and 7.2 percent in 2011 from the 11 percent in 2007. The argument also overlooks the dramatic fall in commodity, food and energy prices: if the economy were unchanged, imports would have gone down, boosting the surplus further (they account for 28.8 percent of total import). Persistent domestic demand, holding up much better than exports and by doing so limiting the fall in imports, seems to be the best explanation for a falling, not rising surplus. Of course, the reported stockpiling of commodities by China's large state-owned corporations could have played a role too.

Secondly, the composition of China's imports suggests domestic consumption is changing. Parsing the data, when one separates imports used to produce exports primarily for the United States from imports destined for domestic demand an interesting dynamic emerges. Imports for production of exports fell much sharper than imports for domestic demand. The fact that this trend has persisted over almost two years—since mid-2007—implies China's economy is being restructured.

Thirdly, recent figures suggest that real household spending is nine percent higher than a year ago, resulting in a hike in private consumption's share of total demand. Retail sales are rising even more—15 percent year on year—though this includes government purchases. On this basis it is plausible to assume that household spending together with government programs should prevent a fall in China's GDP growth below the six-to-eight percent bracket.

Household spending together with government programs should prevent a fall in China's GDP growth below the six-to-eight percent bracket.

The room to maneuver for stimulatory measures is still available for China. But this is not the case for the United States and Japan, where public budget deficits have reached the breaking point with further measures likely to undermine whatever confidence in the economies are left. The United States is running a deficit estimated at 13.2 percent of GDP and Japan looks forward to as much as 11 percent according to the pessimists.

In the end, the world cannot expect the United States to lead the way out of recession and rebalance the global economy. On July 10, Larry Summers, Director of the U.S. President's National Economic Council said to *Financial Times,* "I don't think the worst is over" and added "The global imbalances have to add up to zero and so, if the United States is going to be less the consumer importer of last resort, then other countries are going to need to be in different positions as well." To rebalance the world economy we need to look to growth from countries like China instead of the United States.

The world cannot expect the United States to lead the way out of recession and rebalance the global economy.

Moreover, as the rising savings rate in the United States is likely to slow down the recovery, it will be easier to reduce balance of payments imbalances that have harassed the world for so long. Indeed U.S. exports rose and imports fell in May resulting in the lowest trade deficit for nearly nine years. If this trend persists, and basic economic figures suggest it will, U.S. borrowing will fall, inducing global capital to flow into productive investment rather than U.S. treasury bonds. (Of course, mounting healthcare cost, additional stimulus and greater welfare benefits could alter the situation.)

A reallocation of capital to healthier economies would make the goods and services market work in tandem with the capital market. This would not only benefit the global economy, harmed by the financial crisis, but also help weak economies overcome their imbalances. Most important of all: it would achieve a rebalancing without cutting global demand thus avoiding a global slump. But the United States must pay a price. China would begin to lead the global economy replacing the United States—a bitter pill, indeed.

Joergen Oerstroem Moeller is Visiting Senior Research Fellow, Institute of Southeast Asian Studies, Singapore and Adjunct Professor at Singapore Management University and the Copenhagen Business School.

Critical Thinking

1. Explain why many believe that U.S. economic growth cannot depend on private consumption any longer.
2. Do you think it is a good or bad thing that the U.S. no longer is seen as having the clout to pull the world out of recessions?

From *YaleGlobal Online*, July 28, 2009. Copyright © 2009 by Yale Center for the Study of Globalization. Reprinted by permission of Yale Center for the Study of Globalization. www.yaleglobal.yale.edu

Can the BRICs Become a Bloc?

... equity market performance is just one manifestation of the staggering rise in BRICs' importance to the global economy ... Our 'BRICs dream' that these countries together could overtake the combined GDP of the G7 by 2035—first articulated in our 2003 *Global Economics Paper* "Dreaming with BRICs: the path to 2050"—remains a worthy 'dream' (Goldman Sachs 2007: 5).

Timothy M. Shaw

A mid-2010 OECD (2010) study confirms that the balance in the world economy is shifting from North to South with, by 2020, the emerging and developing economies matching those of the OECD. Within another two decades—by 2030—the OECD expects the South to account for 60% of world GDP. In response, the OECD is encouraging a handful of countries to join the 30-member group. At the core of these emerging economies is a burgeoning proportion of multinational corporations (MNCs) from the Global South, including 'new' icons like Cemex, Embraer, Infosys, Lenovo, Tata, Vale (BCG 2009, Goldstein 2007, van Agtamel 2007). In addition, most Sovereign Wealth Funds (SWFs) are located in the South, especially in the Middle East and Asia (e.g. Brunei, Malaysia, Singapore and Taiwan). But it is the corporations and markets of the so-termed BRICs (Brazil, Russia, India and China) that are leading the global economic reversal (Xu & Bahgat 2010).

Together the BRICs are central features of the profound, current shifts in 'global governance.' Their emerging respectability, if not centrality, was recognised mid-decade through the Heiligendamm Process, which formalised the presence and participation of the 'Outreach Five' (O5)—which includes the BRICs, Mexico and South Africa —at the annual G8 summits. This, arguably facilitated the turn-of-the-decade emergence of the G20 (Shaw, Cooper and Antkiewicz 2007). With the latter advancing from only a meeting of finance ministers and central bankers to include government leaders, the incumbent 8 + 5 formula of the G8 summits has since become somewhat redundant.

The BRICs may lie at the core of a new 'global middle,' but how cohesive are they as emerging economies/ markets/powers and societies? Further, whose interests do they represent in the evolving multilateral forums and alliances of the day?

Aside from distinctive histories, geographies and ecologies, the BRICs divide along several salient dimensions: two are federal democracies with established capitalist economic structures and ubiquitous civil societies; the other pair are at best semi-capitalist democracies. The new multilateralism increasingly involves a trend from inter-governmental to non-governmental relations and coalitions, and from club to network diplomacy (Heine 2006) involving new actors and technologies. Brazil and India, with relatively developed private companies and civil society organisations (such as think tanks) can practise and exploit 'public diplomacy'; the more statist regimes of China and Russia cannot. Conversely, Brazil and Russia are major exporters of raw materials whereas China and India are major importers. And three out of four are nuclear powers, with just Brazil being the exception in the nuclear-free southern part of the western hemisphere. Such differences have become more pronounced around the current global economic crisis.

Finally, there are profound and exponential societal imbalances in some of the BRICs, especially China (124 male births to 100 female) and India (108 to 100), with long-term implications for human and regional developments and security (*The Economist,* 2010).

The BRICs and the Evolving International System

The BRICs are large, complicated, federal political economies so their interests may be multiple. Thus, no one direction may be apparent: some communities, including diasporas, corporations, regions or cities head in one direction, others in another.

Such tensions are apparent in the BRIC Summits which are coming to cover a broad canvas, reflective of a diversity of interests and institutions. Conversely, aside from subgroupings, the BRICs have deepened their collaboration by developing a range of inter-governmental networks, spanning finance ministers and central bank governors, cooperatives, development banks, judicial and statistical officials, along with business forums and think tanks.

In addition, the BRICs are of growing importance not just for industrial production but increasingly for agriculture too, especially Brazil. While agricultural output is set to stagnate in the North, it will expand by over 25% in the trio of BRICs other than Brazil, where it is anticipated to rise by 40% after 2020. This explains the rising centrality of agricultural production for energy rather than food (UN-FAO 2010). Such trends inform the BRICs' policy on, say, the BASIC environmental alliance (which includes Brazil, India and China and South Africa) or the G20 Cairns Group. To some extent the BASIC alliance reflects common interests around climate change and constitutes the BRICs' response to diplomatic pressure on the matter arising from the Copenhagen Summit of end-2009.

Finally, the impact of the BRICs, especially China, on those 'fragile states' which have a concentration of energy and minerals has been profound. In Africa, support for state leaders from Equatorial Guinea, Sao Tome, Angola and the Sudan has come from Chinese and other state energy and mining companies, leaving little competitive space for local civil society or even the private sector (Cheru & Obi 2010, Shaw, Cooper & Antkiewicz 2007). Thus the continent is increasingly divided into state regimes heavily supported by China and those with relatively developed and autonomous NGOs and MNCs with fewer linkages with the Asian power.

But China's readiness to overlook others' criteria or conditionalities, such as prevailing environmental, governance and human rights norms, means it can exert its own leverage. Whether this amounts to a 'Beijing Consensus' coming to succeed that of Washington remains contentious.

In all, as emerging powers the BRICs can contribute to new multilateralism, especially given the decline of United States unilateralism. Yet, although they constitute an embryonic bloc, they are unlikely to become much more cohesive or unanimous given historical and structural differences, distinctive societal values and norms, and economic and diplomatic competitiveness.

References

BCG (2009). 'The 2009 BCG 100 New Global Challengers' (Boston, January).

Cheru, Fantu & Cyril Obi (eds) (2010). *The Rise of China & India in Africa* (London: Zed for NAI).

Goldman Sachs (2007). *BRICs & Beyond* (New York, November).

Goldstein, Andrea (2007). *Multinational Companies from Emerging Economies: composition, conceptualization & direction in the global economy* (London: Palgrave Macmillan)

Heine, Jorge (2006). 'On the Manner of Practising the New Diplomacy' (Waterloo: CIGI, October. Working Paper #11)

OECD (2010). 'Perspectives on Global Development: shifting wealth' (Paris, June)

Shaw, Timothy M, Andrew F Cooper & Agata Antkiewicz (2007). 'Global and/or Regional Development at the Start of the 21st Century? China, India & (South) Africa' *Third World Quarterly* 28(7): 1255–1270

The Economist (2010). 'Gendercide' Vol 394, No 8672, March 6: 13 & 77–80

UN-FAO (2010). 'Agricultural Outlook 2010–19' (Paris, June)

van Agtmael, Antoine (2007). *The Emerging Markets Century: how a new breed of world class companies is overtaking the world* (New York: Free Press)

Xu, Yi-chong & Gawdat Bahgat (eds) (2010). *The Political Economy of Sovereign Wealth Funds* (London: Palgrave Macmillan, forthcoming).

Critical Thinking

1. Identify the BRIC member countries and make a list of their common international interests.

2. Identify two important international policy areas where BRIC countries disagree on what should be done in the future.

3. After compiling the list of common international interests of the BRIC countries, explain why you feel these interests will or will not be enough to allow these nation-states to operate as a bloc on at least a few international issues.

TIMOTHY M. SHAW is Professor Emeritus & Director of the Institute for International Relations at the University of the West Indies, St. Augustine Campus, Trinidad and Tobago.

This article first appeared in *The China Monitor,* June 2010, pp. 4–6, published by the Centre for Chinese Studies, Stellenbosch University, South Africa. Copyright © 2010 by Timothy M. Shaw. Reprinted by permission of Timothy M. Shaw and CCS at Stellenbosch University.

UNIT 11

Globalizing Issues

Unit Selections

Learning Objectives

- Identify and explain key factors that will determine how the world's population affects global stability.

- Describe some of the predicted trends and consequences in the world due to increased population by 2050.

- Explain why water in the future will as important a geo-strategic resource as oil is today.

Student Website
www.mhhe.com/cls

Internet References

Worldometers—real time world statistics
www.worldometers.info

World Overpopulation Awareness (population)
www.overpopulation.org

World Water Council
www.worldwatercouncil.org

The UN Millennium Project
www.unmillenniumproject.org

CIA Report of the National Intelligence Council's 2020 Project
www.cia.gov/nic/NIC_globaltrend2020.html

Commission on Global Governance
www.sovereignty.net/p/gov/gganalysis.htm

Global Footprint Network
http://footprints@footprintnetwork.org

Global Trends 2005 Project
www.csis.org/gt2005/sumreport.html

RealClimate
www.realclimate.org

At the beginning of the 21st century, there was a noticeable increase in efforts to predict important changes and to understand new patterns of relationships shaping international relations. For more than a decade, the UN–sponsored Millennium Project has been assessing the future state of the world by tracking changes in a set of 15 Global Challenges identified and updated by over 2,000 futurists, business planners, scholars, and policy advisers. They provide a framework to assess global and local prospects and make up an interdependent system: An improvement in one challenge makes it easier to address others; deterioration in one makes it more difficult. A recent State of the Future Millennium Report warned "that the world is facing a series of interlinked crises which threaten billions of people and could cause the collapse of civilization." The bleakest warning is on the danger of the climate chaos being caused by pollution, 15 wars, and the fact that three billion people will be without access to adequate water by 2025. Some of these predictions are eerily similar to those of another global prediction project undertaking by the Global Footprint Network. In a 2009 report, this organization, sponsored by several government aid agencies, warned that if current population and consumption trends continue, several dozen nation-states will exceed their "biocapacity within the next twenty years." The report goes on to predict that a number of countries, including Senegal, Kenya, and Tanzania, are set to reach their threshold of biocapacity in less than five years!

© Stockbyte/PunchStock

These and other predictions about the future depend on a number of core parameters such as when and how the world's population stabilizes, whether there continues to be adequate supplies of food and water for this future population, and the nature and impact of future climate change. In "The New Population Bomb: The Four Megatrends That Will Change the World," Jack A. Goldstone notes that while the world's population will probably stabilize around 2050, "twenty-first-century international security will depend more on how the global population is composed and distributed....and how demographics will influence population movements across regions." Goldstone's analysis is useful for identify four key probable trends including: (1) a "reversal of fortunes" for people in the West as their economies become less dynamic; (2) the aging population of Western countries, Japan, South Korea, and even China; (3) increasingly youthful populations in Africa, Latin America, and the Middle East; and (4) urban sprawl. These trends and resulting consequences will pose serious challenges and require creative foreign and domestic policies. Goldstone also believes that "the strategic and economic policies of the twentieth century are obsolete, and it is time to find new ones." This need is made more pressing by the continuing global slowdown.

During the fall of 2009, before the Copenhagen summit on climate control, there were already signs that the conference would fail to achieve its target goals in terms of reducing greenhouse-causing emissions. While most developed countries now support the targets agreed to at earlier UN conferences in terms of reducing global warming gases, few nation-states in the developed world are willing to pay to allow developing countries to continue their efforts to become economically developed nation-states, there is no support among the richest countries, who are also the largest emitters of greenhouse gases, for a carbon tax or government and only weak support for a market-based cap-and-trade system. In the absence of such agreements pollution and global warming will continue.

In the meantime the majority of the world's population will continue to be poor and live in regions of the world that will be hit hard by the effects of climate change and rising sea levels. Yet most of the governments in the developing world lack the human and resource capacities needed to manage future catastrophes. These conditions are one set of reasons why many futurists are now predicting that state collapse, civil war, and mass migration will be inevitable in a warming world. While military superiority may aid Americans in struggles over vital resources, it will not be able to protect Americans against the ravages of global climate change. The recent rise of piracy off the East Coast of Africa may be a preview of one type of violent behavior that is likely to increase in the future. Increasingly complex emergencies after major hurricanes and other more virulent weather disturbances is another type of international phenomenon that is likely to command more attention and resources in the future.

To date, much less agreement has been reached on the extent that global warming and dwindling natural resources are likely to combine to increase violent conflicts over land, water, and energy. However, the evidence is becoming much clearer that certain root causes of violent political conflicts such as environmental degradation and resource scarcities create the preconditions that facilitate future violence among groups. Many analysts now are warning that global climate change and dwindling natural resources are combining to increase the likelihood of violent conflict over land, water, and energy. The inadequate capacity of poor and unstable countries to cope with the effects of climate change is likely to result in state collapse, civil war, and mass migration.

The New Population Bomb
The Four Megatrends That Will Change the World

Jack A. Goldstone

Forty-two years ago, the biologist Paul Ehrlich warned in *The Population Bomb* that mass starvation would strike in the 1970s and 1980s, with the world's population growth outpacing the production of food and other critical resources. Thanks to innovations and efforts such as the "green revolution" in farming and the widespread adoption of family planning, Ehrlich's worst fears did not come to pass. In fact, since the 1970s, global economic output has increased and fertility has fallen dramatically, especially in developing countries.

The United Nations Population Division now projects that global population growth will nearly halt by 2050. By that date, the world's population will have stabilized at 9.15 billion people, according to the "medium growth" variant of the UN's authoritative population database World Population Prospects: The 2008 Revision. (Today's global population is 6.83 billion.) Barring a cataclysmic climate crisis or a complete failure to recover from the current economic malaise, global economic output is expected to increase by two to three percent per year, meaning that global income will increase far more than population over the next four decades.

But twenty-first-century international security will depend less on how many people inhabit the world than on how the global population is composed and distributed: where populations are declining and where they are growing, which countries are relatively older and which are more youthful, and how demographics will influence population movements across regions.

These elements are not well recognized or widely understood. A recent article in *The Economist*, for example, cheered the decline in global fertility without noting other vital demographic developments. Indeed, the same UN data cited by *The Economist* reveal four historic shifts that will fundamentally alter the world's population over the next four decades: the relative demographic weight of the world's developed countries will drop by nearly 25 percent, shifting economic power to the developing nations; the developed countries' labor forces will substantially age and decline, constraining economic growth in the developed world and raising the demand for immigrant workers; most of the world's expected population growth will increasingly be concentrated in today's poorest, youngest, and most heavily Muslim countries, which have a dangerous lack of quality education, capital, and employment opportunities; and, for the first time in history, most of the world's population will become urbanized, with the largest urban centers being in the world's poorest countries, where policing, sanitation, and health care are often scarce.

Taken together, these trends will pose challenges every bit as alarming as those noted by Ehrlich. Coping with them will require nothing less than a major reconsideration of the world's basic global governance structures.

Europe's Reversal of Fortunes

At the beginning of the eighteenth century, approximately 20 percent of the world's inhabitants lived in Europe (including Russia). Then, with the Industrial Revolution, Europe's population boomed, and streams of European emigrants set off for the Americas. By the eve of World War I, Europe's population had more than quadrupled. In 1913, Europe had more people than China, and the proportion of the world's population living in Europe and the former European colonies of North America had risen to over 33 percent.

But this trend reversed after World War I, as basic health care and sanitation began to spread to poorer countries. In Asia, Africa, and Latin America, people began to live longer, and birthrates remained high or fell only slowly. By 2003, the combined populations of Europe, the United States, and Canada accounted for just 17 percent of the global population. In 2050, this figure is expected to be just 12 percent—far less than it was in 1700. (These projections, moreover, might even understate the reality because they reflect the "medium growth" projection of the UN forecasts, which assumes that the fertility rates of developing countries will decline while those of developed countries will increase. In fact, many developed countries show no evidence of increasing fertility rates.)

The West's relative decline is even more dramatic if one also considers changes in income. The Industrial Revolution made Europeans not only more numerous than they had been but also considerably richer per capita than others worldwide. According to the economic historian Angus Maddison, Europe, the United States, and Canada together produced about 32 percent of the world's GDP at the beginning of the nineteenth century. By 1950, that proportion had increased to a remarkable 68 percent of the world's total output (adjusted to reflect purchasing power parity).

This trend, too, is headed for a sharp reversal. The proportion of global GDP produced by Europe, the United States, and Canada fell from 68 percent in 1950 to 47 percent in 2003 and will decline even more steeply in the future. If the growth rate of per capita income (again, adjusted for purchasing power parity) between 2003 and 2050 remains as it was between 1973 and 2003—averaging 1.68 percent annually in Europe, the United States, and Canada and 2.47 percent annually in the rest of the world—then the combined GDP of Europe, the United States, and Canada will roughly double by 2050, whereas the GDP of the rest of the world will grow by a factor of five. The portion of global GDP produced by Europe, the United States, and Canada in 2050 will then be less than 30 percent—smaller than it was in 1820.

These figures also imply that an overwhelming proportion of the world's GDP growth between 2003 and 2050—nearly 80 percent—will occur outside of Europe, the United States, and Canada. By the middle of this century, the global middle class—those capable of purchasing durable consumer products, such as cars, appliances, and electronics—will increasingly be found in what is now considered the developing world. The World Bank has predicted that by 2030 the number of middle-class people in the developing world will be 1.2 billion—a rise of 200 percent since 2005. This means that the developing world's middle class alone will be larger than the total populations of Europe, Japan, and the United States combined. From now on, therefore, the main driver of global economic expansion will be the economic growth of newly industrialized countries, such as Brazil, China, India, Indonesia, Mexico, and Turkey.

Aging Pains

Part of the reason developed countries will be less economically dynamic in the coming decades is that their populations will become substantially older. The European countries, Canada, the United States, Japan, South Korea, and even China are aging at unprecedented rates. Today, the proportion of people aged 60 or older in China and South Korea is 12–15 percent. It is 15–22 percent in the European Union, Canada, and the United States and 30 percent in Japan. With baby boomers aging and life expectancy increasing, these numbers will increase dramatically. In 2050, approximately 30 percent of Americans, Canadians, Chinese, and Europeans will be over 60, as will more than 40 percent of Japanese and South Koreans.

Over the next decades, therefore, these countries will have increasingly large proportions of retirees and increasingly small proportions of workers. As workers born during the baby boom of 1945–65 are retiring, they are not being replaced by a new cohort of citizens of prime working age (15–59 years old). Industrialized countries are experiencing a drop in their working-age populations that is even more severe than the overall slowdown in their population growth. South Korea represents the most extreme example. Even as its total population

is projected to decline by almost 9 percent by 2050 (from 48.3 million to 44.1 million), the population of working-age South Koreans is expected to drop by 36 percent (from 32.9 million to 21.1 million), and the number of South Koreans aged 60 and older will increase by almost 150 percent (from 7.3 million to 18 million). By 2050, in other words, the entire working-age population will barely exceed the 60-and-older population. Although South Korea's case is extreme, it represents an increasingly common fate for developed countries. Europe is expected to lose 24 percent of its prime working-age population (about 120 million workers) by 2050, and its 60-and-older population is expected to increase by 47 percent. In the United States, where higher fertility and more immigration are expected than in Europe, the working-age population will grow by 15 percent over the next four decades—a steep decline from its growth of 62 percent between 1950 and 2010. And by 2050, the United States' 60-and-older population is expected to double.

All this will have a dramatic impact on economic growth, health care, and military strength in the developed world. The forces that fueled economic growth in industrialized countries during the second half of the twentieth century—increased productivity due to better education, the movement of women into the labor force, and innovations in technology—will all likely weaken in the coming decades. College enrollment boomed after World War II, a trend that is not likely to recur in the twenty-first century; the extensive movement of women into the labor force also was a one-time social change; and the technological change of the time resulted from innovators who created new products and leading-edge consumers who were willing to try them out—two groups that are thinning out as the industrialized world's population ages.

Overall economic growth will also be hampered by a decline in the number of new consumers and new households. When developed countries' labor forces were growing by 0.5–1.0 percent per year, as they did until 2005, even annual increases in real output per worker of just 1.7 percent meant that annual economic growth totaled 2.2–2.7 percent per year. But with the labor forces of many developed countries (such as Germany, Hungary, Japan, Russia, and the Baltic states) now shrinking by 0.2 percent per year and those of other countries (including Austria, the Czech Republic, Denmark, Greece, and Italy) growing by less than 0.2 percent per year, the same 1.7 percent increase in real output per worker yields only 1.5–1.9 percent annual overall growth. Moreover, developed countries will be lucky to keep productivity growth at even that level; in many developed countries, productivity is more likely to decline as the population ages.

A further strain on industrialized economies will be rising medical costs: as populations age, they will demand more health care for longer periods of time. Public pension schemes for aging populations are already being reformed in various industrialized countries—often prompting heated debate. In theory, at least, pensions might be kept solvent by increasing the retirement age, raising taxes modestly, and phasing out benefits for the wealthy. Regardless, the number of 80- and 90-year-olds—who are unlikely to work and highly likely to require nursing-home and other expensive care—will rise dramatically. And even if 60- and 70-year-olds remain active and employed, they will require procedures and medications—hip replacements, kidney transplants, blood-pressure treatments—to sustain their health in old age.

All this means that just as aging developed countries will have proportionally fewer workers, innovators, and consumerist young households, a large portion of those countries' remaining economic growth will have to be diverted to pay for the medical bills and pensions of their growing elderly populations. Basic services, meanwhile, will be increasingly costly because fewer young workers will be available for strenuous and labor-intensive jobs. Unfortunately, policymakers seldom reckon with these potentially disruptive effects of otherwise welcome developments, such as higher life expectancy.

Youth and Islam in the Developing World

Even as the industrialized countries of Europe, North America, and Northeast Asia will experience unprecedented aging this century, fast-growing countries in Africa, Latin America, the Middle East, and Southeast Asia will have exceptionally youthful populations. Today, roughly nine out of ten children under the age of 15 live in developing countries. And these are the countries that will continue to have the world's highest birthrates. Indeed, over 70 percent of the world's population growth between now and 2050 will occur in 24 countries, all of which are classified by the World Bank as low income or lower-middle income, with an average per capita income of under $3,855 in 2008.

Many developing countries have few ways of providing employment to their young, fast-growing populations. Would-be laborers, therefore, will be increasingly attracted to the labor markets of the aging developed countries of Europe, North America, and Northeast Asia. Youthful immigrants from nearby regions with high unemployment—Central America, North Africa, and Southeast Asia, for example—will be drawn to those vital entry-level and manual-labor jobs that sustain advanced economies: janitors, nursing-home aides, bus drivers, plumbers, security guards, farm workers, and the like. Current levels of immigration from developing to developed countries are paltry compared to those that the forces of supply and demand might soon create across the world.

These forces will act strongly on the Muslim world, where many economically weak countries will continue to experience dramatic population growth in the decades ahead. In 1950, Bangladesh, Egypt, Indonesia, Nigeria, Pakistan, and Turkey had a combined population of 242 million. By 2009, those six countries were the world's most populous Muslim-majority countries and had a combined population of 886 million. Their populations are continuing to grow and indeed are expected to increase by 475 million between now and 2050—during which time, by comparison, the six most populous developed countries are projected to gain only 44 million inhabitants. Worldwide, of the 48 fastest-growing countries today—those with annual population growth of two percent or more—28 are majority Muslim or have Muslim minorities of 33 percent or more.

It is therefore imperative to improve relations between Muslim and Western societies. This will be difficult given that many Muslims live in poor communities vulnerable to radical appeals and many see the West as antagonistic and militaristic. In the 2009 Pew Global Attitudes Project survey, for example, whereas 69 percent of those Indonesians and Nigerians surveyed reported viewing the United States favorably, just 18 percent of those polled in Egypt, Jordan, Pakistan, and Turkey (all U.S. allies) did. And in 2006, when the Pew survey last asked detailed questions about Muslim-Western relations, more than half of the respondents in Muslim countries characterized those relations as bad and blamed the West for this state of affairs.

But improving relations is all the more important because of the growing demographic weight of poor Muslim countries and the attendant increase in Muslim immigration, especially to Europe from North Africa and the Middle East. (To be sure, forecasts that Muslims will soon dominate Europe are outlandish: Muslims compose just three to ten percent of the population in the major European countries today, and this proportion will at most double by midcentury.) Strategists worldwide must consider that the world's young are becoming concentrated in those countries least prepared to educate and employ them, including some Muslim states. Any resulting poverty, social tension, or ideological radicalization could have disruptive effects in many corners of the world. But this need not be the case; the healthy immigration of workers to the developed world and the movement of capital to the developing world, among other things, could lead to better results.

Urban Sprawl

Exacerbating twenty-first-century risks will be the fact that the world is urbanizing to an unprecedented degree. The year 2010 will likely be the first time in history that a majority of the world's people live in cities rather than in the countryside. Whereas less than 30 percent of the world's population was urban in 1950, according to UN projections, more than 70 percent will be by 2050.

Lower-income countries in Asia and Africa are urbanizing especially rapidly, as agriculture becomes less labor intensive and as employment opportunities shift to the industrial and service sectors. Already, most of the world's urban agglomerations—Mumbai (population 20.1 million), Mexico City (19.5 million), New Delhi (17 million), Shanghai (15.8 million), Calcutta (15.6 million), Karachi (13.1 million), Cairo (12.5 million), Manila (11.7 million), Lagos (10.6 million), Jakarta (9.7 million)—are found in low-income countries. Many of these countries have multiple cities with over one million residents each: Pakistan has eight, Mexico 12, and China more than 100. The UN projects that the urbanized proportion of sub-Saharan Africa will nearly double between 2005 and 2050, from 35 percent (300 million people) to over 67 percent (1 billion). China, which is roughly 40 percent urbanized today, is expected to be 73 percent urbanized by 2050; India, which is less than 30 percent urbanized today, is expected to be 55 percent urbanized by 2050. Overall, the world's urban population is expected to grow by 3 billion people by 2050.

This urbanization may prove destabilizing. Developing countries that urbanize in the twenty-first century will have far lower per capita incomes than did many industrial countries when they first urbanized. The United States, for example, did not reach 65 percent urbanization until 1950, when per capita income was nearly $13,000 (in 2005 dollars). By contrast, Nigeria, Pakistan, and the Philippines, which are approaching similar levels of urbanization, currently have per capita incomes of just $1,800–$4,000 (in 2005 dollars).

According to the research of Richard Cincotta and other political demographers, countries with younger populations are especially prone to civil unrest and are less able to create or sustain democratic institutions. And the more heavily urbanized, the more such countries are likely to experience Dickensian poverty and anarchic violence. In good times, a thriving economy might keep urban residents employed and governments flush with sufficient resources to meet their needs. More often, however, sprawling and impoverished cities are vulnerable to crime lords, gangs, and petty rebellions. Thus, the rapid urbanization of the developing world in the decades ahead might bring, in exaggerated form, problems similar to those that urbanization brought to nineteenth-century Europe. Back then, cyclical employment, inadequate policing, and limited sanitation and education often spawned widespread labor strife, periodic violence, and sometimes—as in the 1820s, the 1830s, and 1848—even revolutions.

International terrorism might also originate in fast-urbanizing developing countries (even more than it already does). With their neighborhood networks, access to the Internet and digital communications technology, and concentration of valuable targets, sprawling cities offer excellent opportunities for recruiting, maintaining, and hiding terrorist networks.

Defusing the Bomb

Averting this century's potential dangers will require sweeping measures. Three major global efforts defused the population bomb of Ehrlich's day: a commitment by governments and nongovernmental organizations to control reproduction rates; agricultural advances, such as the green revolution and the spread of new technology; and a vast increase in international trade, which globalized markets and thus allowed developing countries to export foodstuffs in exchange for seeds, fertilizers, and machinery, which in turn helped them boost production. But today's population bomb is the product less of absolute growth in the world's population than of changes in its age and distribution. Policymakers must therefore adapt today's global governance institutions to the new realities of the aging of the industrialized world, the concentration of the world's economic and population growth in developing countries, and the increase in international immigration.

During the Cold War, Western strategists divided the world into a "First World," of democratic industrialized countries; a "Second World," of communist industrialized countries; and a "Third World," of developing countries. These strategists focused chiefly on deterring or managing conflict between the First and the Second Worlds and on launching proxy wars and diplomatic initiatives to attract Third World countries into the First World's camp. Since the end of the Cold War, strategists have largely abandoned this three-group division and have tended to believe either that the United States, as the sole superpower, would maintain a Pax Americana or that the world would become multipolar, with the United States, Europe, and China playing major roles.

Unfortunately, because they ignore current global demographic trends, these views will be obsolete within a few decades. A better approach would be to consider a different three-world order, with a new First World of the aging industrialized nations of North America, Europe, and Asia's Pacific Rim (including Japan, Singapore, South Korea, and Taiwan, as well as China after 2030, by which point the one-child policy will have produced significant aging); a Second World comprising fast-growing and economically dynamic countries with a healthy mix of young and old inhabitants (such as Brazil, Iran, Mexico, Thailand, Turkey, and Vietnam, as well as China until 2030); and a Third World of fast-growing, very young, and increasingly urbanized countries with poorer economies and often weak governments.

To cope with the instability that will likely arise from the new Third World's urbanization, economic strife, lawlessness, and potential terrorist activity, the aging industrialized nations of the new First World must build effective alliances with the growing powers of the new Second World and together reach out to Third World nations. Second World powers will be pivotal in the twenty-first century not just because they will drive economic growth and consume technologies and other products engineered in the First World; they will also be central to international security and cooperation. The realities of religion, culture, and geographic proximity mean that any peaceful and productive engagement by the First World of Third World countries will have to include the open cooperation of Second World countries.

Strategists, therefore, must fundamentally reconsider the structure of various current global institutions. The G-8, for example, will likely become obsolete as a body for making global economic policy. The G-20 is already becoming increasingly important, and this is less a short-term consequence of the ongoing global financial crisis than the beginning of the necessary recognition that Brazil, China, India, Indonesia, Mexico, Turkey, and others are becoming global economic powers. International institutions will not retain their legitimacy if they exclude the world's fastest-growing and most economically dynamic countries. It is essential, therefore, despite European concerns about the potential effects on immigration, to take steps such as admitting Turkey into the European Union. This would add youth and economic dynamism to the EU—and would prove that Muslims are welcome to join Europeans as equals in shaping a free and prosperous future. On the other hand, excluding Turkey from the EU could lead to hostility not only on the part of Turkish citizens, who are expected to number 100 million by 2050, but also on the part of Muslim populations worldwide.

NATO must also adapt. The alliance today is composed almost entirely of countries with aging, shrinking populations and relatively slow-growing economies. It is oriented toward the Northern Hemisphere and holds on to a Cold War structure that cannot adequately respond to contemporary threats. The young and increasingly populous countries of Africa, the Middle East, Central Asia, and South Asia could mobilize insurgents much more easily than NATO could mobilize the troops it would need if it were called on to stabilize those countries. Long-standing NATO members should, therefore—although it would require atypical creativity and flexibility—consider the logistical and demographic advantages of inviting into the alliance countries such as Brazil and Morocco, rather than countries such as Albania. That this seems far-fetched does not minimize the imperative that First World countries begin including large and strategic Second and Third World powers in formal international alliances.

The case of Afghanistan—a country whose population is growing fast and where NATO is currently engaged—illustrates the importance of building effective global institutions. Today, there are 28 million Afghans; by 2025, there will be 45 million; and by 2050, there will be close to 75 million. As nearly 20 million additional Afghans are born over the next 15 years, NATO will have an opportunity to help Afghanistan become reasonably stable, self-governing, and prosperous. If NATO's efforts fail and the Afghans judge that NATO intervention harmed their interests, tens of millions of young Afghans will become more hostile to the West. But if they come to think that NATO's involvement benefited their society, the West will have tens of millions of new friends. The example might then motivate the approximately one billion other young Muslims growing up in low-income countries over the next four decades to look more kindly on relations between their countries and the countries of the industrialized West.

Creative Reforms at Home

The aging industrialized countries can also take various steps at home to promote stability in light of the coming demographic trends. First, they should encourage families to have more children. France and Sweden have had success providing child care, generous leave time, and financial allowances to families with young children. Yet there is no consensus among policymakers—and certainly not among demographers—about what policies best encourage fertility.

More important than unproven tactics for increasing family size is immigration. Correctly managed, population movement can benefit developed and developing countries alike. Given the dangers of young, underemployed, and unstable populations in developing countries, immigration to developed countries can provide economic opportunities for the ambitious and serve as a safety valve for all. Countries that embrace immigrants, such as the United States, gain economically by having willing laborers and greater entrepreneurial spirit. And countries with high levels of emigration (but not so much that they experience so-called brain drains) also benefit because emigrants often send remittances home or return to their native countries with valuable education and work experience.

One somewhat daring approach to immigration would be to encourage a reverse flow of older immigrants from developed to developing countries. If older residents of developed countries took their retirements along the southern coast of the Mediterranean or in Latin America or Africa, it would greatly reduce the strain on their home countries' public entitlement systems. The developing countries involved, meanwhile, would benefit because caring for the elderly and providing retirement and leisure services is highly labor intensive. Relocating a portion of these activities to developing countries would provide employment and valuable training to the young, growing populations of the Second and Third Worlds.

This would require developing residential and medical facilities of First World quality in Second and Third World countries. Yet even this difficult task would be preferable to the status quo, by which low wages and poor facilities lead to a steady drain of medical and nursing talent from developing to developed countries. Many residents of developed countries who desire cheaper medical procedures already practice medical tourism today, with India, Singapore, and Thailand being the most common destinations. (For example, the international consulting firm Deloitte estimated that 750,000 Americans traveled abroad for care in 2008.)

Never since 1800 has a majority of the world's economic growth occurred outside of Europe, the United States, and Canada. Never have so many people in those regions been over 60 years old. And never have low-income countries' populations been so young and so urbanized. But such will be the world's demography in the twenty-first century. The strategic and economic policies of the twentieth century are obsolete, and it is time to find new ones.

Critical Thinking

1. What is the world's population size today and when is population increase projected to stabilize if present trends continue?
2. Explain which of the following two demographic trends are likely to be most important for future peace and stability in the international system: the aging population in most developed countries or the youth bulge in most countries in the developing world? Be sure you have specific examples or facts to support your position.

JACK A. GOLDSTONE is Virginia E. and John T. Hazel, Jr., Professor at the George Mason School of Public Policy.

From *Foreign Affairs*, vol. 89, no. 1, January/February 2010, pp. 31–43. Copyright © 2010 by Council on Foreign Relations, Inc. Reprinted by permission of Foreign Affairs. www.ForeignAffairs.com

The World's Water Challenge

If oil is the key geopolitical resource of today, water will be as important—if not more so—in the not-so-distant future.

ERIK R. PETERSON AND RACHEL A. POSNER

Historically, water has meant the difference between life and death, health and sickness, prosperity and poverty, environmental sustainability and degradation, progress and decay, stability and insecurity. Societies with the wherewithal and knowledge to control or "smooth" hydrological cycles have experienced more rapid economic progress, while populations without the capacity to manage water flows—especially in regions subject to pronounced flood-drought cycles—have found themselves confronting tremendous social and economic challenges in development.

Tragically, a substantial part of humanity continues to face acute water challenges. We now stand at a point at which an obscenely large portion of the world's population lacks regular access to fresh drinking water or adequate sanitation. Water-related diseases are a major burden in countries across the world. Water consumption patterns in many regions are no longer sustainable. The damaging environmental consequences of water practices are growing rapidly. And the complex and dynamic linkages between water and other key resources—especially food and energy—are inadequately understood. These factors suggest that even at current levels of global population, resource consumption, and economic activity, we may have already passed the threshold of water sustainability.

An obscenely large portion of the world's population lacks regular access to fresh drinking water or adequate sanitation.

A major report recently issued by the 2030 Water Resources Group (whose members include McKinsey & Company, the World Bank, and a consortium of business partners) estimated that, assuming average economic growth and no efficiency gains, the gap between global water demand and reliable supply could reach 40 percent over the next 20 years. As serious as this world supply-demand gap is, the study notes, the dislocations will be even more concentrated in developing regions that account for one-third of the global population, where the water deficit could rise to 50 percent.

It is thus inconceivable that, at this moment in history, no generally recognized "worth" has been established for water to help in its more efficient allocation. To the contrary, many current uses of water are skewed by historical and other legacy practices that perpetuate massive inefficiencies and unsustainable patterns.

The Missing Links

In addition, in the face of persistent population pressures and the higher consumption implicit in rapid economic development among large populations in the developing world, it is noteworthy that our understanding of resource linkages is so limited. Our failure to predict in the spring of 2008 a spike in food prices, a rise in energy prices, and serious droughts afflicting key regions of the world—all of which occurred simultaneously—reveals how little we know about these complex interrelationships.

Without significant, worldwide changes—including more innovation in and diffusion of water-related technologies; fundamental adjustments in consumption patterns; improvements in efficiencies; higher levels of public investment in water infrastructures; and an integrated approach to governance based on the complex relationships between water and food, water and economic development, and water and the environment—the global challenge of water resources could become even more severe.

Also, although global warming's potential effects on watersheds across the planet are still not precisely understood, there can be little doubt that climate change will in a number of regions generate serious dislocations in water supply. In a June 2008 technical paper, the Intergovernmental Panel on Climate Change (IPCC) concluded that "globally, the negative impacts of climate change on freshwater systems are expected to outweigh the benefits." It noted that "higher water temperatures and changes in extremes, including droughts and floods, are projected to affect water quality and exacerbate many forms of water pollution."

Climate change will in a number of regions generate serious dislocations in water supply.

As a result, we may soon be entering unknown territory when it comes to addressing the challenges of water in all their dimensions, including public health, economic development, gender equity, humanitarian crises, environmental degradation, and global security. The geopolitical consequences alone could be profound.

Daunting Trends

Although water covers almost three-quarters of the earth's surface, only a fraction of it is suitable for human consumption. According to the United Nations, of the water that humans consume, approximately 70 percent is used in agricultural production, 22 percent in industry, and 8 percent in domestic use. This consumption—critical as it is for human health, economic development, political and social stability, and security—is unequal, inefficient, and unsustainable.

Indeed, an estimated 884 million people worldwide do not have access to clean drinking water, and 2.5 billion lack adequate sanitation. A staggering 1.8 million people, 90 percent of them children, lose their lives each year as a result of diarrheal diseases resulting from unsafe drinking water and poor hygiene. More generally, the World Health Organization (WHO) estimates that inadequate water, sanitation, and hygiene are responsible for roughly half the malnutrition in the world.

In addition, we are witnessing irreparable damage to ecosystems across the globe. Aquifers are being drawn down faster than they can naturally be recharged. Some great lakes are mere fractions of what they once were.

And water pollution is affecting millions of people's lives. China typifies this problem. More than 75 percent of its urban river water is unsuitable for drinking or fishing, and 90 percent of its urban groundwater is contaminated. On the global scale, according to a recent UN report on world water development, every day we dump some 2 million tons of industrial waste and chemicals, human waste, and agricultural waste (fertilizers, pesticides, and pesticide residues) into our water supply.

Over the past century, as the world's population rose from 1.7 billion people in 1900 to 6.1 billion in 2000, global fresh water consumption increased six-fold—more than double the rate of population growth over the same period. The latest "medium" projections from the UN's population experts suggest that we are on the way to 8 billion people by the year 2025 and 9.15 billion by the middle of the century.

The contours of our predicament are clear-cut: A finite amount of water is available to a rapidly increasing number of people whose activities require more water than ever before. The UN Commission on Sustainable Development has indicated that we may need to double the amount of freshwater available today to meet demand at the middle of the century—after which time demand for water will increase by 50 percent with each additional generation.

Why is demand for water rising so rapidly? It goes beyond population pressures. According to a recent report from the UN Food and Agriculture Organization, the world will require 70 percent more food production over the next 40 years to meet growing per capita demand. This rising agricultural consumption necessarily translates into higher demand for water. By 2025, according to the water expert Sandra Postel, meeting projected global agricultural demand will require additional irrigation totaling some 2,000 cubic kilometers—roughly the equivalent of the annual flow of 24 Nile Rivers or 110 Colorado Rivers.

Consumption patterns aside, climate change will accelerate and intensify stress on water systems. According to the IPCC, in coming decades the frequency of extreme droughts will double while the average length of droughts will increase six times. This low water flow, combined with higher temperatures, not only will create devastating shortages. It will also increase pollution of fresh water by sediments, nutrients, pesticides, pathogens, and salts. On the other hand, in some regions, wet seasons will be more intense (but shorter).

In underdeveloped communities that lack capture and storage capacity, water will run off and will be unavailable when it is needed in dry seasons, thus perpetuating the cycle of poverty.

Climatic and demographic trends indicate that the regions of the world with the highest population growth rates are precisely those that are already the "driest" and that are expected to experience water stress in the future. The Organization for Economic Cooperation and Development has suggested that the number of people in water-stressed countries—where governments encounter serious constraints on their ability to meet household, industrial, and agricultural water demands—could rise to nearly 4 billion by the year 2030.

The Geopolitical Dimension

If oil is the key geopolitical resource of today, water will be as important—if not more so—in the not-so-distant future. A profound mismatch exists between the distribution of the human population and the availability of fresh water. At the water-rich extreme of the spectrum is the Amazon region, which has an estimated 15 percent of global runoff and less than 1 percent of the world's people. South America as a whole has only 6 percent of the world's population but more than a quarter of the world's runoff.

At the other end of the spectrum is Asia. Home to 60 percent of the global population, it has a freshwater endowment estimated at less than 36 percent of the world total. It is hardly surprising that some water-stressed countries in the region have pursued agricultural trade mechanisms to gain access to more water—in the form of food. Recently, this has taken the form of so-called "land grabs," in which governments and state companies have invested in farmland overseas to meet their countries' food security needs. *The Economist* has estimated that, to date, some 50 million acres have been remotely purchased or leased under these arrangements in Africa and Asia.

Although freshwater management has historically represented a means of preventing and mitigating conflict between countries with shared water resources, the growing scarcity of water will likely generate new levels of tension at the local, national, and even international levels. Many countries with limited water availability also depend on shared water, which increases the risk of friction, social tensions, and conflict.

The Euphrates, Jordan, and Nile Rivers are obvious examples of places where frictions already have occurred. But approximately 40 percent of the world's population lives in more than 260 international river basins of major social and economic importance, and 13 of these basins are shared by five or more countries. Interstate tensions have already escalated and could easily intensify as increasing water scarcity raises the stakes.

Within countries as well, governments in water-stressed regions must effectively and transparently mediate the concerns and demands of various constituencies. The interests of urban and rural populations, agriculture and industry, and commercial and domestic sectors often conflict. If allocation issues are handled inappropriately, subnational disputes and unrest linked to water scarcity and poor water quality could arise, as they already have in numerous cases.

Addressing the Challenge

Considering the scope and gravity of these water challenges, responses by governments and nongovernmental organizations have fallen short of what is needed. Despite obvious signs that we overuse water, we continue to perpetuate gross inefficiencies. We continue to skew consumption on the basis of politically charged subsidies or other supports. And we continue to pursue patently unsustainable practices whose costs will grow more onerous over time.

The Colorado River system, for example, is being overdrawn. It supplies water to Las Vegas, Los Angeles, San Diego, and other growing communities in the American Southwest. If demand on this river system is not curtailed, there is a 50 percent chance that Lake Mead will be dry by 2021, according to experts from the Scripps Institution of Oceanography.

Despite constant reminders of future challenges, we continue to be paralyzed by short-term thinking and practices. What is especially striking about water is the extent to which the world's nations are unprepared to manage such a vital resource sustainably. Six key opportunities for solutions stand out.

First, the global community needs to do substantially more to address the lack of safe drinking water and sanitation. Donor countries, by targeting water resources, can simultaneously address issues associated with health, poverty reduction, and environmental stewardship, as well as stability and security concerns. It should be stressed in this regard that rates of return on investment in water development—financial, political, and geopolitical—are all positive. The WHO estimates that the global return on every dollar invested in water and sanitation programs is $4 and $9, respectively.

Consider, for example, how water problems affect the earning power of women. Typically in poor countries, women and girls are kept at home to care for sick family members inflicted with water-related diseases. They also spend hours each day walking to collect water for daily drinking, cooking, and washing. According to the United Nations Children's Fund, water and sanitation issues explain why more than half the girls in sub-Saharan Africa drop out of primary school.

Second, more rigorous analyses of sustainability could help relevant governments and authorities begin to address the conspicuous mismanagement of water resources in regions across the world. This would include reviewing public subsidies—for water-intensive farming, for example—and other supports that tend to increase rather than remove existing inefficiencies.

Priced to Sell

Third, specialists, scholars, practitioners, and policy makers need to make substantial progress in assigning to water a market value against which more sustainable consumption decisions and policies can be made. According to the American Water Works Association, for example, the average price of water in the United States is $1.50 per 1,000 gallons—or less than a single penny per gallon. Yet, when it comes to the personal consumption market, many Americans do not hesitate to pay prices for bottled water that are higher than what they pay at the pump for a gallon of gasoline. What is clear, both inside and

outside the United States, is that mechanisms for pricing water on the basis of sustainability have yet to be identified.

Fourth, rapid advances in technology can and should have a discernible effect on both the supply and demand sides of the global water equation. The technology landscape is breathtaking—from desalination, membrane, and water-reuse technologies to a range of cheaper and more efficient point-of-use applications (such as drip irrigation and rainwater harvesting). It remains to be seen, however, whether the acquisition and use of such technologies can be accelerated and dispersed so that they can have an appreciable effect in offsetting aggregate downside trends.

From a public policy perspective, taxation and regulatory policies can create incentives for the development and dissemination of such technologies, and foreign assistance projects can promote their use in developing countries. Also, stronger links with the private sector would help policy makers improve their understanding of technical possibilities, and public-private partnerships can be effective mechanisms for distributing technologies in the field.

Fifth, although our understanding of the relationship between climate change and water will continue to be shaped by new evidence, it is important that we incorporate into our approach to climate change our existing understanding of water management and climate adaptation issues.

Sixth, the complex links among water, agriculture, and energy must be identified with greater precision. An enormous amount of work remains to be done if we are to appreciate these linkages in the global, basin, and local contexts.

In the final analysis, our capacity to address the constellation of challenges that relate to water access, sanitation, ecosystems, infrastructure, adoption of technologies, and the mobilization of resources will mean the difference between rapid economic development and continued poverty, between healthier populations and continued high exposure to water-related diseases, between a more stable world and intensifying geopolitical tensions.

Critical Thinking

1. Give three examples of how water issues have already been the source of international conflict in relations between two or more countries in the world.

2. Explain why you believe there will or will not be water wars in the future in one region of the world.

ERIK R. PETERSON is senior vice president of the Center for Strategic and International Studies and director of its Global Strategy Institute. **RACHEL A. POSNER** is assistant director of the CSIS Global Water Futures project.

Test-Your-Knowledge Form

We encourage you to photocopy and use this page as a tool to assess how the articles in *Annual Editions* expand on the information in your textbook. By reflecting on the articles you will gain enhanced text information. You can also access this useful form on a product's book support website at www.mhhe.com/cls

NAME: _____ DATE: _____

TITLE AND NUMBER OF ARTICLE: _____

BRIEFLY STATE THE MAIN IDEA OF THIS ARTICLE:

_____

LIST THREE IMPORTANT FACTS THAT THE AUTHOR USES TO SUPPORT THE MAIN IDEA:

_____

WHAT INFORMATION OR IDEAS DISCUSSED IN THIS ARTICLE ARE ALSO DISCUSSED IN YOUR TEXTBOOK OR OTHER READINGS THAT YOU HAVE DONE? LIST THE TEXTBOOK CHAPTERS AND PAGE NUMBERS:

_____

LIST ANY EXAMPLES OF BIAS OR FAULTY REASONING THAT YOU FOUND IN THE ARTICLE:

_____

LIST ANY NEW TERMS/CONCEPTS THAT WERE DISCUSSED IN THE ARTICLE, AND WRITE A SHORT DEFINITION:

We Want Your Advice

ANNUAL EDITIONS revisions depend on two major opinion sources: one is our Advisory Board, listed in the front of this volume, which works with us in scanning the thousands of articles published in the public press each year; the other is you—the person actually using the book. Please help us and the users of the next edition by completing the prepaid article rating form on this page and returning it to us. Thank you for your help!

ANNUAL EDITIONS: World Politics 11/12

ARTICLE RATING FORM

Here is an opportunity for you to have direct input into the next revision of this volume.
We would like you to rate each of the articles listed below, using the following scale:

1. **Excellent: should definitely be retained**
2. **Above average: should probably be retained**
3. **Below average: should probably be deleted**
4. **Poor: should definitely be deleted**

Your ratings will play a vital part in the next revision.
Please mail this prepaid form to us as soon as possible.
Thanks for your help!

RATING	ARTICLE	RATING	ARTICLE
_____	1. The Age of Nonpolarity: What Will Follow U.S. Dominance?	_____	20. Organized Crime in Iraq: Strategic Surprise and Lessons for Future Contingencies
_____	2. America's Edge: Power in the Networked Century	_____	21. Africa's Forever Wars
_____	3. Europe, the Second Superpower	_____	22. Profiling: Sketching the Face of Jihadism
_____	4. Is Beijing Ready for Global Leadership?	_____	23. Al-Shabab's Agenda in the Wake of the Kampala Suicide Attacks
_____	5. The Elephant in the Room	_____	24. Three Pillars of Counterinsurgency
_____	6. Europe and Russia: Up from the Abyss?	_____	25. Combating Terrorism with Socioeconomics: Leveraging the Private Sector
_____	7. In the Koreas, Five Possible Ways to War		
_____	8. Obama's Nuclear Policy: Limited Change	_____	26. Defining Success in Afghanistan: What Can the United States Accept?
_____	9. After Iran Gets the Bomb		
_____	10. Evolving Bioweapon Threats Require New Countermeasures	_____	27. All Counterinsurgency Is Local
		_____	28. Millennium Development Goals: At a Glance
_____	11. Obama's Foreign Policy: The End of the Beginning	_____	29. The African Standby Force, Genocide, and International Relations Theory
_____	12. In Search of Sustainable Security: Linking National Security, Human Security, and Collective Security to Protect America and Our World	_____	30. Rethinking the Responsibility to Protect
		_____	31. China to the Rescue: Growing out of the Financial Crisis
_____	13. A Hidden World, Growing beyond Control		
_____	14. DOD's Energy Challenge as Strategic Opportunity	_____	32. Can the BRICs Become a Bloc?
_____	15. The OSCE and the 2010 Crisis in Kyrgyzstan	_____	33. The New Population Bomb: The Four Megatrends That Will Change the World
_____	16. Chinese Military Seeks to Extend Its Naval Power		
_____	17. The False Religion of Mideast Peace	_____	34. The World's Water Challenge
_____	18. The Next Empire?		
_____	19. Obama and Latin America: New Beginnings, Old Frictions		

NO POSTAGE
NECESSARY
IF MAILED
IN THE
UNITED STATES

BUSINESS REPLY MAIL
FIRST CLASS MAIL PERMIT NO. 551 DUBUQUE IA

POSTAGE WILL BE PAID BY ADDRESSEE

McGraw-Hill Contemporary Learning Series
501 BELL STREET
DUBUQUE, IA 52001

ABOUT YOU

Name _____   Date _____

Are you a teacher? ☐ A student? ☐
Your school's name _____

Department _____

Address _____   City _____   State _____   Zip _____

School telephone # _____

YOUR COMMENTS ARE IMPORTANT TO US!

Please fill in the following information:
For which course did you use this book?
_____

Did you use a text with this ANNUAL EDITION? ☐ yes ☐ no
What was the title of the text?
_____

What are your general reactions to the Annual Editions concept?
_____

Have you read any pertinent articles recently that you think should be included in the next edition? Explain.
_____

Are there any articles that you feel should be replaced in the next edition? Why?
_____

Are there any World Wide Websites that you feel should be included in the next edition? Please annotate.
_____

May we contact you for editorial input? ☐ yes ☐ no
May we quote your comments? ☐ yes ☐ no

NOTES

NOTES